We Know Who We Are

We Know Who We Are

MÉTIS IDENTITY IN A
MONTANA COMMUNITY

MARTHA HARROUN FOSTER

UNIVERSITY OF OKLAHOMA PRESS : NORMAN

Library of Congress Cataloging-in-Publication Data

Foster, Martha Harroun, 1945–
    We know who we are : Métis identity in a Montana community / Martha Harroun Foster.
       p.   cm.
    Includes bibliographical references and index.
    ISBN 0–8061–3705–3 (alk. paper)
      1. Métis—Montana—Lewistown—Ethnic identity. 2. Métis—Montana—Lewistown—History. 3. Métis—Montana—Lewistown—Social conditions. 4. Lewistown (Mont.)—History. 5. Lewistown (Mont.)—Social life and customs. I. Title.

E99.M47.F67 2006
305.8'0597009078629—dc22

2005043971

The paper in this book meets the guidelines for permanence and durability of the Committee on Production Guidelines for Book Longevity of the Council on Library Resources. ∞

Copyright © 2006 by the University of Oklahoma Press, Norman, Publishing Division of the University. All rights reserved. Manufactured in the U.S.A.

1 2 3 4 5 6 7 8 9 10

In memory of Martha Heim Groff

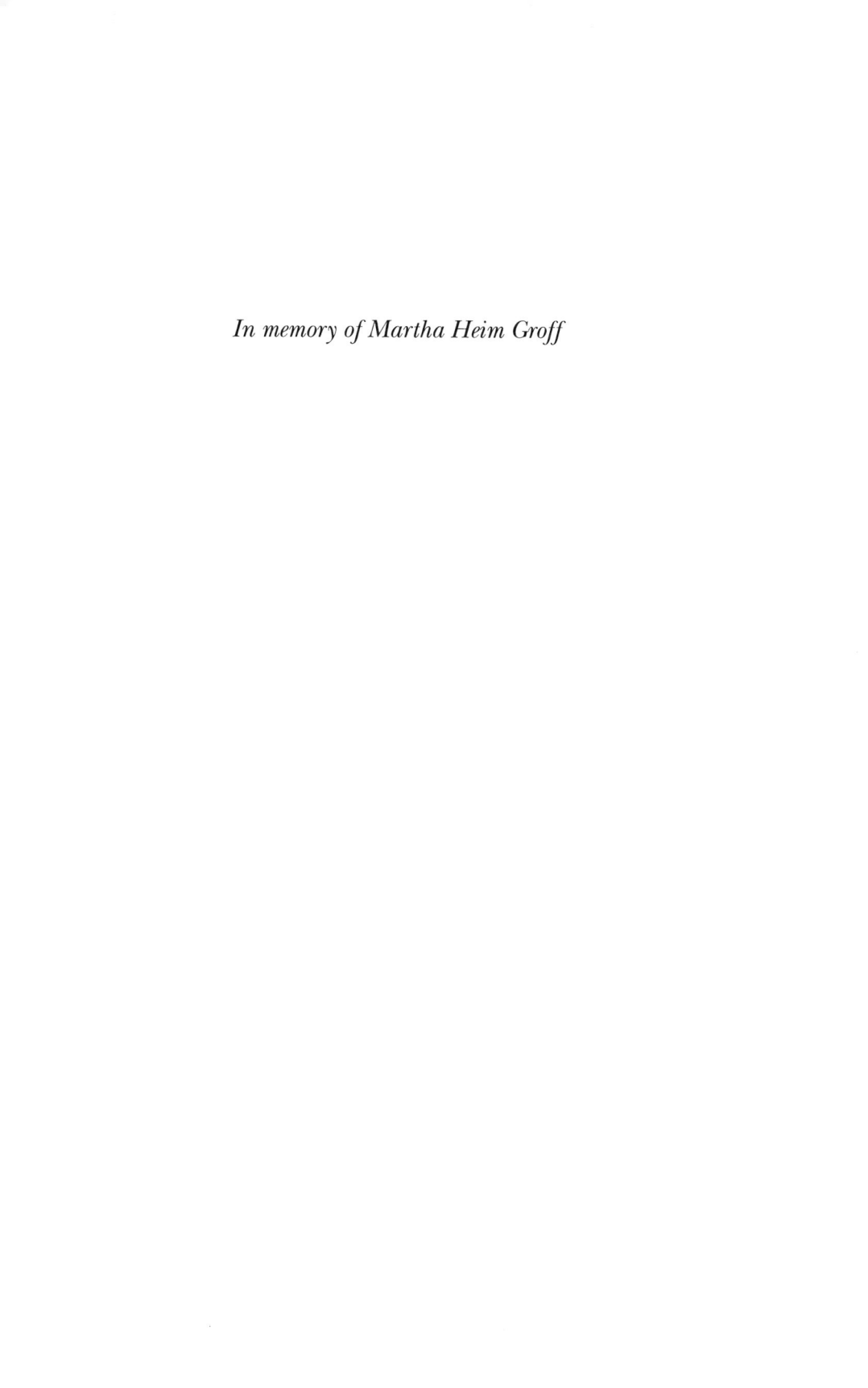

Contents

List of Illustrations	ix
Acknowledgments	xi
Introduction	3
Chapter 1. The Development of Métis Identity and the Diverging Paths of the U.S. Métis, 1670–1864	15
Chapter 2. "Following the Buffalo Trails," 1864–1880	51
Chapter 3. A New Homeland: The Judith Basin and Spring Creek Settlement, 1879–1884	90
Chapter 4. Ethnic Labels: Confronting an Indian/White Dichotomy, 1885–1899	136
Chapter 5. Métis, Indian, and White: Ethnic Negotiation in the Twentieth Century, 1900–1919	179
Conclusion. "Piyish Tout Ni Pouyoun"	222
Appendix. Signatories of Petition to N. A. Miles, Musselshell River, August 6, 1880	227
Abbreviations	229
Notes	231
Bibliography	265
Index	291

Illustrations

PHOTOGRAPHS

Pierre Laverdure	70
Pierre and Judith Wilkie Berger	80
Red River Carts at 5th and Broadway, Lewistown, Montana	138
Bone hide-scraping tool used by Mary Ernestine Wells Fleury	140
Beadwork by Mary Ernestine Wells Fleury	141
Beadwork by Mary Ernestine Wells Fleury	142
Moccasins made by Mary Ernestine Wells Fleury for her granddaughter	142
Ben Kline in Lewistown, Montana	183

MAPS

Red River and Upper Missouri River Drainage	2
Métis Homestead Applications, 1880–1885, Township 15 North, Range 18 East, Fergus County	107
Métis Homestead Applications, 1880–1899, Township 15 North, Range 18 East, Fergus County	108
Métis Homestead Applications, 1880–1885, Township 15 North, Range 19 East, Fergus County	109
Métis Homestead Applications, 1880–1899, Township 15 North, Range 19 East, Fergus County	110
Métis Homestead Locations, Judith Mountains Area, 1880–1899	111

TABLES

Spring Creek Band Family Name Locations	49
Métis Homestead Applications, 1880–1899	105
Spring Creek/Lewistown-Area Métis Families, *1900 Montana Census*	184
Members of the Spring Creek Métis Families Listed as White in the *1900 Montana Census*	188
Métis Homestead Applications, 1900–1915	192

DIAGRAMS

Spring Creek Band: Charlotte Adam LaFountain Network	83
Spring Creek Band: Virginia Laverdure Janeaux Network	84
Spring Creek Band: Judith Wilkie Berger Network	85

Acknowledgments

Many people have helped to make this work possible, but it is the Métis people themselves to whom I owe the greatest debt. I will never know the names of some who graciously added their knowledge and experiences and joined many fruitful discussions.

Residents and former residents of the Lewistown, Montana, area, both Métis and non-Métis, were particularly helpful. They informed this work as well as generously provided friendship, support, and lodging. Ken Doney, Sue Eastman, Marie Ehlert, Robert LaFountain, Treena LaFountain, Frances Morgan Shoup, Donna LaFountain Walraven, Gloria Wells, Anna Zellick, and Helen Zilba all participated in interviews and answered endless questions. Members of the Lewistown Genealogical Society, especially Lil Zwolle, and the librarians of the Lewistown Public Library (Nancy Watts, Nancy Sackett) were wonderful sources of information. Emma Burleigh, Gail Doney, and Julia Jackson, among many others, provided information, assistance, and hospitality. Treena LaFountain shared wonderful beadwork and hide-working tools that belonged to her great-grandmother, Ernestine Wells Fleury. John Haverson of Billings provided photographs of these artifacts. The Lewistown Library staff generously lent the other photographs.

Neither would this work have been possible without the support of UCLA faculty, especially the patience and wisdom of Norris Hundley. Other members of my Ph.D. committee, Duane Champagne, Melissa Meyer, and Albion Urdank, gave of time, advice, and encouragement throughout the project. History department faculty, including Ellen Dubois, Gary Nash, and Michael Salman, provided an atmosphere of inquiry that helped shaped the project.

Other scholars were more than generous with their knowledge and helpful suggestions. Jennifer Brown, Heather Devine, and anonymous readers read all or parts of the manuscript, made many excellent suggestions, and gave valuable advice. Conversations with Tanis Thorne encouraged me through the long process. Larry Burt, Gerhard Ens, Melinda Jette, Gail Morin, Jeremy Mumford, Ruth Swan, and Nicholas Vrooman shared information and ideas and, in general, lent support for the project.

I must also thank the faculty of Montana State University's History, Anthropology, and Native American Studies departments. Special thanks goes to Leslie B. Davis for his many years of helpful advice. By happy coincidence Les was a friend and colleague of Verne Dusenberry, who, so many years ago, was the first academic to take an interest in the Montana Métis. I also owe thanks to Karen Leech, who was always ready with support and hospitality, and to Fred Cady, who, many years ago, saved me from destroying my computer and giving up completely!

My colleagues at Middle Tennessee State University also supported me through the project. The Women's Work Group read parts of the manuscript and generously offered realistic advice. Vincent Armstrong patiently redrew and streamlined the maps, and the History Department provided time to complete the manuscript.

I could never have attempted this project without the holdings and staff of many libraries. The resources of UCLA, University of California Davis, and Montana State University were essential. The libraries of St. Leo's Roman Catholic Church in Lewistown, Montana, the Catholic Parish Center Archives in Great Falls, the Ursuline Center Archives (Great Falls), and the volunteers at the Latter Day Saints Family History Center in Stockton, California, provided help and information. The collections and assistance of the staff at the Lewistown Public Library, the Lewistown Genealogical Society, the Mansfield Library Special Collections (University of Montana, Missoula), the Montana Historical Society Archives, the State Historical Society of North Dakota, and the University of North Dakota Library were especially helpful.

Last of all, I want to thank my children, Theran, Sarah, and Cindy, for their support over the years. Extra thanks goes to Cindy, who read parts of the manuscript and was my chief fetch and copy assistant.

We Know Who We Are

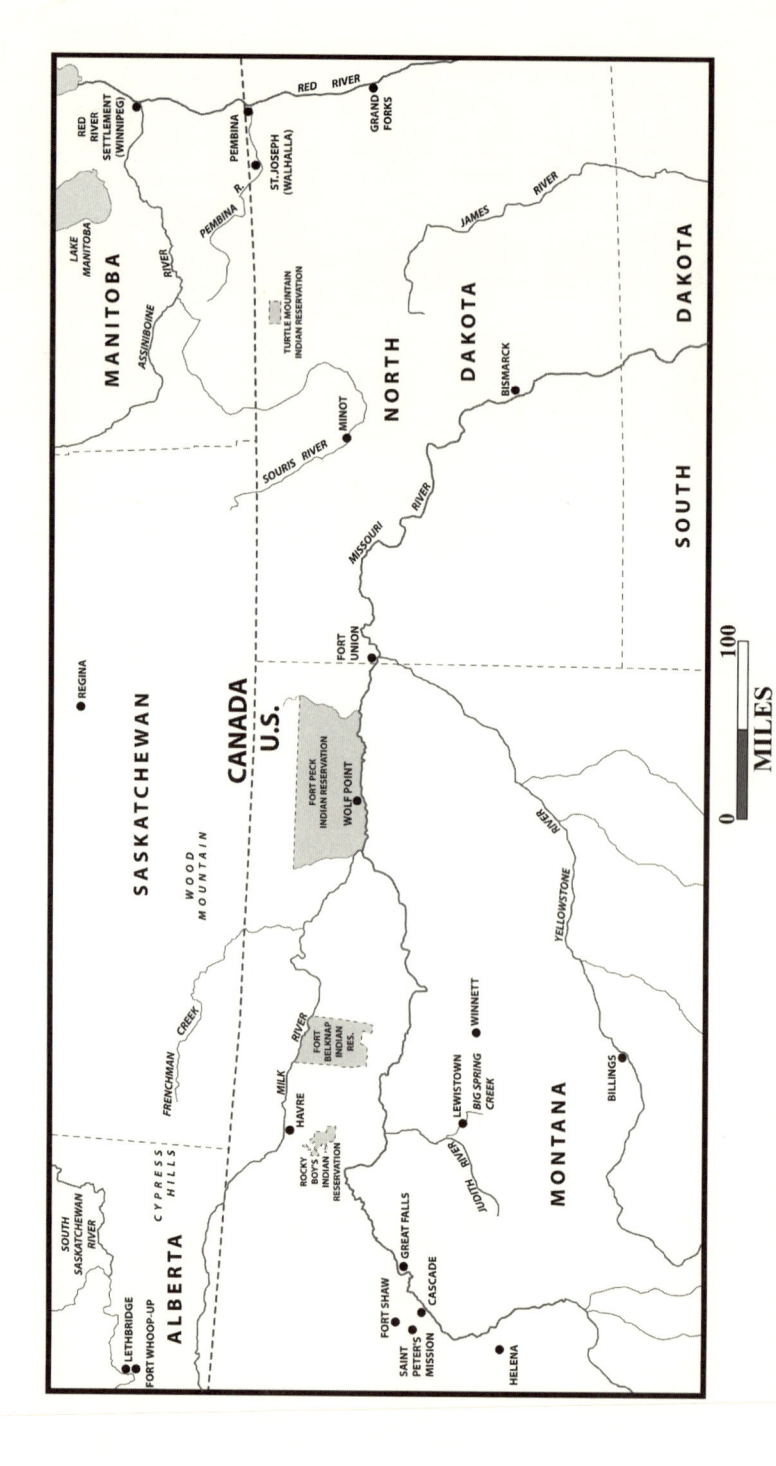

Red River and Upper Missouri River Drainage. Map by Vincent Armstrong.

Introduction

In 1979 the people of Lewistown, a small central Montana community, held a Métis Centennial Celebration in recognition of the town's 1879 founding by Métis settlers. The celebration honored the mixed-descent people of Montana, the Dakotas, and Canada with cultural demonstrations and a locally published history documenting their unique culture and common past. Hundreds of Métis, Indians, and non-Indian people attended events ranging from panel discussions to Métis dances, fiddling, and a powwow. One organizer of the celebration was the newly elected mayor of Lewistown, Robert E. LaFountain. That LaFountain was the first Métis elected to city government in the town's one hundred–year history underscored the celebration's significance.[1] A casual visitor might assume that both the celebration and the election marked the social acceptance of Métis people, the acknowledgement of their considerable historical contributions, and recognition of their ethnic difference. However, the social position of the Métis, their history, and their ethnicity are not so easy to categorize. In fact, the multifaceted and multilayered complexity of the Lewistown-area Métis community, its relationship with non-Métis, and the nature of Métis ethnicity are unraveled only slowly.

The reality of being Métis in Montana is to live with an ethnic dilemma caused by racial stereotypes that either denigrate or ignore mixed-descent people. Métis face both white prejudice toward "breeds" and discrimination against Indians. On the other hand, they also sometimes experience the rejection of enrolled Indians because, as Métis, they have no land base and no official tribal recognition. As with their relationship to the white community, Métis-Indian relations are more complex than they seem at first glance. For example, LaFountain, like a number of other

Métis, is also an enrolled Turtle Mountain Chippewa. Surprisingly, not all of his family is enrolled; he has relatives of equal Indian descent who are not members of any recognized tribe. In fact, his wife, Treena, who, he declares, "is more Indian than I am," has no ties to any Indian group. Nevertheless, like many Montana Métis, she has suffered lifelong discrimination against both "breeds" and Indians. Montana Métis seldom forget that many non-Métis see them as neither white nor "real" Indians, yet, at the same time, often fail to recognize them as a distinct people. Against this backdrop of prejudice are related Métis families who have joined the Euro-American community despite pervasive negative attitudes toward people of Indian descent. Some of these families consider themselves to be "white" and Métis; some are "white" with Métis or Indian relatives. Others have "forgotten" any Indian ancestry or kinship connection, perhaps recognizing only a "French Canadian" great-grandfather or great-grandmother.[2]

Being Métis in the United States is truly ambiguous. Métis people are not quite invisible, but unlike Métis in Canada, who have received government recognition, U.S. Métis, as a people, are virtually unseen, unrecognized, and anonymous. Nevertheless, for Robert, Treena, and others like them, a unique sense of being Métis lives on. In 1979 they celebrated both the Métis founding of Lewistown and their survival as a people.

A MONTANA MÉTIS COMMUNITY

Lewistown is Montana's longest continuously occupied Métis settlement. The story of those Métis who settled on the tributaries of Spring Creek and founded Lewistown begins long before 1879, but in that year a band of related Métis families established homes there. These families, referred to here as the Spring Creek band, are more often known today as the Lewistown Métis. To avoid confusion with later arrivals and since not all of the families lived within Lewistown (many settled along the tributaries of Spring Creek well outside the present-day city limits), I will refer to the original related Métis families as the Spring Creek band.[3]

The Spring Creek families and their relatives who remained on or returned to the Milk River formed the kinship network that has come to be known as the Lewistown/Havre/Glasgow triangle or the Lewistown/Milk River triangle. Other of their relatives traveled southwest from the Milk River to settle at St. Peter's Mission, where Canadian Métis and Crees joined them after 1885. These families established settlements along the Front Range of the Rocky Mountains and became the second principal cluster of Métis families in Montana. Members of the two networks, related before they settled in Montana, preserved and extended their common ties. Despite challenges to their identity as Métis and their flexible acceptance of a variety of ethnic labels, they continued to celebrate their culture, history, and identity as Métis.[4]

MÉTIS ETHNIC IDENTITY

This study explores Métis ethnic identity in Montana by closely examining the families who established the long-lasting Spring Creek Métis community. The band had arrived on Spring Creek with a sense of their difference from both whites and Indians. Their Red River (Manitoba, North Dakota, and Minnesota) ancestors had developed a distinct Métis ethnic identity by the early 1800s. The Judith Basin of central Montana, of which Spring Creek and Lewistown are a part, presented these families with a new series of challenges to this identity. As they watched the buffalo disappear, experienced the arrival of great numbers of Euro-American settlers, suffered discrimination as "Canadian Cree," and sought recognition as Native people, they struggled to maintain their unique sense of self and their Métis identity.[5]

Though the Métis experience is characterized by diversity, a close study of one community lends insights into the nature of Métis identity and the challenges to that identity throughout the United States and Canada. This work examines factors that affected the development and maintenance of Métis identity and follows the changing nature of this identity in a region where there were no obvious advantages to its maintenance. In the process, it explores the role of self-ascription, ascription, kinship, economic factors, institutional pressures, government policy, gender, and discrimination in the development and maintenance of ethnic identification among persons of mixed descent.

The survival of a separate Métis identity in the United States raises fundamental questions about the nature of ethnicity, including the identification of factors that support ethnic persistence and adaptation despite challenges. It illuminates how ethnic identity evolves and develops, continuously adjusting to changing conditions, yet remaining distinct and recognizable to its members and neighbors. Central to this study of Métis identity are issues concerning the special challenges that people of mixed descent face when asserting a unique ethnic identity, especially in the United States. In what ways does a group lacking formal organization and obvious public cultural difference assert and preserve its distinctiveness as a people?

What is the nature of this distinctiveness? To what extent and in what ways do their neighbors perceive their difference? How was this identity forged, and surviving a hundred years in the Spring Creek area, how was it maintained without apparent economic, legal, institutional, or social support and in the face of intermittent pressure to merge with Euro-American or Indian society?

Related to all of these questions is the issue of how attitudes toward Native people and definitions of "Indian" complicate, obscure, and sometimes deny a mixed-Indian-descent identity. Enrollment policy, federal recognition of tribes, and notions of authenticity, of "pure blood," and of what constitutes a "real" Indian are only a few of the issues that affect not only Indian but also Métis identity. In addition, Euro-American prejudice toward Indians has affected Métis ethnic identity. To what extent has this prejudice "spilled over" onto the Métis, preventing their acceptance by the larger community? Was Métis identity sustained only because the Euro-American community denied them a white identity, and because they had neither Indian support for nor legal rights to an Indian identity? Are they, therefore, Métis by default? And, in any case, how have the Métis worked within a system of racial discrimination to create and preserve their ethnicity? What has the effect of this process been on them personally and as a group? Clearly, issues that affect Indian identity invariably affect Métis as well.

All of these questions hold special relevance in a nation, indeed, to all nations of the Americas, where many of us are of mixed-ethnic descent. Examining the experiences of a people for whom ethnic identity has been rooted in a multiethnic heritage speaks to the nature of what it is to be American. There is a pride today among people of multiethnic and bi- or triracial descent that was not present on such a large scale even twenty years ago. The new millennium may be one in which the relatedness of all people is truly recognized.

As intermarriage between ethnic groups becomes increasingly common, multiethnic-descent young people question what it means to be white, Indian, Hispanic, or, for that matter, American. In looking to the past, we see that the Americas have always been the site of joining peoples, have always been multiethnic. To examine the experiences of peoples of mixed descent is to address one of our most pressing issues, the question of identity in the postmodern world.

This is the story of how one group of Métis families negotiated their ethnic identity over time. An inclusive, multiethnic, multicultural people, they constantly reformulated what it meant to be Métis, collectively and individually interpreting and reinterpreting their experiences. This work explores and documents the development of an ethnic identity derived from a variety of ethnic sources, in which dynamic ethnic evolution and redefinition paralleled and, in varying degrees, responded to powerful forces of changing ascribed identity. Despite changing self-ascribed and ascriptive ethnic definitions, an intricate and powerful web of kinship connected these families, providing social and economic stability and a strong sense of who they were. It is the history of the evolution of a distinct mixed-ethnic/racial corporate identity that proved to be, and was historically, a viable and satisfying option. It is, above all, the story of their adaptive response to enormous challenges.

REAL LIVES AND THEORIES OF ETHNICITY

An exploration of the factors involved in the evolution of ethnic identity raises questions about current theories of ethnicity. For example, hypotheses that posit special interest as the essential ingredient in the development of an ethnic identity do not appear to be supported by this Métis example. Superficially at least, it would seem that the economic and social interests of Métis people would be better served by a more concentrated effort to join Euro-American or Indian groups. Likewise, this study questions the dominance of political and legal factors in the development and maintenance of ethnic identity. The Lewistown Métis had little political power in their first hundred years of residence in Montana. Neither have they a separate legal identity or rights that would benefit and sustain the membership of the community. As their identity as Métis survived, it did so without long-term legal or political advantage. Political and legal factors did influence and circumscribe their ethnic alternatives, but the results were, in turn, strongly influenced by other factors, such as the kinship group's sense of who they were.[6]

Theories that stress cultural factors are also of questionable relevance to the Métis situation in the United States. The Spring Creek Métis no longer use the Métis language (Michif); they seldom practice or display distinctive cultural difference; they belong (for the most part) to the local Catholic church, attend community schools, and participate in the larger community's affairs. Demonstrable cultural factors do not seem to play a significant part in the nature of the people's sense of separate identity. Yet they see themselves as distinct. The symbolic nature of their religious faith, of the family, of the purpose of work, and even of the foods they prepare is subtly different from both their Indian and Euro-American neighbors. It is such seeming contradictions that lie at the heart of this study.

Métis distinctiveness yet relatedness to groups of Euro-Americans and Indians makes an examination of the flexible boundaries of Métis ethnic identity a useful vantage point for the study. In its emphasis on the boundaries, however permeable, that define an ethnic group, this study is informed by the work of Fredrik Barth. The focus, here, is on the nature of the boundaries themselves. For the Métis, who have historically manipulated and negotiated them, the boundaries sometimes seem so porous, flexible, and additive as to scarcely exist. Yet, constantly renegotiated and relayered, they signal what it means to be Métis in Montana. Although the boundaries shift and the meaning of being Métis changes, a sense of relatedness to one another and difference from others remains. Montana Métis might easily echo the words of Earl Mills, a Mashpee Wampanoag, inspired by a struggle for ethnic recognition. When asked during a 1977 federal tribal recognition hearing how his youth was different from that of any other small-town youth, he replied: "We were different. We knew we were different. We were told we were different." It is the nature of this difference, and of the negotiated, multifaceted, and multitiered boundaries of Métis ethnic identity that this study explores.[7]

Earl Mills's comment also points to the tension between volition and social assignment in the negotiation of ethnic identity. Sociologist Joane Nagel has noted the volitional aspect of both the "extent and content" of ethnicity, arguing, as does Barth, that "ethnicity results from a combination of self-identification and social assignment." Volition is limited by social constraints involving ascription by a varied audience that may include such disparate elements as a larger racist community or the memory of one's grandmother and her view of who she and her family were. Volitional ethnicity is circumscribed by the outside community, but also, as this study argues, by the kinship group. In multiethnic families, ethnic identity is contested and negotiated within marriages and families in response to the pressures of the larger community.[8]

Identities shift, they are layered, and they change in response to conditions. Nagel views ethnicity as "a dialectic between internal identification and external ascription" in a "socially negotiated and socially constructed status that varies as the audiences permitting particular ethnic options change." The Métis example supports this view but, at the same time, demonstrates the persistence and adaptability of ethnic identification in the face of outside forces. If outside forces circumscribe possible ethnic identities, groups may, and often do, resist. They may respond formally and publicly to pressures that they cannot overcome or do not wish to resist because of benefits derived, but continue to maintain a private conviction of difference from the ascribed identity. In a sense, the disputed identity may go underground in the face of overwhelming challenges, while quietly persevering until social conditions are again more favorable to its public expression. This study argues that kinship systems are the center of such identity maintenance and sustain the sense of difference in a safe, supportive atmosphere.[9]

Alternative identities are most striking to an outsider when they involve public identities. For Métis, public identities tend to be situational. Discrimination, federal policy, and economic necessity are just a few of the factors that have encouraged Métis ethnic flexibility on the public level. Spring Creek Métis continue to publicly name themselves (and allow others to name them) in such a way that allows the most gain and avoids the most trouble. Many mixed-descent peoples move between formal categories that cannot represent their total experience. There are often no optional identities that reflect the reality of complex ethnic combinational variety. To an extent, being Métis is to be part of a network of ethnic identities that permeate each other at certain levels, but which remain relatively autonomous at others.

For the Métis, ethnicity is fluid, permeable, multilayered, situational, and open to both individual choice and to change. The evolution of ethnicity is especially situational for people of mixed descent, who may have choices as to their ethnic identification. Montana Métis, like their fur trade ancestors, have employed different self-identifiers in different contexts for economic as well as social and political reasons. The Métis have constantly renegotiated their public identity. But this does not mean that they "forget" who they are. Alternative, overlapping identities are secured by a core of kinship ties so that rather than actually switching among a repertoire of discrete identities, individuals shift outward symbols and emphasis but do not lose their sense of self. The core remains constant. Emphasis on facets of a multifaceted and multilayered identity shift or sometimes meld, flowing easily and naturally as almost automatic situational responses. Hence, it is possible for the same individual to be white *and* Métis or Métis *and* Indian with sincerity and apparent ease. Ascripted labels are absorbed into the whole. As one Métis explained to a gathering at the 1997 Lewistown, Montana, Métis Celebration, "It doesn't matter what you call us, we know who we are."[10]

The study of one Métis community allows the examination of ethnic issues on an individual, family, and community basis. It is at the family level that many decisions about ethnic identity are made, especially for a mixed-descent people. Such questions as where to live, what language to teach the children, where to send them to school, and what name to call oneself are debated at the family level. The meaning of larger structures of kinship organization and religion are also worked out within the family. As Barth maintains, both the boundaries and content of ethnic identity are "contested within the crucible of the family." This is not to dismiss the importance of legal, political, and economic factors. But how these macro considerations affect the community must be understood through individual and family responses. Although it is essential to understand the forces that affect ethnic identity on the macro, median, and micro levels of social organization, the micro level, while connected and interdependent, as Barth argues, "is required to model the processes effecting experience and the formation of identities." An examination at this level is essential to understanding the negotiation of possible identities and the evolution of ethnic identity itself.[11]

In addressing such issues, this study brings attention to some of the problems that confront people of mixed-Indian descent in gaining recognition for and in asserting their ethnic identity. On a larger scale, I hope to raise questions that are relevant to all persons of mixed descent who are confused as to who they are and what to call themselves. As our nation becomes what historian Gary Nash has called "Mestizo America," mixed-descent persons are increasingly interested in the long history of others who have faced the task of winning recognition and respect for their unique ancestry and the right to celebrate all aspects of their heritage. This examination of the development, maintenance, and evolution of Métis ethnic identity in a small group of Métis who, despite a lack of legal and historical recognition, and in spite of poverty and prejudice, have maintained a sense of community and common history since the early nineteenth century raises questions about the nature of ethnicity that are of interest to ethnic groups everywhere.[12]

FINDING MONTANA MÉTIS IN MÉTIS HISTORY

To appreciate the need for a study of a group of Montana Métis and their place in U.S. and Canadian history, it is helpful to note the irregular development of the field of Métis history in the United States. Until the

1970s, U.S. Métis history was subsumed under the topic of the fur trade as a barely noticed aspect of U.S. West or American Indian history. Occasionally historians alluded to the Métis in discussions of Catholic French-Canadians, who early scholars, such as Francis Parkman, dismissed as a less significant, if not a degenerate, aspect of the true story of the U.S. and Canadian settlement. Even in studies of the fur trade, Euro-American males seemed to operate independently of Indians, wives, or mixed-descent communities. Although the first non-Indian families to settle in much of the Great Lakes region and Missouri drainage were métis of mixed Indian and European ancestry, their history has received very little attention in the United States until recently.[13] The fur trade, of which they were an integral part, frequently has been examined with only a brief, often derogatory, mention of "half-breeds" and almost no recognition of their complex social organization or their contribution to U.S. history.

The seminal works on the U.S. fur trade, including Hiram Chittenden's classic, *The American Fur Trade of the Far West*, which drew attention to the importance of the fur trade in U.S. history, emphasized the rendezvous and white male participation. This tendency has persisted; even today most histories of the early northern plains pass over the métis presence with a brief mention of "Canadians" or "Squaw men." Surprisingly, works valued for their multicultural perspective also ignore or diminish the métis role. Richard White's *History of the American West* and *Middle Ground; Indians, Empires, and Republics in the Great Lakes Region, 1670–1815*, for example, make little mention of métis participation at the heart of Great Lakes and western settlement. State and local histories also minimize the métis role. Michael P. Malone, Richard Roeder, and William Lang's *Montana* mentions "French frontiersmen" on the Missouri River and "mixed-blood trappers" in Montana, but does not discuss the significance of their early presence or the fact that many of the trappers and traders in Montana were métis or were part of métis families. Their emphasis, like that of Chittenden, is on Euro-American mountain men and the rendezvous, and on high-level company employees and partners, rather than on the métis families who were at the heart of the northern plains fur trade.[14]

Because of the more visible Métis role in Canada, Métis history has its origins there with very early works, such as Alexander Ross's *The Red River Settlement* (1856). By the 1970s, there was a resurgence of interest in Métis history in Canada, as the rights of Canada's Native people were vigorously debated. While the politics of race and ethnicity escalated, and discussion of the legal position of Indians, Inuits, and Métis reached national proportions, the historical literature reflected the growing public interest. In fact, for all three groups, historical accounts were essential to the arguments supporting separate legal status. As Canadians debated the rights and definition of its Native peoples, the question of the nature of being Métis received increasing interest.

During the 1980s, the study of Métis history flowered in Canada. Interest was heightened by the passage of the 1982 Constitution Act (section 35), which defined Canada's aboriginal peoples as Indian, Inuit, and Métis. Though seemingly straightforward, the act raised as many questions as it answered. Scholars, lawyers, and politicians alike now struggle with such questions as who has the right to call themselves Métis. Resulting discussions led to a need for historical information about Métis origins, common history, and shared culture, all of which occasioned an enormous outpouring (at least for the field of Métis history) of scholarly work.

In response to this extraordinarily significant event in the Métis peoples' long struggle for recognition, the *American Indian Culture and Research Journal* (*AICRJ*) published a path-breaking series of articles that included discussions of Métis ethnogenesis and the emergence of a distinct Métis identity. The *AICRJ* essays prepared the way for the decade's most important compiled work on the Métis people, Jacqueline Peterson and Jennifer S. H. Brown's anthology, *The New Peoples: Being and Becoming Métis in North America*. *New Peoples* attracted attention on a level that few previous Métis studies achieved and established directions for Métis research.[15]

One *New Peoples* article that is especially relevant to the study of Montana Métis is anthropologist Verne Dusenberry's "Waiting for a Day That Never Comes: The Dispossessed Métis of Montana" (1958). Dusenberry had a lifelong interest in Indian and mixed-descent people of the northern plains. He was instrumental in founding Indian studies programs at the University of Montana, Montana State University, and at the Glenbow Foundation in Calgary, Alberta. His 1958 article was the first scholarly work to call attention to the Montana Métis experience. Unfortunately, it is also the only historical work devoted to the Montana Métis.[16]

Verne Dusenberry (1950s), Pat Morris and Bob Van Gunten (1979), and Robert Franklin and Pamela Bunte (1997) have studied the Little Shell Chippewas, a group that is closely related to the Métis. Also, Larry Burt (1986 and 1987) and Michel Hogue (2002) have looked at the complexities of the Montana Cree experience, which has implications for the Métis. However, only Dusenberry's 1958 article focuses on the Montana Métis.

INTRODUCTION

No work has examined the Montana Métis at length or explored the relationship of their history to that of Canada or the United States.[17]

This study responds both to the absence of historical work and to the appeals of Métis historians for further study. An investigation of this community helps answer the need to explore the diversity of the Métis experience, especially in the United States. Factors that affect ethnic identity are played out in the United States in different combinations and with a different emphasis than in Canadian Métis communities. The duration of the Lewistown Métis community allows an examination of economic, class, and gender issues on a micro level that can lend fresh insights into the evolution and negotiation of ethnic identity.

A NOTE ON TERMINOLOGY

The use of certain terms in this discussion calls for explanation. The word "Indian" is preferred, in most cases, rather than Native American, First Peoples, or other appropriate terms, especially when attempts are made to distinguish between Indian and Métis. Since the Métis are also "Native," the term Indian, even with all of its colonial baggage, seems to generate less confusion. It is also the term employed historically and legally in the United States. The term "white" is also problematical, but in this study refers to a socially constructed category whose exact definition and inclusiveness changes with location and time. Nuances in the meaning of "Métis" and of "Indian" often cannot be discerned without concurrent discussion of what it means at a particular time and place to be "white."[18]

Another troubling term is "half-breed." The term is offensive to many because of its historical and contemporary pejorative connotations. Originally, the term "half-breed" simply meant a person of mixed-Indian descent. Louis Riel, famed Métis leader, used it as the English equivalent of Métis when speaking or writing in English.[19] Even today, some Montana Métis use the term, respectfully, to distinguish themselves from whites or Indians. I use "half-breed" in this same sense unless exploring its historical usage.

A less offensive term, yet one that has caused much emotionally charged discussion, is "Chippewa." My use of "Chippewa" (rather than Anishinaabe or other, and perhaps more appropriate, self-identifiers in reference to the Ojibwa people) stems from current and historical use in Montana. There, many Turtle Mountain Chippewas, Little Shell Chippewas, and Rocky Boy Chippewa Crees currently use the term, as they have since the beginning of their treaty struggles with the U.S. government. Also, it is important to note that the Chippewas and Crees have had a long history of friendship and intermarriage and that many individuals of Chippewa and Cree descent (and a great many non-Indian Montanans) refer to people of that ancestry as "ChippewaCree," as though it were one inseparable word. Alternatively, many Montanans, both past and present, refer to all Métis, Chippewas, and Crees indistinguishably as "Cree."

In any discussion of Métis people, it is necessary to distinguish between the terms "métis" and "Métis." Lower case "métis," as employed here, refers to all people of mixed American Indian and European descent. The term "Métis," with a capitalized "M," refers, more specifically, to an ethnic or social group that is, or is in the process of becoming, distinguishable from others. I do not intend to make a statement as to the date that the Métis people became an identifiable ethnic group. Ethnogenesis is a process, and I find it counterproductive to attempt to determine an exact moment when a group fits a specific definition and qualifies, in some way, as an ethnic group. Therefore, in this paper, "Métis" is used to refer to those people of mixed-Indian descent who take part in the process leading to a distinct Métis ethnic development.[20]

And, finally, a note on the spelling of Métis names. Historically the spelling of Métis names has been somewhat arbitrary. Since many Métis did not read or write, no consistent spelling of family names developed. When names were recorded it was often by priests of diverse nationality and training. They attempted Latin equivalents or spelled according to their own phonetic principles. English-speaking census takers and local officials created spelling according to their own notions and experience. I have tended to use the spellings favored by the Spring Creek Métis and their descendants. In specific cases, however—for example, in census data—I use the spelling employed by the recorder or as found in public documents.

CHAPTER 1

The Development of Métis Identity and the Diverging Paths of the U.S. Métis, 1670–1864

The ancestors of the Spring Creek band of central Montana Métis participated at the very heart of Métis development. Their story illuminates important variations in the conditions that Métis people faced and in the options that they utilized to consolidate a viable identity and maintain their economic and social integrity. The Métis south of the U.S.-Canadian border experienced different economic, social, and political pressures from those Métis to the north. The experience of the parents and grandparents of the Spring Creek band members illustrates some less-known aspects of Métis history and reveals a complexity of experience that has sometimes been overlooked.

Métis people of Indian and European descent, including ancestors of the Spring Creek band, established communities throughout Canada, the northern United States, and the Mississippi Valley. A unique Métis ethnic identity grounded in a multiethnic, multicultural openness has its roots in the very beginning of Indian-European contact in northern North America. It is from these roots that the ancestors of the Métis celebrants in Lewistown developed their unique sense of self.

As the mixed-descent people of the North began to establish a distinct identity, economic and environmental factors encouraged their steady movement westward. By the early 1800s, beaver depletion gradually destroyed the traditional economic foundation of Métis communities in the Great Lakes region, upper Mississippi Valley, and eastern Canada. It was on the great western plains, with its plentiful supply of beaver and game, that the Métis established new communities. Here they created interconnected social and cultural centers on the rivers and streams that flow to the Red River of the North. Throughout the first half of the nineteenth century, the Red River Métis, as the mixed-descent peoples of the Red River trade area came to be known, survived enormous challenges to their economic, legal, and social integrity. In meeting these challenges, their ethnic identity matured and they flourished, all the while absorbing new peoples and extending their vast kinship networks.[1]

Much of the existing Métis historical literature has dealt with the Métis experience north of the U.S.-Canadian boundary. The movement of the Hudson's Bay Company (HBC), North West Company (NWC), and Canadian and Great Lakes independent traders onto the Canadian portion of this area is well documented. South of the forty-ninth parallel, which did not exist for the Métis until the 1820s (and then only peripherally), they had an equally long history.

In reality, the history of the northern U.S. fur trade is so tied to that of the métis that one cannot be told without the other. Neither can the story of the Red River Métis be understood without an appreciation of the métis presence below the border. For many years Pembina, now part of North Dakota, was a larger community than Red River Settlement (present-day Winnipeg). It had the first Red River school and church, and it was here that the great Métis buffalo hunts originated. But Pembina did not develop in isolation. The Pembina Métis had strong ties to Red River Settlement, especially to the community of St. François Xavier. Kinship ties bound the families tightly and were far more central to the Métis sense of who they were than place of residence or birth. The Métis considered the entire Red River drainage theirs, and while Hudson's Bay Company officers and clergy continually attempted to bound the Métis to small Red River Settlement plots, many resisted. They continued to pursue a mobile economy based at first on beaver and then on buffalo products, maintaining their economic freedom and distinctive lifestyle.

When, in the 1820s, the U.S. and British governments pressured the Métis to recognize the international boundary line, the Métis continued to keep their options open. As trade competition between the countries increased, Métis movement across the border became more difficult and costly, and gradually, by the 1840s, they were forced to choose between U.S. or Canadian residency. Those Métis who remained south of "the line" faced different conditions and choices than their northern relatives. Whereas in present-day western Canada, a Métis ethnic identity solidified, strengthened by a united stand against threats to their economic and social well-being, ethnic identity was challenged differently in the United States. Here, the Métis confronted a polarized racial situation in which the legal position of biracial people did not have the benefit of backing by a strong, organized community. In the United States, centuries of slavery and acquisition of Native lands had determined rules for inclusion into the major non-European racial categories, Indian and African American, while at the same time discouraging the development of biracial identities. The Métis resisted official invisibility, attempting to maintain a distinct identity while asserting their rights both as Native people and as Euro-Americans. At the same time, they retained their ties to the north, unwilling (and sometimes unable) to establish a specific Canadian or American identity. By midcentury, the option of a dual (or nonspecific) national identity closed for the Métis people. International law, company competition, and U.S. Indian policy forced families to choose not only a national identity, but a restrictive racial one as well.

THE DEVELOPMENT OF A MÉTIS IDENTITY, 1670–1800

The story of the Métis people began long before the U.S.-Canadian boundary became a reality. Two fur trade regions and the organization of the trade in each contributed to the Métis view of themselves as a distinct ethnic group. In the Great Lakes region and in Rupert's Land (the Hudson Bay watershed comprising much of central Canada, northern Minnesota, and North Dakota), people of mixed ethnic/racial descent faced diverse conditions and made different ethnic decisions.

In the Great Lakes area, the changes in fur trade organization, the need for a bilingual, bicultural presence, and the growing independence of fur traders, combined with a dramatic weakening of Native matrilineal groups, created a fertile climate for the development of a distinct mixed-descent population. The overriding importance of the fur trade put a premium on the services of a uniquely qualified people who had grown up in the trade and had both Native and European skills and kinship ties. In the Great Lakes area, rather than identify as French or Indian, people of mixed-descent "began to look upon themselves and to be recognized by outsiders as representing a distinctive blend of . . . cultures." Historian Jacqueline Peterson describes this new society as one "in flux," continually absorbing varied Natives and Europeans, yet "also a society whose members—if not self-consciously métis before 1815—were a people in the process of becoming."[2]

People of mixed descent had a long history in the Great Lakes area working both for the Montreal fur companies and independently. *Coureurs de bois* (wood runners), "free" or "illegal" traders who were not employees of the large fur-trade companies and often were not licensed to trap or trade, were regularly trading at Sault Ste. Marie and Mackinac before 1670. They settled there and along the Great Lakes permanently between 1702 and 1714. A pattern of illegal, unlicensed trade accompanied by intermarriage with Native and métis women became prevalent throughout the area and encouraged feelings of cohesiveness, independence, and "otherness." The social patterns, appearance, and economic organization of these communities reflected a lifestyle that developed, not only here, but also throughout the fur country of Canada and the Mississippi drainage.[3]

Although the métis founded larger settlements, particularly numerous were semipermanent hamlets that developed as small trading outposts. Usually the residence of an extended family group, including a trader and related engagés (fur trade employees who were often canoemen), spouses, and children, these small villages were located close to Native kin who provided furs and supplies. This band-type residential organization was prevalent in the Great Lakes region, becoming an important aspect of Métis society later in the West, including Montana. Band organization functioned as a chief source of fur trade families' structured mobility. When the scarcity of fur-bearing animals forced a move, the band provided stability and held the group together. Much like Native band organization, this kinship group was an efficient economic and social unit that survived geographical change.[4]

The band placed a premium on kinship ties through marriage. As an important method of expanding trade networks, marriage united traders not only with Indian suppliers, but also with other trade families. Rather than the picturesque lone trapper in the wilderness, it was such kinship ties that were at the heart of the Canadian and northern U.S. fur trade and characteristic of métis life. Organization of bands was family based and women had defined roles (as in Indian society), which were essential to the success of the venture. Métis social and economic organization had a complexity that belied the popular image of a European-style, male-controlled extended family served by passive, often overworked, and sometimes mistreated Indian and métis women. Métis women descended from an Indian tradition of relatively high status and contributed valued knowledge and skills (as their mothers had before them) to the success of the trade enterprise.[5]

After 1790, powerful British trade organizations took control of the fur trade from French speakers (métis and French Canadian) who had long dominated it. The French-speaking population suffered a loss of social and economic influence, but the mixed-descent residents of communities such as Green Bay and Chicago, as well as many small, remote villages, continued their traditional lifestyle despite increasing economic and social pressure. By 1815, métis settlements dotted the land from Detroit and Michilimackinac to the Red River Settlement at present-day Winnipeg. Dozens of small towns and cites in the Great Lakes area, including Sault Ste. Marie, Prairie du Chien, Green Bay, Detroit, Chicago, Saginaw, Grand Rapids, South Bend, and Milwaukee, began as métis communities in the early 1700s and flourished from 1725 to 1825. As we will see later in the chapter, many Montana Métis families trace their ancestry to these communities.[6]

Only in the late 1830s, as U.S. and Canadian fur traders moved west to secure new fur supplies and agricultural settlers inundated the area, did these towns lose their métis character. With the collapse of their economic base in the fur-depleted Great Lakes, the métis had at least three options. They could take up agriculture, wage labor, or other Euro-American occupations and assume the corresponding lifestyle. They could join their Indian relatives on the new reservations, or they could move west with the fur trade. The incoming Euro-American majority absorbed unknown numbers of mixed-descent people who remained in the area. These métis enriched the culture and influenced the growth of their communities in ways that later historians ignored in their desire to celebrate the Euro-American "pioneer" conquest of the "wilderness." Many métis families joined Indian relatives and their names are still found on tribal rolls today. Other Great Lakes métis joined relatives and friends farther west in Red River drainage communities that were very much like their former homes. Great Lakes family names found among Red River–area Métis include Boyer, Charette, Charboneau, Dagneau, Delorme, Doney, Fleury, Gervais, Janeaux, Lafontaine, Laframboise, LaRoque, Laverdu, L'éveillé, LeDuc, Moran, Poitra, Pelletier, Parent, St. Pierre, Turcotte, and Wells, all of which also become well known farther west in Montana.[7]

The towns and villages of the Canadian west that was known from 1670 to 1870 as Rupert's Land were similar, in many ways, to the fur trade communities of the Great Lakes. However, in Rupert's Land, two great fur trade companies as well as numbers of small companies and freetraders influenced the development of a distinct mixed-descent population. Social repercussions of the management practices of the Hudson's Bay Company and the Montreal partnerships (which would consolidate by 1779 to form the first North West Company) helped shape Métis ethnic development. Because these organizations so dominated the social and economic life of

Rupert's Land, establishing its laws, hiring practices, and marriage policies, the companies had a powerful role in determining the nature of fur trade communities.[8]

The area that was to become Rupert's Land gained the attention of European fur traders in the seventeenth century. By the 1660s, French traders Médard Chouart, Sieur Des Groseilliers, and Pierre Esprit Radisson had found a way to secure the valuable Cree trade of the north and to bypass Native intermediary tribes that had long controlled these goods. In 1670, Charles II issued a charter giving authority over "all the lands drained by the rivers entering the [Hudson's] Bay" to the king's cousin, Prince Rupert, and the other Hudson's Bay Company proprietors. Henceforth known as Rupert's Land, this as yet undefined area covered more than 300,000 square miles in the plains and subarctic regions of Canada and included parts of present-day Minnesota and the Dakotas. Significantly for U.S. Métis, the charter would effectively pull the Milk River drainage of present-day northern Montana and the Red River drainage of what is now Manitoba, Minnesota, and North Dakota into the Canadian (rather than the U.S.) fur-trade network.[9]

As the HBC expanded and grew more profitable, the French Montreal companies began to consolidate. By the 1750s, Montreal-based French merchants had extended their trade and kinship networks to a variety of Indian groups south of Hudson Bay. A French fur-trade elite dominated Montreal socially and economically until the 1763 British conquest of Canada. As the British took control of the Montreal trade, they employed many of the methods, forms of organization, and individuals of the French fur trade. French-speaking employees remained, but in lower-ranking positions such as voyageurs. The HBC posts radiated from the Bay in the north, while the old French Montreal-based trade, now made up of companies controlled by British subjects, competed vigorously with them to the south and west.[10]

These large companies influenced both the opportunities and the identity of the fur trade's mixed-Indian descent children. During the eighteenth century, HBC policies in addition to Cree child-rearing and custody practices ensured that most of the descendants of these HBC marriages and temporary relationships integrated into Native bands. Until the end of the century, no separate identity developed for mixed-descent children of the company; they were considered to be Indian. Because there were no missionaries, schools, or other social structures that encouraged a white identity, and because, at first, fathers could not retire in fur country and remain with their children, an Indian identity was not challenged. An indicator of the situation was that most offspring kept their Indian names and had no separate designation as a group.[11]

Eventually, new HBC policies signaled an important shift away from a strict dichotomy of English or Indian identity. A group of men and women gradually emerged who could be distinguished from both the Homeguard Crees and from the British. The company increasingly employed these men in positions that were not available to the Crees, while mixed-descent women married company employees more frequently. Moreover, fur-trade children began to keep their British surnames, and it is by these names that they were identified in company records. Nevertheless, a distinct mixed-descent identity developed far more slowly and at a later date in HBC-controlled areas than it did in the Great Lakes.[12]

Unlike the HBC, North West Company policy, organizational structure, and relationships with Native people encouraged a separate ethnic identity. The NWC perpetuated the mixed-descent trade niche inherited from its French predecessors. Moreover, culture and lifestyle reinforced class difference, and in fur-trade country, cultural differences were pronounced. Most voyageurs were French speaking and frequently of part-Indian descent. Characteristic values, customs, lifestyles, music, and clothing marked them as distinct. Also contributing to the strained relations between the two groups was the voyageurs' independence and lack of servility. Unlike Hudson's Bay employees, who served for long periods of time, NWC voyageurs served only one- to three-year contracts. Not only were their terms short, but since they often had Native families and fur-trade experience, they could, and often did, leave company service to trade on their own as freemen. NWC's lack of control over employee marriage and child-rearing practices and its class and ethnic stratification encouraged the emergence of a mixed-descent population that recognized both its Indian and European ancestry while developing an identity that was distinct from both.[13]

In addition to the large companies, two other associated fur-trade groups, the independent traders and freemen, influenced the development of Métis ethnic identity. Sometimes known as *Gens libres* or *hommes libres*, the freemen were often part-time employees of the Montreal trade, or were retired from that trade. Freemen were more closely associated with the NWC and former XY Company than with the HBC because of company retirement policies. The NWC could not force its workers to retire in Britain or eastern Canada, and many remained with their Native families in fur-trade country after their term of service. These former NWC men often joined the ranks of freemen, using their fur-trade skills to trade independently, or supported themselves by supplying company posts. Unlike the freemen, the independent traders were not in the service of an established company. Throughout Rupert's Land, the Mississippi drainage, and the Great Lakes area, both groups comprised a vital component of the métis population. Described by historian of the Métis, Marcel Giraud, as "nearer to the Indian than to the employee in the post," the freemen and independent traders differed from fur-trade employees in that they became "more intimately associated with [the Indians'] nomadic ways" and let themselves "be absorbed irrevocably into the country where the voyageurs [company employees] were often content with temporary residence."[14]

By the last quarter of the eighteenth century, Great Lakes and St. Lawrence freemen and independent traders had spread over Canada and much of the Mississippi drainage. A few years later they moved into the Red, Saskatchewan, and Assiniboine river areas of present-day Manitoba, Saskatchewan, Alberta, North Dakota, and Minnesota. The Crees, Ojibwas, and other bands with whom they rapidly became connected by marriage, trade, and mutual defense accepted them as family members and trade partners, calling them "O-tee-paym-soo-wuk" (their-own-boss). Along the Red River, a growing lack of interest on the part of Cree, Chippewa, and Assiniboine post suppliers opened a provisioning niche to these traders. As the Indians shifted to full-time buffalo hunting, company personnel were happy to be supplied by freemen.[15]

Independent traders, freemen, and their families established many small communities throughout the Red River drainage. Before the 1812 formation of the Selkirk Settlement, a proposed Scottish agricultural community that would become home to both retired HBC and NWC employees, these families were already in the area. As Red River Settlement grew, many more independent trader and freemen families settled there and, with the families of retired NWC personnel, formed an increasingly organized and vocal métis population.

Along the Red River and in much of Rupert's Land, the unique social and economic circumstances of the independent traders, freemen, and HBC and NWC employees encouraged differing ethnic options ranging from Euro-Canadian, with no recognition of Indian ancestry, to Indian, with no recognition of Euro-Canadian ancestry, and almost every conceivable option in between. Later, these ethnic options became particularly significant to the Métis who settled in Montana. It was in Rupert's Land where the conditions of the fur trade allowed space for a distinct mixed-descent ethnic identity to mature. In western Canada and the northern plains of the United States, a Métis identity flourished as it had nowhere else. But well before they made their dramatic 1816 stand at Red River, complete with a flag and anthem, they had already developed as a distinct people. The discontent of the early nineteenth century served to unite the Métis more closely, but their sense of uniqueness, and separateness from both Indian and Canadian/European society, predated their political flowering.[16]

THE PRE-1821 MÉTIS OF THE RED AND UPPER MISSOURI RIVERS

The Spring Creek band's roots lie deep in the Red and Missouri rivers' fur trade. The vast Red River trade region in which the nineteenth-century Métis flourished extended from Red Lake and Lake of the Woods, in present-day Minnesota and Ontario, to the Rocky Mountains on the west, and from northern Saskatchewan and Alberta south to Minnesota, the Dakotas, and Montana, including the upper Missouri River. Various unrecorded trappers probably reached the heart of this region, the Red River drainage, in the early 1700s. By 1743, Pierre Gaultier de Varennes, Sieur de La Vérendrye, had established two posts in the Red River basin, one at present-day Winnipeg and another near Portage de Prairie.[17] At least five related groups followed the early traders and allied themselves to resident Native peoples creating a rich mix, the Red River Métis. These five groups have particular relevance to the development of Métis identity in western Minnesota, North Dakota, and Montana. The ancestors of the Spring Creek band included representatives of each, and in a country that did not recognize the Métis as a separate people, this varied ancestry contributed much to Euro-American confusion and assumptions as to Métis identity.

One of the five groups, the Great Lakes Métis, had been moving their small, independent, kinship-based networks farther west since the British conquest and the fall of Michilimackinac in 1763. Another group, those freemen and company employees associated with the Montreal trade, also moved west in search of new fur sources. A third group, one with roots in Montreal and the Great Lakes, was the métis of the Missouri River trade who steadily pushed upriver as they opened the Missouri markets. All three competed directly with HBC traders, who had close ties to resident

Cree bands in control of much of the area. The western-moving bands of Chippewas were the fifth distinctive, but related, people coming to this region. Already associated with the Great Lakes Métis, many North West Company employees, freemen, independent traders, and resident Cree bands, the Chippewas followed the beaver west, bringing with them innovative technology, such as steel traps.

The movement of members of these groups onto the upper Missouri River portion of the Red River trade area began before 1683. In that year, Sieur de La Salle reported two such men already living with the Missouri River tribes. By 1704, groups of French-speaking voyageurs traveled the Missouri River backcountry. When La Vérendrye's sons visited the Mandan villages on the upper Missouri in 1742, French-speaking people already resided in the area. Within a few years, freetraders from Michilimackinac and Prairie du Chien, as well as representatives of the HBC and the NWC, initiated trade with the Mandans on the upper Missouri River. The Spanish, based in St. Louis and employing many French speakers from the Montreal and Great Lakes fur trade, also competed for influence on the upper Missouri River. By the end of the century, the upper Missouri villages traded directly with the métis, British, French, and Spanish. The competing companies all employed French-speaking workers who accompanied trade expeditions to the upper Missouri. The children of these workers and their Indian wives would be in a unique position to carry on the work of the upper Missouri fur trade.[18]

After 1805 and the journey of the Lewis and Clark party, the fur trade of the upper Missouri came slowly under the control of U.S.-licensed companies. In reality, many of the same company owners dominated the trade. The workers, too, changed little; the tripmen of the upper Missouri were the same métis and French Canadians as before. It is estimated that at least four-fifths of the engagés (working men under the rank of clerk) were métis or native-born French Canadians. Also during this period, St. Louis traders began to dominate the upper Red River (present-day Dakotas and Minnesota) trade. The availability of markets, the formal establishment of the U.S.-Canadian boundary, and the eventually effective imposition of tariffs drew the Pembina and St. Joseph (North Dakota) trade centers away from the control of Canadian companies and the Montreal market. Throughout the period beaver remained the primary trade item, although after 1815 the demand for buffalo robes gradually rose.[19]

Many of the métis participating in the early Missouri trade settled permanently on the river, some becoming closely associated with the Missouri

River tribes. Others moved north to the Red River, taking part in the establishment of the earliest communities in that area. Pre-1804 Missouri fur-trade records note several family names that occur repeatedly on the upper Missouri and eventually reappear among the Spring Creek band. Pierre Berger, for example, accompanied Missouri Company trader Jean Baptiste Truteau up the Missouri River in 1794. Apparently Berger had been in the area for some time because he spoke a Missouri River language (Ponca). In a position of responsibility, he acted as a trader for Truteau and was second in command if Truteau should be incapacitated. Berger's race or nationality is not mentioned, but elsewhere Truteau wrote that his employees were "Canadian" or "Creole," terms that in the West were often synonymous with métis. There is no way to positively ascertain whether this Berger was a relative of the Pierre Berger who, in 1879, led twenty-five Métis families into central Montana. However, his presence and the repeated mention of one or more Pierre Bergers in the fur-trade records indicate that the family was established in the upper Missouri Valley very early.[20]

An additional name that appears often in the early history of the Missouri and reappears later in central Montana is that of Charbonneau (Charbonneaux). A Charbonneau, described by Don Charles Dehault Delassus, lieutenant governor of upper Louisiana, as a St. Louis "primeras letras" (school teacher), signed a protest letter against exclusive trade in 1801. This Charbonneau had connections to Manuel Lisa, who opened a post on the mouth of the Bighorn River (Montana) in 1807. A better-known individual of this name was the interpreter and guide, Toussaint Charbonneau, the husband of Sacagawea, whom Lewis and Clark hired at the Mandan villages during the winter of 1804–1805.[21]

By the 1820s, métis workers permeated the upper Missouri fur trade. They were the first non-Indians to make the area their permanent home. Many of these métis had close ties to relatives in Canada but also a long history of their own south of the boundary.[22]

Another of the five groups to migrate into the Red River trade area, the Ojibwas, has special relevance to U.S. Métis history. It is through these bands that the U.S. government negotiated land title to the southern portion of the Métis Red River homeland. The Ojibwas, like their Cree allies, also directly influenced Métis economic and social organization through a longstanding relationship extending back to the Great Lakes fur trade. In the U.S. West, the Chippewas, as the Ojibwas were known there, had a continuing influence on Métis customs as both adjusted to plains life. Even today, numerous Montana Métis, as well as many descendants of the Spring Creek families, are members of Chippewa bands.[23]

Chippewa permanent residency on the Red River began in comparatively recent times. In the last decade of the eighteenth century, while the St. Louis traders made their way up the Missouri River, and the HBC, NWC, and independent trappers moved west onto the Red, Chippewa bands also migrated into the upper Red River area. Searching for new territories rich in fur-bearing animals, they continued trading practices already familiar to generations of Montreal and Great Lakes traders. Temporary hunting parties made the first forays to the Red River. As their numbers increased, the Chippewas allied with resident Cree and Assiniboine bands against the Sioux, who also claimed hunting rights in the southern Red River drainage. Although relations between the Chippewas and the already-allied Crees and Assiniboines were not always friendly, they maintained a solid front against the Sioux, traded and hunted together, and intermarried extensively.[24]

The upper Red River trade opened directly to Europeans in the early 1790s when Peter Grant wintered in the Pembina region, near the confluence of the Pembina and Red rivers in present-day northeastern North Dakota. Here he established trade with the Chippewa bands. Business must have been profitable, for in 1797 Charles Jean Baptiste Chaboillez, an NWC trader, opened a post close to the same location. By winter there were three posts at the mouth of the Pembina River, two belonging to the NWC and one to the HBC. The Chippewas made the most of company competition, trading at each of the competing posts.[25]

Eventually those Chippewas who remained on the Red River became known as the Pembina band of Chippewa, a name derived from the Chippewa word *anepeminan* (high-bush cranberry). The area in which they settled (now the northeast corner of North Dakota) and the river that traverses it also took that name. By 1805 Lewis and Clark, traveling to the south of Pembina, referred to the Chippewas "of river Pembena," as one of the three main divisions of "Chipaways."[26]

Freetraders and company men, some with ties to the old Great Lakes trade and already connected to Chippewa families, frequently married women from the Pembina band. As Métis continued to hunt and intermarry with the Pembina Chippewas, Chippewa band and hunt organization helped shape Métis social, political, and military development, and eased their transition from the river-oriented beaver trade to the plains buffalo economy. Semipatrilocal residence with close ties to the wife's family, parental arrangement of first marriages, and a gendered division of labor that left traders dependent upon Indian women's skills all encouraged the development of a Métis society that retained many Chippewa customs and encouraged Chippewa-Métis bonds.[27]

As the Chippewas and the other four groups came together along the Red and Missouri rivers, one village, Pembina, played a decisive role in the development of Métis ethnicity in what became U.S. territory. Here, the Pembina Chippewas and their Red River Métis relatives faced serious challenges to their Métis and Indian identities, their lifestyle, and their economic survival. Settled originally as a Chippewa trading post, Pembina eventually became the center of the upper (southern) Red River fur trade. In 1801, Alexander Henry of the NWC built a post near the ruins of the early Grant and Chaboillez forts. Just after Henry arrived, the XY Company established a post below his, followed a year later by an HBC post at the Grand Passage on the Pembina River. Long before the settlements on the lower Red River became Métis centers, Pembina anchored the southern end of what would become the Red River Métis homeland.

The trade around Pembina flourished, and by 1805 the scattering of company posts became a village, its population supplemented by former company and independent trader families. The 1804 merger of the XY Company with the NWC and the subsequent firing of excess employees resulted in an increase in independent trappers, many of whom settled at Pembina.[28]

Inevitably, however, as the population in the region grew, the pressure of increased trapping depleted the beaver. Scarcity forced Chippewa trappers into new territory despite the risk of encountering enemy Sioux hunters. As beaver became scarce and the Sioux became more aggressive, the Chippewas began to move away from Pembina. Some returned to their former homes near the Great Lakes; others moved farther west. One band settled in the Turtle Mountains of what is today north-central North Dakota. Members of this group had probably been in the Turtle Mountains since 1800 or 1801 and called themselves Mikinakwatshu-anishinabe. They flourished in this area of abundant game, protected by the mountains from both enemies and the fierce prairie winters.[29]

The Chippewas who remained on the western plains adopted year-round buffalo hunting as did their Cree and Assiniboine allies. As the

Chippewas turned to buffalo hunting, these animals satisfied most of their needs, and they became less interested in the beaver trade and the provisioning of posts. Gradually, Métis freemen and independent traders replaced them as the dominant hunters and trappers for the posts.[30]

Drawn by the new opportunity, more Métis freemen and independent traders settled near Pembina. As it grew, the village's character changed. By 1818, it resembled a typical Métis village, with a church and school served by the Catholic priest, Father Sévere Dumoulin. His congregation numbered about three hundred, much larger than that of the first Red River Settlement church built at St. Boniface in 1820, and his school educated sixty students. Pembina priests assured Catholicism's success by accompanying the buffalo hunts, providing religious services and educating the children during the long periods of time that the Métis were away from the settlements.[31]

It is these Pembina Métis and other Métis along the Red and upper Missouri rivers that included the parents and grandparents of many of the families that later settled on Spring Creek in central Montana. The Spring Creek families had deep roots in the five groups who intermarried with local Native peoples and became the Red River Métis. Their ties to Pembina, the NWC, and the Missouri River trade are especially apparent. In fact, family names that appear together in NWC records reappear, still closely associated, later in Montana. Individuals with Spring Creek band names (or those of their mother's family) are actually found in the same canoe seventy years before they settled together in central Montana. For example, in June 1808, a Houle, a Charbonneau, and a Fleury manned a Pembina River canoe. A list of NWC employees, made just after the merger of that company with the rival XY Company, includes twenty-four individuals with Spring Creek band names all working on the Red River. By 1821, all but eight of the Spring Creek band family names are found in the Red River trade area. The majority of those who appear in the Red River and upper Missouri trade region between 1804 and 1821 were NWC employees or independent traders. Most were low-level voyageurs, a smaller number were interpreters, guides, or *contre-maitres* (foremen), and a few enjoyed high-ranking positions of bourgeoisie or clerk. Of the NWC families, many worked out of Pembina and some settled permanently there, joining a growing number of freemen and independent traders. Many of the families that came together on the plains of Montana had a long association in the fur trade of the Red and upper Missouri rivers (see table 1 at end of chapter).[32]

THE RED RIVER COMMUNITIES AND THE EMERGENCE OF MÉTIS NATIONALISM, 1812–1821

After the Métis established themselves in the Red River area, a change in HBC policy created new tensions that had wide-ranging implications for the Métis as a people. By 1812, the HBC had dropped its longstanding policy against retirement in fur country and supported a planned agricultural settlement at the confluence of the Assiniboine and Red rivers near Fort Rouge (the present site of Winnipeg). News of the colony raised fears among NWC employees and freetraders, already settled at Pembina and the Red River area. They viewed it as a threat not only to the fur trade, but also to their dominance in the region. Ignoring or unaware of area residents' hostility, HBC stockholder, businessman, and philanthropist Thomas Douglas, Earl of Selkirk, initiated and backed the project.[33]

After a slow start, the colony's population began to grow, supplemented by Métis freemen, independent traders, and provisioners who headquartered there. Those workers not employed directly by the companies supported themselves by hunting and provisioning the company posts with pemmican, a dried buffalo meat product that their women relatives specialized in making.[34]

After the Selkirk Colony became somewhat established, many Hudson's Bay employees began to consider it an attractive alternative to retiring in the East, a difficult decision that usually necessitated separation from Native families. Although several Native groups disputed actual control of the area, the colonists sought and obtained consent for a settlement from local Chippewas and Crees. As more retired HBC employees moved to the colony, inevitable conflict between NWC employees (together with allied Métis) and the agricultural settlers (supported by the HBC) escalated, endangering the settlement.[35]

By the spring of 1815, trouble over the Métis' right to hunt and trade as they pleased spilled over into violence. They demanded respect for their traditional rights, based on their Indian and European descent, and their long-term residence in the area. A dispute concerning the transportation of pemmican and the shooting death of the new governor, Robert Semple, and twenty others led to what became known as the Pemmican War. This battle and the raids that preceded and followed it proved to be a major milestone in the consolidation of Métis identity to which many historians date the emergence of Métis nationalism. It certainly united the Métis of the Red River area and brought them a publicity they had never experienced. As historian Jacqueline Peterson notes, in 1815 the Métis seemed to "burst upon the historical stage. . . . So sudden was the birth of métis consciousness that it seemed almost autochthonous, an unpredicted welling up from the soil of nationalistic aspirations." But as that same scholar points out, though the battle marked the first organized, public declaration of Métis identity, the roots of that identity stretched well beyond Red River. The Battle of Seven Oaks and the Pemmican War, however, brought recognition that the "New People" of Red River were "not merely biracial, multilingual and bicultural, but the proud owners of a new language; of a syncretic cosmology and religious repertoire; of distinctive modes of dress, cuisine, architecture, vehicles of transport, music, and dance; and after 1815 of a quasi-military political organization, a flag, a bardic tradition, a rich folklore, and a national history."[36]

REORGANIZATION OF THE FUR TRADE, 1821–1830

In addition to bringing attention to the Métis as a distinct group, the Pemmican War highlighted the ethnic differences that corresponded to company background. The social and cultural variation between the NWC and HBC descendants of mixed-Indian descent stood out in stark relief. It was apparent that the "English halfbreeds" of the HBC had not developed the same political consciousness or social distinctiveness as the independent Métis traders, freemen, and NWC employees. However, an event in 1821 ended much of the tension between these two groups of mixed-Indian descent peoples, emphasized their common interests, and set the stage for a new era of Métis development. In that year the NWC and the HBC merged, ending a competition that had shaped events in the valley since the arrival of the first fur traders. The diminished company rivalry allowed the mixed-descent population to recognize their common social and economic position. As all suffered from the discrimination in company policy that became more conspicuous in the 1820s, race became a uniting factor for them. When racial prejudice was exacerbated by widespread layoffs, mixed-descent families found common ground and a common need to protect their social and economic position.[37]

The layoffs following the NWC-HBC merger destroyed the traditional means of support for a large number of families. In response, the HBC attempted to ameliorate the situation by settling retired and dismissed employees as agriculturists in Red River Settlement. It was in the company's interest to prevent its former workers' return to the fur trade as competing independents. Company officials hoped that as farmers, the laid-off workers would present less of an economic threat to the company and would provide the post with needed provisions. Many took up this offer and settled in Red River Settlement. A large number did not, turning instead to part- or full-time independent trading and supplying of the posts. Consequently, despite HBC efforts to the contrary, the layoffs greatly increased the freetrader population.[38]

Because Pembina lay nearer the buffalo herds, many laid-off families joined the freetraders there. Already, by 1819, the population of Pembina was at least forty families, about three hundred people, quite large for early communities of the northern plains. As the Pembina community grew, however, developments to the south put its future in doubt. An international treaty had recognized the forty-ninth parallel as the boundary between Canada and the United States in 1818, but not until the 1823 expedition of Major Stephen Long had anyone actually attempted to mark the boundary's exact location in the Red River area. In August 1823, Long's party found the international border to be just north of Pembina, locating the entire community in U.S. territory.[39]

Governor George Simpson realized that a large Métis population south of the boundary could become an economic, political, and military threat to Red River Settlement. Several factors concerned him and other company officials. They recognized that U.S. traders would attempt to use Métis hunters in an effort to compete effectively against the HBC. In addition to this economic risk, they foresaw several military problems. Principally, Simpson and others feared that a large Métis settlement to the south, hunting so close to Sioux-controlled territory, would escalate tensions with this powerful group and pose a threat to the colony. Simpson also perceived a military danger in the large number of "nomadic" Métis living in what he considered "an uneducated and savage condition." After the Pemmican War, Simpson and the allied Catholic clergy agreed that the only way to eliminate the potential threat was to settle these mobile bands near the Settlement. They hoped that here the hunters would become sedentary farmers under the control and influence of HBC officials and the clergy.[40]

In addition to enlisting the aid of Catholic clergy, Simpson devised a plan to settle the Métis under the leadership of Métis Cuthbert Grant. He reached an agreement with Grant whereby the latter was given a large tract of land west of the colony on the White Horse Plains. Grant was to encourage the Pembina Métis and other semimigratory groups to settle permanently at Grantown (later known as St. François Xavier), well north of the boundary.[41]

Many of the Pembina Métis did follow Grant's lead and settled on the White Horse Plains, greatly adding to the population of Red River Settlement, then only a few hundred people. At the same time, with friends and relatives still in Pembina, the new settlers of Grantown retained their close association with the Pembina Métis. They continued to visit and hunt together, often furthering their close kinship ties by additional intermarrying. They also joined for the large, biannual buffalo hunts that originated and were organized in Pembina. By no means all Pembina Métis located at Grantown, and for many others it was a brief hiatus before a return. Even members of Cuthbert Grant's family kept their ties to Pembina, some later moving to Montana with other Pembina Métis and eventually becoming part of the Spring Creek band. To maintain, as U.S. officials soon would, that the gradual migration back to Pembina from the Settlement was the illegal wandering of Canadians, was an oversimplification, indeed a distortion of a more complex truth.[42]

NEW DEMANDS, NEW RESPONSES, 1830s AND 1840s

By the 1830s Red River Settlement communities were becoming the cultural and economic center of Métis society. Despite differing origins and cultural backgrounds, the biracial descendants of the fur trade established a distinctive lifestyle supported by subsistence farming on narrow river lots and organized their seasons around biannual buffalo hunts. Whether Catholic or Protestant, whether descended from NWC, HBC, or independent trader ancestors, whether identified as "English half-breeds," Métis, Crees, or Chippewa Métis, these people settled in communities bound by kinship and a distinctive way of life. Their restricted economic opportunities and the social limitations imposed from the outside by their biracial background supported a common ethnic identification. Historian Gerhard Ens maintains that by 1835, the Métis communities of Red River Settlement, "regardless of their origins . . . came to be united by common land tenure, economy, and social structure." Company leases (the HBC held title to the land) and a tradition of squatter's rights based on occupation typified Red River land tenure. Most Métis claims to the land were traditional and unofficial, formed by decades of successful, informal implementation and centuries of Native landholding practices. The river-lot organization of narrow holdings, with homes, barns, and cropland near the river and pastures extending back into common-held land, originated in both Scottish and French-Canadian farm practices. Indian-style subsistence gardening, combined with the sale of surplus products to the HBC, buffalo hunting with the sale of pemmican, and part-time labor for the company, structured economic life.[43]

A distinctive Métis culture also flowered. In language, dress, music, and decorative styles, Métis borrowed from French, Scottish, Chippewas, Crees, and other groups to forge unique creations of their own. Men favored bright, finger-woven Assumption sashes, which set off blue or black pantaloons, jackets (capotes) and beautifully beaded leggings, moccasins, and tobacco pouches. The beadwork and embroidery designs often included the "Chippewa rose," a floral pattern accented by traditional Indian linear designs. More plainly dressed, Métis women often wore dark dresses, sometimes accented by brightly embroidered leggings and colorful shawls. Métis fiddlers, in their dark pants, decorated leggings, and bright sashes, played their fast-paced music for ever-popular and frequent dances. Scottish-based jigs and reels with intricate steps were interspersed with French ballads. Their language, too, included both French and Indian aspects. Built on a Cree grammatical foundation, it employed a largely French vocabulary sprinkled liberally with Chippewa and Cree.[44]

As mentioned above, by no means all of these Métis families lived in Red River Settlement communities. Many, while residing part-time in the settlements and selling their pemmican and, perhaps, garden surpluses there, wintered in outlying areas closer to supplies of game and to Indian kin. A great many others lived in villages dispersed throughout the area. Various degrees of association with Indian relatives lent both distinctiveness to Métis society and diversity within it. In some Métis communities, such as Pembina, the residents never depended to any extent on farm produce. These "nomadic" Métis, as both contemporaries and later historians would call them, had organized their economic life around the buffalo.[45]

Observers commented on the distinctive lifestyle at Pembina, noting the colorful, exciting aspects of the hunting-based community. Nevertheless, unfavorable attitudes toward residents' "nomadic" habits, aggravated by new perceptions of race and an increasingly pervasive racial ideology, colored their views. Belief in a scientific racism, which promoted the notion of an innate Caucasian superiority, spread, crystallizing by the mid-nineteenth century. A growing number of proponents considered the inferiority of other races to be genetically inevitable, and therefore condemned the "mongrelization" of superior strains by interracial marriage.

Consequently, attitudes toward people of mixed descent hardened. Terms used by Métis people themselves in a neutral, self-descriptive manner, such as "half-breed," "michif," "Métisse," and "Métis," took on, for non-Métis, a pejorative connotation. Notions of mixed-descent degeneracy and social inferiority became almost universal. Race prejudice intensified throughout the United States and Canada, but hit the Métis people particularly hard because of their biracial background. By 1831, popular publications such as Caleb Atwater's, *The Indians of the Northwest*, portrayed the Métis as a "mixed breed," a "miserable race of men" who were "as motley a group of creatures (I can scarcely call them human beings) as the world ever beheld."[46]

Such views underlay the judgments of many contemporary Euro-Canadian/American observers. William H. Keating, arriving at Pembina in August 1823 when many of the residents were away on the summer hunt, described Pembina in this way:

> The settlement consists of about three hundred and fifty souls, residing in sixty log houses or cabins; they do not appear to possess the qualifications of good settlers; few of them are farmers; most of them are half-breeds, who having been educated by their Indian mothers, have imbibed the roving, unsettled, and indolent habits of the Indians.

Later scholarship, especially the work of French ethnologist Marcel Giraud, took up the theme of Pembina nomadism and indolence. In a typical passage, Giraud wrote, "The same kind of farming without ambition, always secondary to the nomadic life, characterized the Métis groups established on the verges of the colony, and especially at Pembina." Thus the image of the Métis as restless, semicivilized nomads followed them well into the next century.[47]

Euro-Canadian and Euro-American commentators, who viewed permanent residence and property ownership to be hallmarks of respectable citizenship and doubted Métis commitment to a civilized life style, misunderstood the nature of the Métis migratory, buffalo-based economy. Métis buffalo hunters participated in a complex production economy that provided a security unavailable through farming and land ownership. Natural disasters from locusts to droughts, unsatisfactory wheat varieties, and the difficulty encountered in attempting to winter cattle and sheep made agricultural efforts precarious. The needs of the Red River communities were met with buffalo products far more often and securely than with those from the farm.[48]

But a buffalo-based economy had unique requirements, including the proximity of large herds. As the towns and villages on the Red River grew, economic and environmental developments inevitably led to changes in Red River–area lifestyle. The Métis soon exhausted nearby game supplies, and individual, close-to-home hunting no longer provided sufficient provisions for the communities. By the 1830s, the game disappeared along the Red River, and short-duration, small-group hunts close to the settlements and villages became impractical. In response, large-scale, organized buffalo hunts to distant areas became more prevalent. As before, meat, pemmican, and robes from these hunts supplied the Métis throughout the year, while surpluses (especially of pemmican) were sold to the HBC, which provided a small but constant market.[49]

An additional development fundamentally changed the nature of the Red River buffalo trade after 1830. Kenneth McKenzie, a former NWC employee working for the American Fur Company at Fort Union (in present-day western North Dakota), realized that great profits could be made if the U.S. fur trade were opened along the entire length of the Missouri River. The stumbling block had always been the hostility of the Blackfeet on the northern tributaries of the river, who traded with the HBC. McKenzie was familiar with this trade. A former employee of the NWC, let go like so many others after the company merged with the HBC in 1821, he understood a basic weakness of the HBC trade. He knew that the company could not, at this time, profitably trade in buffalo robes. The high cost of travel to Canadian markets, which were two thousand miles away by difficult-to-navigate waterways, made the transport of bulky, heavy buffalo robes prohibitive. The company could only make a profit on the sale of smaller, high-quality furs. Taking advantage of the much easier and cheaper transportation routes of the Missouri drainage, McKenzie in 1827 opened a post on the White River (in what is now North Dakota). The returns of this trade encouraged him to open another post in 1829 (Fort Union), this one on the mouth of the Yellowstone River. McKenzie sent messages to the Assiniboines, Crees, and Chippewas of the region asking for their business. These groups, plus "many half-breed families" who traveled with them, found in McKenzie a market for their robes in addition to lower prices for the goods they bought. With his initial success at Fort Union, McKenzie attempted the next logical steps, the opening of trade to the Blackfeet and to the friendly Crows farther up the Yellowstone. The Blackfeet had long resented and reacted violently to American incursions into their trade area. To accomplish the dangerous task of meeting with the Blackfeet,

McKenzie selected an experienced Métis employee, Jacque Berger, probably the father of Pierre Berger of the Spring Creek band. Berger proved an excellent choice, for he knew the Blackfeet, their customs, and their language, having traded with them while working for the HBC. With Berger, McKenzie sent a small group of French Canadians and Métis who, as French speakers, he hoped would be less offensive to the Blackfeet than English-speaking Americans. Barely surviving the dangerous mission, Berger succeeded in bringing a Blackfeet trading party to Fort Union, thereby opening that profitable trade.[50]

As U.S. companies reached the farthest tributaries of the Missouri River, and the buffalo trade became established on the northern plains, Métis and Indian hunters found that they could make better profits by dealing with American traders. The U.S. market for robes was strong. Popular as bedding, wraps, boots, coats, and military clothing, the robes found an American market eager to absorb all that the Métis produced. In response to the demand, trader Norman Kittson established a post at Pembina in 1844 and actively courted the Métis buffalo robe trade. The forty-ninth parallel as yet made little difference to the hunters, who ignored it. No one enforced tariffs, nor could they in such a vast area still under Native control.[51]

With a good market established by the 1840s, the buffalo hunt took on grand proportions, becoming the principal support of many Red River drainage families. Red River carts, each carrying up to one thousand pounds, hauled the robes to river ports. Joseph Kinsey Howard, journalist and historian, wrote a classic description of this vehicle:

> The cart was built entirely of wood and the noise of its wheel hubs as they rubbed on the axle, which usually was an unpeeled poplar log, was a tooth-stabbing screech which was never forgotten by anyone who heard it; it was as if a thousand fingernails were drawn across a thousand panes of glass.

Hundreds of these carts now rolled across the prairie, carrying provisions to the hunt and products to market.[52]

Alexander Ross, Protestant Scottish resident of Red River Settlement, reported disapprovingly of the dramatic increase in the buffalo trade. He recorded that accompanying the 1820 summer hunt were 540 carts, and with the 1825 hunt, 680. The numbers steadily increased to 1,210 carts in the 1840 summer hunt. Such numbers reflected the growing Métis participation in the biannual hunts and the central position they assumed in the Red River economy.[53]

Ross described the June 1840 hunt in detail. A well-organized and expensive undertaking, it included 1,630 people (620 men, 650 women, and 360 children) as well as the 1,210 carts. Ross estimated that the cost of the hunt, including supplies and labor, was £24,000 at a time and place where a gun cost £2, a draft ox six, and a hunter's wages were ten shillings per day. Red River Settlement families traveled to meet friends and relatives at Pembina, "the great rendezvous on such occasions" and the center for organization of the hunt. After roll call and review of hunt rules and regulations, the hunters held council to nominate leaders. They elected several captains, each with ten "soldiers" under his command to assist in enforcing the rules of the hunt. Most important, they appointed "the great war chief or head of the camp."[54]

On the 1840 hunt, as often before and after, the Métis elected Jean Baptiste Wilkie, a respected Pembina leader whom Ross described as "an English half-breed, brought up among the French," to be chief of the hunt. Thirteen years later, Governor Isaac Stevens of Washington Territory, then with a railroad survey and exploration party, found Wilkie still leading the hunt. "I was much pleased with Governor Wilkie, who is the head of the expedition," he wrote, and he noted Wilkie's "fine appearance and pleasant manners." Wilkie's leadership role was continued by his descendants when, in 1879, his daughter, Judith Wilkie Berger, and her husband, Pierre Berger, led twenty-five families to central Montana in search of the few remaining buffalo. (Relatives of Wilkie's wife, Amable Azure, also moved to Montana. They later settled near St. Peter's Mission, about 150 miles to the west of the Spring Creek band's new home.)[55]

As hunt chief in 1840, Wilkie's responsibilities included acting as president on all public occasions, settling disputes, and returning lost objects to their rightful owners (a practice on which the Métis prided themselves). As with their Native relatives, the Métis chief enjoyed only specific, limited powers. Ten guides shared responsibility for the hunt during the day. They made the important decisions and directed the progress of the hunt. When the camp flag was lowered in the evening, the captains and soldiers took responsibility for setting up camp, no small undertaking. As Ross described, the camp, which "occupied as much ground as a modern city," was "formed in a circle; all the carts were arranged side by side, the trams outward." He wrote:

tents were placed in double, treble rows, at one end; the animals at the other in front of the tents. This is the order in all dangerous places; but where no danger is apprehended, the animals are kept on the outside. Thus the carts formed a strong barrier, not only for securing the people and their animals within, but as a place of shelter and defense against an attack of the enemy without.[56]

The hunting party established clear rules and punishments, the most serious offenses being theft and hunting ahead of the group (which would disturb the herd and make hunting difficult for everyone). These regulations were similar to those of the Métis' Chippewa and Cree relatives, as well as many other Plains Indian groups. In fact, though some of the terminology was European, hunt organization was largely Plains Chippewa. With the exception of the carts, the methods and technology were also similar. What differed most was the economic importance of the hunt for the Métis. For Métis families, the purpose of the hunt was large-scale production of robes (during the winter hunt) and pemmican for sale to the posts. They were dependent upon the fur-trade system and ultimately upon international fur prices for their well-being. Most of their Indian neighbors, and plains groups in general, had economies that were more diversified and less dependent upon European markets.[57]

As the buffalo herds decreased in number and moved farther from the Red River, tensions among groups dependent upon them rose. The rendezvous for the semiannual Métis hunts shifted from Pembina west to the Turtle Mountains, where the animals were still plentiful. The Chippewas, who had moved there in the first years of the century, claimed the Turtle Mountain region as their hunting territory. Though at first they did not mind Métis relatives joining their hunt, they insisted on their right to control the harvesting of game. Regulating the number of buffalo taken became a particular concern as the herds diminished. Major Samuel Wood, commanding an expedition to the area in June 1849, mentioned "old men" among the Chippewas who witnessed a one-half decline in the numbers of buffalo within their lifetimes. They feared that the herds would disappear altogether from the region. While the Chippewas were still socially and militarily allied to the Métis, tensions over territorial rights grew. On September 14, 1852, Way shaw wush koquen abe (Green Setting Feather) of the Turtle Mountain Chippewa band addressed this longstanding dispute, complaining to Isaac Stevens of the Office of Indian Affairs that the Métis were killing too many buffalo, wasting the meat of those that they killed, and driving the herds away. Despite tensions, the Chippewas and Métis had too many ties of kinship and were too dependent upon one another for protection from their common enemy, the Sioux, to allow these grievances to drive them apart. The well-publicized Indian complaints damaged the Métis reputation, however, and, ignoring all other factors, many Euro-Americans and Indians alike blamed a supposed Métis wastefulness for the destruction of the herds.[58]

Meanwhile, both Chippewas and Métis had to travel farther to find the herds as the animals' range decreased. Métis bands traveled west, creating new communities in western Manitoba, Saskatchewan, and western North Dakota. Many Red River Settlement Métis also moved south across the U.S. boundary. Four principal factors caused this southwestern migration from the Settlement. First, the Métis had found it increasingly difficult to succeed, or even find more than part-time work, in the HBC. Second, by the 1840s, buffalo robes replaced beaver as the main trade fur, and a large, profitable market flourished in the United States. The third factor was the free trade movement in the Red River region that expanded an already brisk trade across the boundary. Last, U.S.-Canadian border tension, caused by expansionist dreams and fears in both nations, inevitably involved the Métis. For Americans interested in expanding U.S. territory, the Métis became a welcome ally against the British HBC, which was suspected of similar designs on U.S. territory and trade.[59]

Exacerbating deteriorating U.S.-Canadian relations was the increase in illegal trade across the border. An alliance between Norman Kittson, the American trader at Pembina, and the Rupert's Land freetraders enhanced an already lively cross-border trade. Tensions between the freetraders and the HBC mounted as the Métis flagrantly disregarded HBC regulations forbidding trade with competing posts. Defiance of the attempted HBC trade monopoly was so widespread that when Métis freetrader Guillaume Sayer was brought to trial for smuggling in 1849, judges dared not defy intense public pressure and, although they found him guilty, were forced to set him free. Sayer's release met with cries of "Le commerce est libre" and signaled the end of HBC control of the Red River trade. The inability of the HBC to enforce effectively its regulations opened trade with U.S. markets, increasing Métis commodity production and ushering in a new period of Métis prosperity.[60]

Throughout the 1830s and 1840s, the Métis on both sides of the boundary retained their traditions of joint hunts while maintaining kinship ties and frequently visiting back and forth. A Red River Métis could easily have been born on the prairie, have been married in Pembina, have had a home and garden in St. François Xavier, and have spent most of his or her life west of all of these places. As long as tariffs were not enforced or could be avoided, the U.S.-Canadian border meant little to these people. But the situation could not remain so for long. In the summer of 1845, Captain Edwin Sumner warned the Métis that hunting and trading across the "line" would soon become illegal. By the 1850s, like their Indian relatives, the Métis would be forced between lines on a map, pressed to decide if they were Canadian or American, Métis or Indian, Pembina or Lake Superior Métis, or a variety of other categories, any of which some of their number could rightfully claim their own.[61]

TREATY YEARS: U.S. GOVERNMENT ASCRIPTION OF MÉTIS ETHNIC IDENTITY, 1850–1864

The Métis population south of the boundary continued to grow. A U.S. Army officer assigned to the Pembina region, Major Samuel Wood, reported in June 1849 that two thousand Métis lived south of the boundary line. At Pembina he noted 177 families, including 511 males and 515 females, totaling 1,026 individuals. Father G. A. Belcourt, longtime Pembina resident, found five thousand Métis living in the region, explaining that "the half-breeds are much more numerous than the Indians in this Dept" (Red River and tributaries south of the forty-ninth parallel). He wrote that the Pembina Métis were "the descendents of thirteen different bands . . . which spread themselves from the stony mountains to the Atlantic Ocean," adding that "the very great majority are of Cree or Chippewa extraction."[62]

An 1850 description of the Pembina Métis in a St. Paul newspaper indicates that they had not only retained a unique lifestyle, but that Euro-American attitudes toward their perceived difference were hardening. The characteristic most frequently commented upon, as in this article, was Métis resemblance to Indian society.

> Their dress is half-way between that of the whites and Indians. . . . They wear wild-looking fur caps, blanket coats, pants secured around the waist by a belt, and deer-skin moccasins. Their complexion is swarthy, their hair and eyes black. Their language is an impure French, though all probably talk Indian, besides.

Others commented on their Indian-like lifestyle, noting that for "most of the year they were wanderers, devoting themselves to the interests of trapping and the chase and living in tents or lodges like those of the aborigines." The Euro-American focus on appearance and the lifestyle occasioned by a mobile economy ignored both the demographic growth and political development of Pembina. Although flooding caused many Métis to move west a day's journey to St. Joseph (present day Walhalla), Pembina and St. Joseph remained the economic and social centers of Métis life south of the boundary. In recognition of this fact, in 1858, twelve hundred Métis St. Joseph residents, led by Father Belcourt, petitioned for the organization of the Dakota Territory with St. Joseph as its capital. Although this effort failed, St. Joseph continued as a center of Dakota Territory political life, hosting northern Dakota's first public election in 1867.[63]

Throughout the development of Pembina and St. Joseph, and long before the organization of Dakota Territory, the families that would later make up the central-Montana Spring Creek band were at the heart of Pembina social and economic life. The 1850 Minnesota Territory census and Spring Creek band kinship records show that many of the families had close ties to Pembina and to each other. For example, individuals from each of the Spring Creek family groups (see family diagrams, chapter two) could trace their ancestry to the Pelletier family, whose Pembina presence dates to 1805. Charlotte Pelletier (successively married to Andre Millet dit Beauchemin and Antoine Azure) was ancestor or godmother to many Pembina residents and, thus, connected the Spring Creek families even more tightly to other Pembina Métis.[64]

The 1850 census confirms these ties. Although the census information is limited because census takers visited the Pembina region in late summer when many Métis were away hunting or visiting relatives, it does reveal the residence of many of the families or their parents, who later made up the central-Montana Spring Creek band. Representatives of each of these extended families, which included the relatives of married women and the in-laws of their sons and daughters, were in residence at Pembina during September 1850. For example, Judith Wilkie Berger, daughter of respected elder and hunt chief Jean Baptiste Wilkie, her husband Pierre Berger, and their children lived in the Pembina district. This large family later provided the core and leadership of the Spring Creek band. Included in the census were Judith's father and her mother, Amable Azure. Their son, Judith's brother, Alexander Wilkie, also joined the Spring Creek band in the company of his daughters' families. Judith Wilkie's grandfather was Pierre Azure, brother-in-law of Charlotte Pelletier Azure, thus connecting the Wilkies to many of the other Spring Creek families. Catherine Charette and her husband, Pierre Laverdure, were later members of the Spring Creek band, as were their daughters Virginia (whose husband Francis Janeaux became the band's principal trader and community leader) and Eliza (whose daughter married Janeaux's employee, Paul Morase). Virginia and Eliza were related by their brother's marriage to the Azures and Wilkies. Nearby lived Michel and Madeleine Klyne, the parents of Ben Kline (also spelt "Klyne"), another of the band's traders. Madeleine was the daughter of Charlotte Pelletier and Andre Millet dit Beauchemin and therefore a half-sister of several Azures. Two houses from the Klynes, Isabelle McGillis and her husband, Edward Wells, resided. Their son, daughter-in-law, and grandchildren also later joined the band. Joseph Fagnant, half-brother of Charlotte Adam Lafontaine (mother and sister of several band members), and his wife, Marguerite, were neighbors of Judith and Jean Baptiste Wilkie. The Fagnants and Lafontaines were connected to the Wilkies, Azures, and many other Pembina families through Charlotte Pelletier's sister Josephte, who married Antoine Fagnant. The Fagnants' daughter, Madeline, married Joseph Larocque and accompanied cousins and other relatives in the band to Spring Creek in 1879. These extended families (including in-laws and later marriages) living in the Pembina district in 1850 represented all the original Spring Creek band families and associated traders. (A diagram of the kinship networks may be found in chapter two.)[65]

The location of these families' homes illustrates their close relationship. Census enumerators' instructions included directions to number consecutively both the "dwelling houses" and families in order of visit. The recorded numbers provide an indication of a family's closest neighbors and of families living together (or perhaps on an extended visit) at the time of the census. Representatives of all the Spring Creek band families lived in dwellings that numbered somewhere between 59 and 108, and the "elders" of the group lived even closer, between 59 and 94. The association of these families, noted in the fur-trade records before the 1821 consolidation of the HBC and the NWC, continued into the 1850s.[66]

In 1851, another U.S. government effort to enumerate the Métis provided an additional indication of the extent of Montana Métis roots in Dakota Territory and of their determination to preserve their Métis identity. During the 1850s, as the population of the Pembina River area grew and pressure to enforce border regulations increased, the U.S. government initiated a series of treaty negotiations intended to settle the Indians and half-breeds on reservations. The granting of reserves to mixed-Indian-descent peoples had been a part of U.S. government policy since the end of the War of 1812. It was a popular policy in the Old Northwest, where the United States needed the support of the large French/Indian population. By the late 1840s there had been two proposals to settle the half-breeds on territory purchased from the Indians. Father Pierre de Smet, an early Catholic missionary concerned about the métis of the Missouri River, advocated a "mixed-blood" colony in 1849 and again at the Fort Laramie Treaty negotiations in 1851.[67]

In the Red River Valley, any effort to establish a permanent settlement for the Métis had to include the Chippewas. Their claim to the area, while vigorously disputed by the Sioux, Assiniboines, and Crees, had been recognized by the Hudson's Bay Company and the British government since the Selkirk Treaty of 1817 and was acknowledged subsequently by the U.S. government. When, in 1851, Governor Alexander Ramsey of Minnesota Territory negotiated a treaty at Pembina to acquire land for Métis and Euro-American settlement, he chose to negotiate with nearby Chippewa bands rather than with the contesting parties (most of whom did not live in the area at the time). Two hundred and fifty Red Lake and Pembina Chippewas and "several hundred half-breeds" from the Red and Pembina river villages attended, joined by a smaller number of Pillager Chippewas. Alexander Ross, whose comments were often somewhat biased against both Métis and Americans, commented acerbically but with accuracy on the negotiations.

> If we may judge from the mode of concluding the present compact, the Americans are not very particular in forming their treaties with the Indians. Pembina was disputed ground. The Assiniboine, Crees of the plains, and the Saulteaux [Chippewa] of the woods, all laid claim to it as their land; but the title of the last has always been the most disputed: yet, being found on the spot, they were, without hesitation or inquiry, recognized as the lords paramount of the soil, and with them the treaty was concluded; nor were the principal Chippewa chiefs themselves present—they were distrustful and lukewarm—not willing to sell their lands, and therefore declined to attend.[68]

Ramsey not only failed to include most of the interested Indian parties and recognized Chippewa leaders in the negotiations, but also refused to allow the Métis to participate. Throughout the treaty negotiations, he sharply distinguished Indians from Métis. He acknowledged that the half-breeds had asked to be allowed to participate in treaty negotiations, but he denied their request, citing as his reason their status as "quasi citizens." Ramsey apparently made no attempt to determine the actual citizenship status, place of birth, or length of residence of the Métis involved. His motivation appears to have been his distrust and fear of the influence that the Métis exercised over their Indian relatives. Wanting to keep control of the negotiations, he excluded the Métis, many of whom, like Jean Baptiste Wilkie, were experienced negotiators.[69]

Prevented by Ramsey from participating in the treaty negotiations, the Métis failed to secure an agreement for a Métis reserve. In the end, Congress refused to ratify the 1851 treaty, but the Métis recognized another chance three years later. In negotiations for the Chippewa Treaty of 1854 with the Lake Superior and the Mississippi Chippewas, the Pembina Métis, as descendants of Lake Superior Chippewas, attempted to exercise their rights as Native people and to secure title to land that they considered theirs. This time the ratified treaty included a half-breed provision stating, "Each head of a family or single person over twenty-one years of age . . . of the mixed-bloods, belonging to the Chippewas of Lake Superior, shall be entitled to eighty acres of land."[70]

Several Pembina Métis applied for and received land. But by July 8, 1856, after approving initial land and scrip distribution, the Department of the Interior reinterpreted the entitlement provisions to apply only to those "mixed-bloods of Chippewas of Lake Superior as resided among or contiguous to the various bands of those Indians." This strict residency provision effectively eliminated all the Pembina Métis from entitlement. Nevertheless, scrip continued to be issued regardless of residence for some time. It seems there was disagreement within the department as to what restrictions should apply. In the midst of this confusion, many families later associated with the Spring Creek band applied for land or scrip. The vagueness of the instructions and the various interpretations caused years of delay, turmoil, and charges of fraud.[71]

During the investigations following the fraud accusations, the department assembled lists of those who received land or applied for scrip. Included were the surnames of most of the Spring Creek band families or those of their parents. Specific individuals are difficult to identify because, unless officials recorded comments, names appeared without additional information. Nevertheless, certain members of the Spring Creek band can be identified. In most cases, they did not deny being Pembina Métis, but claimed rights to Lake Superior scrip through their parents. All seemed to have been residing in the Red River Valley, not the Lake Superior area, at the time of application. Familiar names stand out in the lists of applicants. Again, the Pierre and Judith Berger family, the Edward Wells, Sr., and Jr. families, and Amelia and Louise Wilkie (wives of Jean Baptiste and Alexander, respectively) applied. The parents and a half-brother of other band members can be tentatively identified as well.[72]

Authorities rejected many of the scrip applications from Pembina Métis because, upon investigation, these individuals were determined to be Pembina mixed-bloods and not directly associated with the Lake Superior Chippewas. Officials even rejected persons who claimed membership through their parents because they could not prove the required direct association. The reasoning was specious and its application uneven, causing a great deal of controversy. Although some Pembina Métis with Lake Superior Chippewa ties had moved into the Red River area as early as the turn of the century, others came later, and there had been much moving back and forth. There is no question that Pembina Chippewa roots lay with the Lake Superior bands and that many Pembina Métis claimed association with both bands.

Significantly, rather than seeking aboriginal land rights as Indians, many Métis chose to secure title as "mixed-bloods." The testimony on ascertaining the rights of individuals to scrip or land indicates clearly that the applicants themselves, and those testifying as to their identity, considered them to be mixed-bloods. The argument centered not on their dual heritage—both the Métis and the outside communities recognized it—but on the Indian band to which they belonged. Henceforth, the government identified them not as an independent mixed-descent community, but as separate groups associated with specific Chippewa bands.

This identification process was reinforced nine years later, in 1863, when the Department of the Interior attempted to deal with Pembina Métis claims through a treaty negotiated with the Red Lake and Pembina Chippewas. Negotiations took place at Old Crossing on the Red Lake River near present-day Crookston, Minnesota, with Governor Ramsey representing the United States. "Today the Pembina Indians arrived," Ramsey complained, "bringing in their train nearly twice their own number in Half-breeds from Saint Joseph, who insisted in regarding themselves as individually and collectively the guardians and attorneys of the Pembina Chippewas in all matters touching the disposition of their landed interests." Ramsey could not prevent the Métis' coming to Old Crossing because the Chippewas insisted that they participate. Ramsey recognized, as he had in

1851, that the Métis considered themselves, "to a certain extent, the real owners of the soil, and as having even a greater interest in any treaty for its purchase than its far less numerous or powerful aboriginal occupants."[73]

Despite Chippewa demands and Métis claims, Governor Ramsey again refused to include the Métis in the treaty deliberations. This time his rationale centered on the claim of aboriginal title. Only the Indians, he maintained, could cede land based on such title and the half-breeds could not be considered to have aboriginal claims to the land. Ramsey feared the Métis' perceived dominant position in the Pembina area. They clearly outnumbered their Chippewa relatives and were a powerful force. By negotiating only with certain Chippewas, Ramsey managed to bargain from a position of strength without interference. In dividing the Métis and Chippewas during negotiations and in the settlement, he weakened both groups and reached an agreement very favorable to the government's interests. Ramsey again used the tactic of ignoring powerful Chippewa leaders who opposed his aims, and he employed the same tactic to negate the power of the Métis by excluding experienced Métis intermediaries. Ramsey's strategy forced the Chippewas to negotiate from a position of weakness, without all their leaders and without their western-educated relatives.[74]

Although excluded from negotiations, the treaty did include the Métis in its provisions. In addition to setting aside reservations for the "full-bloods," the treaty, in article 8, provided that each half-breed, "related by blood to the ... Chippewas of ... Red Lake or Pembina bands who has adopted the habits and customs of civilized life, and who is a citizen of the United States," was entitled to 160 acres of land. In March 1864 a U.S. Senate resolution modified article 8 of the treaty to provide scrip (to be exchanged for land elsewhere) "in lieu of all future claims for annuities." Métis applicants had to prove both residence and citizenship, difficult for a people with a mobile lifestyle and economic base. Despite the problems involved, many of the families of the Spring Creek band applied for scrip under the provisions of the 1863 treaty. Representatives of all of the extended Spring Creek families, except the Edward Wells II family (which received scrip under the 1854 treaty), applied for and received scrip as Pembina mixed-bloods.[75]

Table 1 indicates that, in the 1850s and 1860s, representatives of the families considered themselves, and were considered by others, to be Pembina mixed-bloods. Many also claimed membership in the Lake Superior Métis band or had parents who were associated with that group. They asserted their rights as Natives and residents of the Pembina region by applying for land or scrip under Chippewa treaty provisions. Thus, they also acknowledged their Chippewa ancestry and close ties to that tribe.

Although superficially seeming to support a unified Métis identity, the 1854 and 1863 treaties' mixed-blood provisions, rather than encouraging an all-encompassing mixed-descent community, fragmented the Métis by forcing them to identify themselves in terms of their various Chippewa ancestries. Thus, government policy divided the U.S. Métis into small groups whose land rights and legal identity were dependent upon their relationship to specific Chippewa bands. The treaties recognized no separate, independent Métis Native rights. Such limited (and temporary) recognition served only to divide the Métis and to void their rights as a separate Native people. Henceforth, many would hold their land in severalty, relinquishing any Native claims or hopes for a Métis land base. Despite the fact that even Ramsey understood that the Métis considered themselves to be "the real owners of the soil" and sought to retain control of the region with their Chippewa relatives, the treaties had a far different effect. The allocation of small, discrete parcels of land or scrip not only left the Métis prey to speculators, who descended immediately, but also scattered Métis holdings, effectively destroying their hopes for a homeland.[76]

The treaties also demonstrated the power of the U.S. government to ascribe identity to small groups. Negotiations forced the Pembina Métis and the bands that evolved from them to seek recognition by identifying themselves according to their relationship to the Chippewas regardless of their perceived self-identification. Most of these individuals also had Cree ancestry in addition to various other combinations of Native lineage, ranging from Iroquois to Assiniboine. However, the U.S. government allocated land or scrip to Métis not on the basis of their Native rights, but upon their rights as Chippewas, ignoring their separate history, lifestyle, language, and religion, their very identity as Métis.

Although identifying the Métis in terms of their Chippewa relatives, the 1854 and 1863–1864 treaties' provisions ironically encouraged a separation between the Métis and the Chippewas. Not only did the chief negotiator for two of the treaties, Governor Ramsey, refuse to negotiate with those whom he identified as mixed-bloods, thereby promoting their difference, but the treaties themselves distributed land to Métis and Indians in a different fashion and according to different criteria. The Métis, if able to provide evidence of a "civilized" lifestyle, citizenship, and European ancestry, were offered (in fact, had no choice but to accept) individual title to a set number of acres. They were physically separated from Indian relatives, who eventually settled on reservations that sometimes excluded their Métis relatives.

• • •

After a half century of Métis ethnic solidification in the Red River area of both the United States and Rupert's Land, the reality of the international boundary signaled a divergence of paths. During the 1850s and 1860s, Métis ethnic development on the northern plains of the United States took a different turn than in Canada. Inept HBC and British policy alienated the Métis and threatened their livelihood. It gave the mixed-descent people of Rupert's Land a common grievance and reason to work together to protect their common interests. Events there defined and politicized Métis identity. On the other hand, in the United States, government policy encouraged the Métis to seek protection of their lands through treaty mechanisms already in place to deal with Indian land. Their only option was to seek Native rights as mixed-bloods associated with a tribe already recognized by the government, not on the basis of Métis Native rights. The allocation of land or scrip to persons identified as mixed-bloods associated with a particular, recognized Indian group came as close as the U.S. government ever would to recognizing the Métis as a distinct people with Native rights. Rather than promoting Métis cohesiveness, the treaty provisions resulted in a fragmentation and effective isolation of the Métis.

Despite outside efforts to alternately define or ignore Métis identity, Métis families adapted, taking advantage of U.S. policy and their relationships with Indian kin to protect their economic base. They were flexible in their acceptance of superficial identification by outsiders, using their inclusive, complex ancestry to best advantage according to the requirements of the time. They did this as extended family units, always conscious of their kinship ties to the larger group. Thus, their self-ascribed identity, though sometimes changing in name, remained essentially the same. The kinship ties and economic networks, which sustained the mobile community, while threatened, remained strong.

TABLE 1
Spring Creek Band Family Name Locations

Family Name[1]	Gt. Lakes	NWC	1850 Pembina Census	Chippewa Treaties	Redriver Settlement
Adam	X			X	X
Berger		X	X	X	
Bottineau		X	X	X	X
Charboneau		X		X	X
Charette	X	X	X	X	X
Daniels/Daignon	X	X	X[2]	X	X
Desmarais		X		X	X
Doney/Lonais/Lyonnais	X	X	X	X	X
Fayant		X			X
Fleury	X	X		X	X
Gardepie/Gardepee			X	X	X
Gayion					
Gourneau			X[3]	X	X
Janeaux	X				[4]
Kiplin				X[5]	
Kline		X	X	X	X
LaFountain	X	X		X	X
LaFramboise	X	X	X	X	X
LaRocque	X	X	X	X	X
LaTray				X	X
Laverdure	X	X	X	X	X
Ledoux		X		X	X
Moran/Morin	X	X	X	X	X
Morase					
Ouellette/Wallet		X		X	X
Ross		X		X	X
St. Pierre	X	X	X	X	X
Turcotte	X	X		X	X
Wells	X	X	X	X	X
Wilkie		X	X	X	X

1. Spellings of Métis names vary. The spellings used here are those found in contemporary documents. Spring Creek family names include the maiden names of married women.
2. 1860 Pembina Census.
3. 1860 Pembina Census.
4. The name Jannot is found in Sprague and Frye's *Genealogy*.
5. Paul Kipland.

TABLE SOURCE: Sources for Great Lakes families include: Baird, "Recollections," 197–221; Fonda, "Reminiscences of Wisconsin," 205–84; Grignon, "Recollections," 197–295; Lockwood, "Early Times"; Morice, *Dictionaire*; Pratt, "Reminiscences"; Russell, *Michigan Censuses*; Thwaites, "Mackinac Register of Marriages," 18:469–513, 19:149; "Fur Trade on the Upper

Lakes," 234–374; "Fur Trade in Wisconsin," 375–487; and "Commercial History of Milwaukee," 253–89; *1830 Michigan Census; 1850 Wisconsin Census.*

Sources for NWC families include: Bradbury, *Travels*; Coues, *New Light*; Stewart Wallace, *Dictionary*; Fleming, *Minutes*; Hafen, *Mountain Men*; Masson, *Les Bourgeois*; Nasatir, *Before Lewis and Clark*; Thwaites, "Mackinac Register of Marriages," 18:469–513, 19:149.

1850 Minnesota Territorial Census, Pembina District; "treaty with the Chippewa . . . 1854," Ex. Doc. 193; Wub-e-ke-niew, *We Have the Right.*

Included in the last column are those with family names found in Red River Settlement. Many, as those of Pembina, also lived elsewhere during their lifetimes (Sprague and Frye, *Genealogy*).

For additional information, see Martha Harroun Foster, "We Know," 143–46, 225.

CHAPTER 2

"Following the Buffalo Trails," 1864–1880

We roamed the prairies . . . just camping here and there without thought of settling permanently in any place, just following the buffalo trails.
CLEMENCE GOURNEAU BERGER,
"MÉTIS COME TO JUDITH BASIN," 1943

Accelerated environmental and economic changes of the 1860s and 1870s presented the Métis with new challenges to their economic well-being, and to their identity as Métis. As Métis families made the decision to follow the buffalo onto the plains of Montana, both the U.S. government and the fast-growing Euro-American population questioned their ethnic/racial, legal, and national identity. They met these challenges as they had in the past, using their flexible band structure and extensive, effectively bilateral kinship networks to maximize the advantages of the new conditions and to buffer themselves from their most harsh effects.

THE BUFFALO ROBE TRADE

During the nineteenth century, a growing market for buffalo products encouraged the production of meat, pemmican, and robes as the Red River Métis families' economic mainstay. By intensifying their profitable buffalo trade, the Métis committed themselves to a mobile, environmentally sensitive resource. Experienced in this regard, having participated in the beaver trade for generations, they adapted quickly to the changing circumstances of buffalo availability and varying market conditions.

The focus of the buffalo market shifted over the century. Until the 1840s, provisioning of post employees, cart drivers, and boat crews with meat products provided the principal market. The HBC depended upon a steady supply of pemmican to maintain the personnel of its far-flung posts. Even after agriculture became common in Red River Settlement, the dependable supplies of easily transported buffalo meat continued to be essential to HBC operations. Any threat to the buffalo hunt endangered the company.

So great was the company's demand for buffalo meat that it absorbed the production of both the Pembina and St. François Xavier hunters. But though it provided a market for meat products, the HBC had long ignored the trade in buffalo robes. This situation changed in the 1840s as the U.S. robe market grew and the Métis turned their attention to that profitable trade. The HBC was forced to accept more robes in order to prevent the loss of suppliers who could sell both meat products and robes to U.S. posts. Company records reflect the change in policy. In 1857 the HBC collected only 4,320 robes from the Red and Swan River areas; by 1865, it had responded to the market and sent out eighteen thousand robes. Métis drivers overcame the difficulties of transporting bulky, heavy robes by using Red River carts to move them as far as St. Peter (now Mendota, Minnesota) and St. Paul, where they were loaded on boats for St. Lawrence and Atlantic coast markets.[1]

The Minnesota trade centers had the advantage of cheap, efficient water transportation. Since 1819 St. Peter had attracted the Red River trade and competed effectively with the Canadians by offering merchandise at competitive prices. After N. W. Kittson opened his Pembina post in 1845, this trade expanded westward. In 1857 Kittson alone sent over four thousand robes to Mendota. The robe market grew steadily, and by 1865 carts from Red River Settlement conveyed nearly twenty-five thousand robes to St. Paul. Pembina and then St. Joseph thrived during these years as centers for the cart trails that led to Mendota, St. Paul, and the Mississippi Valley.[2]

Not only the Red River drainage, but the Missouri River area as well, supplied robes for eastern markets. The Missouri, in addition to providing an inexpensive means of transportation, flowed through the heart of the northern plains herd. The Métis were quick to take advantage of the Missouri River posts. Charles Larpenteur, a Fort Union clerk, reported Métis trading at, and working for, Fort Union as early as 1830. After 1832, as more steamboats reached Fort Union (near the confluence of the Yellowstone and Missouri rivers), the transport of heavy robes became easier, cheaper, and more profitable. The Métis supplied traders who brought robes down the Missouri from river posts as far west as Fort Benton in west-central Montana. Estimates indicate that between 1841 and 1870 traders transported the products (robes, skins, meat, and tongues) of approximately 115,000 buffalo a year down the Missouri River, far surpassing the HBC's seventeen thousand a year. In 1858 Fort Benton shipped close to twenty thousand robes. The HBC, St. Paul markets, and the Missouri River trade allowed the Métis buffalo hunters to enjoy competitive markets and good prices.[3]

The success of the buffalo trade depended on an efficient means to move products to ports where they could be shipped cheaply by boat or barge. The transportation of bulky robes, meat, and pemmican overland for great distances across the roadless plains necessitated specialized freighting techniques. Red River carts, organized into long trains, provided the Métis with a cost-effective and efficient mode of transport. The Métis, already experienced in organizing distant buffalo hunts, were expert at avoiding or overcoming the difficulties and dangers of prairie freighting.

The problems encountered by the Hatch expedition, a battalion of Minnesota volunteers, illustrate the expertise needed for the successful transport of personnel and supplies across the northern plains. Major Edward A. Hatch, who, in the fall of 1863, led three hundred men overland from St. Paul to Pembina, followed a route traveled regularly by hundreds of Métis carts; nevertheless, they met almost insurmountable difficulties and ultimately were unsuccessful in transporting their supplies. Snowstorms and periods of melting made travel difficult for the party. Major Hatch could not find enough pasture, hay, or grain for his horses and oxen. Even though his troops confiscated the winter supplies of Métis whom they encountered along the route, they lost half of their stock to starvation and cold. Eventually, his men and animals near exhaustion, Hatch abandoned the supplies and, taking only the best horses, managed to reach Pembina. Unfortunately, arrival at the settlement did not end the suffering of his troops. Temperatures that winter ranged from twenty to forty below zero, with a record of sixty below on January 1, 1864. Frostbite hindered efforts to construct cabins, and the men, unable to secure vegetables, developed scurvy. Horses, too, died from a lack of hay, grain, and protection, for they were not conditioned to survive on the prairie as Métis stock routinely did. The Hatch expedition failed to move supplies and stock across a route that the Métis with their carts had used for decades. The Métis had developed an expertise that enabled them to profit from expanding buffalo product markets in an area where traditional freighting techniques could not succeed. Their ability to move heavy goods across the plains allowed them the freedom of following the buffalo into new areas without substantial disruption or change in their production and transportation methods.[4]

ENVIRONMENTAL CHANGE AND THE ROBE TRADE

The Métis prospered as the demand for buffalo products expanded, but changes in the 1860s also presented new difficulties that altered the nature of Red River Métis life. During these years, despite the opposition of HBC and church officials, environmental conditions in the Red River area led increasing numbers of Métis to leave farming and engage full-time in buffalo product production and trade. Frost, floods, birds, locusts, mice, and other pests, in addition to droughts in 1863 and 1864, destroyed Red River–area crops during much of the decade. Starvation became a real possibility, forcing relief organizations to aid Red River Settlement. Farther south, the Pembina-area Métis fared better. They depended far less upon agricultural products, and as buffalo hunters, continued to prosper. The message seemed clear to the Métis; given the climate of the northern plains, it was from the hunt, not agriculture, that a dependable living could be made.[5]

As the agricultural disasters of the 1860s reinforced a Métis economic commitment to the production of pemmican and robes, a more long-lasting environmental change altered the very nature of the Red River communities. By the mid-1860s, while the prices received for robes climbed and hunting increased, the buffalo disappeared from the Red River vicinity. Many observers had been commenting on the disappearance of the herds for years. The failure of the animals to return to the immediate area of Red River Settlement underlay tensions that resulted in the Pemmican War of 1814–1816. Diminishing herds also caused dissension between the Métis and their Indian relatives, as demonstrated by Way shaw wush koquen abe's 1852 St. Joseph speech, in which the Chippewa leader accused the Métis of overhunting. In 1857, the Plains Crees of the Qu'Appelle River also complained of the scarcity of buffalo, which they blamed on white and Métis hunters. Again in 1858, the Crees reported the buffalo "very scarce." Many agreed with Edwin Denig, the trader in charge of Fort Union on the Missouri River, who noted that the buffalo "appear in full as great numbers at this time, 1855, as at any period during the last 20 years, *though there is little doubt but the whole number is rapidly decreasing and those remaining confined to a small range, having entirely abandoned other sections where a few years back they were found in abundance.*"[6]

In the 1850s and 1860s, travelers such as naturalist Ferdinand V. Hayden, who was on the upper Missouri several times during those years, attempted to discern the reasons for the disappearance. Hayden wrote:

> As near as I could ascertain, about 250,000 individuals [buffalo] are destroyed every year, about 100,000 being killed for robes. At the present time the number of males to females seems to be in the ratio of ten to one, and this fact is readily accounted for from the fact that males are seldom killed when cows can be obtained. Skins of females only are used for robes, and are preferred for food.[7]

Indian and Métis preference for young cows surely had consequences for the herds' ability to recover from intense hunting. Other contemporary observers blamed half-breed "improvidence" for the "reckless destruction." They condemned Métis butchering practices, including the "wanton revelry [of] taking only their skins and tongues."[8]

Modern scholars continue to debate the causes of the buffalo's near extinction. Hayden's explanation of overhunting, especially of cows, has long been favored as the most obvious, but recently historians of the period have suggested other factors as well. The sheer numbers of buffalo taken are staggering. However, as large as these numbers were, the enormity of the herds enabled them to sustain great losses. Unfortunately, at the same time that the herds suffered increased hunting pressure, they also had to compete for habitat with Indian horse herds and encroaching cattle ranchers and agriculturists. Droughts that plagued Red River farmers also further diminished buffalo pasture, and probably weakened the herds' reproductive capability. Loss of habitat brought another danger in its wake. As domestic animals came in closer contact with the buffalo, new pathogens accompanied them. Although documentation is difficult, the buffalo, having no natural resistance to these diseases, certainly suffered enormous losses. Métis winterers had noticed many sick buffalo on the northern plains. Victoria Callihoo, whose family hunted in the Edmonton area, recalled that "before the buffalo disappeared, hundreds of dead ones were seen on the plains. People said they died of black-leg."[9]

Settlers inadvertently introduced many new pathogens capable of destroying both cattle and buffalo herds. Abortion-causing diseases such as bovine brucellosis, leptospirosis, infectious bovine rhinotracheitis (IBR), and bovine virus diarrhea (BVD) are just the more common of forty or so diseases and agents known to cause abortion in cattle. Cattlemen have long known that by disrupting the reproduction cycle, these diseases could destroy an entire herd. Fatal diseases also threatened the animals. Deadly anthrax and tuberculosis are known to infect twentieth-century herds. Nineteenth-century cattle diseases such as pleuropneumonia, Texas fever, vesicular stomatitis, rinderpest, and hoof-and-mouth disease spread through cattle, causing epidemics such as the Texas fever outbreaks of the 1870s and 1880s. In buffalo, with no immunity, the losses must have been overwhelming. Eventually, the animals may have developed immunities and recovered their numbers, but increased hunting and habitat pressure did not give them an opportunity.[10]

Regardless of the cause, or more likely the combination of causes, the decimation of the great herds challenged the resourcefulness of the Métis. Buffalo extinction on the Red River forced the hunters to travel farther and farther west. During the 1850s, it was still possible to winter in St. Joseph and be close enough to the herds, but by then Red River Settlement and Pembina were too distant. A few years later the animals moved even too far from St. Joseph for hunters to live there year-round. By the 1860s the large organized hunts could no longer leave from the Red River, for the great herds' range had shrunk to an area more than five hundred miles to the west. Western wintering camps, which had become prevalent in the 1840s, increasingly became necessary as centers from which to conduct the hunts.[11]

The wintering communities, strung out from Lac la Biche some hundred miles northeast of Edmonton, Alberta, to the Milk River of northern Montana and southern Alberta, gradually became year-round villages. As distances became too great for regular travel, the hunters no longer returned to the Red River towns. Most of the winterers relocating in the new settlements were the already related families from St. François Xavier, Manitoba, and the Pembina-St. Joseph, North Dakota, area. The Métis population of these towns correspondingly shrank as the buffalo hunting families moved west.[12]

Whatever caused the herds to diminish, the result was a dramatically altered Métis environment in the 1860s. The Métis people responded quickly, adopting coping strategies that led them far west of Red River. But not all of the challenges that the Métis faced in the 1860s were environmental or economic. As they moved west, they could not escape a hardening racism among the growing Euro-American population. Non-Métis attitudes toward and perceptions about people of mixed-Indian descent would have enormous consequences for Métis relations with U.S. government officials, businesspeople, and settlers.

"REJECTING CIVILIZATION"

In the non-Métis mind, wintering emphasized the nomadic, Indian–like aspects of Métis society. As the Métis migrated into what is today western Saskatchewan, Alberta, and Montana, the non-Métis public viewed them not as businesspeople, successfully extracting a profit from area resources, but as nomads who, unable to succeed as agriculturists, had reverted to their dominant primitive instincts. Most Euro-Canadians and Euro-Americans viewed wintering as a retreat to nomadism, a tragic inability to meet the challenges of the modern world. Though the profits available in the buffalo trade were obvious to the Métis, others were sharply critical of the accompanying lifestyle, especially as the hunting families gave up farms and gardens to pursue a semisedentary life. Already by the 1860s the image of the Métis in the popular mind, especially in the United States, was one of carefree indolence, lack of responsibility, and disregard for property.[13] This image had serious repercussions for the Métis as the non-Métis majority debated their suitability as responsible, fully entitled citizens and welcome neighbors.

Indicative of popular attitudes, contemporary popular literature solidified common perceptions. A *Harper's New Monthly Magazine* article, published in 1860, provides a glimpse into that decade's middle-class Euro-American attitudes toward the Métis.[14] The article's depiction of Métis society is typical of the period, and its large, transnational readership meant that such notions reached even the most remote corners. Unflattering representations of Métis life in popular literature ensured that the Métis would face the additional challenge of discrimination as they came into more frequent contact with a growing non-Métis, Indian-fearing population.

In his *Harper's* article, "To Red River and Beyond," author Manton Marble provided beautiful descriptions of the Red River countryside and exciting tales of buffalo hunts. He marveled at the skill and bravery of "half-breed" hunters. Despite those exciting and colorful images, Marble's admiration for the Métis fell short of respect. For example, gentle ridicule, faint praise, and innuendo riddled his description of Métis community leader, trader, business owner, and representative to the Minnesota Territorial Assembly, Joe Rolette. After implying that Rolette's political past could not bear close scrutiny, Marble belittled his generosity. Marble described him as "hospitable and generous beyond reckoning, [but] reckoning on equal unselfishness in return; giving you his best horse if you ask for it, and taking your two mules if he needs them." Rolette, moreover, was "too generous to his debtors to be just to his creditors." Generosity is a Métis trait mentioned by most commentators. Yet the characteristic is almost never allowed to stand alone as a compliment, but is instead followed by a qualifier, as Marble did here. The article portrays Métis generosity not as selfless sacrifice, but as a lack of responsibility and an absence of good judgment. Also typical of the article is the humorous but unfair description of Rolette as "a good Catholic, believing especially in absolution." Rolette was not presented as one in whom trust could be placed. He was colorful but not stable, generous but not to be trusted, hardly an example of industrious virtue or the material of solid citizenship.[15]

Marble had an even less favorable opinion of the hunting families. To him they seemed "semi" aboriginal in their pleasures and lifestyle. He saw the leaders, too, as somewhat closer to savagery than civilization. When he observed Baptiste Wilkie, "President of the Councilors of St. Jo," and his party returning from a treaty-making expedition to the Dakota, he described not a distinguished team of negotiators, but a "motley crowd" who, when greeted, shouted "halloos that could come from none but semi-civilized throats."[16]

Marble's regard for the women of these families was especially low, ranging from disapproval to pity. Since to many Euro-Americans the condition of women in a society provided a significant indicator of that group's level of civilization, his unfavorable description of Métis women served to distance all Métis from "polite society." Marble was especially offended by his observations during a Métis dance. He was unpleasantly surprised to find women there with no hoops in their skirts (this was the era of Scarlett O'Hara styles). Worse, several women were breast-feeding in full view of everyone, and, beyond his comprehension, those not dancing sat unceremoniously on the floor! Drawings accompanying the article also accentuated Métis otherness. Whereas elsewhere in the issue, well-dressed, respectable Euro-American women stand decorously in corseted gowns made from yards of material spread wide by large hoops, this article depicts Métis women vigorously dancing, unkempt hair flying, and unhooped skirts reaching only to the knees of their fast-moving, well-exposed legs.[17]

The noted lack of propriety and consequent suggestion of sexual permissiveness reinforced an implied lack of control that Métis women had over their bodies and their lives. Though thought to be kindly treated by the more civilized Métis upper-class men, ordinary Métis women were portrayed as drudges whose position and welfare were tenuous and dependent upon the uncertain nature of their husbands.[18]

Although Marble compared the Métis to their Indian relatives, he did not confuse the two. His characterization of nearby Indian bands (whose tribe he never mentioned) indicates that he considered these people to be in an entirely different category than the Métis. His description of a band camping near Fort Ellice has a far different tone than that of the bemused, mocking portrayal of the Métis. In the Indian camp, "villainous vermilion, lamp-black, and yellow-ochre disfigured their earthly habitations with hideous symbols." "Repulsive representations of the Deity" adorning some lodges offended the author rather than producing a sense of spiritual kinship. On visiting a trading post, Marble again utilized the Indian custom of sitting on the floor to indicate their level of barbarity. In this case, unlike that of the Métis, where at least some individuals sat in chairs, the Indians not only rested, but also, to his disgust, preferred to eat while sitting upon the floor. Even in the home of their employer, trader William McKay, while their "betters" dined at a well-set table, the Indian employees sat on the floor of a back room, putting themselves not only "below the salt" but also outside it. The author apparently found no human commonality or connection with the Indian band. Whereas the Métis did not measure up to Euro-American standards, the Indians were beyond measuring. From this article, one is left with the impression that if the Métis worked hard at it, they could possibly achieve respectability. The potential, at least, existed. The author found Indians, on the other hand, totally outside any potential for civilized behavior.[19]

It was such ambivalent attitudes that the Métis met as they moved west and came into increasing contact with Euro-American officials and settlers. In the early 1860s popular literature, like the half-breed provisions of the 1854 and 1863–1864 Chippewa treaties discussed in chapter 1, recognized the Métis as a people closely associated with, but separate from, their Indian relatives. Increasingly, this literature, like government policy, defined not only what it was to be Métis, but also the degree to which the Métis people were part of the Euro-American or Indian communities.

THE MILK RIVER YEARS, 1865–1879

The . . . country is notable primarily for its weather, which is violent and prolonged; its emptiness, which is almost frighteningly total; and its wind, which blows all the time in a way to stiffen your hair and rattle the eyes in your head.

WALLACE STEGNER, *WOLF WILLOW*, 1955

When the Métis first moved to the plains of Saskatchewan, Alberta, and Montana to be nearer the ever-decreasing buffalo herds, Euro-Canadian and Euro-American attitudes toward them played little part in their decision. They did not expect to confront either prejudice or threats to their identity in isolated wintering communities. Their concerns were the proximity of the buffalo and the availability of traders to take their produce and provide supplies. At first the wintering sites were temporary communities where families lived in lodges. Occasionally they would build rough cabins, but as these camps lasted only as long as the herds remained nearby, they would abandon the sites after a winter or two. The camps varied in size, as did the hunting bands that occupied them. Sometimes just one extended family traveled together; other times several bands, as many as two hundred individuals, would congregate. Band membership constantly shifted as groups broke up and reformed. The Métis spent summers following the herds, making jerky and pemmican from the meat. In the fall, after the buffalo coats became prime, the families went out again for robes and fresh meat. In 1873, George Dawson, a member of the U.S.-Canadian boundary survey, noted Métis wintering camps at Wood Mountain and Cypress Hills, and along the Milk and the Whitemud rivers. Dawson described a summer camp that resembled the hunting camps of the 1840s. The circle arrangement protected the band, their stock, and supplies. Priests often accompanied the hunting parties to say Mass, perform marriages, and educate the children. In the winter, the band that Dawson observed moved to Wood Mountain, where they had already erected cabins. He reported that rather than returning to Red River markets, these Métis sent their robes out on the Missouri River, fifty or sixty miles to the south.[20]

By the early 1870s, wintering sites included the older ones of Turtle Mountain, Wood Mountain, and Qu'Appelle River as well as more than a dozen others scattered throughout present-day Alberta, Saskatchewan, North Dakota, and Montana. Many of these camps grew into permanent communities, and ones such as St. Laurent (Batoche) played important roles in Métis history. Many remain Métis communities to this day. A favored wintering site, especially for the Pembina Métis and a number of their St. François Xavier relatives, was along the Milk River and its tributaries. The Milk River winds across the Canadian-Montana border, through the vast semiarid grasslands of north-central Montana and southern Alberta. This seemingly stark and forbidding country, which looked much like a desert to early Euro-American and Euro-Canadian agriculturists, was among the last refuges of the buffalo.[21]

Although the northwestern plains through which the Milk River flowed attracted buffalo hunters, its weather had discouraged most others. Modern weather statistics give an indication of the conditions encountered by those living in the region. On the western edge of the plains, near Helena, Montana, the coldest official temperatures recorded in the contiguous United States were logged at Rogers Pass, 130 miles south of the Milk, where it reached seventy degrees below zero on January 20, 1954. Temperatures are also extremely variable and unpredictable there. At Browning, Montana, about thirty miles south of the Milk's headwaters, temperatures dropped from forty-four degrees above zero to fifty-six below in a twenty-four-hour period in January 1916. Summer temperatures routinely pass one hundred degrees on the eastern Montana plains, and 110 is not unusual. As extreme as the weather is, it was the infrequent rainfall, rather than the heat and cold, that most discouraged settlers. Rainfall throughout the area is light, decreasing as one travels east on the river. Ranging from fourteen inches a year near the Rockies to between eleven and twelve inches in the present-day Havre, Chinook, and Malta areas, precipitation often falls in the form of snow or all at once in violent thundershowers or hail. The region's semiarid conditions preclude the survival of most crops. Early observers' belief that agriculture could not succeed in the area was realistic. It was not until modern grain varieties, farming techniques, and equipment enabled that most hardy of all grains, wheat, to grow in select areas that agriculture could consistently support communities there. Twentieth-century novelist Wallace Stegner echoed the opinion of all but the buffalo hunters and later land speculators when he wrote of his boyhood home near Frenchman Creek, a tributary of the Milk: "If you owned it, you might be able to sell certain parts of it at a few dollars an acre; many parts you couldn't give away."[22]

Regardless of its weather and agricultural potential, as long as the buffalo thrived on the Milk River drainage, Indian and Métis hunters prospered with them. Métis were already making a living on the Milk River in 1835. Charles Larpenteur, a Fort Union employee, noted that half-breeds frequented the river valley, "which abounded with beaver." By 1853 the beaver were gone, but Euro-American travelers wrote of Métis buffalo hunters pushing into the traditional territory of the Milk River peoples (Assiniboine and Gros Ventre). Organized bands of Métis buffalo hunters were hunting on the Milk River by 1866 when Ben Kline, a Pembina Métis, found many already living there. Louis Shambow, with another group of "Half Breeds," had arrived in 1866. Two years later, in 1868, Turtle Mountain

Métis Baptiste Gardipee and his family also left their game-depleted Dakota home and passed through the Milk River area.[23]

With a group of ten families (thirty people) and thirty carts, the Guardipee family joined Tom Lavatta, a Métis trader who had been living near Fort Benton, Montana. The band accompanied four hundred other Métis carts traveling west to hunt. When the Guardipees reached the Milk River, they found a "great camp of breeds . . . somewhere in the vicinity of where Dodson [Montana] is now." Before traveling on to Fort Benton, farther west on the Missouri River, the Lavatta party spent a few weeks resting, visiting, and hunting. Eli Guardipee, the young son of Baptiste, later recorded his memories of the Milk River Métis camp.[24]

> It was truly a happy life that these people were living. The camp was in the midst of the buffalo herds and they hunted and worked hard during the day but when night came they danced and sang the old French songs, until the late hours, arranged for many and divers horse races for the following day,—then slept the sleep of people who had no cares for the moment.[25]

Other accounts also stress the good life that the Métis led on the Milk River, recounting the fun that they had, the plentiful buffalo, and their relative prosperity. Clemence Gourneau Berger described her life as a winterer years later for the *Lewistown (Montana) Daily News*. Born in Pembina in 1842, she was the oldest of Red River Métis couple Joseph and Judith McMillan Gourneau's eleven children. Her parents had moved to Pembina from Red River Settlement before her birth. Clemence Gourneau married Isaie (Isaiah) Berger, son of Pierre and Judith Wilkie Berger, at St. Joseph in 1870. After their marriage the couple traveled extensively in Dakota, Montana, and Canada, as Clemence put it, "just camping here and there without thought of settling permanently in any place, just following the buffalo trails." Clemence's first two children were born at Wood Mountain (southern Saskatchewan), where her husband's family was hunting buffalo. They did not stay long in any one place. From Wood Mountain they moved back to the Milk River and then to the Cypress Hills (southern Saskatchewan and Alberta). As the herds became harder to find, they stayed longer in Montana, remaining in the Milk River area continuously for about six years before moving as part of the Spring Creek band to the Judith Basin.[26]

Clemence Berger remembered that "for . . . supplies we generally had some trader with us, like Francis Janeaux and others, who always had a supply of tea, sugar, tobacco and so forth." While the men did the hunting, "women did all the tanning of the buffalo hides, made jerky meat, pemmican and moccasins." Although her memories were pleasant she noted:

> We endured many hardships, too. There were times when we could not find any buffalo or other game, and occasionally even water was hard to find. Yet, somehow, we were all happy and, with all our miseries, we never heard any complaints.[27]

Like many observers, she remembers Métis cheerfulness in the face of deprivation.

While they "roamed the prairies," Berger noted that she and her husband were "always in the company of people of part Indian blood" who traveled in "many groups."[28] Her portrayal is consistent with traditional Métis band structure as well as that of their Chippewa and Cree ancestors. But although band organization and lifestyle had many similarities to that of Indian relatives, Clemence Berger was careful to point out the differences between her people and the Indians.

> You might think that we lived the life of real Indians, but one thing we had always with us which they did not—religion. Wherever we were we had some Jesuit missionaries with us. They baptized our children and instructed them in the Catholic faith, and we always did try to live in accordance with their teaching. In fact, in those early days, I believe people generally were more deeply religious than they are now. Every night we had a prayer meeting. Just before a buffalo hunt, we would see our men on bended knee in prayer.[29]

Berger further underscored the distance her people felt from Indian groups when she described the Nez Perce, whom she witnessed fleeing toward Canadian territory in 1877. The pity she feels for the Nez Perce emphasizes the comparative security and freedom of the Métis and her own identification, despite this sympathy, with U.S. officials.

> We were there [in Montana] when Chief Joseph and his fleeing band of Nez Perce were being pursued by *our* United States Army. These poor Indians were about starved, they traded their good horses for any amount of dried meat, and also bedding. It was a most pitiful site to see their little children, heads sticking out of some sacks made for the purpose and fastened on each side of the mother, riding on horseback.[30]

The Indians' plight disturbed her, but Berger had no doubt as to which was "our" side in the matter.

A large part of Clemence Berger's perceived difference from her Indian neighbors and relatives was her Catholicism. She mentioned that missionaries traveled long distances to accompany the Métis winterers. Some of these priests came south from the wintering communities in Saskatchewan and Alberta; still others traveled east from the Blackfeet mission of St. Peter's. St. Peter's Mission, which after several moves, was located near present-day Cascade (west-central Montana) provided for the religious needs of a large section of Montana. Priests from this mission were baptizing Métis children and performing marriages at Fort Benton, on the Missouri River, as early as 1858 and on the Milk by the 1870s. When priests were not present, Métis elders would take over certain of the responsibilities. For example, Virginia Janeaux's father, Pierre Laverdure, led the frequent community prayers in the absence of a priest. In 1877, Joseph Gardepi performed Marie Selma Gardepi's baptism, which was later sanctified by Rev. Camillus Imoda, S.J., a St. Peter's missionary.[31]

Other accounts round out a picture of everyday life on the Milk River that underscores the differences between Métis community life and that of their Euro-American and Indian neighbors. The Métis had what amounted to an organized government, much like that developed years earlier for the large buffalo hunts. Samuel O'Connell, bookkeeper for Francis Janeaux (Juneaux), noted that the Métis on the Milk River "had a code of laws and were governed by a council of Twelve, under their chosen [leader] Gabriel Ausur [Azure]." The laws, he remembered, were "in some cases very severe." For example, punishment such as "flogging and confiscation of their horses, carts, buffalo, etc." resulted if "one of their number use[d] disrespectful language towards any of the women, or girls or offer[ed] any insult." Although strict, O'Connell continued, "there [were] not many occasions to administer the law as the infractions . . . were very few."[32]

In addition to explaining camp government, O'Connell described Métis women's dress during the period. He remembered that "their garb was quite picturesque always clean and neat." The older women "wore dark colored dresses and double width broadcloth cloaks—with black handkerchiefs around their raven black hair," while the younger women and girls "wore head gear of brighter colors." The women "always wore the insignia of their faith, a German Silver Cross about 5 inches long."[33]

In his recollections of an 1860s Milk River Métis camp, Louis Shambow, like so many commentators before him, noted what "a happy people" the Métis were and what good times they had. He reported that one "of the first things they would do when they got in a permanent camp was to build a dance house." They constructed the building from hewn cottonwood logs with hides stretched tightly over them to make a good floor for the dancing. He remembered that "the fun that we had was beyond telling." The dances were so important to the Métis community that, according to Shambow, "the Priest could do anything with them but stop [the] dancing."[34]

Unfortunately, life on the Milk River was not quite so carefree as the young Eli Guardipee, Clemence Berger, and Louis Shambow fondly remembered. The Métis were not the only occupants of the area, and competition among hunters and traders, plus a growing and suspicious military presence, caused continual trouble for the Métis. When Ben Kline returned to the Milk with a trading party in 1866, territorial law officers harassed his group almost immediately. U.S. marshals, led by X. Biedler of Helena, accused the party of selling ammunition to "hostile" Lakotas. Biedler confiscated their goods, which Kline valued at fifteen thousand dollars, and set fire to their cabins. The marshal then forced traders Antoine Gladue and James Francis across the border into Canada, but allowed the others to remain in U.S. territory. The loss of their cabins, goods, and traders left the remaining families without supplies or protection for the winter. Since the marshal also confiscated their ammunition, the band had no means to provide these essentials. Upon complaining to Biedler that they would starve without means to secure provisions, Biedler granted Francis Avila Janeaux, a trader known to the band from Dakota Territory, a license to trade with them on the Milk River.[35]

Little is known of Janeaux's background. Although he was very vague about his past after settling on Spring Creek, a few things can be pieced together. According to local newspaper articles, Janeaux was born in Montreal. While some descendants insist that he was of European descent, he was more likely a member of the well-known Milwaukee métis trade family of the same name. Janeaux spent at least part of his early years on the Missouri River, where he gained extensive experience in the fur-trade business, first with the American Fur Company and later with Durfee and Peck of Leavenworth, Kansas. By 1866 he was at Fort Stevenson, North Dakota, and soon thereafter moved to the Milk River.[36]

Because of Janeaux's experience with U.S. fur-trade companies and because he was one of the few on the river who spoke English, Biedler employed him to help control the Milk River trade. In March 1868 or 1869, after Biedler arrested a relative of the Milk River hunters, Frank Ouellette, for smuggling, the marshal appointed Janeaux deputy detective to help him gather information about other illegal traders in the area. The campaign to deport Métis traders bringing in Canadian goods was, in part, the result of genuine fears that they were supplying arms and ammunition to Lakotas, whom the government considered hostile. The 1862 Minnesota Sioux uprising caused a widespread paranoia concerning these roaming bands, and the refusal of many Lakotas to remain on their designated reservations aggravated this fear to the point of hysteria.

U.S. Army correspondence indicates that the Métis-Lakota trade was of great concern to officers in Dakota and Montana. In January 1865, Col. C. Dimon accused Canadian Métis of trading with Lakotas, writing that the Lakotas were "rejecting all overtures of peace and being incited to unlawful acts and encouraged by presents and munitions of war by certain parties, said to be from the Red River of the North." He concluded his letter by requesting permission to "break up these trading parties" and prevent their trading with the Indians. On receipt of this report, Major-General John Pope concluded, "It seems impossible to restore quiet among the Northwestern Indians until some steps are taken to prevent interference of English subjects."[37]

In addition to military concerns, Montana businessmen—especially in the trading center of Fort Benton—wished to eliminate those Canadian competitors who operated without licenses and smuggled goods in from Canada (Rupert's Land was annexed to Canada in 1870). Federal licenses to trade with resident Indians were a sought-after commodity and, if secured, ensured financial success. Two business owners, Charles A. Broadwater and Thomas C. Power, went to the extraordinary lengths of agreeing to give up their profitable, but illegal, liquor business to guarantee the receipt of a federal license. When James Wright, superintendent of Indian Affairs in Helena, Montana, threatened these businessmen with the loss of their licenses if they did not give up the "whiskey trade," they saw the wisdom of discontinuing the practice. Power and Broadwater even took on a newfound respectability, condemning the business that had supported them for so long.[38]

Despite their recent involvement in the liquor sales, Fort Benton business people, in order to discourage competition from Métis traders, routinely encouraged lurid articles concerning supposed "Canadian" Métis traders' illegal liquor trade and sales of ammunition to Indians in local newspapers such as the *Benton Record*. In 1879, the editor of the *Record* wrote that "a half-breed camp is nearly as great an attraction for hostile Indians as a herd of buffalo is to a pack of famishing wolves, and while the half-breeds are permitted to roam at will, the hostiles will never want for ammunition or whiskey, or cease to prowl on the outskirts of civilization and rob the white settlers of life and property." The editor complained that the Métis enjoyed "more privileges than are allowed white families who are not permitted to reside upon Indian reservations, much less to carry on an illicit trade with hostile savages." Early articles such as this one established the notion in Montana that all Métis were illegal immigrants from Canada who made a living from supplying arms and liquor to "hostiles."[39]

Francis Janeaux probably survived the political intrigue because of his long association with U.S. fur companies, his continuing ties to licensed companies, and his cooperation with U.S. marshals. Eventually, in partnership with the Euro-American trading firm of Leighton Bros., Janeaux built a substantial post near the mouth of Frenchman Creek. The post, known as Fort Janeaux, or Medicine Lodge, consisted of a stockade and several log cabins, one of which Janeaux reserved for himself and another for his clerks and interpreters, including Ben Kline. Janeaux traded for buffalo robes, furs, meat, and pemmican with traveling bands of Missouri River Indians and with about a hundred families of Red River Métis. After a few years at the mouth of Frenchman Creek, Janeaux followed the Métis hunters downriver to a site near present-day Saco. As Kline explained, "It was necessary, of course, as you know, to follow the buffalo."[40]

The survival of Janeaux's business depended upon retention of a trading license. Janeaux's awareness of his complete dependence upon the good will of Deputy Marshall Biedler in this matter is illustrated by the following incident related by Ben Kline years later. Kline recalled that although federal trading licenses prohibited the sale of liquor, Janeaux, like almost everyone in the area, including Biedler himself, "was . . . very fond of liquor." One day, according to Kline, a bootlegger "arrived at the trading post and gave Juneaux [Janeaux] a few bottles of liquor." Not wishing to jeopardize his license, "Juneaux, who was sort of a deputy marshal under Biedler, find [sic] the bootlegger $10.00." Then, in order to not unduly discourage a valued liquor supplier, Janeaux "pulled a $10.00 gold piece out of his pocket and paid the fine himself." Janeaux immediately "dispatched Kline to the headquarters of X. Biedler with a letter and the $10.00." Reportedly, Biedler "was very much delighted with the transaction." Janeaux and Kline were also quite pleased with the arrangement, and Kline noted that "thereafter they had no trouble with X. and his deputies." Understanding the political realities of the time was essential for a successful trading-post operation.[41]

The need to compete in the business climate of Montana Territory left most Métis traders at a disadvantage. Not having the political contacts, money, or English-language skills necessary to gain influential contacts, they could seldom secure the federal licenses. Because they frequently traveled back and forth across the border, U.S. businessmen and government officials suspected them of importing goods without paying required duties. Moreover, rather than an advantage as in the past, their Indian heritage and contacts caused suspicion in a territory where most Euro-American communities still feared Native raiding parties. Nor were the handicaps under which the Métis labored offset by the traditional middleman role between white and Indian, a position no longer relevant now that reservation and military officials communicated directly with their "charges."

Although the Métis traders faced a hostile business climate in the United States, the new conditions strengthened their role as leaders in their own communities. Having to constantly negotiate the right to hunt and trade on traditional Indian land and on reservations now controlled by territorial officials, the Métis found it useful to select leaders who were politically adept, could prove U.S. citizenship, were western educated, and spoke at least some English as well as the common Métis language, Michif, and a number of Indian languages. The current situation on the Milk River put traders in an especially elevated position within the band, as they often were the only English speakers and were more likely to understand the realities of dealing with territorial regulations. This situation accentuated the traditional respect with which the Métis, as well as their Chippewa and Cree relatives, held traders and strengthened their leadership role. The following contemporary observations by H. M. Robinson illustrate a Euro-American view of wintering camp traders' position in Métis society.[42]

> [The trader] is looked up to by his fellow as a kind of Delphic oracle upon all disputed points, on account of this superior wealth and standing. . . . He assumes an air of vast importance as the head man of the camp. He becomes the arbiter in all petty disputes, the umpire at horseraces, and general referee in knotty and vexatious games of grand-major, poker and the moccasin-game. His authority is second to none save the priest, who, as the spiritual leader of the camp assumes the first place by right of eminent fitness and propriety.[43]

Although Robinson's comments are overstated and ignore the buffalo hunters' long tradition of elected leadership, he was correct in his observation that traders enjoyed great respect. As he noted, they were usually men of above-average wealth because trading among the winterers required a greater outlay of capital than had been necessary for earlier freetraders.

Only prosperous Métis could afford the expense of outfitting the necessary trading party and traveling to the distant winterers.[44] The restriction of trading to those of at least moderate wealth and the increased prestige of the position widened the economic and social distance between traders and hunters. When Janeaux established his trading post, his relative prosperity and the respect traditionally accorded traders positioned him as a community leader and placed him and his employees socially and economically above the common hunter.

Though respected by the Métis, a trader's success ultimately required kinship ties to his customers. Janeaux cemented his relationship with the Milk River bands by his marriage to Virginia Laverdure, daughter of Métis elder Pierre Laverdure. Pierre Laverdure was born in Pembina around 1819. He was listed in the 1850 Pembina census and was issued scrip as a Pembina Métis under the 1863–1864 Chippewa Treaty. Pierre Laverdure and his wife, Pembina Métis Katherine Charette, like many Milk River families, had ties to both Pembina and St. Francis Xavier Métis and were related to many (perhaps all) of the Milk River bands. By establishing his post among his wife's relatives, Janeaux extended his influence to the surrounding related bands. He then strengthened his family ties by hiring his wife's relatives. When, in the late 1870s, as part of the Spring Creek band, he built a trading post on Spring Creek in the Judith Basin, all of his associates and employees were members of his wife's family.[45]

Janeaux's marriage to Virginia Laverdure allied him to her parents and the families of her brother and two sisters, who traveled with other relatives on the Milk River. Virginia's brother François was married to Marie Turcotte, whose brother, Vital Turcotte, married Adele Berger, daughter of Pierre Berger and Judith Wilkie Berger. The Turcotte/Berger marriage joined the Laverdures and Janeauxs to those large and important families who also hunted on the Milk River. Another marriage reinforced the trader-band ties. Virginia Laverdure's sister Eliza married Frank Daniels (Daignon) and the Daniels's daughter Margaret married Paul Morase, who worked for Janeaux. Although scholars and commentators have often described Métis families as patriarchal and assumed that band formation centered on a male leader, his sons, and their wives, this is not true of the Laverdure/Janeaux families. Janeaux became part of an extended family that included his wife's respected, elderly parents, her two sisters' families, and that of one brother. The senior Laverdure daughters' relationships to their father and brother, as well as their sisters, mother, and niece (daughter) were as significant in determining band membership and residence as

Pierre Laverdure (identity not verified). Courtesy of Lewistown (Mont.) Public Library, Brenner Collection.

those of male members. Through female band members, the Laverdures allied themselves with two traders (Janeaux and his employee, Paul Morase) and with at least three other Milk River families (Turcotte, Berger, and Daignon). These marriages connected the Laverdures to many of the other Milk River families and to all of the families that would move south together to Spring Creek in the Judith Basin.

Janeaux and the Laverdures had maintained a traditional social organization that was familiar to generations of Métis. The Métis traveling to Milk River did so as bands, much like their Cree and Chippewa relatives, and spread their camps miles apart along the Milk and its tributaries.[46] Related groups moved and settled in small, flexible units bound by kinship but dividing and reorganizing for particular purposes or by individual choice, yet always retaining ties to the larger group. Although band membership was fluid, most members were related by consanguinity, marriage, or fictive (usually adoption) kinship designations. Only the priest and sometimes the trader might not be related to the band. The trader, however, if he wished to succeed, would soon need to establish kinship bonds, either fictive or by his own or his children's marriages.

The move to Montana replayed well-established Métis band organization and wintering customs. Emigration caused little upheaval. Residences were portable, meat sources mobile, and wild edible plants widespread on the prairie. Social organization was flexible enough to adjust to a variety of economic situations, and kinship systems were extensive enough to provide endless possibilities for resource utilization. Later immigrants needed only to join already established kin, in a chain migration pattern that left no isolated individuals without community support. Probably only Indian groups moved into new areas with such ease and with so little dislocation. Additionally, the Métis' flexible system for formally and informally selecting leaders allowed the bands to pick the best individuals to meet current problems. Thus, when they met new challenges on the Montana plains, they included such men as Janeaux among their respected leaders. The bands selected other leaders for their ability to organize the large hunts and maintain order in camp, as Jean Baptiste Wilkie had done in the 1840s.

Wilkie's son-in-law, Pierre Berger, held such a position of responsibility on the Milk River. Traveling with the family of his wife's brother, Pierre Berger had been on the Milk since the 1860s. Born in Red River Settlement, he had moved to Pembina in 1845. He, his wife Judith, and three of their children had applied for land as Pembina half-breeds under the 1854 Treaty with the Lake Superior and Mississippi Chippewas, and he and his son Pierre, Jr., were issued land scrip as Pembina half-breeds under the 1863–1864 Treaty with the Chippewas of the Red Lake and Pembina Bands. His marriage to Judith Wilkie united him with a respected Pembina family. Judith's father, Jean Baptiste Wilkie, had led the great buffalo hunts of the 1840s. The marriage of the daughters of Judith Wilkie Berger's brother, Alexander, united the Wilkies and Bergers to the extended Calixte and Charlotte Adam LaFountain family. Magdalena Rose and Josephine Wilkie married the brothers, Octave and Bernard LaFountain, sons of Calixte and Charlotte. Judith's sister, Betsy, married Antoine Fleury and that family also joined the band. Judith and Pierre Berger's children provided the family with additional kinship ties as noted in the following diagrams. Especially important to the band when they moved to Spring Creek were the marriages of Jacque Berger to Philomena Ouellette, Anabel Berger to Frank Ouellette, and Adele Berger to Vital Turcotte. These unions, and those of the other sons and daughters, tied the Berger family to the bands on Milk River and provided the membership of what would soon be the Spring Creek band.[47]

THE BOUNDARY

Membership in the Milk River bands depended on kinship ties, rather than on residence, place of birth, or nationality. But questions of citizenship loomed ever larger for the Métis as they attempted to deal with territorial regulations and to ensure their rights on the Milk River. Because buffalo hunting on the Milk River led the Métis back and forth across the boundary, officials in both countries questioned Métis citizenship. In fact, the Milk River bands consisted of related Pembina, Missouri River, and Canadian (usually St. François Xavier) families. Most of the older members had lived part of their lives on both sides of the boundary. As Joseph Kinsey Howard explained so well, the Canadian border was an artificial line that meant little to the Métis. "The forty-ninth parallel, that 'imaginary line' drawn across an open plain, was a wholly artificial boundary; the idea of a purely political barrier which should obstruct the free movement of men and goods was regarded as absurd on both sides." Howard knew that, to the people living in the area, "the boundary just did not make sense, and doesn't yet. It sought to separate the sparse populations of a hazardous frontier, to stay the essential interchange among people whose needs were similar and who were socially compatible." It was no wonder that "the people ignored the line, flouted the law, and dodged the enforcement agents." National identity had little meaning. "For many years," observed Howard, "the conviction of interchangeable citizenship, or no citizenship at all, persisted. Even today, with customs and immigration patrols grimly awaiting a misstep, border residents regard 'the line' as merely a nuisance which slightly delays their arrival at Saturday night dances." Howard recognized that the Métis were "continually in trouble because they cannot, or will not, provide proof of their citizenship." The Métis, at first, had little concept of being either British subjects or U.S. citizens. Many genuinely did not know on which side of the line they had been born. As Howard argues, proof of place of birth "was not easily obtained by the last generation. A half-breed born during a buffalo hunt had a hard time determining which country could claim him if the hunt occurred, for instance, along the Milk River—or the Red, the Souris, Poplar, Pembina, or other streams which flow in both Canada and the United States." Nor did they necessarily live their lives on the side of the line to which they were born. Most buffalo-hunting families had children born on both sides.[48]

When forced to adopt a national identity, many Métis remained ambivalent. Twentieth-century residents of the Milk River drainage echo the confusion that the Métis felt about national identity. Wallace Stegner, whose parents homesteaded just north of the line, wrote, "Our homestead lay . . . right on the Saskatchewan-Montana border—a place so ambiguous in its affiliations that we felt as uncertain as the drainage about which way to flow."[49]

NEW CHALLENGES ON THE MILK RIVER

The problems faced by the Métis on Milk River were compounded when, during the 1870s, greater numbers of Métis moved onto the plains of Saskatchewan, Alberta, and Montana. Several factors influenced this migration, including changing conditions in Red River Settlement after the 1869–1870 Manitoba Resistance. The conflict had resulted, in part, from fear of a proposed Canadian government takeover of Rupert's Land (which was still under HBC control and in the process of being sold to Britain). The Métis resisted this move, insisting on protection of their rights as residents and petitioning for local self-government, recognition of the French language and Catholic religion, protection of their landholdings, and free trade with the United States. After Louis Riel's provisional government negotiated for provincial status, most of these demands were met formally by the passage of the 1870 Manitoba Act. However, the hostility of a growing number of Protestant settlers from eastern Canada undercut the act's provisions. Their persecution, from which the government provided little recourse, unresolved land ownership disputes, and diminishing economic opportunities persuaded many Métis families to move from Red River Settlement.[50]

As noted earlier, economic and environmental factors had encouraged many Métis to move west of present-day Manitoba and eastern Dakota long before 1870. By this date, however, the buffalo had withdrawn so far from Red River that it was impossible to accompany the hunts while maintaining Red River–area farms. More and more families chose to move closer to the herds on the plains of Saskatchewan, Alberta, Montana, and western Dakota, where the remaining buffalo still grazed in enormous numbers. The Métis presence in Montana became particularly visible because of the profitable markets located on the Missouri River, where barges and steamboats provided the cheapest transportation to Mississippi River ports. One of the trading centers, Fort Benton, became an important export point for the robes gathered in Montana, southwestern Saskatchewan, and southern Alberta. However, as the increase in unregulated cross-border trade came to the attention of tariff collectors, the transport of robes across the boundary became both more expensive and more dangerous. The Métis had traditionally avoided the 10 percent duty on robes by smuggling them across the unpatrolled border. By 1874, laws not only increased the duty to 20 percent but also encouraged more effective enforcement.[51]

Though the Métis had pressing reasons to leave Red River Settlement and the Pembina-St. Joseph area during the 1870s, many non-Métis interpreted the move as an inability to adapt to the changing environment. The Métis rejection of farming and "reversion" to hunting seemed to agriculturists and outsiders of the 1870s, like earlier observers, to be a primitive people's rejection of civilization. As in previous years, the harsh response of non-Métis ignored the fact that the move was a rational economic decision. The widespread criticism that the Métis met when they abandoned farms in favor of the migratory life involved in robe production influenced the attitudes of Montana business people and government officials toward them. Particularly damaging was the anger and distress of the Catholic clergy in Red River Settlement, Pembina, and St. Joseph. In the 1870s, faced with wholesale abandonment of their parishes (especially in Pembina and St. Joseph), the priests reacted with stinging criticism. St. Joseph's Father Le Floch lamented about the Métis moving west, "These are people over whom civilization has no hold," and they will "lose themselves among the savages." Religious leaders complained bitterly of the failure of the Métis to heed their advice and settle down to farming, and predicted dire consequences from the abandonment of Red River farms. Indeed, many Métis families did lose their land to neighbors, who took advantage of their absence. Le Floch noted that even if the wintering Métis locked their Red River homes and nailed shut the windows and doors, new European and Canadian immigrants broke into the empty homes and stole whatever they could use, disregarding the unwritten laws that governed Métis communities and had previously protected their property. The Métis often lost what was left of their farms to delinquent taxes. The new immigrants quickly bought Métis land at tax sales, and even the Catholic Church accumulated Métis farms when the owners did not return in time to pay overdue taxes.[52]

The criticism of the disappointed priests reinforced an image of irresponsibility that lowered Euro-American opinion of the Métis, especially after the Manitoba Resistance. Worse for the long term, attitudes toward the Métis suffered when historians, using the most accessible sources, based their interpretations of the period on diocese letters. Thus, Marcel Giraud's authoritative history of the Métis echoes the sentiments of the Red River religious leaders and presents the period as a reversion to nomadism from which the Métis "entered into . . . [a] phase of social decay," rather than as a logical, informed economic decision. Most other historians of Canada followed suit with descriptions of Métis dislike of agricultural labor and their failure to succeed even when they tried, since their "efforts at husbandry had always been feckless and destructive of the soil." Historians' images of the Métis as "indolent, thoughtless and improvident, unrestrained in their desires, restless, clannish and vain" followed them into Montana and into the present.[53]

Euro-American impressions of the Métis as irresponsible nomads and rebellious troublemakers became particularly relevant as Montana military and territorial officials acted on suspicions concerning the activities of the growing Milk River Métis population. The need to control the border and enforce tariffs, concern over preserving the remaining buffalo for local tribal use, and fear that Métis traders were supplying hostile Indian bands, all encouraged a surveillance of Métis activities and, in some cases, actual harassment. Furthermore, reservation Indians and their agents complained that the Métis were overhunting and driving away the herds upon which they depended. At the same time, because the Métis often camped, traveled, and hunted with Cree relatives and were usually well armed, the military and reservation agents viewed them as an undependable and possibly dangerous appendage to the Indian community. As tensions between the immigrating Euro-Americans and disgruntled "hostile" Indian bands further polarized racial attitudes, additional suspicion centered on the Métis.[54]

Especially troubling to new Euro-American settlers was the growing number of Sioux. The Sioux had been moving into Montana since early in the century as agricultural settlement and the disappearance of the buffalo forced them west. During the 1870s, like other peoples dependent upon the buffalo, they moved into Montana in greater numbers. Francis Janeaux's bookkeeper, Samuel O'Connell, nervously reported many Sioux bands hunting and trading on the Milk River in 1875. "There are over 300 lodges of Yancktonai Sioux camped here," he worried, "who are saucy, independent, and, it might be truly said, hostile. They move camp in a few days, nearer to the trading post [Ft. Turney]," and, he warned, "the consequences of this move will be the destruction of the few whites who inhabit the post. This would be certain now were it not that our 150 lodges of half breeds are camped here."[55] Only in the company of large numbers of well-armed Métis did Euro-American traders risk working on the Milk. Because of their "openly and defiantly hostile" behavior, the incoming Sioux bands caused even more consternation than the growing number of other Indians, including Crees and Canadian Blackfeet and Bloods.[56]

Not knowing the source of the well-armed Sioux warriors' supplies, guns, and ammunition, U.S. government suspicion centered on Métis traders and the illegal traffic in merchandise from Canada. Several investigations were launched to uncover any Métis plot to sell provisions, guns, or ammunition. In May 1874, Indian agent William W. Alderson sent an investigator to "the trading post and Indian camps in the vicinity of Medicine Lodge and French Creek . . . [to investigate] the illegal trade in arms and ammunition and the reported whiskey traffic in the half-breeds camps near the boundary line." The next year, in March 1875, Major N. B. Sweitzer of Ft. Ellis forwarded the report of an agent sent to uncover Sioux movements and trade arrangements. After investigating "a settlement of these Half Breeds [that] has been made on Milk river some 40 or 60 miles from Ft. Peck," agent D. E. Clapp accused the "Red River halfbreeds" of conducting "a trade for arms and ammunition." He recommended "campaigns against hostile camps and tribes until they are destroyed or broken up, and impoverished and compelled to submit to the Government." The danger of the Sioux was obvious to Agent Clapp, who maintained that "these Indians hold complete control of the Yellowstone and Powder River Country." By the March 23, Brigadier General Alfred Terry had become concerned enough about supposed Métis provisioning of hostile bands that he ordered Colonel John Gibbon to "break up" the "halfbreed settlement" if it was found illegally camped within reservation lands. The reservation agents cared little for the rights of U.S. Métis who, as non-Indian U.S. citizens, could lawfully hunt off reservation land—they wanted all Métis expelled, no matter where they were found. But the army, on this occasion, gave more consideration to the disputed citizenship of the Métis and was only willing to deport those families found hunting on reservation land (thereby breaking the law) or proven to be Canadian citizens.[57]

Matters worsened for the Métis after the 1876 army defeat at the Battle of the Little Bighorn. As military historian Michael Koury puts it, "There were two definite periods in the life of the military in Montana—before the Little Big Horn, and after." Before Colonel George A. Custer's dramatic 1876 defeat, there were only seven hundred troops in Montana Territory; by 1877 there were thirty-three hundred. Sioux paranoia swept Montana, and the military felt compelled to establish control over the Indian situation. Suspicion again centered on Métis traders, who were thought to be supplying the Sioux with goods brought in illegally from Canada.[58]

Compounding the pressure to remove the Métis for military reasons were renewed complaints from reservation agents and U.S. trading company personnel demanding that the army expel all "Canadian" Métis. Tirades appeared in Montana newspapers, including the *Benton Record*, whose editor accused the Métis of carrying "on an illicit trade with hostile savages." "These Canadian half-breeds pay no taxes," he claimed. "They produce nothing but discord, violence and bloodshed where ever they are permitted to locate, they are a worthless, brutal race of the lowest species of humanity, without one redeeming trait to commend them to the sympathy or protection of any Government." In response, the army complained to the Canadian government about "British half breeds and Indians on United States soil." But Canadian officials, in the person of British minister to the United States, Sir Edward Thornton, argued that since U.S. Indians and Métis were allowed to hunt in Canada, the reverse was only fair. In spite of Canadian objections, the army removed many Métis to Canada, where the Canadians disagreed as to their nationality. Superintendent Walsh of the North West Mounted Police believed that "all the half-breeds on the Milk River are Canadian and are entitled to take up lands on this side of the line." But in that same year, 1879, the Canadian Indian commissioner noted that "about 140 half-breeds have been arrested by the Americans on the other side of the line," and most of them insisted that they were U.S. citizens. Canada was willing to accept only those Métis who declared Canadian citizenship. The commissioner reported that "all but ten" of the arrested Métis "said that they were Americans" and that those "who had declared themselves American were advised to go to the Gudath [Judith] Basin. Many did so, and have settled there." The Métis who remained in the United States were probably the Milk River Métis whom General Nelson A. Miles "escorted" part way to the Judith Basin later that year.[59]

There was a great deal of confusion in both countries not only as to the nationality of the Métis but also as to their rights as individuals. In general, those Métis who had not become enrolled members of a tribe assigned to a reservation were not considered Indians or wards of either government. However, as such, if not already U.S. citizens, they should have been able to immigrate and register their intention to become citizens before a county judge—the same rights accorded other Canadian immigrants. But their association with Indians in the minds of both the Canadian and U.S. governments led officials to deny them basic liberties. Their civil rights were often violated in the United States during the 1870s by reservation agents and government officials who arbitrarily sentenced them to expulsion and destroyed their possessions without due process. Nor did they receive protection from or compensation for Indian depredations. When, for example, Lakota raiders stole the Milk River Métis' horses, they faced starvation. They were neither compensated for their lost property, as Euro-American settlers would have been, nor did the army help them retrieve their stolen property. On the other hand, since they were not federally recognized as Native people, they did not receive rations to help get them through the winter. Territorial and army officials had devised no fair, uniform policy that acknowledged the Métis as non-Indian citizens enjoying full rights, nor had they provided them with benefits similar to those of Indians. Conservatively, there were more than thirty thousand Métis in western Canada and the northwestern United States, but neither government had developed a consistent policy to deal with their rights and needs.[60]

MOVING TO THE JUDITH BASIN: THE SPRING CREEK BAND FAMILIES

As the army stepped up its program to expel Canadian Métis, many Métis were already leaving the Milk River region of their own accord. The number of buffalo in the area declined sharply in the late 1870s. In the summer of 1878 fires had destroyed much of the grass in the Milk River region on both sides of the boundary, causing the herds to move south toward the Judith Basin of central Montana. Consequently, Métis bands were starting to break up and move away. Some returned to Dakota Territory or Canada, while others traveled to new locations in Montana. Canada was a poor option because the buffalo had already disappeared from there and many Canadian Métis and Indians were suffering from starvation. The Judith Basin of central Montana seemed the best choice, but it was becoming crowded. Andrew Garcia, a freetrader working in the Musselshell Valley, just east of the Judith Basin, reported that Assiniboines, Crees, Bloods, Gros Ventres, Piegans, Pend d'Oreilles, and Métis were already hunting in the region. Garcia's own experiences underscore the popularity of the area and its multiethnic character during the late 1870s. Of Mexican or Mexican American descent himself, he married a Nez Perce woman in a large Cree-Métis hunting camp on the Musselshell in 1878. As the presence of Garcia and his marriage indicate, central Montana was attracting a diverse collection of hunters and traders. In addition to the peoples mentioned, bands of Crows and Lakotas also traveled through the Judith Basin, and as many as two hundred Métis families in small wintering bands joined Métis already there.[61]

It was in early May 1879 that a group of related Milk River families, under the leadership of Pierre Berger, formed what may be informally termed the Spring Creek band and moved toward the Basin. Like others, they had heard of the area's plentiful game and buffalo. The army encouraged, but apparently did not force, the band to make this decision. Nevertheless, to ensure that the band reached the Judith Basin, Captain Williams of Fort Benton sent two soldiers and two civilians to accompany them.[62]

Band members included Pierre Berger, his wife Judith Wilkie Berger, their four unmarried children, four married sons and their families, two married daughters and their families (Turcotte and Ouellette), and a married granddaughter (Wells) (see following kinship diagrams). Judith Berger's brother, Alexander Wilkie, and his married daughters (LaFountain) and Judith's sister, Betsy Wilkie Fleury, and her married son and family also accompanied them. Two Doney families, the wife in each case a sister of the husbands of Alexander Wilkie's daughters (LaFountain), and the families of three Fagnant brothers and a sister (LaRocque), all half brothers or the half sister of Charlotte Adam LaFountain (mother-in-law of the married daughters of Alexander Wilkie) also joined the band. The John Ledoux family, which was probably related to the LaFountains and Fagnants, the Gayion family, and Ben Kline, employee of Francis Janeaux, and Kline's childhood friend, Mose LaTray, and family (Kline and LaTray were both connected to the Wilkies though the Charlotte Pelletier family) made up the body of the initial party. The band traveled from the Milk River to

Pierre and Judith Wilkie Berger. Courtesy of Lewistown (Mont.) Public Library, Brenner Collection.

Fort Benton, where they crossed the Missouri River by ferry. They then continued on to the Judith Basin accompanied as far as Cottonwood Creek by their military escort. From Cottonwood Creek the band traveled southeast to Spring Creek and camped at a site north of the later-day Great Northern freight depot in present–day Lewistown.[63]

After the band arrived on Spring Creek, Ben Kline remembered that two hunters were sent out almost immediately to search for buffalo. From Black Butte (a prominence several miles to the east commanding a view of the surrounding countryside) they sighted the herds. The band moved again toward the buffalo. Ben Kline noted that the hunting was good and that the men "killed lots of them." The families then continued in a southeasterly direction toward Flat Willow Creek and followed that stream west. In July, on Flat Willow, they met the Laverdures, Daniels (Daignon), and Janeauxs, who had traveled south from Fort Benton. Together they circled south of the Snowy Mountains to the "Gap in the West," probably what is now called Judith Gap, where the Judith River makes its way between the Snowy and Little Belt mountains. Here Ben Kline remembered that they killed so many buffalo that it took them a "whole week to dress and dry the meat." Upon returning to Spring Creek, they met trader Paul Morase (grandson-in-law of elder Pierre Laverdure and employee of Janeaux) camped with his family on Spring Creek at Reed's Fort, near the present site of Lewistown. In August, the Antoine Ouellette and Edward Wells families crossed the Missouri by ferry at the mouth of the Musselshell and also moved south to join relatives on Spring Creek. Edward Wells's brother was married to Philomene Ouellette, sister of Frank Ouellette who, in turn, was the husband of Anabel Berger. By the end of the summer, the Spring Creek band consisted of a substantial party. All of the families were closely related, with the possible exceptions of the Gayions (whose positive identity is not known).[64]

On the surface, band membership seems to have been composed of discrete patriarchal nuclear families. Surviving documents that list the male heads of families making up the band reinforce such an image. When observed from this perspective, band membership appears random and disjointed. Only when one looks below the surface of patronymic surnames does a connecting pattern appear. Family reconstruction with careful attention to the premarriage names of grandmothers, mothers, and married daughters reveals webs of intermarriage that link band families through maternal lines.

While Pierre Berger and, sometimes, Francis Janeaux, are referred to as the band leaders, band membership did not stem from these men. As noted above, except for a possible relationship to Philomene Jannot, who married Antoine LaFountain (a brother of a Spring Creek band member, but a person who did not move to Spring Creek himself) and probable early-century family ties, Janeaux's kinship to the band depended entirely on his wife's parents' and siblings' connections. At first glance, the Pierre Berger/Judith Wilkie Berger and Calixte LaFountain/Charlotte Adam LaFountain extended families have a closer resemblance to a traditional patriarchal family than does Janeaux's. In both cases, sons and their families accompanied their parents. However, in determining band membership, the daughters' marriages are equally important, as are the relatives of the sons' wives. Furthermore, it is the siblings of the wives, Judith Wilkie Berger, Charlotte Adam LaFountain, and Virginia Laverdure Janeaux, who account for the kinship links to all of the band members except the couple's own children, who of course, are related to both parents.

The following diagrams demonstrate that band membership consisted of wives' and daughters' relatives and in-laws as often as those of husbands and sons. Indeed, the entire band membership can be traced through three women, Judith Wilkie Berger, Charlotte Adam LaFountain, and Virginia Laverdure Janeaux. The Spring Creek band was not patriarchal in the sense of being organized around and controlled by related fathers and their sons. Although the political leaders were men, they did not determine the band's composition. The bonds provided by wives, sisters, and daughters cemented the band and provided its form, flexibility, and durability. The following diagrams illustrate the intricate, overlapping nature of these families' ties.[65]

These findings are at odds with a popular image of patriarchal Métis bands. They support, instead, the findings of Susan Sleeper-Smith and Lucy Eldersveld Murphy, who have assessed the role of Catholic mixed-descent women in the building of Great Lakes kinship systems and communities. An examination of Spring Creek band family organization illustrates the role of women's kinship ties in the formation and maintenance of band organization and flexibility. Their experience suggests a bifocal, effectively bilineal, system in which the kin of both spouses formed the threads of the interlocking kinship web.[66]

As noted in chapter 1, the association of the Spring Creek families was no recent occurrence. Almost all of the family names belonging to Spring Creek band members or their parents can be found among those working for the North West Company in the Northwest before 1821. The majority of the family names of the Spring Creek band can also be found among families of Great Lakes Métis as shown in table 1 (chapter 1). The families of Pierre and Judith Berger, Edward and Marie Wells, Calixte and Charlotte Adam LaFountain, Pierre and Katherine Laverdure, and Alexander and Louise Wilkie, as well as Peter Charboneau, John Charette, Frank Daniels, Joseph Doney, Joseph LaRocque, and John Ledoux were Pembina Métis who had applied for land scrip under the 1854 and 1863–1864 Chippewa treaties. Although some Métis moved to the Milk River from St. François Xavier (part of Red River Settlement), including the large LaFountain family, these Pembina and St. François Xavier families were closely related. Many Pembina Métis had lived part of their lives in Red River Settlement. The band cannot be defined or limited in terms of geographical origins, except in a large regional sense. Kinship bonds united the band to Missouri River, Great Lakes, Canadian Plains, and Pembina Métis. These bonds survived repeated separations and diverse residences. When the band formed for yet another move, it was the bonds of family, organized to

SPRING CREEK BAND
(members in bold type)
Charlotte Adam LaFountain Network

KEY

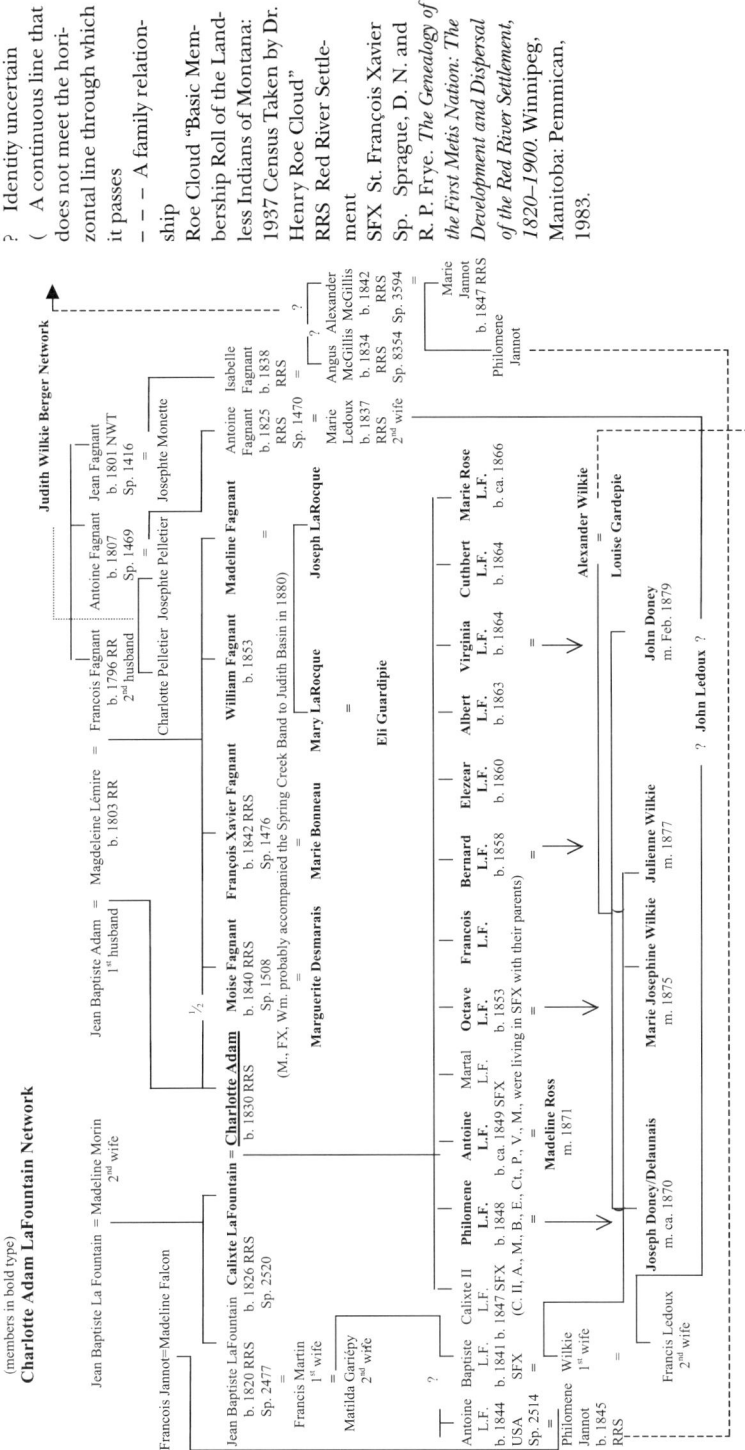

? Identity uncertain

(A continuous line that does not meet the horizontal line through which it passes

– – – A family relationship

Roe Cloud "Basic Membership Roll of the Landless Indians of Montana: 1937 Census Taken by Dr. Henry Roe Cloud"

RRS Red River Settlement

SFX St. François Xavier

Sp. Sprague, D. N. and R. P. Frye. *The Genealogy of the First Metis Nation: The Development and Dispersal of the Red River Settlement, 1820–1900.* Winnipeg, Manitoba: Pemmican, 1983.

SPRING CREEK BAND
(members in bold type)
Virginia Laverdure Janeaux Network

KEY
? Identity uncertain
(A continuous line that does not meet the horizontal line through which it passes
– – – A family relationship
Roe Cloud "Basic Membership Roll of the Landless Indians of Montana: 1937 Census Taken by Dr. Henry Roe Cloud"
RRS Red River Settlement
SFX St. François Xavier
Sp. Sprague, D. N. and R. P. Frye. *The Genealogy of the First Metis Nation: The Development and Dispersal of the Red River Settlement, 1820–1900*. Winnipeg, Manitoba: Pemmican, 1983.

Joseph Laverdure = Theresa Villebrun

Jean Baptiste Charette = Josette Monette (Bellehumeur)   **Judith Wilkie Berger Network**

Pierre Laverdure
b. ca. 1815 Pembina

Charlotte Pelletier
=
Andre Millet dit Beauchemin

Katherine Charette
b. ca. 1820 Pembina

Michel Klyne Jr.= Madeleine Beauchemin

Judith Wilkie Berger Network

?

Jean Baptiste Charette = Angelique Petit
b. ca. 1810   b. ca. 1821

Jean Baptiste Turcotte = Angelique Pocha/Patien
b. 1837
Sp. 4726

Pierre Berger = **Judith Wilkie Berger**

Jean Baptiste Laverdure
=
Marie Azure
b. 1852

David Daniels = Marie Diserly

Mary Ann Laverdure

Virginia Laverdure

John Charette
b. 1843

Vital Turcotte

Adele Berger
m. Jan. 1879 Milk River

Eliza Laverdure
b. 1847 Pembina

Frank Daniels/Daignon
b. 1839 Canada

Francis Janeaux
b. 1839 Montreal

Charlotte Adam LaFountain Network
(Jamot ?)

employee

Benjamine Kline
b. 1845 Devil's Lake, N.D.

Judith Wilkie Berger Network
Antoine Azure = Charlotte Pelletier
b. ca. 1792

Francois Laverdure
b. ca. 1853 Pembina
=
Marie Turcotte
m. Jan. 1879 Montana

Judith Wilkie Berger Network
Antoine Azure = Charlotte Pelletier
b. ca. 1792

Margaret Daniels/Daignon
b. 1860 Dakota

Paul Morase
b. 1848 Canada
(employee of Janeaux)

Angelique St. Pierre

Arsene Azure= Adalaide Larivee
b. 1833

Charles Azure = Nancy Grant
b. ca. 1821

Felix LaTreille = Marguerite Jolisbois

Louis Napoleon LaTraille
=
Mose LaTray = Susan Moran
(Raised with Ben Kline)

Sara Azure
b. 1859

SPRING CREEK BAND
(members in bold type)
Judith Wilkie Berger Network

KEY
? Identity uncertain
(A continuous line that does not meet the horizontal line through which it passes
– – A family relationship
Roe Cloud "Basic Membership Roll of the Landless Indians of Montana: 1937 Census Taken by Dr. Henry Roe Cloud"
RRS Red River Settlement
SFX St. François Xavier
Sp. Sprague, D. N. and R. P. Frye. *The Genealogy of the First Metis Nation: The Development and Dispersal of the Red River Settlement, 1820–1900*. Winnipeg, Manitoba: Pemmican, 1983.

Jacques Berger = unknown

Pierre Azure   Antoine Azure = Charlotte Pelletier

Jean Baptiste Wilkie = Amable Elise (Annabelle) Azure Wilkie
b. 1803 Pembina   b. 1808 Pembina

Pierre Berger   **Judith Wilkie**
b. Canada   b. Canada

Alexander Wilkie   Betsey Wilkie   Madeline Wilkie   Antoine Wilkie
b. 1831   b. 1836 Pembina b. 1837 Pembina   b. 1847 Pembina
  =   =
Louise Gardepie/Gariépy   Antoine Fleury I   Esther Gladue   Gabriel Dumont
b. 1830 Dakota   b. ca. 1840   b. 1837 St. Boniface

Marie Josephine Wilkie   Julienne/Julia Wilkie   Antoine Fleury II
                            =
                          Bernard LaFountain
                          m. Dec. 1877 Milk R.

Antoine Azure = Charlotte Pelletier
Antoine Azure = Victoire Larivie

Antoine Ouellette = Angelique Bottineau
b. ca. 1835   b. 1838

Edward Wells (Wills) I = Isabelle McGillis

Octave LaFountain

Isadore Ouellette = Mary Bottineau
Margaret Gourneau=Paul Kiplin

Jacque B.   Bernard B.   Adele B.   Anabel B.   Catherine B.   Frances B.   Marie B.
b. 1851   b. 1855   =
Pembina   Pembina   Frank Azure
  =   b. 1856
Philomena Ouellette   m. Jan. 1878 Milk R.

Vital Turcotte   Frank Ouellette   Philomene Ouellette
                  b. 1868 N.D.   b. Willow Bunch, Ca.
                  Roe Cloud 398

John Wells   Edward Wells II
b. ca. 1855   b. 1838
              =
              Marie Demontigny
              b. 1841, m. 1863

Pierre B. Jr.   Francois Xavier B.   Isidore B.   Jean Baptiste B.
b. 1842   b. 1844   b. 1846   b. 1849
RRS   RRS   Pembina   Pembina
  =   =   =
Clemence Gourneau   Domitilla Laframboise   Betsy Kiplin
b. 1847 N.D.
m. 1870 St. Joseph

← Charlotte Adam Network

← Virginia Laverdure Janeaux Network

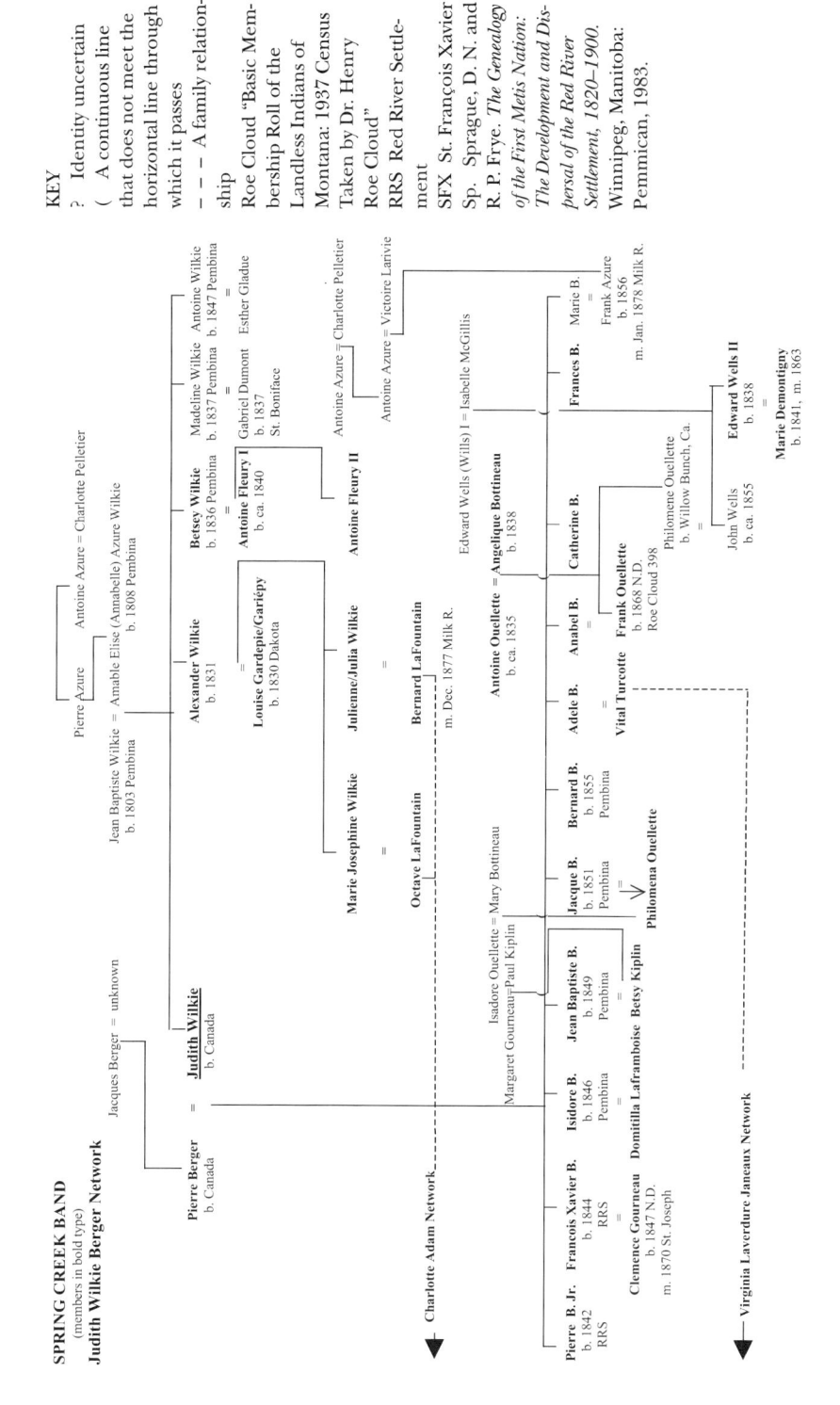

accomplish a common economic goal, that provided membership, structure, and almost instant stability.

THE MÉTIS ARE EXPELLED FROM MILK RIVER

The Spring Creek band seems to have left the Milk River just before public pressure to force all Métis from the area resulted in military action. In the midst of the confusion among officials and the non-Métis public as to who the Métis were racially and nationally, General Nelson A. Miles took matters into his own hands. In the fall of 1879, he broke up the remaining Milk River Métis camps, forcing many Métis across the line into Canada. He was concerned about raiding parties that had come down from Sitting Bull's camp north of the Canadian line during the winter. By summer Sitting Bull's bands moved south of the line, where Lieutenant W. P. Clark of the Second Cavalry encountered them on Frenchman Creek. The ensuing "sharp engagement" convinced Miles that something had to be done about the Lakotas. He believed that the "location of such a large camp of hostile Sioux near the border was a menace to the peace and welfare of the citizens of the United States in that vicinity."[67]

Miles's campaign against the Lakotas involved depriving them of supplies, especially weapons and ammunition, in U.S. territory. To this end, he informed Canadian officials that in the "future all property—horses, carts, and cargoes—of any Canadian halfbreed found trading ammunition with United States Indians will be confiscated." He noted later that "living in that country [were] a body of people known as 'Red River half-breeds,' half French and half Indian." He assumed them to be "practically British subjects, living most of the time on Canadian territory." His concern about the Métis centered on reports that "this people had been a disturbing element for some time.... They were in close communication with the hostile Sioux under Sitting Bull, and it was reported to me that they were supplying those Indians with ammunition." Miles, therefore, "determined to break up the traffic." His troops surrounded the Métis camps and "gathered them together on one field to the number of over a thousand people, together with their eight hundred carts, herds of horses, tents and other property.... These were all sent out of the country after being kept for some time, thus breaking up one of the means of supply to the camp of Sitting Bull."[68]

In treating the Métis as foreign-arms suppliers to hostile Indians, Miles justified their expulsion and the confiscation of their goods without due process. Even later, as he faced the protests of U.S. Métis and the Canadian government, he insisted that the majority of Métis in the Milk River region were Canadian subjects. Miles defended his operation, maintaining that, even thought his actions primarily affected Métis bands, much of the country south of the U.S.-Canadian border was reservation land, and he would allow no one, Indian, Métis, or white, onto the land without a permit.[69]

Although army records are not specific on the point, Miles did not send all of the Métis to Canada. He proposed to settle at least one band in the Judith Basin, where game was still plentiful and the land somewhat more suitable for cultivation. The Judith Basin was also far enough from reservation land to prevent illegal trading with reservation Indians and competition over their game supplies. Ben Kline's version of these events differs somewhat from that of Miles. Kline maintained that Miles "rounded up the breeds along the Milk River for trading with the Sioux and gave them their choice either to go to Canada or the Judith Basin." In any case, about fifty families did travel to the Judith Basin. Kline remembers that Miles's soldiers "escorted" the families, who with their Red River carts and possessions crossed the Missouri by steamboat near the mouth of the Musselshell River. This party probably included the Wells and Ouellette families, who settled with their already established relatives near Spring Creek.[70]

An "amusing" story recounted to Kline by a member of the military party escorting the families indicates the attitudes of the soldiers toward the Métis and the prejudice that would confront them in their Judith Basin home. Kline heard the tale from B. E. Stack, who accompanied the soldiers as a muleskinner. During the move, an accident occurred somewhere between the Milk and the Missouri rivers:

> The breeds were lined up in their carts single file extending about a mile in length. The soldiers and some of the breeds started a run on a bunch of buffaloes. The buffaloes, in order to escape in a group, made a run towards the line of breed carts, puncturing the line and knocking the breeds and their carts where they struck them over like a bunch of ten pins. In making inquiry of Mr. Stack whether or not any breeds were injured, he stated that he did not know because they did not take enough interest in the proceeding to even inquire, as at that time they were considered simply breeds and subject to the white traders and marauding Indians.

"Mr. Stack," who later became a "prominent capitalist of Lewistown" (the town that the Métis founded on Spring Creek) apparently regarded the

Métis as altogether alien and their fate of no interest. His reaction to the accident foreshadowed one more challenge that the Spring Creek Métis would face in their new home.[71]

General Miles's efforts to remove the Métis from the Milk River area were short-lived. His campaign resulted in a dramatic but temporary disruption of the Milk River Métis communities, but soon, despite the army's efforts, the Métis returned. Even today, the Milk River of north-central Montana secures the northern base of an inverted triangle, reaching to Lewistown in the south, that is home to the many descendents of the Milk River bands.

• • •

The 1860s and 1870s presented serious social, legal, and economic threats to Métis identity. Economic and environmental realities, as well as the discrimination and harassment that they encountered, reinforced traditional Métis band structure and dependence on kinship bonds. The Métis survived migration and resettlement with very little social or economic disruption by moving in fluid but organized kinship groups. In this way the families were able to effectively respond to new conditions while preserving their sense of themselves as a distinct people.

In following the buffalo west, the Métis made rational economic decisions based on realistic evaluations of agricultural and buffalo markets. Meanwhile, south of the U.S.-Canadian boundary, they encountered numerous challenges to their identity as Métis. Confusion over their racial, legal, and national identity compromised their social and economic position. Lack of support for a distinct Métis identity was pronounced in the non-Métis community, where criticism of Métis lifestyle, a disregard of Métis economic achievements, and an ignorance of Métis history led to a misunderstanding or denial of Métis identity. Moreover, Euro-American criticism of the Métis for being "too Indian," for being irresponsible, and for their perceived rejection of the benefits and responsibilities of "civilization" encouraged a social distancing by the Euro-American community. The close relationship with Indian relatives that the Métis enjoyed (especially the Chippewa and Cree bands with whom they hunted, visited, and intermarried) caused suspicion and fear among Euro-Americans, who reacted by denying Métis civil rights. Nor were they accorded the rights and benefits of reservation Indians. They received neither reservation land, nor annuities, nor recognition as a distinct people. U.S.-Canadian border tensions also led to difficulty. Métis ties to Canada, their frequent cross-border travel, and the publicity of the Manitoba Resistance caused a popular impression that the Métis were Canadian, not U.S., citizens. This confusion resulted in challenges to both their national identity and to their civil rights as citizens.

The unwillingness of the U.S. government to recognize the Métis people as a distinct group led to a contrived invisibility. The Métis were often referred to as Indians or as "breeds." The term "breed," as used by the Euro-American settlers, was not synonymous with Métis. A "breed" was not white, Indian, or Métis. Such people were assumed to have lost their inheritance, reduced by the fact of their biracial birth to a condition beneath that of either parental group. "Breed" signified a part-Indian ancestry without recognition of Métis culture, lifestyle, or history, especially history.

When the Métis presence became suspect or inconvenient, as it did in Montana during the Lakota troubles, Euro-American settlers emphasized the Métis' Canadian background. By ignoring their long history in U.S. territory, Montanans were able to rationalize Métis removal to Canada. Although this scheme ultimately failed, the perception of Métis as illegal aliens lived on. Even historians picked up the notion that all Métis were Canadian. M. A. Leeson's influential 1885 *History of Montana* dated the arrival of the Métis in Montana to the post-1869–1870 Resistance exodus, writing that "after the Red River troubles of 1871 a small number of half-breeds moved from the Canadian side to Montana, and made their settlements on Milk River." Although briefly noting an earlier Métis presence (without using the word "Métis"), his statement served to legitimize both the notion that Métis numbers were small and that the Métis in Montana were Canadian. Later historians, such as John Ewers, continued this theme, identifying the Métis as recent arrivals from Canada. As Canadians with Indian ties, Métis expulsion from Montana was easily justified. Ultimately, designation as Canadian rather than as a people with a long history in the United States led to Métis invisibility in the history of the U.S. West. Euro-Americans who settled in Montana and the Dakotas after the 1860s were celebrated as "pioneers." The Métis, who made the area home years earlier, were labeled "Canadians."[72]

CHAPTER 3

A New Homeland

*The Judith Basin and
Spring Creek Settlement, 1879–1884*

> We came . . . to the famous Judith Basin which was, indeed a paradise land of plenty; game of all kinds, lots of good water and timber. What more could we want?
> CLEMENCE GOURNEAU BERGER,
> "MÉTIS COME TO JUDITH BASIN," 1943

During the early 1880s, the Spring Creek Métis settled in their Judith Basin home. Despite continued harassment of the Métis hunters who remained on the Milk River, the band and their Milk River relatives adapted to Montana law, politics, and military regulations, using them to advance their struggle for rights as aboriginal citizens. Taking advantage of their relatively large numbers, experienced leadership, and still-viable economic position, they worked toward securing a Montana homeland. As the buffalo disappeared from the Montana plains and Euro-American cattlemen took over the range, they faced new challenges to their economic and social survival as a community.

CONTINUED MÉTIS HARASSMENT ON MILK RIVER

While the Spring Creek band settled on the tributaries of Spring Creek in the heart of central Montana, the difficulties encountered by their relatives still hunting on the Milk River continued. Those Métis whom General Nelson Miles had expelled to Canada in the summer of 1879 almost immediately returned to U.S. soil. Tensions over their presence intensified as the Lakotas who had escaped to Canada after the Sioux War of 1876 also drifted south across the border, forced back, like the Métis, by the disappearance of the buffalo from the Canadian plains. Noticing the movement, army officers reported "hostile Sioux" on the Montana portions of the Milk River in the fall and winter of 1879. Lieutenant Colonel H. M. Black, commander of Fort Assiniboine on the Milk River, received information that as many as 730 lodges of Lakotas, including followers of Sitting Bull, were camped on French Creek about twenty miles from the Milk River. They had "committed . . . no depredations," he noted, "except it was thought a few of them had crossed the Missouri to the Judith Basin and stole some horses from some Half Breeds living there." These were probably the horses stolen from the Spring Creek Métis, but as his observation suggests, army officials did not come to the band's aid or assist in recovery of their animals. Although the army ignored Lakota raids on the Métis, they did take seriously charges that the Métis were supplying Sitting Bull's followers.[1]

As tensions mounted, a dispute over the legality of Métis residence on the Milk River broke out among army officers and reservation agents. Fort Peck agent Ned Porter "emphatically" asserted that the Métis were on the river illegally since they were "all Canadian Half-Breeds, a portion of them being the same that were captured by Gen. Miles in the summer of 1879." Porter insisted that he was "authorized by [Indian] Commissioner Hayt to call on the military for assistance to remove all Half Breeds from this reservation." Informed that there were Métis on the Big Bend of the Milk River, he demanded that the military "see they are removed." Lieutenant Colonel Black's informant assured him, however, that the Métis whom Miles had captured and deported were now in the Judith Basin on Warm Spring Creek, and that those presently on the Milk were not the same band. Furthermore, the informant continued, those Métis now on the Milk were starving and in such "destitute condition" that they could not travel.[2]

Not only was there confusion concerning the identity of the Métis on the Milk River, but the area in which they could legally hunt was in question. The boundaries of the reservation, which marked that land set aside for the exclusive use of enrollees, were not clearly drawn. Despite these problems, the assistant adjutant general, stationed in St. Paul, Minnesota, ordered Lieutenant Colonel Black "to act in the matter of the half-breeds near Big Bend on Milk River." His directive was superficially clear: "If these halfbreeds be Canadian they will be put over the line. If they be American halfbreeds they can be ejected from reservation excepting [in the] case they are of the blood of the Indians owning the reservation."

The directive failed to address the heart of the problem, that of establishing the nationality of the Métis then on the Milk River. Black, unlike Agent Porter, believed that "nearly all" of the Métis on the Milk River were "American Half Breeds, having been born along the Missouri River." He added, moreover, that many of those on reservation land were legally employed, working for the military or U.S. trading companies hauling grain, hay, and fuel, and providing a valuable service. Black, therefore, recommended against removal or, if removal was deemed necessary, simply requesting of the Métis that they move elsewhere. The use of force, he believed, was unnecessary, stating in a letter to the assistant adjutant general that "if those Half Breeds are intelligently informed they must move from the Ft. Peck reservation, they will go without resorting to force."[3]

The lieutenant colonel had additional concerns. Questioning the advisability of deportation, he wondered "whether the Government can afford to drive these Half Breeds back across the line and at the same time allow, or at least tacitly permit, the immense number of British Indians to remain hunting and trapping on this side."[4] Unlike reservation officials, he did not dispute the right of Canadian Indians to hunt on the Milk River, stating that "from what I can learn it has been customary to follow the Buffalo on either side of the line, by Indians from both sides." It was apparent to him that the Indians and Métis hunted south of the line because of necessity, since many were starving and were reportedly reduced to eating their dogs. Black argued that sending the Métis back across the line while allowing large numbers of Canadian Indians to hunt in Montana was grossly unfair and would be sure to worsen the already tenuous relations with the Canadian government. He also feared that if the Métis were forced to move to Canada, many would perish from a lack of food and shelter.[5]

Black had high-level support for his position. General William T. Sherman, in an advisory opinion on the matter, also questioned the logic of forcibly removing the Métis to Canada. He wrote to army headquarters in January 1880.

> I see no good reason why Indians and half-breeds may not earn a bare existence by killing the buffalo, which do not care for National boundary lines. Also half-breeds have a right to immigrate to our soil, if they commit no crimes and do not actually molest our subjects. Surely in that vast uninhabited Region, the few Indians along the Upper Missouri can find enough land to cultivate, if so disposed—or room to hunt if they will not work—without [inciting] our little garrisons into a fight with 4000 hostiles.[6]

Sherman realized that if the Métis were not deemed to be legally Indian, with rights to hunt on Indian land, then they must be entitled to the same immigration privileges as any non-Indian Canadian. Many non-Métis Canadians were also moving south of the boundary and, as immigration law provided, simply registered their intention to become citizens.

Despite top-level support, Black's hope that the Métis be left in peace met with ultimate rejection. Under pressure from Montana reservation agents and business interests, the acting assistant adjutant general ordered the removal of the Canadian Métis near the Big Bend of the Milk River. In deference to conditions on the plains, he added a provision that "eviction could be postponed since they are in such destitute condition and the snow [is of a] depth that many would probably perish if compelled to move at once."[7] The directive underscored the ambiguous legal standing of the Métis people. These Métis suffered a legal no-man's-land in which they could prove neither a Euro-American nor an Indian identity and, as Métis, had the rights of neither.

LOUIS RIEL JOINS THE CENTRAL-MONTANA MÉTIS

Unknown to army officials, as they debated the fate of the Métis still hunting in the Milk River country, the revered leader of the Manitoba Resistance, Louis Riel, joined the Milk River Métis. Riel had been in hiding since his escape from Manitoba. When released from a Quebec mental hospital in January 1878, he quietly left Canada and joined friends in New York. Still deeply concerned by the condition of his people and eager to build a coalition of anti-British interests, he attempted to enlist the aid of visiting Fenian revolutionaries. Unsuccessful in efforts to build an Irish alliance and unable to secure other support in New York, Riel resolved to move west, hoping to find greater sympathy for his cause closer to the Red River. With the encouragement of friends, Riel next sought the help of Bishop John Ireland, founder of the Catholic Colonization Bureau. Ireland planned to establish Catholic towns across western Minnesota in an effort to improve the condition of impoverished European Catholics. But Ireland, like the Fenians, disappointed Riel by rejecting his schemes. Finding neither work nor aid, and with his personal financial situation worsening, Riel moved farther west to the Pembina Métis community on the Red River in Dakota Territory.[8]

On reaching Pembina, Riel determined to reestablish his position as Métis leader with yet another bold strategy. He envisioned a confederacy of northern plains Indians and Métis, using an Indian coalition in place of the Irish alliance he had previously attempted to build. The discontent of the western tribes in Canada and the United States; the large numbers of Métis in Manitoba, Saskatchewan, Montana, and Dakota; and the strained relations between the U.S. and Canadian governments gave him hope of success. While he waited in Pembina for a chance to meet with Indian leaders such as Sitting Bull he renewed friendships. In May 1879 he wrote to his mother that he had visited Madame Félix Latreille. This was probably the mother of Spring Creek band Métis Moise Latreille, whose family had lived in Pembina sometime between 1850 and 1870 and had spent the 1870s hunting on the Milk River in north-central Montana. From such friends Riel surely learned that many former Pembina residents, as well as the Dakota-area Indians, had followed the remaining herds to the Milk River. After a few weeks in Dakota Territory, Riel joined the Milk River hunt, planning to confer with Métis and tribal leaders while in Montana.[9]

By October 1879, Riel was in a Milk River Métis hunting camp of thirty lodges, perhaps comprising 150 to 210 individuals. Writing to his mother in October, he described vast herds of buffalo whose bugling (*mugissement*) could be heard at all hours of the day and night. "Il y a beaucoup de Buffalo," he wrote, "J'en ai vu des quantités immenses." These were the herds, no longer found in the Dakotas or Canada, that had attracted the Pembina Métis to Montana. Because they were hunting north of the Missouri River on what was then, in part, Assiniboine, Gros Ventres, and Sioux reservation land, the Métis needed permission from the reservation agents. Not to receive such permission left them, like other Milk River hunters, in danger of expulsion to Canada.[10]

Following traditional hunt organization patterns, the Milk River Métis camp, by then consisting of 150 families, elected Riel as leader to represent them and secure needed permission. Riel successfully obtained hunting rights for the winter of 1879–1880, but agency officials demanded that the Canadian hunters return home in the spring. As already mentioned, reservation agents opposed the wintering of Canadian Métis and Indians in the Territory. They anticipated an accompanying increase in illegal trading, but primarily they objected to the additional pressure that these hunters put on the diminishing herds. Furthermore, although some military officers believed that a strong Métis presence would discourage Indian warfare, military and reservation officials both feared that Riel might unite the Indians and Métis and become a military threat in the region. A November 15, 1879, letter of Fort Belknap agent W. L. Lincoln reflected this suspicion.

The Half Breeds are . . . in force on the Milk River. They also have been very importunate in regard to staying in this country, and latterly one Riel (the leader of the trouble in Manitoba in 1869) has acted as their ambassador. . . . He can wield the Half Breeds at will, and also probably the Crees.

Indeed, as Lincoln feared, Riel asserted his influence by actively attempting to organize a confederation of Indians and Métis. He met with Sioux, Blackfeet, and Cree leaders, but again his effort to win allies, in addition to the already friendly and closely related Crees, failed.[11]

EFFORTS TO ESTABLISH A MÉTIS HOMELAND IN MONTANA

Riel did not return to Canada after the 1879–1880 winter hunt. The Canadian government failed to grant him a hoped-for amnesty, and he had no choice but to remain in the United States. To prevent deportation, Riel declared his intention in May 1880 to become a U.S. citizen. By August, he was south of the Missouri, traveling with the Spring Creek band and their friends and relatives in the Musselshell River drainage just east of the Judith Basin. Without entirely giving up the idea of a Native confederation, Riel joined other Métis leaders in a new project, an effort to secure a Montana land base for the Métis people. He prepared a petition, signed by the adult males then hunting in the area, asking for a "special reservation . . . for the halfbreeds." Again, as in the Chippewa treaty negotiations, the Métis identified themselves as "half-breeds," using the word, as Riel did here, as an English translation of the French word "métis," and with none of the pejorative implications commonly associated with the word.[12]

Because Riel wrote the petition himself but did not record information concerning the document, we do not know what role other Métis played in its creation. Since the Métis usually decided important matters by mutual consent, it seems probable that many took part in the effort, especially the respected hunt chief Alexander Wilkie and his sister's husband, Spring Creek band leader Pierre Berger. Both Wilkie and Berger had experience with half-breed land allotments, having applied for such grants under the 1854 and 1863–1864 Chippewa treaties as Pembina Chippewa half-breeds and descendants of the Lake Superior Chippewas.[13]

The signed petition, delivered to Colonel Nelson A. Miles in August 1880, not only requested land but also funds for schools, agricultural implements, seeds, and animals. The proposed reservation would be distinctly

Métis. Riel made it clear that the Métis did not wish to live on an Indian-style reservation and intended to be self-supporting once established on land of their own. His people, he wrote, "would have no need for the clothes and provisions annually issued to Indians by Government." He also requested that the Métis be allowed to own their land individually as other settlers did, writing, "We ask that all Halfbreeds . . . shall own that land according to the homestead, preemption or timber acts or such other way as the government may desire." Riel understood that his people wished to live near one another, with a recognized land base, much as their Indian relatives did, but that they also wanted to own their land according to European custom and law. The Métis had learned from hard experience in Canada and Dakota that not to do so endangered their community. Riel's western-educated background also influenced him to seek private allotments for the Métis. To him, a nomadic lifestyle led only to moral degeneration. He saw the future of the Métis people in terms of European-style settlements made up of privately owned farms.[14]

To bolster his case for a Métis reservation, Riel pointed out the advantages of having a Métis presence near Montana's Indians. "As halfbreeds," he wrote, "we stand between the civilized and uncivilized man; and are closely related with the several tribes of the northwest, owing to which fact we indirectly exercise some influence and from the indian blood in our veins, we are inclined to believe that indians will listen to us more favorably than to the majority of those who are not connected by family ties with them."[15] Riel felt justified in asking the government for a reservation both on the basis of Métis aboriginal rights and in return for the services that the Métis were uniquely able to render the government. The Métis presented themselves as a distinct group, neither Indian nor Euro-American, but closely tied to both and in a position to work closely with either. This was a sophisticated plan that made use of U.S. fears of Indian unrest and the Euro-American supposition that permanent agricultural communities were a prerequisite to civilization. It took advantage of both U.S. Indian policy and mainstream Euro-American values manifested in the Homestead Act.

Supporting the plan and signing the petition were members of the Spring Creek band who had settled on Spring Creek the summer before (see the list of signatories in appendix). Other signatories were their friends and relatives, most of whom eventually settled to the north in the Milk River/Havre/Zortman area, or to the west at St. Peter's Mission near present-day Cascade and along the Front Range of the Rocky Mountains. Historian of the Métis, Thomas Flanagan, has identified many of the signatories, and others can be traced through the Pembina censuses and the 1854 and 1863–1864 Chippewa treaties, as well as through genealogies of the Spring Creek band.[16] Of the 101 men who signed the petition, twenty-four were members of the Spring Creek band, five more settled with the band in the 1880s, and at least ten others were parents, siblings, children, or cousins of band members (see appendix). Of the remaining signatories, all but ten had known kinship ties to each other or to Spring Creek band members. The petition signatories did not come together in a temporary arrangement of convenience for an important goal. The hunters who signed the petition had deeper connections and were seeking to preserve an existing community based on kinship ties.[17]

As discussed in chapter 2, the Spring Creek band families were related through the women of their families as often as through the men. Family relationships between the signatories also become more apparent when women's networks are uncovered. While at least twelve family groups among the petition signers included a father and sons or brothers, the cohesiveness of the group as a whole depended upon women's family ties. It is essential to note the bilineal nature of Métis band kinship patterns, for if viewed as discrete patrilineal families, the complex kinship relations of the entire collection of signatories are lost.

An investigation into the kinship relations of the families also illuminates their Pembina ties. All of the family names except those of Beauchamp, Leclaire, and Norwest can be found either in the 1850 or 1860 U.S. censuses for the Pembina District, or as Lake Superior and Pembina half-breed applicants for land script under the 1854 and 1863–1864 Chippewa treaties. Individuals are more difficult to pinpoint. Many have common names, making positive identification difficult. Others are missing from these records because of age. As Thomas Flanagan has pointed out, the hunters in the Judith Basin were a noticeably young group.[18] As such, many were too young to have signed the Chippewa treaties, and others were not yet born. Similarly, many were born after the 1850 census, yet their families had already moved west, out of range of the census takers by 1860. Nevertheless, by counting family name groups (which are not necessarily nuclear families, but who, in most cases, can be shown to be closely related), at least one member, and often more, of twenty-three of the family name groups out of the thirty-eight represented by the signatories can be tentatively identified in a Pembina census or Chippewa treaty. Of the remaining family name groups, most contain only an individual signatory whose family connections are not clear and who was probably too young to have been counted in the above sources. The relationship of the Spring Creek band signatories to the Pembina community is even closer than that of their other relatives in the Judith Basin. As noted in chapter 2, almost all of the Spring Creek families have direct Pembina ties, and intermarriage brought such ties to those few families who had no previously known Pembina connections.

Every family of a petition signer who can be positively identified had relatives who considered themselves to be Pembina half-breeds and/or had lived in the Pembina community. This is not to deny their connections to Red River Settlement. Some were born there, but all also had strong residential, kinship, and community ties to Pembina and were recognized in U.S. documents as claiming Pembina residence or Pembina or Lake Superior Chippewa half-breed status. These were families that had been claiming their rights to U.S. soil for more than twenty-five years.

The petition came very close to success. Colonel Miles of Fort Keogh, charged with pacifying the area, thought the idea had merit. Knowing that a large Métis presence would diffuse intertribal conflict, he hoped that they might also set an example for the tribes. Unfortunately for the Métis, the influential Crow Indian reservation agent, A. R. Keller, vigorously opposed the plan. He objected to the suggestion of Riel's and others' that part of the Crow reservation be appropriated for the settlement. Knowing that the Crows would not be willing to further reduce their territory, the agent protested on several grounds by raising issues that, although unfounded, reflected and intensified pervasive fears concerning the Métis. The Métis were British citizens, the descendants of Canadian Cree Indians, he argued, and therefore, had no right to U.S. land. Furthermore, he accused the Métis of being poor citizenship material, citing their reputed connections to the whiskey trade. Agent Keller's opinions reflected widely held beliefs, but he was incorrect on both counts. As already shown, most of the petition signatories had kinship ties to the Pembina, Dakota, community. He also ignored the fact that the largest whiskey suppliers in the region were non-Métis companies based in Fort Benton.[19]

Unfortunately, agent Keller's objections gave ammunition to cattle, land, and mining interests then pressuring the government to open existing reservations to white settlement. The Indians had no need for such large tracts of land, Montana business people insisted, while Euro-American settlers would "improve" the land and make better citizens at the same time. Cattlemen especially, such as future Territorial Council President

Granville Stuart, opposed setting aside more land for Native use; rather, they wanted the current amount drastically reduced. In response to this pressure, and on the strength of Keller's information, the Indian commissioner failed to recommend the petition, causing the Department of the Interior to reject it. The chance for a Métis reservation in Montana was lost.[20]

MÉTIS HUNTERS IN THE JUDITH BASIN, 1880–1881

After the petition's rejection, Riel continued to represent the interests of the Métis hunting in the Judith Basin. Unlike the Milk River reservation agents, Judith Basin military personnel were happy to have large groups of Métis on the plains as a deterrent to Indian raids and hoped that the Métis could help keep peace in an area where so many different tribal groups hunted in close proximity. The commanding officer of Fort Maginnis, the new post near Spring Creek, granted Riel, as representative of the Métis, permission to hunt in the area through the winter. "The Major Commanding this Post Advises the Half-Breed Hunters to go + hunt + winter together as usual + as of old to Protect themselves + Horses against Raiding Indians," he ordered in September 1880. The commander expected the Métis hunters to protect themselves against Indian attack without army aid, and, at the same time, to help prevent Indian raids in the area. "In Wintering all in a body they will be in a measure to stand + resist any Difficulty with the Indians as of old," he believed. Furthermore, "in being their own safeguard without forfeiting any laws of the Country they might Save an Indian Expedition + being in a Large body by themselves would Doubtless prevent such."[21]

With permission to hunt from the Fort Maginnis commander, Riel continued as spokesman for the central-Montana Métis. He supported himself as a trader for Thomas O'Hanlon, an Irish Catholic employee of T. C. Power and Co. O'Hanlon operated out of Carroll, a wild and rough-hewn trading town once described as "a squalid collection of mud and log huts, too small and too dirty even to be called cabins," about sixty miles north of the Spring Creek colony on the Missouri River. Riel's friendship with O'Hanlon began a period of cordial relations with the T. C. Power company that would survive his later indictment of Montana traders for their sale of liquor to Indians and Métis. By fall, Riel became subagent for another trader, James Willard Schultz. Later well known for his depiction of Montana frontier life, Schultz had recently expanded his independent trading operation by opening a post at Carroll. Like others, he had noticed that the disappearance of the Canadian buffalo herds brought an unusual number of

Native hunters to central Montana. Near Carroll, the Crees, Blackfeet, and Bloods from north of the boundary joined what Schultz described as a large number of half-breeds to whom they were related. Schultz hoped for a profitable trading season with so many hunters in close proximity and hired Riel to bring in the Métis and Cree trade.[22]

Schultz's memoirs lend sobering insights into attitudes that the Métis encountered as they interacted with the growing Euro-American population of Montana Territory. "It was not for their looks that I disliked them so much as it was their habits and customs," wrote Schultz, expressing a common regional view. "They ate dogs, for one thing; they pretended to be faithful and zealous members of the church, but were the worst set of liars and thieves that ever traveled across the plains; they hated the Americans as much as they did the English, and in their bastard French cursed us." His comments are puzzling since his Blackfoot wife's relatives' customs were similar in many ways to those of the Métis, yet he was not critical of them. His claim that the Métis "hated" Americans cannot be supported. In fact, as noted, many Métis were U.S. citizens, and others had applied for citizenship. Furthermore, Schultz's trusted assistant, Berry, was Métis, and his own children were "half-breeds." However seemingly irrational, Schultz's attitude toward the Métis was not uncommon, and this attitude was noticeably more virulent among the increasing number of new arrivals.[23]

Regardless of his views, Schultz was more than willing to profit from Métis hunts and to employ their leader as his subagent for the winter of 1880–1881. Hiring Riel ensured the business of the large Métis band wintering on the Flat Willow, southeast of Spring Creek. Schultz's business that winter was good. He reported "a banner season," receiving twenty-eight thousand dollars for four thousand buffalo robes, plus five thousand dollars for more than four thousand other skins and pelts. But by summer, the buffalo were not as plentiful. Most Indian hunters moved on, while the Crees and Métis continued to supply Schultz with pemmican.[24]

As Schultz noted, in 1880 and early 1881 the buffalo were still numerous in the Judith Basin, and most of the Métis in Montana hunted there. Other Métis families lived to the west in the Fort Benton area and on the upper Teton River. Plains Indian historian, John C. Ewers, estimated the number of Métis in the Fort Benton and Teton River regions at seventy-nine and sixty-six, respectively, with 229 living in Chouteau County as a whole (the north-central section of Montana, including Fort Benton and a portion of the Teton River). These numbers give an indication of the Métis settlement centers, but they are surely underestimated, as Ewers depended on census population data collected in the summer when most Métis were away hunting. In addition to those Métis mentioned by Ewers, smaller concentrations had settled on the Missouri River near Carroll and Wilder's Landing, north of the Spring Creek settlement, hunting and cutting wood for the steamboats. Others moved west to St. Peter's Mission, where the missionaries had hoped to establish a Métis agricultural community.[25]

All of the Montana Métis, whether traders, wood cutters, trappers, or buffalo hunters, ultimately depended upon the buffalo. The market for buffalo products supported and underlay Montana Métis economic well-being. The Judith Basin, one of the few places where the animals were still plentiful, naturally became the center of the early 1880s hunts.

SPRING CREEK SETTLEMENT

During the winter of 1880–1881, the Spring Creek band settled in the Judith Basin along the tributaries of Spring Creek, using the area as a base from which to conduct their hunts. Various Métis had hunted and traded in the immediate area long before these families arrived. Armell Creek, a few miles to the east of Spring Creek, was named for Augustin Hamell (Armell), a Métis trader and trapper who operated a trading post there around 1845.[26]

Nor was Spring Creek without Euro-American residents when the band arrived. Upon reaching the creek, they found an already established (although short-lived) trading post run by A. S. Reed and John J. "Jim" Bowles. Reed and Bowles sold liquor, tea, tobacco, and clothing, which they traded for buffalo robes, hides, and furs. Bowles was living with a Piegan woman whose relatives were camped to the south at the foot of the Snowy Mountains. No doubt Reed and Bowles made use of her kinship ties to secure the valued Piegan business. Although apparently successful in their trade operations, the two had an "unsavory reputation." Acquaintances told stories of Indians mysteriously disappearing if they unwisely visited the post unaccompanied but in possession of good horses or furs.[27]

Reed and Bowles had relocated Reed's Fort, as the post came to be known, to the Spring Creek crossing of the Carroll Trail. This trail led overland from the village of Carroll, on the Missouri River, to Helena. It had gained popularity in dry years when the Missouri, the only practical route for the shipment of Montana freight, was too low for steamboats to reach the trade center of Fort Benton. Fort Benton was the closest river port to the busy gold fields of Helena (140 miles distant from Fort Benton by an only slightly improved dirt track). Although the trail from Carroll to Helena was longer (210 miles), the terrain it crossed was much gentler and easier for the hauling of large loads. Nevertheless, Carroll could not lure the Fort Benton trade, except on very dry years, because of a major problem—the Carroll Trail ran through the Judith Basin, one of the most popular Indian hunting areas. This region was relatively unprotected by U.S. troops until 1880, when the army established Fort Maginnis, south of the Judith Mountains. In 1874 the army had occupied a short-lived summer camp (Camp Lewis) on Spring Creek, but it was understaffed and did nothing more useful than to eventually provide a new name for the Spring Creek settlement.[28]

SETTLEMENT PATTERNS ON SPRING CREEK

Although the Métis could not have been unaware of its advantages, the importance of the Spring Creek drainage was not its proximity to the Carroll Trail but its abundant game, protected valleys suitable for summer gardens, and the nearby buffalo herds. As they settled in the fall of 1879 and spring of 1880, certain residential patterns became evident. The trader group built homes and a trading post on Spring Creek about three miles south of the crossing of the Carroll Trail. Francis Janeaux, leader of the traders, Paul Morase, Pierre Laverdure, and Antoine Ouellette immediately took advantage of the promising location by applying for homesteads near the post on land that is now within Lewistown city limits. By doing so they became the town's founders.[29]

The hunting families moved a few miles east, dispersing along the small tributaries of Spring Creek, near hills rich in game. Much as they had done on the Milk River and in the Pembina region, these families settled in family clusters, far enough apart to assure adequate pasture for their stock, sufficient garden- or farmland, and plentiful small-game hunting territory, but not so far as to make frequent contact difficult (see homestead maps and table 2). Relatively few of the hunting families applied for homesteads in the first years. The application process required cash for the filing fee (a rare commodity on the plains) and considerable inconvenience. Filing on homestead land entailed traveling over a hundred miles to the southwest around the Little Belt Mountains and across the roadless prairie to White Sulpher Springs, the Meagher county seat. Undertaking such a project required not only an appreciation of the importance of legal title, but also a need for such title. Of the hunting families, only the Bergers and Wilkies applied for homestead land by 1883.[30]

The Berger family settled immediately on arrival, building cabins less than three miles east of the traders on and near a homestead filed by Pierre Berger's son Peter, along what was later called upper Breed Creek. Not until the following spring did the rest of the hunting families build homes, but during the winter they cut the necessary timber. Ben Kline located just to the south of Pierre and Judith Berger and their married and unmarried children, while Judith's brother, Alexander Wilkie, and his daughters' families (LaFountains), settled to the northeast. Wilkie's two-room cabin was the largest in the area, having one room that measured twenty by thirty feet. This was quite a luxurious size for that place and time, but Wilkie planned ahead, knowing that the families would need a large room in which visiting missionaries could conduct services.[31]

Another cluster of families settled just beyond the "Berger place," closer to the Judith Mountains. These families established "a little village" near the head of Blind Breed Gulch. John B. LaFountain, husband of one of Alexander Wilkie's daughters, settled there soon after arrival. LaFountain was partially blind and his condition gave the creek its name. Less is known of these families because fewer obtained title to their homesites.[32]

The band quickly established a trail around the foot of Black Butte on the east end of the Judith Mountains. Known simply as the "half-breed trail," it led to the plains east of the Judith Mountains and to the buffalo, which were plentiful there. This trail passed the homes of the remaining band members. Joe Doney and his wife Philomene LaFountain, and Joe Larocque (LaRocque) and his wife, Madeline Fagnant, half-sister of Charlotte Adam LaFountain and therefore half-aunt of Philomene, located near this trail about twelve miles northeast of the Wilkies and LaFountains. Eli Gardipee and his wife, Mary Larocque (Joe Larocque's sister) made their home even farther to the northeast, at the head of Bear Creek on the northeast side of the Judith Mountains in the midst of buffalo country.[33]

The homestead maps and table 2 illustrate the residential grouping of the Métis families by legal descriptions of homestead entry filings. A number of these families—for example, Francis Janeaux and Paul Morase—also bought land outright, but lived on their homesteads. Map 2 indicates the homestead filings in Township 15/Range 18 (T15/R18) from 1880 to 1885—that is, the filings of those Métis who took action almost immediately upon arrival. The numbers within each entry boundary correspond to the names listed in table 2. Township 15/Range 18 includes the town site of Lewistown. As the numbers on the map indicate, all of the settlers who filed before 1885 within or bordering the eventual city limits of Lewistown were traders, their employees, or close relatives.

The homestead pattern of the hunter families is quite different. Most of them are found on maps 4 and 5 (Township 15/Range 19, adjacent to T15/R18). Their filing dates show that, of the hunters, only the band leaders, the Bergers and Alexander Wilkie, filed before 1886, although between 1886 and 1899, fifteen more individuals filed. Map 6, the areawide homestead location map, indicates the sections (rather than the actual legal description) in which the remaining Métis families settled. None of these ten hunting families filed early—that is, before 1886.[34]

Homestead filings reflect the occupational priorities of the band families. Those concentrating most exclusively on hunting lived farthest from Spring Creek and were the least likely, or the latest, to obtain land title. The trader families clustered closely together, surrounding the trading post. Those who farmed as well as hunted were more likely to file for homestead land and to live closer to Spring Creek.[35] Residential patterns also reflect class differences within the community. The relatively prosperous traders, the band leaders, and the few skilled craftsmen filed on homesteads early and on better agricultural land closer to Spring Creek.[36]

In table 2, early homestead filers (1880–1885) are highlighted in bold. Most filed under provisions of the 1862 Homestead Act (HE). Some individuals filed under the 1841 Preemption Act (Pre), which provided a means for those who settled on land before receiving legal title, often derisively called "squatters," to obtain title for a fee. The numbers in the first column correspond to the numbers included within the individual holdings shown on maps 2 through 6. The third column lists the section in which the homestead was located. The last column lists the filers who met the terms of the Homestead Act by living on their land for five years and making the required improvements. Several filers "commuted to cash"— that is, they purchased the land outright before waiting five years. Of the fifty Métis filings listed in homestead records, thirty-two "proved up" by meeting the Homestead Act requirements and received their final certificate (FC) and deed. Six commuted to cash (CC) and received deed, and six filed under the Preemption Act. Of the five who did not receive title (10 percent), one cannot be positively identified as Métis. This record far exceeds the national average, in which only one-third of those who filed claims proved up and received deeds. Such a percentage is all the more remarkable

TABLE 2
Métis Homestead Applications, 1880–1899

Homesteader # (Maps 2–5)	Name	Section	Type	Disposition
Township 15N/Range 18E (includes town site of Lewistown)				
1	**Wallet, Antoine[1]**	**10**	**HE**	**FC**
2	Juneaux, Evelyn[2]	11	HE	FC
3	Laverdure, Joseph	12	Pre	
4	Azure, Frank	12	Pre	
5	Cline, Ben	12	HE	FC
6	**Berger, John B.**	**12**	**HE**	**FC**
7	**Wells, Edward, Jr.**	**13**	**HE**	**FC**
8	Vadnais, John	13	Pre	
9	Wells, Mary F.	13	HE	FC
10	**Pichette, J. B.***	**14**	**Pre**	
11	Larock, Wm. A.	14	HE	FC
12	**Morase, Paul**	**15**	**HE**	**FC**
13	**Janeaux, Francis**	**15**	**HE**	**CC**
14	**Laverdure, Francis**	**15**	**HE**	**FC**
15	Laverdure, Bernard	23	Pre	
16	Laverdure, Ralph	23	HE	CC
17	Laverdure, Nobar	23	HE	FC
18	Laverdure, Daniel	24	HE	CC
Township 16N/Range 18E				
19	Wells, Edward, Sr.	33	HE	FC
20	Wells, Daniel	34	HE	FC
Township 15N/Range 19E				
21	LaFontaine, John B.	4	HE	FC
22	Rocheleau, Modest*	4	HE	FC
23	Berger, Jacob	4	HE	FC
24	**Wilkie, Alexander**	**6**	**HE**	**FC**
25	Berger, John B.	6	HE	FC
26	**Berger, Peter**	**7**	**HE**	**FC**
27	Berger, John B., Jr.	7	HE	FC
28	Kline, Julia	7	HE	FC
29	Paul, Leonides	7	HE	FC
30	Oulette, Mose	8	HE	FC
31	**Berger, Isaiah**	**8**	**HE**	**FC**
32	Papillon, Joseph*	9	HE	
33	Berger, John B.	9	HE	FC
34	Lavalle, Peter	10	HE	FC
35	Wells, James	10		FC
36	Ouelette, Joseph	11	HE	FC
37	Vadnais, John	12	HE	FC

TABLE 2 (*continued*)
Métis Homestead Applications, 1880–1899

Homesteader # (Maps 2–5)	Name	Type	Section	Disposition
38	Paul, Leonede	17	Pre	
39	**Berger, Isadore**	**17**	**HE**	**FC**
40	**Fleurie, Antoine**	**18**	**HE**	**FC**
41	Wells, Thomas	21	HE	CC
42	Laverdure, Frank	23	HE	CC
Township 16N/Range 19E				
43	Daigneau, Frank	33	HE	FC
Township 15N/Range 20E				
44	Fleury, Louis	7		Can
45	Fleury, Alice	18	Hd	CC
46	Laplant, Louis	19	HE	
Township 16N/Range 20E				
47	Donais, Joseph	3	Hd	
48	Guardipee, Eli	11	Hd	*
	Lefferts, Wm. O.	16	Hd	CC
49	Latray, Mose	29		Rel
	*Description amended			
Township 17N/Range 20E				
50	Larocque, Joseph	34	Hd	FC

1. Early homestead filers (1880–1885) are highlighted in bold.
2. Spellings are as found in the Bureau of Land Management documents.

KEY
Can Cancelled. "Land actions cancelled are done by the Government for failure to comply with law or regulation."
CC Commuted to cash. A cash payment made to receive patent.
CE "A cash sale entry is involved."
FC "This denoted the issuance of a final certificate by local land office officials. The document implies that an entry person has proved up under provisions of the law and is entitled to a patent.
Hd See HE.
HE Homestead Act entry. "Can denote the Homestead Act of 1862, Reclamation Act of 1902, Forest Homestead Act of 1906, Enlarged Homestead of 1909, and some times the Stock-Raising Homestead Act of 1916."
Pre "The land is being taken under the provision of the Preemption Act of 1841.
Rel Relinquishment. "Entryperson voluntarily gives up his/her right to the entry in question."
*Ethnicity unknown

Key source. Bureau of Land Management, District Office, Billings, Mont. For specific dates of homestead entry applications, see Martha Harroun Foster, "We Know," 322–23.

A NEW HOMELAND 107

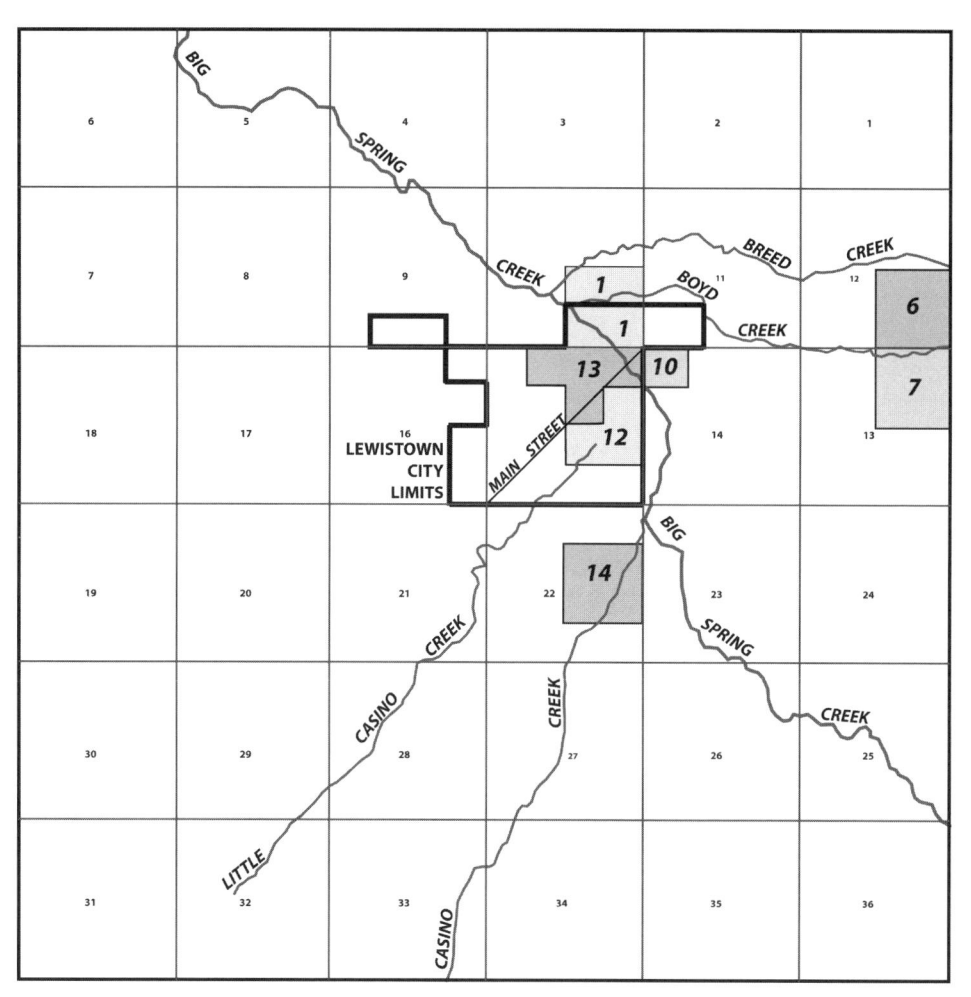

Métis Homestead Applications, 1880–1885. Township 15 North, Range 18 East, Fergus County. Shaded areas: homestead applications. Map by Vincent Armstrong and the author.

because the area receives little rainfall, endures long and harsh winters, and was, in general, unsuitable for the farming techniques then in practice. The Métis proved more successful in obtaining title to their homesteads than later homesteaders because they used their land for gardens, small farms, and pasture, but did not depend on the land for their entire livelihood. They routinely supplemented their incomes with the sale of game products and their diet with quantities of wild meat.[37]

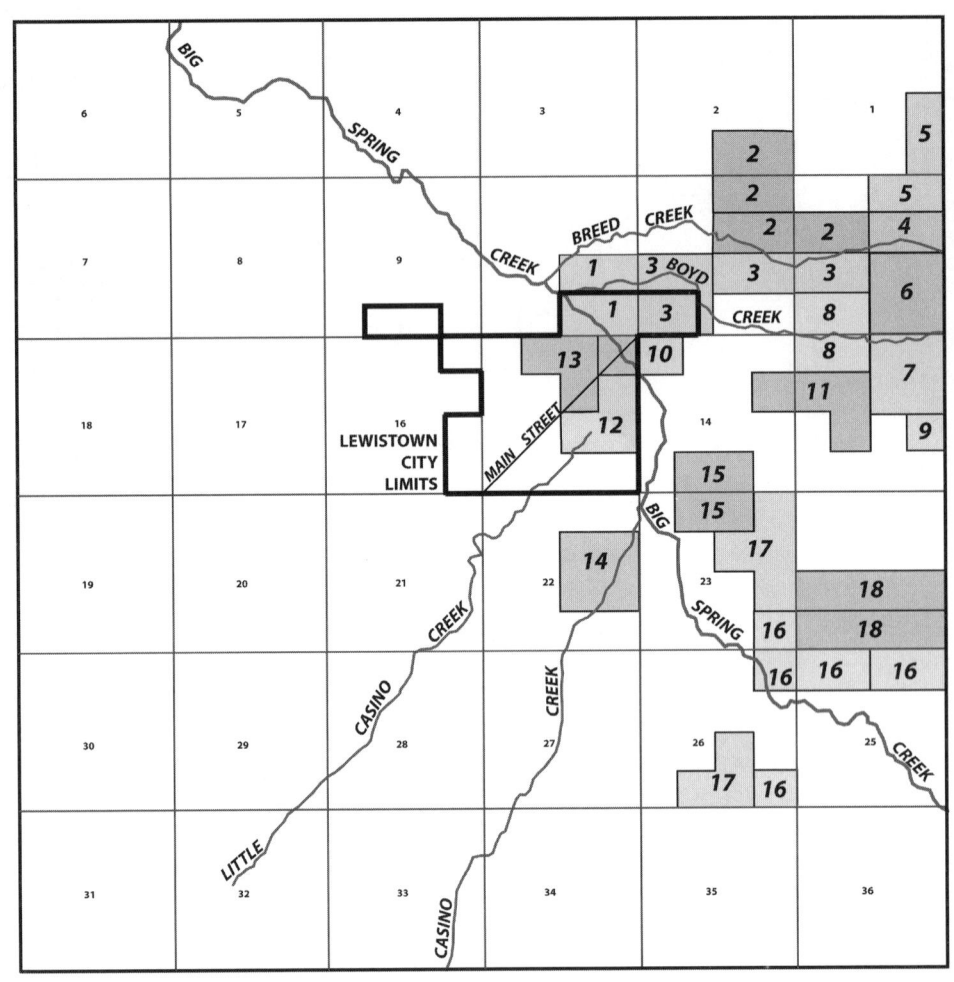

Métis Homestead Applications, 1880–1899. Township 15 North, Range 18 East, Fergus County. Shaded areas: homestead applications. Map by Vincent Armstrong and the author.

In addition to helping visualize the life of the Spring Creek Métis, the homestead records shed light on persistent misconceptions regarding the early history of the Montana Métis. Although, in the first decades of the twentieth century, many Montana Métis become known as Landless Indians, this was not because none applied for or received land title. There is a general impression in Montana that the Landless Indians became so because they were Canadian Indians who, as Canadians, were ineligible for enroll-

A NEW HOMELAND 109

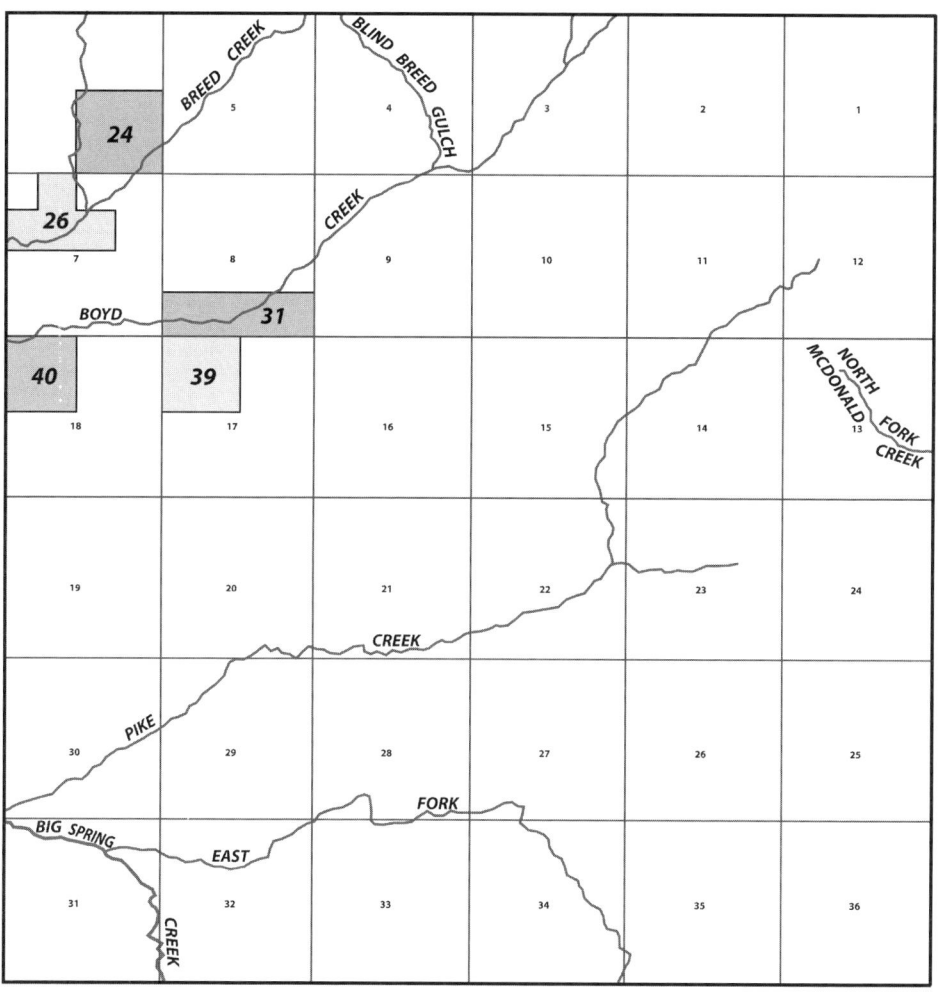

Métis Homestead Applications, 1880–1885. Township 15 North, Range 19 East, Fergus County. Shaded areas: homestead applications. Map by Vincent Armstrong and the author.

ment on Montana reservations. Yet because they were Indian (and presumably eligible for Canadian Indian land) neither could they obtain U.S. homestead land as other Canadian immigrants did—the classic tragic situation of a people caught in between. Indeed, this was the case for some Métis families who immigrated to Montana after 1885, especially if they were identified by authorities as Canadian Crees. But, as shown, the Montana

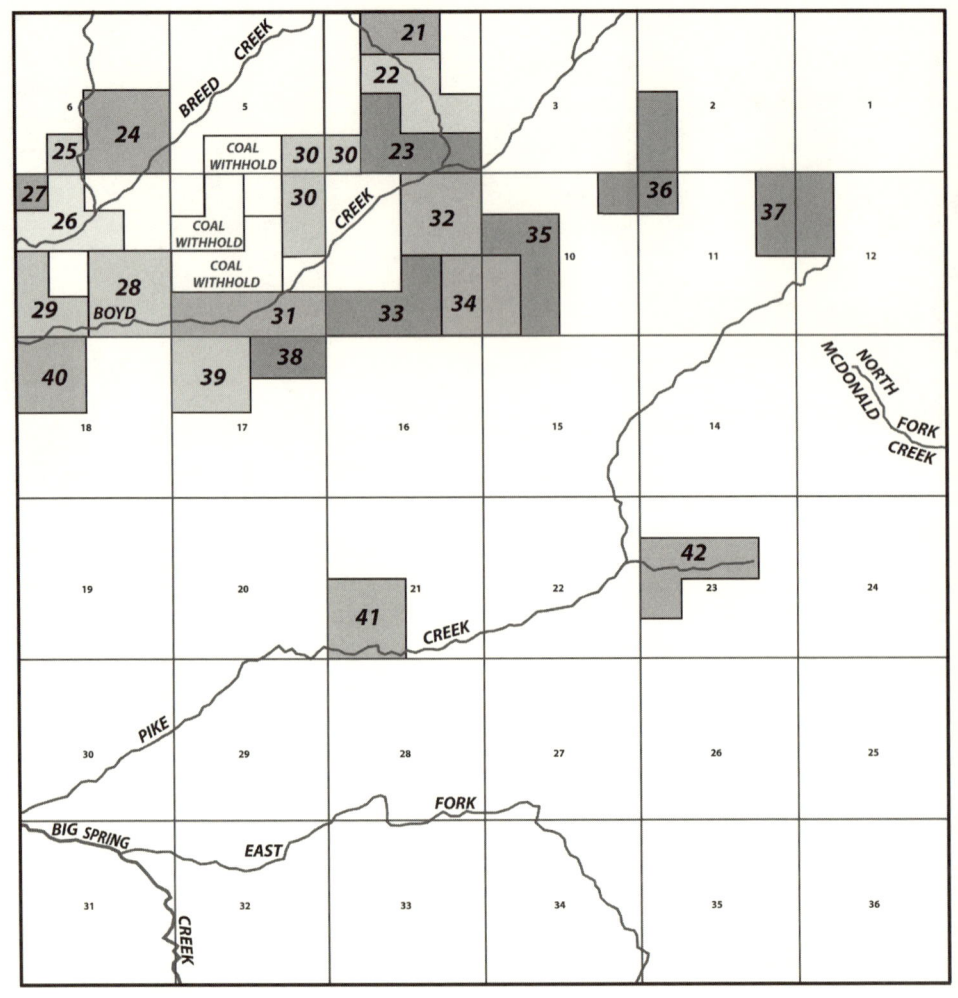

Métis Homestead Applications, 1880–1899. Township 15 North, Range 19 East, Fergus County. Shaded areas: homestead applications. Map by Vincent Armstrong and the author.

Métis could and did take advantage of their rights under the Homestead and Preemption acts. The popular notion that U.S. Métis were excluded from participation in the Homestead Act provisions is not supportable. To the contrary, most of the Spring Creek band did file on homestead land and, in a few years, met the requirements and received their final certificates and deeds.[38]

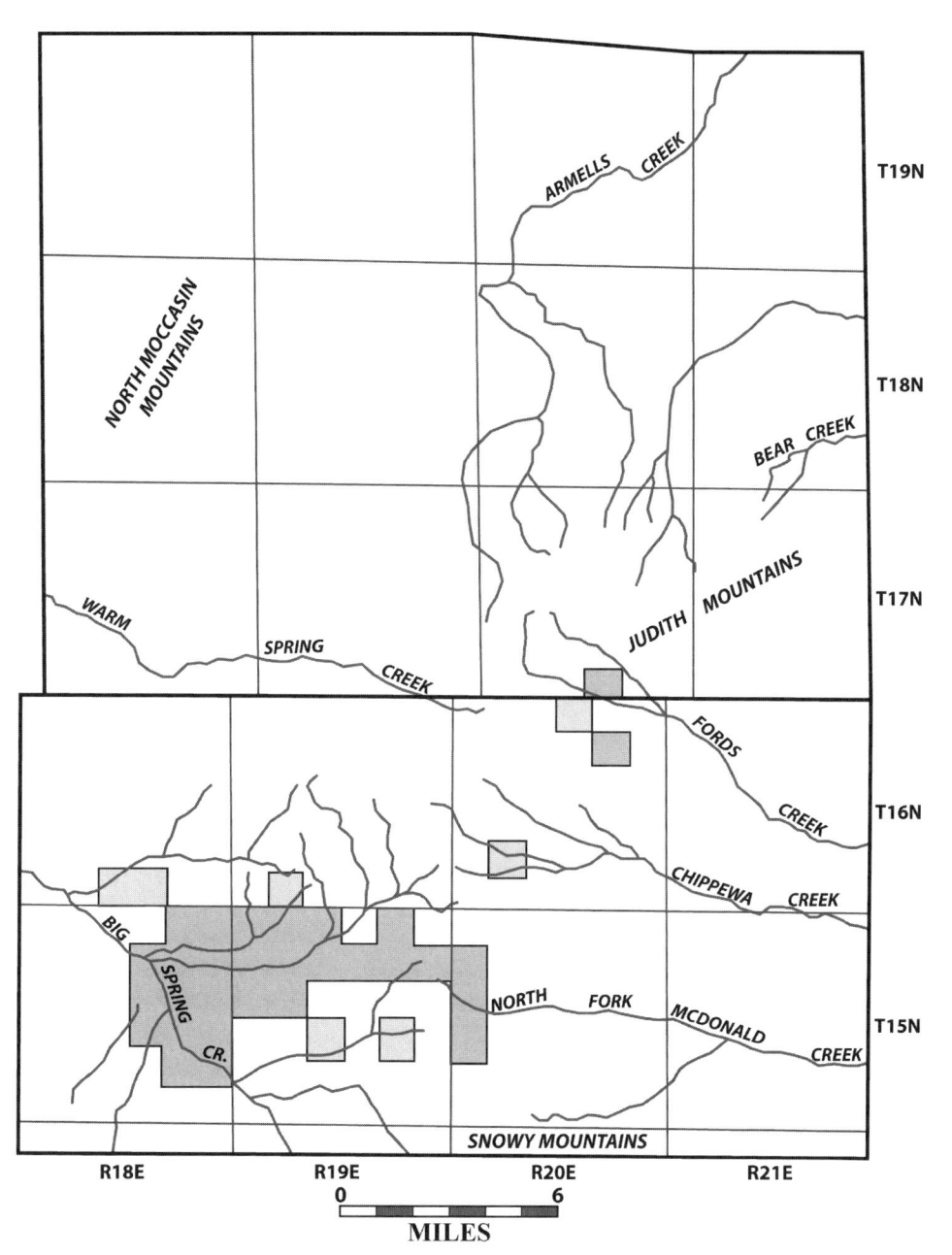

Métis Homestead Locations, Judith Mountains Area, 1880–1899. Map by Vincent Armstrong and the author.

THE SPRING CREEK MÉTIS IN 1880:
A COMMUNITY PROFILE

In the Spring Creek drainage, additional families soon joined those already there. By 1880, the census taker (who prudently did not brave the open plains to count the families temporarily away hunting) found thirty Métis families living in the Spring Creek settlement area that summer. The 1880 census, although excluding many hunting families, provides a profile of the community. As the census indicates, many members of the Spring Creek band older than thirty had been born in Canada. Among a few families, like that of Alexander Wilkie, all individuals had been born in Dakota. But most indicative of the Métis mobile lifestyle and the meaninglessness of the national boundary to the Métis sense of community was the place of birth of their children. Since Métis families were large and the children were often born only a year or two apart, families' movements can often be traced by the birth of their children. The Berger, Wilkie, Daniels (Daignon), and Laverdure children under the age of thirty were born in Dakota. In the case of the Berger family, the oldest children had been born in Canada (Ezra, or Isaiah [Isaie], Berger, age thirty-five, was born there). This typical pattern reflects the fact that many Pembina Métis had lived in Red River Settlement for a period of time before 1850. The LaFountain, Fayant, and Doney (Lonnais) family births tell another story. For example, Alex and Mary Fayant list seven children at home on June 11, 1880, when the census enumerator visited. The oldest child, at sixteen, was born in Canada; Francis, two years younger, in Dakota, and, by the birth of their twelve-year-old, the family was back in Canada. Joseph and Josephine, ages ten and eight, were born in Montana, but the family was again north of the boundary for the birth of Peter, age four, and back in Montana when Mary gave birth to baby Isabel, only a month old. The census illustrates the difficulty of ascertaining the nationality and place of residence of the Spring Creek families. Most had members born on both sides of the boundary line, which until recently had meant nothing to them.[39]

While settling on Spring Creek, these families supported themselves in the traditional manner, hunting buffalo and trading pemmican and robes for supplies. Some had also started farming. In the 1880 census, Alexander Wilkie; Jack, Isadore, and Peter Berger; Joseph and John Doney; Frank Boyer (identity uncertain); Antoine Lafontain; Frank Daignon; Peter Laverdure; and Baptiste Adam list their occupation as farmer. Such a high number of farmers (as opposed to hunters) in residence on Spring Creek in mid-June

A NEW HOMELAND												113

is not surprising. This was planting time in an area where the last snowstorm is very often during the first week of June. Families who were hunting that season had already left for the herds by the time that the enumerator arrived, leaving others, often older members of the community, to plant the crops.[40]

In addition to place of birth and occupation, the 1880 census provided space for the notation of race. In the Montana census "color," as listed there, was a very subjective matter. The census taker in enumeration district twenty-three, which included the Spring Creek area, recorded all the Métis families as Indian. Traders Francis Janeaux and Paul Morris (Morase), who, at least occasionally, presented themselves as white but who were married to Métis women, were also described as Indian. In enumeration district three, Fort Benton, the enumerator handled the subject of "color" differently. He listed a Wells, an Ouellette (Willett), and a Laverdure family, all from Pembina and almost certainly related to the Spring Creek Métis families of the same name, as "white," while tabulating Antoine A. Janeaux and his children as white, but his wife Josephine as Indian. On the other hand, this enumerator described the children of Robert S. Tingley as Indian even though Tingley himself was designated white (his wife Louise was listed as Indian). Class may have entered into designations of ethnicity in Fort Benton, where mixed-descent families had been living off and on since the 1830s. Prosperous farmers, traders, and skilled laborers were invariably listed as white, as were their children. Eli Gardipee, a teamster, and therefore somewhat lower on the local social scale, was entered as "$1/_2$ br" and his wife as Indian. Unfortunately, they had no children to show how the enumerator would have solved that ethnic puzzle. Enumerators in both districts listed hunters and trappers as Indian. The Wells family again illustrates the contradictions inherent in establishing racial and ethnic identity. John Wells, a sixty-four-year-old trapper found by an enumerator in the Musselshell Valley, east of the Spring Creek drainage, reported his parents' place of birth to be Ireland. Nevertheless, the enumerator entered him as Indian, as he did John's wife, Mary, and their children.[41]

Feelings about race ran high in Montana, and not everyone agreed with a family's own or the enumerator's designations. In enumerator district four, Shonkin Creek, Chouteau County, the enumerator's original "w" (white) for Pierre (white) and Rose (Indian) Charboneau's children was heavily overwritten with a large "I." At the side, in different writing is a heavy black "HB" (half-breed). Obviously, three commentators had three separate opinions as to these individuals' "color."[42]

LIFE ON SPRING CREEK

As the census indicates, the Spring Creek settlement was a growing community in 1880. Granville Stuart, an early Montana gold miner and cattleman, traveled through the area that year and described both the new village and the hunters abroad in the Judith Basin. While searching the Basin for cattle grazing land, Stuart met a large Métis hunting party with their fifty carts as they moved from McDonald to Flat Willow Creek (east of the Judith Mountains). The next day, on June 26, he encountered forty more "carts and half-breed families" traveling from Black Butte. Describing "carts with two very large wheels in which the families ride," he remembered their "peculiar 'screechy' noise that [could] be heard for miles." While visiting the Métis, Stuart asked for information about good grazing land. One of the hunting party, Sevire Hamlin, told him of fine pasturage in the Ford Creek area east of Spring Creek. Stuart took advantage of this advice, and after examining the land, established a large cattle ranch there.[43]

In May 1880, when Stuart passed through the Spring Creek settlement, he was favorably impressed with the village, noting that it was "quite a settlement." He approved of the plowed fields and the neatness of the post and homes. His only criticism was of the post's defenses, which he found insubstantial. "The logs are small so that . . . a bullet . . . would go right through them," he complained—an important consideration in an area where Sioux and Blackfeet horse-stealing parties were very active, and where, just three nights before, the Sioux had stolen thirty head of the settlement's horses. The community was far more to Stuart's liking than the rough Missouri River trade towns, and he commented dryly that "the houses of the Red River half breeds are in marked contrast to the posts of the white men through here."[44]

That the Métis had built such a tidy and substantial settlement so quickly is all the more remarkable since they arrived with so little. Presumably Janeaux, as a trader, was well supplied with tools, but most families had only the axes that they always carried on their carts. Just one of the hunting families owned a shovel. Pierre Berger, who had experience in blacksmithing and tin working, had a few metalworking tools and a hoe, and Isaie Berger had a small number of carpentry tools. None had furniture, few had more than one cart, and all had only the few possessions that they were able to carry in their carts.[45]

Cabins were especially difficult to construct with only an axe, and the carts, being too small to haul logs, were no help in this chore. All of the logs had to be dragged, a few at a time, out of the mountains with a horse. Elizabeth Berger Swan described the building of the cabins and their furnishings.

> Building the log cabins was quite a task, they could not have many logs at a time, with only a device of their own, but managed to snake down a few logs each day, being they were skilful with the use of an axe they made all their roofing, flooring, framework and some furniture with smoothly hewn logs. No one had a stove and they cooked in the fire place built on a casing of small timbers and finished with a mortar, made with a mixture of grass and dirt. When the roofing is all up in place the cracks were filled with mortar and the top covered with sod, for the doors and windows the framework was covered with raw hide, was not altogether transparent, still gave plenty light inside and was weatherproof.
>
> The bunks, tables and benches were finished with peg legs, besides the light from the fire place, at night, a lamp was made by melting tallow on a deep receptacle and twisted rag for a wick. The brooms were made of buck brush tied securely on the end of a stick.[46]

From such meager supplies, the Métis quickly built a community. Before long they were ready for their traditional celebrations. Already, by Christmas of 1880, they were celebrating in their accustomed manner. Christmas was a relatively quiet family day, but it began a round of visiting and dancing that lasted until New Year's. On New Year's Day the traditional large, community-wide parties and dances were held. The women worked for weeks cooking enough food for their guests. The entire community was welcome in each home, and groups of celebrants moved from house to house. When evening came, and the meal was finished, they removed the furniture from one or two rooms to make space for dancing. The traditional Métis dances accompanied by Métis fiddlers would continue all night.[47]

In addition to enjoying their traditional celebrations, the Métis differed from their few Euro-American neighbors in other ways. Since most band members spoke no English, language set them apart. Their appearance, too, was distinctive. James Willard Schultz, who, as noted earlier, disliked the Métis, offered this description of the Judith Basin Métis.

> They were not dark, but actually black-skinned, and they dressed in black, both women and men, the latter wearing a bright red sash around the waist. The women's kerchiefs were black. And then the men had such a despicable way of wearing their hair, cut straight off

just above the shoulders, and standing out around the head like a huge mop.[48]

Although the Spring Creek Métis continued their traditional way of life, they also attempted to learn the customs of the trickle of Euro-American settlers making their way into the Judith Basin. They established schools almost immediately, hired English-speaking teachers, and welcomed non-Métis newcomers. Many of the Spring Creek band elders were educated and could speak and read French, as well as speak Cree, Chippewa, and Michif. Several of the younger members of the band had attended school in Pembina and could also read and speak these languages. Most could not speak English, but traders Francis Janeaux and Ben Kline could speak and read English as well as French and several Indian languages. These families valued education and made schools one of their community priorities. They organized the first school in 1880, and by the winter of 1881–1882 had hired Edward Brassey, later Lewistown mayor, to teach. Brassey lived in Janeaux's stockade and taught in a nearby cabin. The cabin had no plank flooring, and the children simply sat on the ground while Brassey managed as best he could with few books and no blackboards. Thirty children attended this early school: the twenty-six Métis and four Euro-American siblings. The next year, in 1882, the community built a one-room schoolhouse with seating for thirty-six students. It was often crowded, with three students sometimes sharing the double seats. In 1883, Mercy Jackson, her brother George, and her cousins, the Day children, were the only non-Métis at the school. George Jackson remembered that his education was not limited to the curriculum. From his Métis classmates he learned a little French and "Indian" and established friendships that lasted throughout his life.[49]

Non-Métis were also welcome to the Spring Creek band religious services. The Métis families had made space and arrangements for these services from the very first. Alexander Wilkie had built his log house large enough to accommodate Mass and religious instruction. A fiddler and singer, he had learned liturgical music in Pembina and St. Boniface. In his new home, he organized a church choir, which sang the old hymns in French or "Cree" (probably Michif). Visiting priests, discouraged by what they considered to be depraved behavior in such towns as Fort Benton and Carroll, were, as Joseph Kinsey Howard later described, "astonished and delighted to find this oasis of gracious worship in what they regarded as a desert of dissent and apostasy."[50]

The first of these visiting missionaries was the Reverend Joseph Damiani of St. Peter's Mission, about 160 miles to the northeast. This was not an unusual distance for the early missionaries to travel. Other priests traveled even farther, some all the way south from Canada to minister to the Métis hunting in the Judith Basin. Stories of the adventures of other missionaries made Damiani's travel and discomforts seem mere annoyances.

Andrew Garcia, a trader who was married in an 1878 Judith Basin hunting camp, described one such missionary's service in a Cree and Métis camp. Attended by many of the tribes in the area, the service must have presented quite a challenge to the priest, Father Landre. Known as "Black Robe of the North," Landre "followed the Cree buffalo camps in Canada and lived in the tepees with them like an Injun, wherever there was a camp in Montana, and said Mass and preached to them in the Cree language." Lacking a church, Landre made an altar from "the tail end of a Red River cart. It was some sight to see," Garcia recalled. "There were many tepees of different tribes, most of them ready to cut each other's throats, and all of them ready to steal and run off the horses of each other. But here today in hypocritical brotherly love, Assiniboines, Crees, Bloods, Blackfeet, Gros Ventres, Piegans and Pend d'Oreilles met together to hear the wise words of the white man's God." The priest kept peace and conducted Mass. "It was certainly a wild and savage scene to see those warriors and some of the bewhiskered long-haired white men with squaws, and plenty half-breeds and their women. All of us knelt down on the ground in the hot sun during Mass."[51]

Reverend Damiani, as difficult as his travel must have been, met a far different assemblage. Before he arrived, indeed the very first winter in the Spring Creek area, the Métis prepared for his arrival. Elizabeth Swan described the activities of that first winter.

> Through the first winter parents seen to it that the children had catholic instructions which was all in French and sent the older children down to Alexander Wilkie who gladly gave his time to prepare them for first communion mostly, as the daily prayers was all taught at home and rosary said on Sunday right after the morning task was done. This latter custom was a general practice of all the older generations.[52]

Swan also described the arrival of Reverend Damiani for his first visit, writing, "In the late spring the Azure boys from St. Peters Mission brought in Rev. Father Joseph Damiani on a red river cart." They celebrated the community's first Mass at Alexander Wilkie's home, where the priest baptized several children and gave first communion to the prepared class. Also at that time, Reverend Damiani performed the settlement's first marriage. This union, between Antoine Fleury, Jr., and Ernestine Wells, daughter of Marie and Edward Wells, was the first of many early marriages between band families in their new community. After this visit, Damiani returned once or twice a year until the village was large enough to attract its own priest. By 1884, Catholic residents also held services in the home of Francis Janeaux. In that year Reverend Damian performed a double marriage, again between members of the Spring Creek band families. Joseph and Daniel Laverdure, sons of Pierre and Katherine, married Pauline Wells (a sister of Edward Wells) and Mary Natalie Wells (daughter of Marie and Edward Wells), respectively. These marriages wove the threads of band kinship into even more complex patterns.[53]

As the band members met the religious needs of the community and strengthened interband ties, they also reached out to the wider Montana community. Those who were not already U.S. citizens made that commitment by registering their intent to do so. A number of the older band members and several others had been born in Canada. Even though they had spent most of their lives in Dakota, and many of their children had been born there, they realized the necessity of citizenship in order to lessen the risk of deportation. They created a community while establishing ties to central Montana. Their adaptability, as it had throughout their history, served them well and enabled them to establish a vibrant new community quickly.[54]

THE MÉTIS, LOUIS RIEL, AND 1882 MONTANA POLITICS

The Métis commitment to their community extended into the political arena as they worked to further their common goals. The Spring Creek band, as well as other Montana Métis, increasingly turned to Louis Riel to represent their interests territory-wide. Riel's ties to the Montana Métis became closer in 1881, after meeting Marguerite Monet dit Bellehumeur, the daughter of a Judith Basin Métis hunter. The Jean Baptiste Monet dit Bellehumeur family, which had ties to the Pembina Métis community, had followed the buffalo south from Fort Ellice, Manitoba. A Jean Baptiste Bellehumeur, probably Marguerite's father, had signed the 1880 petition and Riel most likely met Marguerite near that time. Riel and Marguerite married in April 1881 on the Musselshell River "prairie style," that is, without benefit of a priest. Later, on March 9, 1882, they formalized their marriage before a priest in Carroll. Little is known of Marguerite. Lacking a western-style education, and Indian-like in her ways, she resembled ordinary Métis buffalo hunters more closely than the urbane and western-educated Riel. The marriage caused some comment. As Joseph Kinsey Howard later expressed it, "The romance of the exiled President of Rupert's Land and this dark daughter of a wandering prairie hunter was a strange and pathetic and ultimately tragic affair." Howard recognized that the two had little in common, especially since Marguerite could not read or write, and spoke "Cree" (probably Michif) but very little of Riel's favored French or English. Riel's Indian heritage was not obvious in his appearance, according to Howard, but his wife was "very dark . . . black as a negro." Howard's and others' sense that the marriage was inappropriate reflected not only their attitudes toward "color" as a mark of social and racial distinction, but also the obvious differences of class between Riel and the hunting families. What they did not understand was that, while class differences were quite noticeable among the Métis in Montana, marital ties and kinship bonds frequently crossed class lines. Marriage reflected community and work relationships, and traders often married into the hunting families with whom they traveled.[55]

Another consideration overlooked by those commentators who were surprised by the union was the nature of Métis kinship networks stretching between Red River Settlement and the Montana Métis communities. These ties were so all-encompassing that it is quite possible Riel knew of and was even distantly connected to the Bellehumeur family. Riel's brother and two of his sisters had married children of Frances Poitra and Madeline Fisher. These Poitra siblings were the grandchildren of Marguerite Grant, who had once been married to Michel Monet dit Bellehumeur. A Marguerite Grant and Michel Monet dit Bellehumeur were also the grandparents of Marguerite Monet dit Bellehumeur, Riel's wife, although it is not clear whether they were the same couple. Marguerite, therefore, was possibly related to the Poitras, Riels, and to the St. Dennis and Laverdure families (through marriages of the children of Henry Poitra and Marguerite Grant). Her marriage to Riel may also have linked him to Jean Fagnant, possibly Marguerite's great-uncle and brother of Charlotte Adam LaFountain's stepfather, and thus to the heart of the Spring Creek band. Despite the fact that Marguerite was "dark" and illiterate, there was nothing strange about this marriage; it fell well within the range of typical Métis marriage patterns. Perhaps already related to the Montana Métis through three of his sisters, who were married to a Parisien (Zastre), a Gladu, and a Lavallée,

Riel solidified his bonds to the central Montana families through his own marriage. It is not surprising that many of these same family names turn up as signatories to the 1880 petition.[56]

Now that Riel was even more closely linked to the Montana bands, he could count on their continued support in his efforts to represent their best interests. By 1882 he had noticed deterioration in the Métis condition and was increasingly concerned about the plight of most Montana Métis. Although the Spring Creek settlement prospered, Riel grieved over the impoverishment of others who suffered from a lack of buffalo and restricted hunting ranges. Blaming liquor for his people's problems rather than the harsh economic conditions, Riel campaigned against its sale to Métis. He first sought to enlist the aid of Deputy Marshall X. Biedler. In March or April 1882, he wrote to Biedler informing him "that C.A. broadwater & Co. at wilder's landing [a trading village on the Missouri River near Carroll] have carried on during this winter the illegal practice of selling intoxicating liquor to indians." He was not "inspired by malice" to make these accusations, he insisted, but as a "friend of law"; his only purpose was to stop "the liquor trade with indians and if possible with the halfbreeds who are not citizens." Riel was aware that under U.S. law, Métis were designated as non-Indian and that Indian legislation, such as laws forbidding the sale of liquor, did not apply to them. Despite their non-Indian status, he hoped to use the noncitizen status of some Métis to prevent their buying liquor and, if possible, to change the law allowing such sales to any Métis.[57]

In addition to writing Deputy Biedler, Riel sent at least one letter to the editor of the *Helena Independent* denouncing the illegal whisky trade. The editor declined to publish Riel's letters, but Simon Pepin, a Métis trader in the employ of Broadwater & Co., became aware of the charges and responded with a vigorous, public countercampaign. Meanwhile, the lack of response from either Deputy Biedler or the *Independent* led Riel to write to U.S. Marshall Alexander Botkin of Helena. Commenting on his willingness to make liquor sales an election issue, Riel assured Botkin that he could "reach public opinion . . . in the streets of Helena, if not in the press." After receiving a sympathetic response from Botkin, Riel took the politically dangerous step of initiating a lawsuit against Simon Pepin and C. A. Broadwater & Co., one of the most powerful Montana merchants. He charged the company with illegal sales of liquor to Indians and Métis, but the court ultimately dismissed the suit for lack of proof of such sales to Indians. The judge upheld the position that liquor sales to Métis were legal, thus destroying Riel's hopes of limiting his people's access to liquor and leaving him with no recourse.[58]

Although this was not Riel's intention, his battle with Montana liquor interests led to the legal affirmation of equal rights for Métis people. Riel was willing to risk these rights in his determination to block what he considered to be a greater evil. He seemed unaware of the contradiction between his insistence that the Métis enjoy all rights of citizens (especially the rights to vote and own land) and his position on liquor sales. Neither did he foresee that his emphasis on Métis noncitizen status, a ploy meant to end liquor sales to them, only reinforced a public perception of the Métis as illegal Canadian immigrants. Ultimately, this perception would cause more trouble for the Métis than liquor.

The lawsuit and surrounding publicity in Montana's principal newspapers led Riel, willingly, into the quagmire of Montana politics.[59] A number of factors, including the rivalry between the Republican T. C. Power, with whom Riel had good relations, and his chief competitor, Charles Arthur Broadwater, a staunch Democrat, influenced Riel to favor the Republican party. Most important, Riel's new ally, Republican Marshall Botkin, intended to run against Democratic U.S. House incumbent Martin Maginnis for Montana Territory's congressional seat. When Botkin proved sympathetic to Métis concerns, Riel decided to organize the Métis in support of his candidacy. In an open letter to Martin Maginnis, Riel explained his position, telling him, "Your good friends and supporters have had the idea that I might vote for you, with a number of half-breed voters. . . . But I doubt very much that such will be the case for the following reasons." Riel then accused the Democratic press, especially the *Helena Independent*, of unfairness "in regard to American half-breed citizens" and accused territory Democrats of contempt for his people. Democratic officials had "taken advantage [of this contempt] . . . year after year, to pillage [the Métis] in the most open and scandalous manner." Moreover, the "Half-breed American citizens of Meagher, Dawson and Chouteau counties [in Central Montana] have had during the last three years more than 250 horses stolen from them by the British Indians" and three hundred more by the "Yanktons, of Poplar river" (Sioux). Yet, Riel maintained, the Métis had received no protection from Indian raids and their complaints had been disregarded. Laying the blame for this lack of protection at the feet of the Democrats, Riel argued that "as the democratic party is in power in Montana, they ought to have done at least something to show good will towards those injured people." Furthermore, he accused the Democrats, especially those in the trading firm of Broadwater & Co., of spreading malicious rumors about the Métis and misrepresenting them in Washington, D.C. Summing up his reasons for supporting Botkin and the Republican party, he wrote that Mr. Botkin, who, unlike the Democrats, had shown interest in eliminating sales of liquor to the Métis, was "disposed and willing to protect the best interests of every American citizen, regardless of race or color."[60]

In organizing a Métis voting block, Riel hoped to unite all citizens of part-Indian descent—not only the Red River Métis, but all "half-breeds" in Montana—and to weld them into a powerful political force. "White men married to indian women in Montana are counted by hundreds," he noted in a letter to the editor of the *Helena Daily Herald*. "Their halfbreed sons entitled to vote are themselves twice as numerous as the heads of families. And fathers and sons counted together and won on our side, at the time of election would constitute a favorable item." In a territory whose scant population was concentrated in the west—around Butte and Helena—an organized Métis/half-breed voice would have been a powerful political force in the sparsely populated central and eastern areas. Such an organized political block was no small threat to Democratic election chances in thinly populated Meagher, Dawson, and Chouteau counties, where mixed-descent people concentrated. Even without counting non–Red River people of Indian/Euro-American descent, Riel estimated the Métis population in Montana to be at least 225 families. Since it was not unusual for Métis to have ten or more children, this constituted a large number of potential voters.[61]

It is ironic that the Republican position to which Riel and his Métis supporters committed themselves put them directly at odds with the devoutly Catholic, virulently anti-British, but staunchly Democratic Irish miners of the more populous western Montana counties. As anti-British Catholics, they might have been natural allies of the Métis, and, except for the party difference, Riel might have been able to gain their support in his efforts. Irish miners dominated western Montana mining communities such as Butte, where their animosity to anything or anyone British was well known. It was common knowledge that mine owners made use of this antagonism to divide Irish and British workers in labor disputes.[62] The Irish and Métis not only had religion and anti-British sentiment in common, they also both suffered discrimination in Montana. Many Montanans held the Irish in almost as low esteem as they held half-breeds. Suffering such prejudice might have led the Irish to sympathize with their fellow Catholics' plight. Riel could have taken advantage of these strong feelings to organize a

Catholic, anti-British coalition. Unfortunately, his commitment to the Republican party precluded any chance of alliance.

As Riel set about encouraging Métis to vote Republican, Democrats, especially those involved in the trade companies that Riel had attacked, took advantage of the opportunity to retaliate against his accusations of illegal liquor sales. They found Riel and the Métis easy targets. Because some Métis could not prove citizenship, Democrats charged them with wide-scale illegal voting in the 1882 territorial elections. Riel eloquently defended himself and his people in friendly newspapers, arguing that the Métis voted in good faith. He accused the Democrats of political motives, pointing out that they were angry over the Métis support of Republican candidates. The Métis supported the Republicans, Riel explained, because they had adopted a resolution pledging "to use their influence in favor of American Half-breeds whenever they saw them in danger of being treated unjustly and to help them fairly to get justice as any other citizen." He denied coercing Métis to vote Republican or encouraging them to vote illegally. If the Métis voted Republican, he maintained, it was because it was in their best interest to do so.[63]

It was not only Riel who incurred the "vengeance of the Democratic press." Other Métis, including Spring Creek band trader Francis Janeaux, opposed Maginnis and "exerted [themselves] . . . in favor of the Republican candidate for Congress." Democrats retaliated against Janeaux by accusing him of using his position as election judge to influence the Métis vote. They characterized him as a puppet of Republican merchant T. C. Power, upon whom he was dependent for goods to supply his trading post in Lewistown.[64]

However, it was Riel, as the best known of the organizers, who suffered the most severe attacks. On May 19, 1883, Fort Benton Sheriff J. J. Healey, a Democrat and former whiskey trader, arrested Riel on a bench warrant issued by the district court for "complicity in election frauds." Public opinion in Fort Benton supported the popular Healey's action. The *Benton Weekly Record* described Riel as "the leader of a lot of British half breeds," who "at Rocky Point last election . . . tried to vote almost all of them, but was prevented, and he then went to Carroll and opened polls at two o'clock in the afternoon and voted all of them." The article echoed a familiar complaint—that the Métis who voted "were British subjects and had refused to swear allegiance to the United States." The accusations of British citizenship and refusal of allegiance to the United States were particularly effective in Fort Benton, where the British were extremely unpopular. Fort Benton merchants were still angry over the Royal Mounted Police closure of the profitable but illegal transborder Indian whiskey trade. Mountie patrols on the boundary had put many of the smaller Fort Benton merchants out of business.[65]

In reality, the charges filed against Riel were far more limited than the *Weekly Record* suggested. A Chouteau County (Fort Benton) grand jury indicted Riel for "attempting to incite Urbain Delorme and Jerome St. Matt to vote, he knowing they had not declared their intentions to become citizens of the United States." Opinions about Riel and Métis participation in voter fraud were split, not surprisingly, along lines of party and economic interest. The *Weekly Record*, representing powerful Fort Benton business interests, vigorously criticized Riel and Helena's *Weekly Herald*, which supported him. One typical *Weekly Record* article ridiculed the *Weekly Herald* for describing Riel as "a gentleman and scholar." Rather than a gentleman, the *Weekly Record* editor argued, Riel was "a low scoundrel whose fox-like cunning has alone kept him out of jail for these many years." The editor continued in the tradition of the day, with no regard to fact, accusing Riel of "peddling liquid hell-fire to the Indians in defiance of . . . laws." He further accused Riel of attempting "to blackmail every prominent man in the Northern country." The "blackmail" consisted, it must be assumed, of suggesting that the "prominent" merchants of Fort Benton were guilty of illegal whiskey sales. The writer, after attacking Riel's character, defended the grand jury indictment, claiming that the case had been "carefully examined" and that the decision to indict had "hardly a dissenting vote."[66]

Feelings ran high, providing an outlet for the underlying prejudice against half-breeds that found its way into Montana newspapers. This was not new; tirades against Métis ran regularly in the Fort Benton papers. As noted earlier, a *Benton Record* writer complained in 1879 of "Canadian half-breeds" who were a "brutal race of the lowest species of humanity without one redeeming trait to commend them to the sympathy or protection of any Government." By 1883, such inflammatory pieces appeared more often, frequently presenting Louis Riel as an object of ridicule. In April a reporter noted that Riel had written "another of his absurd epistles to the Helena *Herald*, in which he claims that the half-breed is a man and a brother." The article repeated the portrayal of Riel as having an "animal, fox-like cunning," borrowing a common characterization of half-breeds from the popular literature of the day. Such images reinforced a perception among the Euro-American population of Montana that the Métis, being semi-intelligent but amoral, embodied an unnatural, not quite human hybrid that was more unstable and more dangerous than any of their "pure-bred" parental stock. Widely used Euro-American terms for the Métis, including "breed" and "coyote french" reflect this perception. As a *Great Falls (Montana) Tribune* article expressed it, the half-breed was "the meanest creature that walks. . . . He is never equal in courage to his father. . . . He surpasses his mother in dishonesty and treachery."[67]

Fear of treachery underlay Montanans' anxiety concerning the Métis. Even the most "civilized" Métis inspired fear and uneasiness since their language, customs, and religion seemed foreign to most new settlers. The well-educated and urbane Métis were especially distrusted. Their obvious abilities made them more suspect than the ordinary buffalo hunters and actually increased speculation of illegal Métis activities.

Despite the intense emotional climate, a thorough investigation by the Democrats found no actual evidence of wrongdoing by Riel. Having no basis for the arrest, Healey released Riel and dropped the charges. Unfortunately, the incident inflicted long-term damage on the Métis reputation in Montana: it reinforced the public perception of the Métis as dangerous illegal aliens ready to use any means at their disposal to further their own ends. Despite a public defense of Riel in the Helena *Weekly Herald*, Montanans permanently associated him and the Métis with the whiskey trade, illegal voting, and noncitizenship. The perception that the Métis were illegal Canadian aliens, newly arrived in Montana, solidified after the 1882 elections and has survived to this day. This charge would be used against Métis interests with increased frequency after 1885, when many Canadian Métis took refuge in Montana.[68]

Regardless of the abuse he endured, Riel did not give up his attempt to curb the liquor trade. He persuaded Republican allies to appoint him special deputy marshall, a position that enabled him to bring charges against illegal liquor sales. The Spring Creek Métis supported his efforts, testifying in court on behalf of his cause when needed. In October 1884, Riel subpoenaed Spring Creek Métis Alexander Wilkie, B. Lafontaine, Baptiste Adams, Frank Gladu, Antoine (probably Wilkie), Edward Wills (Wells), and Frank Demers to testify as prosecution witnesses. The Spring Creek Métis continued to support Riel politically and needed no urging to oppose the Democrats in power. They related a list of grievances against Democratic law enforcement officers and the Democratic press that Riel used in his condemnation of the party. The Spring Creek Métis had received no redress after the murder of one of their people, Riel complained, and the Democrats had taken "no interest in the matter and the press of the party mentioned it only to confound the Halfbreeds with the accused indians." Neither had the Spring Creek band been protected from theft of their horses, Riel charged. Furthermore, he related instances where tax collectors ruthlessly and unfairly compelled Métis to pay taxes they could not afford. In one instance an assessor forced the immediate sale of a Métis family's only horse, leaving them stranded "flat poor on the highway." Riel maintained that law enforcement officers used the close association of the Métis with their Indian relatives to dismiss Métis claims of Indian depredations and to refuse protection.[69]

In Riel, the Métis had a strong, nationally known figure through whom they could express their frustrations. His success in bringing attention to his people's plight was due, in part, to his ability to interact with Montana politicians and businessmen in a way that most Métis could not. Riel's family was part of the Canadian Métis upper class who, as well-educated landowners and prosperous traders, tended to emulate French-Canadian lifestyles and values. Riel prided himself on his flawless French and good English, not on his passable Cree, Chippewa, or Michif. He was fervently Catholic and considered Indian religious practices barbaric. Although he acknowledged an Indian ancestry, Riel considered his Indian relatives to be uncivilized.[70] When dealing with Montana authorities, Riel expressed views similar to theirs and enlisted Euro-American support by appealing to values that he and they shared. These values and opinions were not necessarily the same as those of the people he represented. This was most apparent in his attempt to gain a Métis homeland when, to win governmental endorsement, he emphasized a Métis desire to settle permanently and take up agriculture. Many of his fellow Métis, however, were happier living near their Indian relatives and hoped to continue their hunting lifestyle.

Riel's willingness to disregard Métis opinion in his determination to organize them into a coherent political force led him to oppose efforts to establish an organized political alliance with Indian relatives. Reversing his earlier position, Riel opposed a Métis-Chippewa alliance, specifically Métis enrollment in the proposed Turtle Mountain Chippewa reservation in Dakota Territory. The Métis dominated the Pembina, Dakota, area, and Riel realized that if organized and registered to vote, these Métis could play a major role in the 1884 Dakota elections, thereby establishing themselves as a significant political force. As a consequence, he opposed any conditions under which the Métis would lose the right to vote, including Indian status and reservation privileges. To ensure the success of his position, Riel attempted to convince the Republicans who controlled Dakota

Territory that the best interests of the party lay in preventing the Métis from enrolling on the reservation. Political necessity, supported by cultural preconceptions, reinforced his view that a European-style economic and political organization would more likely make the Métis competitive in their new surroundings.[71]

Many Métis broke with Riel on the issue of reservation enrollment and Indian status. They were not prepared to abandon their ties to the Dakota Chippewas. Most, especially the hunting families, had maintained their Chippewa contacts and identity as Pembina Chippewa half-breeds. When treaty negotiations with the Pembina Chippewas at Turtle Mountain took place, these families asserted their right to be involved. Spring Creek leaders such as Alexander Wilkie had maintained close ties to the Pembina Chippewa community, and, by 1886, Wilkie returned to support Chief Little Shell and to take part in the coming negotiations for a Turtle Mountain reservation.[72]

CATTLEMEN COMMANDEER THE RANGE

While the Métis explored political solutions to their problems in Montana and Dakota, a powerful political force developed on the plains. As the army restricted Indians to reservations and the buffalo herds disappeared, vast grasslands opened up. Montana businessmen immediately realized the economic potential of the seemingly empty prairie. Area bankers such as Samuel T. Hauser, of the First Bank of Helena, enthusiastically encouraged investment in cattle ranching, offering potential loan applicants rates of $1\frac{1}{2}$ to 2 percent a month. Hauser assured his clients of success, declaring that the stockmen's "profits are often larger than ours." Painting a picture of easy money, he claimed, "We know that all a man has to do is brand his cattle, and go to sleep until another roundup comes around." An 1879 booklet published at the direction of the Montana legislature not only reprinted Hauser's assurances, but also maintained that "in this vast free pasturage no one need own an acre of land, and thus few have cared to." Early Judith Basin rancher, Con Price, explained the procedure for avoiding the expense of buying land in this way.

> I am going to make a statement here that almost sounds fishy, but I can prove it. I worked for a cow outfit that run twenty-five thousand cattle and three or four hundred saddle horses to handle the cattle with, and they didn't own one foot of deeded land. The land was unsurveyed and belonged to the government. They usually build a

big log house, some corrals and a kind of stable, and called it their ranch, and no one disputed their title. . . . They paid no taxes on this land and as it would be impossible for the assessor to count the cattle in an area of two or three hundred miles, I would say a good honest cattle man might give in one-third of his number. An outfit the size I speak of, would hire about 25 cowboys during the summer months and keep 4 or 5 during the winter. That was the only expense they had, outside of buying saddle horses to mount their cowboys.[73]

Stockmen controlled vast stretches of land simply by occupying it. Sometimes ranchers would homestead or buy small, strategically located parcels from which they could control the area's water. By restricting the waterways to their own use they could eliminate any competition from their vicinity.[74]

Despite bankers' assurances of low costs and high profits, early cattle ranching required a large investment. Cattle were expensive and difficult to bring into the area, branding was labor intensive, and reaching markets involved risk, loss, and skilled labor. Most cattle operations depended on financial support from partnerships or corporations that had ties to the business and political community. Though foreign money played a part, most Spring Creek–area ranchers were Montana businessmen. Some investors, such as the Stuart brothers, were successful former gold miners and had close ties to that group. Montana businessmen Samuel T. Hauser, A. J. Davis, and T. C. Power, as well as other Helena and Fort Benton businessmen, also invested large amounts in the area's cattle industry. Since most Judith Basin cattlemen had both mining and merchant contacts, their combined political power, in a state dominated by mining and business, made securing their interests in the territorial legislature a relatively easy matter.[75]

These political realities affected the Spring Creek Métis and Indian hunters almost immediately. In 1880 two events signaled change in the Judith Basin. In March 1880 the owners of one of the first cattle corporations in the Spring Creek vicinity used their political influence to force the Blackfeet from their traditional hunting grounds. That fall, the Blackfeet had decided to winter where they often did, on the Judith River at the mouth of Warm Spring Creek. When they arrived at the site, they were surprised to find a ranch established, without their permission, in their "favorite winter hunting grounds." On learning that T. C. Power, an acquaintance whom they called Woman Stealer, owned the ranch, the Blackfeet decided to allow the cattle to graze there undisturbed. Power and his employees would not be so accommodating. Noticing the Blackfeet presence, ranch manager Henry Brooks notified Power that Indians were on Warm Spring Creek killing cattle. Power complained about the situation to both territorial and army officials, insisting that the Blackfeet be removed at once. Power's influence was such that soldiers soon arrived. When they attempted to "escort" the Indians back to the agency, the hunters denied killing cattle and claimed that, in any case, the land was theirs. The army gave them no hearing, but insisted that they return immediately to the agency. According to trader James Willard Schultz, who was present, war was only narrowly averted. During a tribal conference, mixed-descent interpreter and trader Joseph Kipp warned those favoring annihilation of the soldiers that such an action, while effective in the short run, might result in a retaliation similar to the Baker massacre of 1870, when nearly three hundred Blackfeet men, women, and children were killed. With no real choice, the Blackfeet made the sad journey back to the reservation and, as Schultz put it, "never again did the tribe hunt south of the Missouri."[76]

The removal of the Blackfeet from their acknowledged hunting lands signaled a change of control in the Judith Basin. Ranchers could now dictate who would travel and hunt on "their" range. To enforce their domination, they pressured the army to construct a fort in the Spring Creek drainage. At the request of stockowners, including A. J. Davis, Samuel T. Hauser, and Granville Stuart, the army established a fort on Ford Creek, at the base of the Judith Mountains. While the soldiers at Fort Maginnis were notably unsuccessful in controlling Indians, their presence, and the army policy of restricting all tribes to reservations or of driving them into Canada, marked the end of open hunting in the Basin.[77]

Poor hunting in the winter of 1881–1882 and the absence of buffalo by 1883 aided the cattlemen's takeover. Though the demise of the buffalo herds opened the range to cattle grazing, it posed other problems for the ranchers. Knowing the Indians' main source of food was growing scarce, cattlemen greatly feared that the hunters would turn to cattle for sustenance. Through newspapers, their congressmen, and influential business allies, Judith Basin cattlemen pressured the army into banning Indians from the range. Protection of their assumed rights to exclusive use was essential to Montana stockmen, for whom a constant presence, fencing, and land ownership were not only impractical but would have substantially cut into profits.

For the Métis, who were dependent upon hunting for their livelihood, access to the range was also essential. They did not have government aid through reservation annuities, which, poor as they were, helped support reservation Indians. Nevertheless, as cattlemen gained control of the Judith Basin, they not only set about eliminating the Indian hunters from the area, but also sought to restrict the Métis. Granville Stuart, manager and part owner of the DHS (D-S) ranch on Ford Creek south of the Judith Mountains, led the fight to remove all Indians and "breeds" from the range. Despite having a Native wife and nine mixed-descent children, Stuart insisted that the "breeds" and Indians must be driven off the range if the livestock industry was to succeed and sent forth a continual stream of angry letters about "trespassing Indians" on "his range." To Stuart, the presumption of Indian and Métis guilt in cattle stealing and the right of cattlemen to govern the range were unquestioned. In July 1881, he wrote to his partner, Samuel Hauser, that although he could not be sure passing Native people had killed any cattle, "the presumption is in favor of their doing so, for there is no game and they can't live on air." Stuart's solution was to restrict all Native people to reservations or to deport them to Canada.[78]

By 1881 Judith Basin ranchers were even more concerned. Stuart estimated his cattle losses that year to Indians at thirteen hundred head. His neighbor, James Fergus, an individual who was often sympathetic to the Indian cause, was nevertheless also concerned about his losses and specifically accused the Spring Creek Métis. In December 1881 Fergus wrote to Stuart charging that "the Big Spring half-breeds are killing our cattle on Dog and Armells Creeks." "We have got rid of the Indians only to find what I suspected all along, that the half breeds are as bad as the Indians," Stuart answered. He assured Fergus that he would contact the army about the losses and suggested that, if they received no satisfaction from the military, they should organize Judith Basin stockmen. The cattlemen could then confront "the breeds" and "warn them to keep off and away from our ranges or we will run them out of the country."[79]

The army responded to the intense pressure from cattle interests and attempted to remove the Métis from the range. Falling back again on the rationale that all Métis were Canadian citizens illegally hunting in the United States with their Canadian Cree relatives, the army campaigned against both the Crees and the Métis. Since the two often hunted, traveled, and camped together, it was convenient for the army to do so. It was also often hard to distinguish them, a confusion that would plague both the Crees and the Métis in the coming years.

One officer described the army's campaign against the Crees and Métis in a letter to his wife. Gustavus (Glen) Doane wrote of burning Métis homes ("100 shacks") in March 1882, an action that must have left at least a hundred families homeless on the prairie with at least two more months of harsh Montana winter to suffer through. In July the same officer's party found a "halfbreed and Cree outfit" from whom they confiscated "19 guns, 9 horses (all the branded ones) all their ammunition." Doane "wanted Major Kelogg to kill all their ponies and burn all the [illegible] but [Kelogg] thought it better to be a little easy on the first lot." Such consideration may have prevented immediate starvation, but even without the confiscation of all the horses, the loss of guns and ammunition ensured hardship and possible starvation for the families. By this time game and buffalo were growing scarce. The buffalo had been hunted to extinction north of the Missouri River and would only last a short time longer to the south.[80]

In addition to the disappearance of the buffalo and harassment by army officials, the Métis faced a new threat that made earning a living by selling buffalo products all but impossible for many. In 1883 the Fort Benton sheriff attempted to levy duties on robes transported into Canada. In the process, he confiscated the robes and goods of those families unwilling or unable to pay. His actions forced more than two hundred Métis families to leave Montana for Canada. Others returned to their former homes in Dakota Territory.[81]

The Métis did not leave their hunting grounds without a struggle. Some reacted by holding U.S. Deputy Marshall J. J. Healy hostage in March 1882. But such actions were ultimately futile; changing conditions weighed against the continuation of a hunting way of life on the Montana plains. The same officer who left us the above account reported that "everything is favorable for doing something which will close up the Cree and halfbreed . . . effectively." Events would prove that he was more correct than he realized.[82]

THE GREAT HERDS DISAPPEAR

Of all the problems with which the Métis struggled, the disappearance of the great buffalo herds from their last large Montana refuge, the Judith Basin, had overwhelming consequences. The loss of this livelihood, around which Métis culture had been built, overshadowed all else. Not only had the fur trade helped define Métis society, but buffalo, since the end of the beaver trade, had been the source of Métis prosperity. The consequences of the irrevocable erosion of their economic base cannot be underestimated. This was truly a new world for the plains Métis and their Indian relatives.

By the winter of 1881–1882 James Willard Schultz reported fewer buffalo. The "Crees and Red River breeds were still with us," he wrote, "but the buffalo were not so plentiful. . . . Their range was also smaller." The animals had completely disappeared from north of the Missouri River and from the Canadian plains. In Canada, the Hudson's Bay trader at Fort Pitt complained as early as February 1877 that people there were starving. In the summer of 1879, an Edmonton House trader wrote that the "Half Breeds" were "living on dogs" and were "starving." By 1881 pemmican was no longer available and the HBC was forced to supply pork to its workers. Desperate Indians moved from Canada to follow the buffalo, as they traditionally had, into land now controlled by the United States. In 1880 the *Weekly Record* complained about Canadian Crees who "were selling their furs and every other article of value to procure food, while women were prostituting themselves, to save their children from starvation." The article reported that "the men were weak and emaciated from hunger, and women and children with rags and filth. . . . The country is entirely destitute of game."[83]

By the winter of 1881–1882, there was large-scale malnutrition and starvation among some Montana tribes. John Ewers estimated that almost a fourth of the Montana Piegans died of starvation in 1883 and 1884. With winter temperatures reaching sixty degrees below zero at St. Peter's Mission, near the Blackfeet reservation, the welfare of the entire tribe was threatened. On better-managed reservations, the immediate impact was not as severe, but life was never again the same. Pretty Shield, a Crow medicine woman, told the story of the end of the buffalo this way.

> We believed for a long time that the buffalo would again come to us; but they did not. We grew hungry and sick and afraid, all in one. Not believing their own eyes our hunters rode very far looking for buffalo, so far away that even if they had found a herd we could not have reached it in half a moon. "Nothing; we found nothing," they told us; and then, hungry, they stared at the empty plains, as though dreaming. After this their hearts were no good any more. . . . We began to stay in one place, and to grow lazy and sicker all the time.[84]

Damage went beyond the loss of a primary source of food and material. Before the buffalo were actually gone, their scarcity hindered the ability of hunting groups to work together in solving common problems. Competition over this essential resource led to intertribal and Indian-Métis tension, making any alliance to further common goals unlikely. It also exacerbated Euro-American ill will as reservation Indians lost the means to support themselves, and discontent mounted. The *Weekly Record* noted the intense competition, blaming Métis interlopers from Canada. The author argued that the Métis had no right to hunt in the United States and exhaust tribal resources, writing, "The Gros Ventres and the Assinaboins will have a feast this year if the soldiers succeed in keeping the half-breeds and Crees across the line."[85]

Although many observers had worried about the decrease in buffalo and had noticed the shrinkage of their range since the 1850s, the actual disappearance came as a surprise. According to estimates, as recently as the 1880–1881 season, traders shipped 100,000 hides from the Yellowstone River alone. Nevertheless, the end can be measured in the decrease in robe sales. Fort Benton merchant I. G. Baker estimated that seventy-five thousand buffalo robes were shipped out of Fort Benton in 1876, twenty thousand in 1880, five thousand in 1883, and none in 1884. By the end of 1883, the herds were gone, even from the Judith Basin.[86]

Estimates in 1889 included only 635 "wild and unprotected" buffalo in North America. The destruction of the buffalo herds was the most significant factor in the change of the Montana Métis way of life. The buffalo had provided an economic niche that was the "social and economic basis of the Metis identity" as it had been known. The poverty of Indian and Métis hunters after the destruction of the herds was the primary factor in their inability to organize to protect their rights and maintain a strong political voice. Competition over the diminishing resource had further divided various tribal and Métis interests, making a united front among all Native peoples impossible.[87]

Despite, or perhaps even because of, the buffalo's disappearance, the Spring Creek Métis community continued to grow. With the addition of new families, the Spring Creek settlement had a population of about 150 Métis families before many Euro-Americans joined the community. By 1883, however, Métis economic and social domination ended in the newly named town of Lewistown. That year Spring Creek band trader Francis Janeaux, unable to meet rising debts, sold out to his creditor and supplier, T. C. Power. It is both significant to Janeaux's financial situation and symbolic of the Métis future that his business failure occurred in the same year that the great herds disappeared.[88]

• • •

The Métis experience in Montana, as earlier elsewhere, was one of adaptive change. Their tradition of inclusiveness encompassed cultural, economic, and ethnic diversity, defying attempts to define or enforce ethnic borders and confusing attempts to define what it meant to be Métis. Laura Peers, in *The Ojibwa of Western Canada*, has emphasized the "constantly shifting balance between cultural continuity and adaptive change" among the western Ojibwas. This is also true of their close relatives, the Montana and Dakota Métis. Central-Montana Métis communities of the early 1880s had a common lifestyle, language, religion, and subsistence activities. Métis people viewed themselves, and were viewed by others, as a distinct people. Yet they shared other languages, cultures, ancestries, and kinship networks with people outside of their core community. Because Métis families maintained close relations with each spouse's kin and were free to live with either set of relatives, Métis families typically had close ties to a variety of communities. Sometimes these communities were quite distant—in another country or with people who spoke different languages (often Cree, Chippewa, French, or English). Frequently, Métis families had close connections to communities that were ethnically diverse. They traveled often and lived and worked with a variety of ethnic groups. Kinship networks simultaneously reached out to new members while growing within, continually becoming more complex. Montana Métis, with their multiple affiliations and loyalties, were simultaneously culturally and linguistically heterogeneous and homogeneous. The apparent contradiction of their diversity, on one hand, and their maintenance of core values and customs on the other, allowed space for a variety of social and economic options. Métis identity, with its porous boundaries, was tolerant of, even encouraged, alternate affiliations. It is no wonder that they had multiple ways to identify themselves or that their neighbors and outside communities would sometimes be confused as to their identity.[89]

Their simultaneous cultural homogeneity and heterogeneity allowed the Spring Creek Métis to establish an open community that welcomed diverse neighbors and adjusted to their customs and language. It permitted a western-educated, French-speaking poet and visionary such as Louis Riel to marry a Michif- and Cree-speaking woman of a seminomadic hunting family. It was also the reason that English-speaking traders such as Janeaux and Morase were not unusual members of the Michif-speaking community and retained close ties to it. It explains why government officials could not always distinguish U.S. Métis from their Canadian Cree relatives and hunting companions. The long tradition of Métis intermarriage and acceptance of diverse ethnic groups, plus a bilateral kinship network in which families maintained close relationships with each spouse's relatives, added a valued diversity to families' networks.

Riel, in an effort to strengthen the Montana Métis social and political position, attempted to impose a bounded identity upon his fellow Métis, which included a strict Catholicism, a sedentary agricultural lifestyle, and an economy based on a Euro-American model. But Métis customs included generations of diversity. Métis identity was characterized by nothing so much as its porous boundaries. Though they accepted Riel as a respected leader, the central-Montana Métis were not willing to surrender ties to their Indian relatives or, for that matter, to their Euro-American neighbors, whom they tried to accommodate in their new community.

Such adaptability served the Spring Creek Métis well. From 1879 to 1883 they successfully established a Métis community. But the extermination of the buffalo herds and the control of the plains by cattlemen with powerful political support in Helena, Montana Territory's capital, precluded Métis economic, social, and political dominance in their new community. Although law confirmed their non-Indian status, socially they were linked, in the Euro-American mind, to their Indian relatives. While the Métis respectfully referred to themselves, when speaking English, as "half-breeds," their Euro-American neighbors came to use the word "breed" to mean something more akin to degenerate Indian. In Montana, references to the Métis emphasized their Indian connections more often than their Euro-American ones, ignoring their distinctive values and lifestyle.

Their ascribed legal and social identities in conflict, the Métis faced the greatest challenge of their long history—the end of the fur trade. Though the Spring Creek band welcomed and accommodated Euro-American newcomers to the most prosperous Métis community in Montana, their life in the Judith Basin had changed forever. By 1884 the Spring Creek Métis had not only lost economic control of their community, but also had witnessed incoming Euro-American settlers reverse their numerical, and consequently, their political advantage. Above all, they watched in dismay as their economic base abruptly disappeared from the plains.

CHAPTER 4

Ethnic Labels

Confronting an Indian/White Dichotomy, 1885–1899

A CHANGING COMMUNITY

I still remember their Red River carts and the squeaking wheels that had rawhide for tires. . . . You would see a squaw sitting down in the bottom of the cart with a papoose on her back.

LULA SCHUFLET, INTERVIEW, 1980

With the disappearance of the great buffalo herds in 1883 and the arrival of numerous Euro-American settlers in the next few years, the Métis confronted the harsh realities of adjusting to a nonbison economy. At the same time, they continued to face challenges to their identity as Métis. While the social dynamics of their central-Montana community changed, the Métis confronted increasing discrimination grounded in a prejudice toward both people of mixed descent and toward Indians. They continued to participate in community affairs, but gradually lost influence in the very institutions that they had helped create. As Métis families negotiated their ethnic identity with powerful representatives of the U.S. government and the Roman Catholic Church, as well as with the general non-Métis population, they continued their close association with Indian relatives and entered into new alliances that altered the way they saw themselves.

In 1885 a Maiden, Montana, *Mineral Argus* article described Lewistown (Spring Creek settlement) as the "Big Spring creek half-breed settlement—the largest in Montana." But the community was changing rapidly. Another

Argus contributor commented upon a different Lewistown. He focused on the town's growth, boasting of its thirty-five buildings, "three-fourths of which have been put up within the last year." Prominent among these structures was T. C. Power's general store, formerly owned by Francis A. Janeaux, and "a substantial school building, the best in the county." The school and trading post, once the pride of the Métis community that established them, were now the centerpiece of a new, non-Métis boosterism. In his article, the Euro-American author exaggerated the village's growth and resources in an energetic promotion of Lewistown as an appropriate site for the future state capital. Arguing that when the "immense Indian reservations to the east of us have been thrown open for settlement . . . centrally located" Lewistown would be a far superior choice for a state capital than a "western" location (Helena). Describing the region as having "the healthiest climate in the world, surrounded by inexhaustible agricultural and miner wealth," Vulcan, as the writer called himself, helped set the stage for the agricultural settlement of the Spring Creek drainage and its consequent growth.[1]

By 1886 Lewistown was the county seat of newly created Fergus County. It had a newspaper (the former Maiden, Montana, *Mineral Argus*), twenty-two "business establishments," and a population of 125. The town continued to grow, having close to four hundred residents in 1888. By then the thirty-six business buildings included a bank, three general stores, two hotels, five saloons, a county jail, the school, a Catholic church, and a new Methodist church, established to serve the growing Protestant population. Employment opportunities included freighting from Missouri River ports and, later, the railheads of Billings and Fort Benton. The nearby mining town of Maiden, as well as Fort Maginnis, provided services and furnished additional work, as did the livestock industry and a small amount of farming.[2]

For the Métis, the new realities had special significance. Few managed to accumulate sufficient financial resources to establish stores, freighting companies, or ranches. They owned none of the new businesses in Lewistown. With the buffalo gone and game depleted, the Métis took what work they could find. Pierre Berger, who had led the band to Spring Creek, and his son John hauled freight from Rocky Point and Fort Benton on the Missouri River to Fort Maginnis, Lewistown, and Maiden, using their own carts or working as drivers for freighting companies. Joe LaTray worked as a ranch hand for G. P. Barnett and the N-Bar ranch, starting a tradition of LaTray horsemanship that continues into the present. Joe's father, Mose, hauled potatoes for the Brooks ranch, on Warm Spring Creek (north of

Red River Carts at 5th and Broadway, Lewistown, Mont. Courtesy of Lewistown (Mont.) Public Library, Brenner Collection.

town). He also built homes in Lewistown, Giltedge, and Maiden, and he constructed the Lewistown post office. At Fort Maginnis, he served as undertaker and, since he spoke five Indian languages plus French, acted as interpreter. Joe Doney scouted for Fort Maginnis and, with Vital Turcotte, carried mail from Rocky Point to the fort. Many Métis turned to chopping wood. Even after the railroads replaced steamboats (which had to be regularly supplied with wood), firewood was in great demand. All of the residences and businesses of Lewistown were dependent upon wood for heat, and, because cold weather might last from early September to mid-June, "wood hawks" always had work. Ironically, it was the buffalo herds, now gone from the plains, that provided the greatest employment opportunity. The bones of these animals still lay strewn across the prairie, and a market for them developed as fertilizer and sugar companies bought all that could be delivered to railheads. Tons of bones were processed into fertilizer or burned to obtain carbon for sugar refining. Con Price, Montana freighter and rancher, remembered that, in the early 1890s, "there was . . . a lot of half breed Indians gathering buffalo bones and brought them there [Big Sandy rail depot] to ship. . . . Most of them drank plenty whiskey and with their families had dances every night. The musician would be some half breed with moccasins on, and he kept time with both feet while he played."[3]

Less is known of the women's work. Métis women, like their Indian ancestors, kept a lower profile and far less often held jobs that brought them into public situations. They continued, as they always had, to participate in family economic activities. They gathered bones, raised large gardens, kept livestock and poultry, tanned hides, and created beautifully beaded or embroidered footwear, clothing, quilts, and decorative pieces. When buffalo and deer leather was no longer available as a base for their beadwork, Métis women used sheepskin, cowhide, or fabric.[4] Mothers raised and fed large families while their husbands, brothers, and sons struggled to find new employment.

Like many Métis women, Mary Ernestine Wells Fleury, wife of Antoine Fleury II, cared for a large family. Mary Ernestine had nine children of her own and adopted at least two others, one after the early death of her husband. She supported her children by cooking for ranchers, using her knowledge of medicinal herbs to provide medical services, and by acting as undertaker when necessary. Providing food for her children in the traditional Métis manner, Mary Ernestine dried meat that she received as payment or that her sons brought home from hunting, kept a large garden, and collected berries and roots.[5]

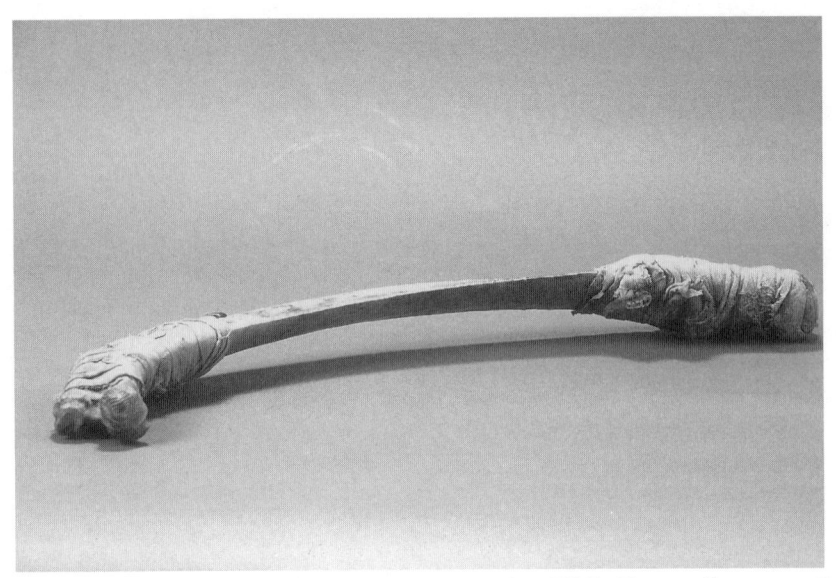

Bone hide-scraping tool used by Mary Ernestine Wells Fleury. Courtesy of Treena LaFountain, Billings, Mont. Photograph by John H. Havener, Jr., Billings, Mont.

Her great-granddaughter remembers stories of long, fun-filled days berry picking. Berrying was a women's project, planned and executed while the men "would go off into town and try to get work." The women and girls prepared days ahead, cooking and collecting supplies. On the appointed day, they worked from dawn to dusk picking chokecherries and sarvestberries (serviceberry or Juneberry), managing, at the same time, to make a joyous picnic of the chore. After gathering the berries, the women spread them out to dry on government-issue tarps elevated by stakes to protect the fruit from animals. Mary Ernestine and her daughters stirred and mixed the berries until they were evenly dry and then packed them into "gunny sacks" for storage in their root cellar. After the first frost the women went out again and lay their tarps under buffaloberry bushes. Buffaloberries were far easier than other berries to pick. All one had to do was shake or beat the bush with a stick (picking was inadvisable because of large thorns) and watch the berries fall onto the tarp. At other times of the year, when they were ready, Mary Ernestine collected roots and herbs, both as food and medicine. She also continued to work hides and to create beautiful

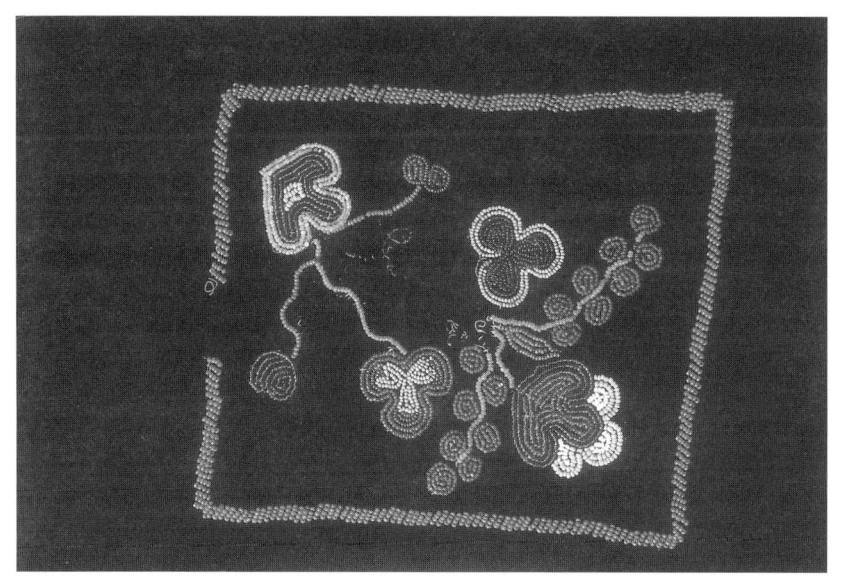

Beadwork by Mary Ernestine Wells Fleury. Courtesy of Treena LaFountain, Billings, Mont. Photograph by John H. Havener, Jr., Billings, Mont.

embroidery, which perhaps supplemented her income. Some of these pieces and her hide-working tools are still treasured possessions of the family.[6]

Because Mary Ernestine was known as a healer, she was often able to add to her family's food supply with provisions given to her in return for her services. Only rarely, her great-granddaughter recalls hearing, was money exchanged. But language was a continuing problem for Grandmother Fleury. A family story, related with much laughter, recalls Mary Ernestine attempting to treat a German farmer who was unable to keep food down. Mary Ernestine, who could speak very little English, and the farmer's wife, who could speak less, attempted to discuss the farmer's problem. With signs and simple English words, the farmer's wife was finally able to convey the nature of the problem. "Down, up, whoop!" she exclaimed, mimicking her poor husband's reaction to food. Understanding the demonstration, Mary Ernestine was then able to prepare a tea of roots that alleviated his symptoms and allowed him to recover.[7]

Mary Ernestine took advantage of a variety of opportunities to support her family. When Turtle Mountain allotments became available, she applied

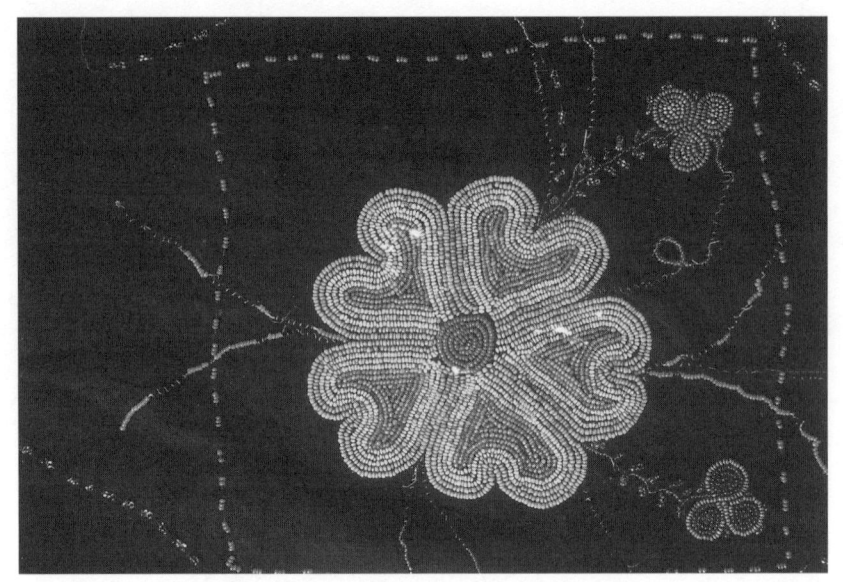

Beadwork by Mary Ernestine Wells Fleury. Courtesy of Treena LaFountain, Billings, Mont. Photograph by John H. Havener, Jr., Billings, Mont.

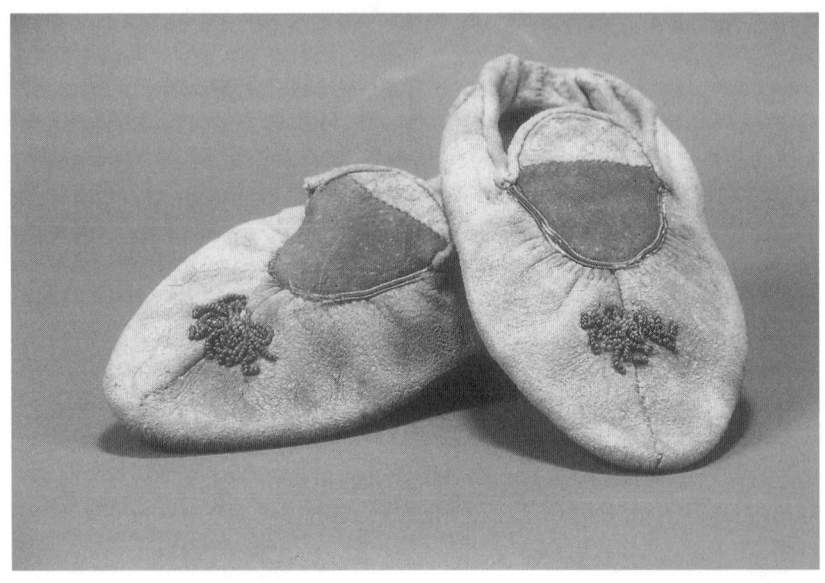

Moccasins made by Mary Ernestine Wells Fleury for her granddaughter. Courtesy of Treena LaFountain, Billings, Mont. Photograph by John H. Havener, Jr., Billings, Mont.

but, like most of the Spring Creek band, was ruled ineligible. Shortly thereafter, taking advantage of the Homestead Act, she homesteaded her own place as "head of family." The land she selected was in the Judith Basin, not near Turtle Mountain, North Dakota, home of many Chippewa and Métis relatives of the Spring Creek band. Although Mary Ernestine acknowledged her Indian ancestry, she never considered reservation life. After seeing reservation conditions firsthand, the postbuffalo-era disease and starvation discouraged her, like other Métis, from joining relatives there. She preferred her own homestead on land of her choosing.[8]

MÉTIS COMMUNITY PARTICIPATION

As the Spring Creek Métis found ways to make a living without buffalo, they continued to participate in Lewistown community activities. They voted in elections, sent their children to school, and supported the Catholic church. Métis had been voting in Montana since the 1864 election to establish Montana as a territory. Familiar family names of Juneau, Lafontain, Lavallie, and LeDoux are found on the 1864 poll lists. In the 1886 Fergus County elections, many Métis again voted, even though the candidates for county office included no Métis and only one French speaker (Dr. L. A. LaPalme, a non-Métis Canadian running on the Democratic ticket). Members of the Laverdure, Wells, Janeaux, Charrette, Daigneault, Morase, Paul, Berger, Fleury, Veiduais (identity uncertain), Kline, and Doney families were among the twenty-two Métis men who voted from the Lewistown precinct. Throughout the 1880s and 1890s the Métis were a strong political force in central Montana. After the death of Francis Janeaux, Ben Kline, one of the few Spring Creek Métis who spoke English well, assumed the position of unofficial Métis community leader. Euro–American residents believed that Kline controlled Métis voting and "directed the political leaning of the entire band." Block voting, even the impression of it, gave the Métis political power in the small communities of Lewistown and the precincts to the east. This strength may account for the readiness of county officeholders to establish schools in Métis districts and for the absence of local discriminatory legislation. Despite their political influence, however, party ticket records indicate that the Métis were not selected as candidates for office. None were asked to serve on an 1887 grand jury or were nominated for the 1899 elections for the newly incorporated city of Lewistown. Whether this was because of racial discrimination or because few of the Métis as yet spoke, read, or wrote standard English, is difficult to determine.[9]

Métis families also gave freely to support missionary work and to establish a local church. Francis Janeaux donated land for Lewistown's first church, and he and his Métis wife, Virginia Laverdure, held early church services in their home. Pierre Berger and his brother-in-law, Alexander Wilkie, held services in their homes for those residents east of town. Antoine Ouellette donated land for Lewistown's first cemetery, and others, including non-Métis Irene Desy, whose wife, Evelyn, was the daughter of Francis Janeaux and Virginia Laverdure, graded a road and fenced the cemetery. Despite Métis generosity and participation, non-Métis settlers quickly took over the organizational aspects of the Catholic parish. The only representative of the Métis community asked to serve on the church construction committee was Janeaux, who donated the land and who many identified as French Canadian.[10]

Contemporary accounts demonstrate the loss of influence Métis suffered as new settlers took over church activities, but they also point to the difficulty of uncovering Métis participation. Few Métis kept records of important events, but many of the new settlers wrote letters, memoirs, and articles for the paper. Their opinions and views of events were everywhere. Typical of non-Métis accounts was Theresa McDonnell's recollections of Lewistown's earliest church. She noted the roles of local non-Métis business and ranch owners with no mention of the Métis except in reference to early church services held in Janeaux's home. In contrast is Elizabeth Berger Swan's version from a Métis point of view, which is unusual in that it exists at all. Unlike McDonnell, Swan places the Métis community at the heart of the church construction effort. "Our little village was progressing fast," she noted. "The catholics started to discuss about having a place of worship. Janeaux, Brooks, Crowleys and others along with our people started to organize and find ways and means, each party to donate time and money for the interprise [sic]. Janeaux donated the ground, John B. Berger got up a subscription amongst his people." Swan remembers Francis Janeaux as "one of the main promoters." Without her memoirs we would know little of Métis participation. Non-Métis accounts note the Métis only in passing (if at all) and more as colorful neighborhood curiosities than as involved and essential components of the community.[11]

The nature of Métis record keeping also made documentation of their participation, even their residence in the county, difficult. Unlike early Euro-Americans, who expected to record all of their significant life events in local newspapers and official county records, the Métis left such record keeping to visiting missionaries and parish priests. As French speakers accustomed to the relatively informal organization of Métis communities, they saw no reason to obtain licenses or to record important events in English-language newspapers. Another factor contributed to this artificial invisibility: many Métis continued to move about within a homeland that extended from the Teton River–area just east of the Rocky Mountains to the Turtle Mountains of North Dakota, north to the Saskatchewan River, and south to just beyond the Snowy Mountains. They also made frequent extended trips to visit distant relatives, leaving their records scattered and difficult to retrieve. After the establishment of St. Leo's Catholic Church, as the Lewistown church would come to be known, the parish priest kept birth, death, and marriage records in one place, but the far-flung kinship networks and the need to travel for employment still made even parish record keeping sporadic.[12]

As Elizabeth Swan's account demonstrates, despite their loss of influence, the local Catholic church and its priests remained an important focal point for the Spring Creek band. The priests, in addition to keeping Métis family records, attempted to serve the special needs of these parishioners. Especially popular was French-speaking Father John van den Heuvel, who became the parish priest in 1893. "Father Van Heuvel, our first resident priest, spoke good french, he was very pleasant, and made many friends among the half breeds," remembered Elizabeth Berger Swan. "During his three and a half years of residence here, he went to say mass at the Pierre Berger home and refused to be brought back in a rig. He said in the old country he had to walk any wheres to his missions and enjoyed it." It was an indication of the ethnic divisions and Métis feelings of estrangement from the new settlers that the Métis so appreciated a priest who accepted their customs and spoke their language.[13]

After Reverend van den Heuvel resigned in 1895, the parish did not again have a permanent priest until the arrival of Reverend James M. Vermaat in 1899. Although Father Vermaat endeared himself to the Métis families by later bringing in Cree-speaking missionary, Father Therien, O. M. I., he was not as comfortable with the Métis as had been Father van den Heuvel. Referring to his parishioners, "the largest number [of which] consisted then of Cree Indians and half breeds," as "my Indians," Vermaat seems to have regarded the needs of his Métis parishioners as an extension of his former missionary work among the Cheyennes, whom he referred to fondly as "those wild children of the mountains."[14]

As the growing Euro-American population relegated the Métis to the periphery of Lewistown-area church life, they responded warmly to those religious leaders who brought with them a familiar language, forms of worship, and habits of everyday life. But formal church organization, control, and even influence were out of Métis hands by 1900. Though they continued to participate, they never again made decisions concerning the larger Catholic community. The church, which might otherwise have provided a source of strength and unity, became another arena in which the Métis experienced displacement and loss of influence.

At the same time, Métis community participation extended beyond political and religious activities. They also supported community education by establishing and attending the area's first schools. In 1889, when a larger school was needed in town, it was Paul Morase and his Métis wife, Margaret Daignon (Daniels), who donated much of the necessary land. As the population increased, the county established rural schools to which Métis parents (most of whom lived to the east of town, outside city limits) sent their children. In 1885 the school district built a school on Half Breed Creek, four miles east of town, for the thirty to thirty-five students of the immediate vicinity, most of whom were Métis. The non-Métis population knew this school as the "Half Breed School" or "Breed School." About ten years later, another school, just east of town, on Boyd Creek, opened to serve predominately Métis students. At first the Métis enthusiastically supported these schools, but as non-Métis county school officials assumed control, the Métis became less convinced that the schools met their children's needs. Ethnic conflicts over educational program content and methods surfaced within the Boyd Creek school. Among teachers and administrators, students at Boyd Creek School had the reputation of being difficult and challenging. The young Métis did not like their "white" teachers and resisted learning English. Frustrated with the students' presumed lack of progress, school superintendent Elizabeth Peebles had by 1902 come to the conclusion that "half breeds should not be allowed to speak any language other than English while in school." This unilateral decision, made without consulting Métis parents, could not have enhanced county schools' popularity.[15]

As in the political and religious arenas, the Métis shared in local educational efforts. However, despite the fact that they supported the school system in comparatively large numbers, their participation, by 1890, was limited to student attendance. They no longer created their own schools, selected the teachers, or determined school policy. In fact, the Métis increasingly attended separate schools, which gained a reputation among the non-Métis teachers as problem schools. No Métis served on the school board and, of the school board members, only Dr. LaPalme spoke French.[16]

Unable to participate fully in the operation of their schools, forced to use an unfamiliar language by unsympathetic and often unpopular teachers, and suffering from Montanans' prejudice toward those of Indian descent, it is not surprising that, in the early 1890s, when a St. Peter's missionary, Father Van Gorp, urged Métis parents to send their children to be educated at the mission school, many took advantage of his suggestion. These parents hoped to provide their children a better education than that found in county schools, and as devout Catholics, were pleased to have their children receive religious instruction. But religious instruction was not the only difference from the Lewistown-area school system that the young Métis students encountered at St. Peter's. Here they found themselves strictly separated from "white" children by their placement in the Indian school. A "big, two-room long house . . . was the home of the native girls and that is where we were assigned," recalled Elizabeth Berger Swan. It had "stairways on both sides so we did not mix in the dormitory." The Indian and Métis children lived, studied, ate, and played while completely cut off from the other children. The only time they encountered students from the white girls' school was at Sunday service, for even their daily prayers were held separately. Neither were the children able to continue the use of their native language. The Indian school strictly enforced the use of English by forbidding any other form of communication. Terribly homesick and upset by the compulsory use of a strange language, Swan later remembered, "What worried me most . . . was that I didn't understand nor speak English and the rule was not to speak anything but English. I'm sure I broke the rules many times when I had a chance between our own band from Lewistown."[17]

The Métis children's curriculum also differed from that of white students. Most significantly, St. Peter's Indian school, unlike its white girls' academy, emphasized agricultural, stock-raising, and household skills. Long on work, the Indian program was noticeably short on academics. While academy girls studied arithmetic, reading, spelling, elocution, geography, history, drawing, and painting, the Métis and Indian children spent most of their time in manual labor. In the spring of 1896, when the diocese bishop visited for confirmation ceremonies, the school limited the Indian girls' participation to giving the vestals, while "the white girls were examined in arithmetic, grammar and stenography."[18]

Swan's memoirs provide an indication of the inadequate academic preparation given the Métis students. Despite her years at St. Peter's, where she learned to milk, churn butter, clean, and cook, Swan received the bulk of her academic education from her brief attendance at the rural (and mostly Métis) Corbly school, east of Lewistown. Especially important to her were the four months spent as a student of teacher Laura Downing. "I give her credit for what little education I have today," Swan wrote years later. In four months of public school, Swan gained more academic training than she had in years of mission schooling. This education served both her and later generations well. The skills learned from Downing made possible her compilation of the most complete record of early Métis life on Spring Creek.[19]

The St. Peter's school not only neglected the academic training of Indian and Métis students, but also instruction in the trades. Instead, the students spent most of their time in chores and unskilled labor. Although the school had an onsite blacksmith shop and carpentry shop, no effort was made to extend training in those skills to Métis and Indian children. The rationale behind this lack of academic and practical training lay deep in perceptions common to the era. In a letter to the superintendent of Indian schools, supervisor William M. Moss noted these views in reference to the Indian boys' department. "I consider that practically nothing is done at the trades," he wrote. "The Superintendent says that his observation is that it does not matter so much what the boys work at as that they work, as but few ever follow their trade after they leave school." As far as the girls were concerned, Moss failed "to see the necessity of any training or education for a girl, without regard to color, which is not given here." In fact, he went on to write, "If I were to make any criticism at all, it would be that everything here is so very fine and nice that when they go home the contrast will be too great for them to bear."[20]

The belief that Indian children needed to learn to work rather than to acquire skills was widespread and generally accepted. This was not necessarily a program instituted by the hardworking teachers at St. Peter's school (whose membership, at one time, included Métis leader Louis Riel). The teachers' instructions were clear, as recounted by L. B. Palladino, S. J., in his history of Montana Catholicism. "The training of our Indians must be of a very rudimentary kind, and, above all, industrial . . . for after religion, next in importance as a factor of Indian civilization, must be placed manual labor," he insisted. "This is all the more true, because our Indians have a deep aversion to real labor." In Palladino's opinion, like that of other respected educators, a "plain, common English education, embracing spelling, reading and writing, with the rudiments of arithmetic, is book-learning sufficient for our Indians. Anything beyond that for the present at least, in our candid opinion, would prove detrimental, rather than beneficial; since it might serve to encourage their natural indolence at the expense of what they need most, industrial education." Not only was the Native student's inclination to work questioned, but also his ability to handle academic subjects intellectually. "Like a weak stomach that can digest but little food at a time, even so is the head of an Indian with regard to book-learning," wrote Palladino, echoing common educational theory of the day. All that was necessary, he believed, was that Indian children learn to support themselves. "But it is not necessary for this that he should become an artist, or a skilful workman, or even a mechanic. For it is obvious," he was sure, "that so long as civilization is not more generally advanced among them, trades cannot be much in demand."[21]

Palladino also recommended against the establishment of day schools for Indian children, wondering "of what practical use for their education can a day school be for wild Indian children who have no real home, and who are destitute of family training?" Boarding schools were necessary, for "how can you civilize these savage beings, except you withdraw them from the blighting influences that encompass them on every side?"[22]

A nationwide Indian educational policy, which had grown out of the Indian reform movement of the 1860s, decided the future of the Lewistown Métis who attended St. Peter's Mission school. Such policy was not limited to Catholic schools but influenced all Indian schools well into the next century. For the Spring Creek band children, these policies ensured that, on completing their education, they would be suited only for jobs involving manual labor. Their reading, writing, and math skills would be insufficient to operate a business or to read and fully understand the terms of bank loans, homestead provisions, or tax laws. It relegated them to the lower economic classes and guaranteed that their education would not match many of their parents'.

The education that the Métis children received at St. Peter's also points to contrasting but fast-changing ethnic definitions in Lewistown and at the mission school. The non-Métis of Lewistown identified local Métis as "breeds," part Indian but not Indian. Non-Métis at St. Peter's identified the Métis as Indian and treated them as such. Because St. Peter's teachers were officials of the church and were respected by the Métis community, this definition could not be overlooked by the Métis people. It became part of the way the younger generation of Spring Creek Métis saw and identified themselves.

From the perspective of the mission personnel, the reasoning behind defining the Métis as Indian lay in the school's dependence on a government contract that paid according to the number of Indian students served. The school risked losing government funds altogether if it could not attract enough Indian students. When the Blackfeet children that the school originally served ceased attending St. Peter's, the school faced closure. The decision to recruit mixed-descent children for the Indian school seemed a sensible solution to the Indian student shortage. It was in response to this need that missionaries encouraged the Lewistown Métis to send their children to St. Peter's. In such mundane ways, an alien ascribed ethnic identity was attached to the Spring Creek Métis. Whereas in Lewistown during the 1880s and 1890s the Métis students were noticeably different and not considered to be quite white, they were not isolated from Euro-American children. At St. Peter's, their placement in the Indian school separated them in their own minds, as well as in the minds of other students, from the Euro-American population. It contributed to a growing sense that the Métis were Indian, if not genuine "full-bloods."[23]

The dramatic differences in type and quality of education make an examination of the ethnic background of the "white" St. Peter's students all the more revealing of the racial categories into whose Procrustean beds the Métis were pressed. Included among the white students of 1885 and 1886 were daughters of the neighboring Lewis, Ford, and Pambrun families. The mother of the Lewis girls, Ed Lewis's wife, Sy-co-was-ta-ca-pa, was Piegan. Contemporary photographs of the Lewis girls show that they, while well dressed and fashionably coifed in Euro-American style, "looked" Indian. Louise and Millie Ford were the children of Sam Ford and his wife, Clementia Lapierre, a Métis and daughter of Métis parents. The parents of the Pambrun girls were also probably members of the well-known Métis family of that name. Yet these girls were all enrolled in the white academy and associated exclusively with white students. They received the higher-quality training and education that the girls' academy provided and were strictly separated from the "Indian" children.[24]

The logic of the arrangement escapes a casual modern observer. But on investigation, it becomes apparent that these part-Indian children were from a very different social background than most of the Métis students. They were the children of prosperous neighboring landowners who gave money, time, and material assistance to the mission. The "white" children spoke English and came from homes dominated, for the most part, by Euro-American males with British-style education and values. Their manners and style of dress reflected their fathers' aspirations for them. Additionally, their mothers were not socially close to the Pembina Métis and, particularly in the case of Sy-co-was-ta-ca-pa Lewis, felt a great social distance from them.[25]

Isabell Lewis Tabor, daughter of Sy-co-was-ta-ca-pa, left memoirs that reveal her mother's feelings about the Métis. She remembers a conversation between Father Camillus Imoda, a St. Peter's priest, and her mother, who was isolated and lonely on her husband's ranch. Father Imoda, Tabor recalled, assured Mrs. Lewis that soon there would be many Catholic families for her to visit. Imoda referred to his plan, initiated in 1878, to bring Catholic Turtle Mountain Métis families to settle near the mission. Mrs. Lewis was not impressed. "But," she replied, "they will all be Crees." What Mrs. Lewis did not mention was the longstanding animosity between the Blackfeet and the Crees with whom many Montana Indians identified the Métis. She regarded the Turtle Mountain Métis as strangers, "squatters" with "their noisy Red River carts." Camping on their small allotments, they could not be considered the social equals of the area ranchers (or of the Blackfeet). Having little respect for the Métis, the Lewis family was not surprised when Imoda's settlement plan did not succeed. "The mixed-bloods," Isabell noted, were "a restless roving race" who "did not take kindly to ranch life."[26] Despite her own mixed ancestry, when Isabell used the term "mixed-blood," her definition did not include persons such as herself. Her understanding of the term had little to do with Indian ancestry, but was socially constructed, based on values characterized in lifestyle choices, especially by apparent nomadism, from which she felt her family free.

Even taking into account such social distinctions, the reasoning behind the mission's ascribed Indian identity of the Spring Creek band trader family children (Wells, Ouellette, Kline, and Morase) is particularly obscure. St. Peter's records acknowledge the part-European ancestry of all but the Kline family, including the Morase, Ouellette (Wallace), and Wells children in their list of boys having "white" fathers.[27] Like the Ford, Lewis, and Pambrun fathers, these Lewistown families were landholders, owned businesses, and were considered prosperous, respected members of the community. Yet these children of "white" fathers were placed in the Indian school.

Perhaps part of the reason was that the Lewistown trader families were not neighboring landowners; nor did they provide essential services to St. Peter's as did the Ford and Lewis families. Probably of more significance, most of these children did not speak English and lacked middle-class,

American-style manners and dress. Their lack of Euro-American household and labor skills made them seem to be in need of the same sort of training that the teachers felt would benefit Indian children. Language, appearance, and manners set them apart, causing them to seem both foreign and Indian-like. Apparently class (as indicated by manners, English-language skills, a certain prosperity, and an ability to financially support the mission) played a determining, if porous and ill-defined, role in racial identification at St. Peter's Mission, while physical attributes and actual genetic heritage was of far less importance.

An 1895 Feast of the Ascension and first communion celebration illustrates the confusion surrounding these ethnic designations. At this event, twenty girls received first communion. Seven "white" girls, including Margaret Lewis, wore white dresses, while thirteen "Indian" girls, including Spring Creek Métis Mary Morase, Mary Ouellette, and H. Cline (Kline), wore pink. That Margaret Lewis's Indian ancestry exceeded that of Mary Morase's, and possibly of the Ouellette and Cline girls as well, escapes comment by school officials. Further underscoring the social distinctions that these definitions imposed was a luncheon following the service. The "white" girls and their parents, including Mr. and Mrs. Lewis, were served lunch together, as guests of the school, while the Indian girls, whose parents were not present and, it seems, not invited, ate lunch separately in the art room.[28]

There was no doubt in the minds of the Métis students attending St. Peter's Mission school that they were not white. It may have been the first time many of them learned that they were Indian. Their parents had considered themselves to be "breeds" (as they were called in English), Métis, or Michif. Nevertheless, the Indian identity ascribed by school and church officials made an enormous impression on the children. After all, their parents, as devout Catholics, had taught them to respect the priests and nuns as God's representatives.

MÉTIS AND HALF-BREED: EVOLVING EURO-AMERICAN ATTITUDES TOWARD THE MÉTIS

Even as a growing number of Euro-Americans identified the Métis as Indian, prejudice toward them as mixed-blood or "breeds" continued. The conferred Indian identification was a double-edged sword, as was evident in contemporary commentary. Writing of Métis residents in 1889, Lewistown settler Lula Schuflet recalled seeing "a squaw sitting down in the bottom of the cart with a papoose on her back." Describing the Métis in Indian terms distanced them from the mainstream Euro-American community. On the other hand, it did not confer the status of "real" Indians. The mention of a cart, a vehicle in which most Montana Indians did not travel, identifies them as "breeds" rather than as "full-bloods."[29]

The Métis suffered both from prevalent attitudes toward Indians and from antimiscegenation sentiment deeply entrenched in nineteenth-century Euro-American thought. Euro-American men who married Indian women faced strong white-community disapproval. Their mixed-descent offspring met with various responses and divergent social prospects, but always faced the possibility of discrimination. Even the most prosperous and socially secure Euro-American fathers could not completely protect their mixed-descent children from the prejudice against them.

Acknowledging the perceived differences and the social reception afforded different groups of mixed-descent people, Andrew Garcia, a trader of Spanish Indian descent, categorized three principal mixed-descent populations in late-1870s Montana. The first he termed variously French Injuns, Crees, or half-breeds. In this category he included those families who often spoke Indian languages and sometimes English, but who had their own language, Michif, which was closely related to French and Cree. These people were usually of French or Scottish descent, as well as Indian, and often had Canadian relatives. Most were descended from generations of mixed-descent peoples. The second group he referred to simply as half-breeds and included any offspring of a white and an Indian parent. Garcia's third category, which perhaps represented his personal viewpoint rather than contemporary realities, included Mexican half-breeds, whom he described as "in a class of their own." Most Montanans probably would not have made such fine distinctions between what Garcia termed Mexican and other half-breeds, but they did recognize distinctions between "French Injuns" and English-speaking, western-educated half-breeds.[30]

Garcia's perspective is that of a white man. Despite being referred to, on occasion, as a "damn half-breed American greaser," he saw himself as Rio Grande Spanish; his conclusions about half-breeds, despite his own heritage, reflect this. Like Euro-American Montanans, he believed in the superiority of "full-bloods," be they white or Indian. For example, in describing the woman he married, he wrote, "Le-oh-lee . . . was no breed . . . but was all the better being a squaw." Furthermore, he maintained that even male "breeds" preferred a "full-Blood squaw" to a woman of mixed descent, and that "the breed women also lean heavy toward the buck Injuns, probably knowing that full-blood stock is the best every time." There is no evidence to support such conclusions; in fact, the contrary is true. Most Montana Métis of the period, as shown earlier among the Spring Creek band families, married other Métis. Nevertheless, many Euro-Americans in Montana would have agreed with Garcia's assumptions.[31]

As did much of contemporary literature, Garcia portrayed people of mixed descent as weak and alcoholic, but crafty. Métis women were invariably "hussies," and only full-blood Indian women were virtuous. In this, his opinions differed little from common thought of the day. As early Fort Benton resident, Euro-American Winfield Scott Stocking put it, "The crossing of the breed increased the good looks, but . . . it seldom improved moral character."[32]

While all people of mixed-Indian descent faced similar attitudes in Montana, the Métis were often singled out. Recent Euro-American settlers and visitors, particularly, avoided close association with them. Mary Hunter Doane, wife of Fort Assiniboine officer Gustavus C. Doane, maintained her sense of propriety and social distance from Métis families even when hundreds of miles out in the prairie. During a journey from Fort Ellis (present-day Bozeman, Montana) to Ft. Assiniboine (near Havre), a difficult trip over hundreds of miles of dirt track, Doane rejected the comforts of a Métis camp. "At Sun River Crossing, we found a half breed family living," she wrote later. "They offered to give us shelter, but I preferred sitting up in the ambulance all night to their hospitality." Her feelings against association with half-breeds were so strong that she sat up all night in a cold, hard wagon rather than share the warm comforts of the Métis.[33]

One reason for the rejection of Métis hospitality and companionship often given by Euro-American settlers was a supposed Métis infestation with lice. Many believed that wherever breeds were to be found, so surely would lice. Such was also thought to be a common condition of Indians, who were assumed to be infested with these pests. The epithet "lousy Indian" was in common use and referred to a very real suspicion. But because the Métis were not confined to reservations and roamed freely in close contact with Euro-Americans, the perceived danger of contracting lice from them was viewed as ever present.

This social distinction by lice led to many hours of hard work for Euro-American housewives and agony for their lye-scrubbed children. To have lice on your person could reduce you socially to the level of Indian, forever ruining the reputation of your family and isolating you from polite company. When an early Montana ranch woman, Nannie Alderson, discovered lice in the ranch hands' blankets, she immediately lay the blame on a visiting half-breed. "The next few weeks were the worst nightmare I have ever experienced," she later remembered. "We boiled those blankets in water with lye in it, but could do only two at a time for it was bitterly cold, and the boys [ranch hands] couldn't be left without covers. We would lift the blankets out of the boiling water with a stick and they would freeze stiff almost before we got the clothespins in them. . . . It took four or five days." Such was the exhausting labor endured to keep one's family free of the stigma attached to "lousy Indians."[34]

Even Garcia used a lice analogy—"that Injun louse"—in referring to a breed who, Garcia felt, falsely represented himself to be French Canadian. This perception of Métis as infectious carriers of lice followed them into the twentieth century. Wallace Stegner remembered playing with Métis children in his early-twentieth-century boyhood home on the Montana-Saskatchewan border. Although his mother allowed the children to play together, she "combed us out somewhat fiercely with fine-combs when we came inside."[35]

The assumption of lice infestation was just one way to distance the Métis from Euro-American society. The scenario played out thousands of times on a daily basis and, in addition to other forms of discrimination, served to separate them from other Montanans. Though lice were probably not racially motivated, Métis families' unique lifestyle did signal actual difference, and, in Euro-American eyes, justified much of the prejudice against them. While traveling, Métis families often lived Indian–style in lodges. As mentioned earlier, many sat on the floor and served their meals there. Their dress was distinctive also, but what set them apart completely was their continued use of Indian languages, French, or Michif. Even central Montanans who were married to Indians or persons of mixed descent, and who, presumably, had no prejudice against half-breeds, found Métis to be foreign. Teddy Blue Abbott, husband of Mary Stuart (daughter of prominent local rancher Granville Stuart, and his Shoshone wife, Arbonnie), apparently felt no less inclined to ridicule the Métis in deference to his wife's ancestry. "God, how I've laughed at those French breeds," he wrote in his recollections, *We Pointed Them North*. "I must have spent hundreds of dollars buying whiskey just to get them to talk. They get everything all mixed up. Like old Mose LaTreille (LaTray)," he remembered, "telling me about the time he 'crossed the Rocky Mon-tanne, by Chris', run away my va-gonne, broke my horses.' That old man," Abbott marveled, "was with white people over fifty years, and at the end of that time he talked just the same as when I first knew him."[36]

DEFINITIONS OF WHITENESS

As the Métis became increasingly estranged from Euro-American society, and were more often identified with their Indian relatives, other central Montanans of mixed descent remained closely identified with the Euro-American population. This phenomenon, noted previously at St. Peter's and Fort Benton, was not restricted to the Rocky Mountain Front Range communities or long-established trading towns.

"Half-breed" was a racial definition in the sense that one must have Indian ancestry to be a member of the group. But race is a social construction uniquely defined in place and time. Not all half-breeds were created "equal." Within the broad racial definition were social boundaries that marked off different positions and possibilities. Some "breeds" were more readily admitted into Euro-American society. Dress, language, lifestyle, education, work habits, land ownership, degree of financial security, values, and world view differentiated those of part-Indian descent and limited acceptance by the "white" community. As at St. Peter's Mission, the position, economic and social, of mixed-descent children's Euro-American parent was often the key to providing acceptance by the Euro-American community.

Many of the cattlemen who came to Montana before the 1880s had married Indian women. Reese Anderson and Granville Stuart, prominent Spring Creek drainage ranchers, for example, married Shoshone sisters in the 1860s. These fathers raised their children in prosperous, middle-class Euro-American style, including the employment of tutors and the purchase of the latest eastern U.S. fashions. Their children, although they faced intermittent discrimination as half-breeds, joined the Euro-American community.

Often, as in the case of the Stuart children, non-Métis persons of mixed-descent had no social contact with the Métis. As Teddy Blue Abbott recalled, the Stuarts were Protestant, spoke standard English, and had the manners of the mainstream middle class. "The Stuart girls were half-breeds, but they were pretty, well-dressed, good dancers and very much sought after," he wrote in his memoirs. "Those girls had every advantage there was to be given in that place and time. Mr. Stuart always had a schoolteacher living at the ranch." Not only were they well educated, but their father bought them the latest fashions in Helena. Sometimes the advantages the Stuart girls enjoyed caused trouble. Abbott noted that "there was a good deal of jealousy on account of it. The Stuart girls had prettier and more expensive clothes than any of the others in that country and was always dressed in the latest style, and it drove the white girls wild."[37]

Mary Hunter Doane also noted the social position of the Stuart girls. As the wife of an army officer, she often attended community social gatherings at and near Fort Maginnis. "We were happy, and had a wonderful summer," Doane wrote of her stay at Fort Maginnis. Everyone was "drawn together from the very fact of our isolation and our dependence upon one another. . . . Our only and nearest neighbor was Granville Stuart. His wife was an Indian squaw who preferred living in a teepee to a house." Despite this shocking situation, Doane noted that "Mr. Stuart had at that time the largest private library in the territory. He had a governess for his children. One daughter at home was grown and a graduate of a college." Doane solved the unusual social predicament with a prim solution that conveyed her judgment: "I visited their home but never met the wife," she wrote. Such comments gloss a complex underlying reality. Doane, who sat up all night in a cold and uncomfortable wagon rather than accept the hospitality of a Métis family, found Granville Stuart's daughters acceptable company; their manners and education included them in polite frontier society. However, Mrs. Stuart, Indian in her ways, was neither visited nor invited. Left unsaid is the fact that, although Doane maintains that Granville Stuart was "our only . . . neighbor," in reality, several Métis families lived close to the fort. Apparently these families did not exist in so far as qualifying for the social round.[38]

Granville Stuart's attitude toward the Métis was clear. He campaigned relentlessly to get half-breeds and Indians off the range. He was not, one would assume, referring to his own children. It can only be imagined what the Stuart children thought of their father and neighbors constantly complaining of thieving half-breeds; but, whatever their personal thoughts on the matter, they identified with the Euro-American community. The high regard in which that community held Stuart's daughter, Mary Stuart Abbott, is reflected by a state senate resolution issued upon her death. The resolution, while honoring her memory and noting her accomplishments, made no mention of her mixed heritage, except to recall her mother, Arbonnie, as a "full-blood Shoshone Indian Princess." As descendants of a "princess" and a respected landowner and legislator, the Stuart children moved into a social world quite separate from that of the Métis.[39]

COWBOYS AND MÉTIS: THE CATTLE INDUSTRY

The social world in which the Stuart children grew up—that of the large, Montana ranchers—had reached central Montana soon after the Spring

Creek Métis arrived. Montana businessmen had not taken long to recognize the region's economic potential. They invested in large cattle herds and pushed steadily into the Judith Basin as the buffalo disappeared and the Indians were forced onto reservations. The Spring Creek band noticed the arrival of the cattlemen as they moved into the basin. They were aware that Henry Brooks, managing for T. C. Power and Co., had driven cattle to Warm Spring Creek, just north of Spring Creek, shortly before they arrived. They also helped Granville Stuart find appropriate grazing land near Spring Creek for his partners' cattle. By 1883 some thirty-three thousand cattle grazed within a twenty-mile radius of Spring Creek, and by 1885 the number of sheep and cattle within sixty miles of the creek had increased to approximately 100,000 each.[40]

With the buffalo gone, the Indians on reservations, and the plains filling with cattle and sheep, the Métis struggled with new realities. They had no reservations or government allotments, however inadequate, to which they could retreat. They faced the changing economic realities of the plains without government aid but also without government restrictions. They could and did apply for homesteads, where they raised gardens and kept their own stock. They sought wage work in town and on ranches. But local livestock owners continued to be suspicious of the Métis, accusing them of killing cattle and stealing horses. After the 1885 Northwest Rebellion and a new influx of Métis and Cree refugees from Canada, stockmen's accusations and hostility increased. Area rancher James Fergus, knowing that game was scarce, wrote, "Half-breeds have killed over a hundred deer. I am afraid they will kill cattle when the deer are gone." His fears were typical.[41]

Métis were not the only targets of ranchers' suspicions. Unhappy with the ineffectiveness of distant law enforcement personnel, local ranchers, reportedly led by Granville Stuart, organized to stop cattle and horse losses, whatever the cause. Their primary target was the organized bands of rustlers who, until then, had easily escaped capture by retreating with stolen stock to the Missouri breaks—the badlands along the Missouri River. After hanging at least fifteen men without trial (some estimates are as high as sixty), the Judith Basin vigilantes, or "Stuart's Stranglers," as they came to be known, brought organized livestock theft in the Judith Basin to an end.[42]

In addition to organized cattle rustling gangs, Stuart suspected that Indians and Métis played a large role in cattle thefts. He wrote in 1885, "Between six and seven hundred Cree Indians . . . with their families [and] without any means of support and of necessity preying on citizens of Montana" lived by eating cattle and stealing horses. "There was nothing left for the stockmen and ranchers to do but to deal with the Indian thieves as we had dealt with the white ones." The vigilantes' hangings had a profound effect upon the Métis community when, in 1884, at least two of their number were executed without trial.[43]

The Métis were especially outraged over the death of Sam McKensie. Particularly galling was the way in which this popular Métis musician was tricked into capture and hanged without trial. Contemporary Isabelle Larocque (LaRocque) heard the story from a brother-in-law. "Eli Guardepie told me that Sam McKensie a half-breed in 1884 was going to a dance, he had his violin with him as he was expected to furnish music." Unaware of the danger, "he was kept playin all night. The so called vigilantes were pretty well drunk . . . [and] they took him in the morning and hung him to a cottonwood tree by the road-way lane West of the D-S [DHS, Stuart's ranch] Ranch." This execution of a well-liked musician exacerbated tensions between the Métis community and local cattlemen.[44]

Not all ranchers supported the vigilantes, however. In fact, Granville Stuart's much-publicized accusations of Métis and Indian depredations were contradicted by other ranchers as well as by county criminal records. Oscar Stevens, a respected and prosperous rancher, opposed vigilante activities and maintained that he had not suffered from Indian theft. Small stockholders in communities along the Missouri River were especially resentful of the vigilantes, whose activities they saw as one more example of large ranchers' unfair and illegal control of the range. Among them were a number of Métis families who had been living along the Missouri years before the cattlemen arrived, making a living as wood hawks by supplying wood to steamboats. They often owned stock of their own and accused the larger operators of stealing as many cattle as the accused thieves.[45]

Nor does the Fergus County Register of Criminal Actions lend support to accusations of Métis horse and cattle theft. The register records only one charge of Métis theft between 1887 and 1909. In September 1887 Alexander Ledoux and Peter Falcon faced charges of horse stealing, but the court discharged the defendants. In fact, the Métis were a remarkably law-abiding group. Of the 525 cases (of all kinds) brought before the court and recorded from 1887 to 1909, only ten concern individuals who can be identified with certainty as Métis, and only three others possibly involved Métis.[46]

Despite the peaceful and law-abiding nature of the Spring Creek Métis, their relations with the cowboys from certain of the area ranches deteriorated. Harassment of the Métis was not confined to organized raids. Ranch hands sometimes casually tormented Métis families as they traveled and camped on the open range. In one incident, reported later by Isabelle Larocque, cowboys fired into a camp of what they assumed to be unaccompanied women and children, busily preparing food. "Eli [Gardipee] told me," Larocque remembered, "one time a group of us [Métis] were camped not too far from the D-S Ranch. The women in our group were cooking our Midday meal in kettles on a fire, outside the tents, when a group of cowboys came along. The cowboys commenced shooting holes through the kettles and raising hell in particular." But, Larocque reported, the cowboys got a surprise of their own. "The men of our camp were mostly inside. They got their guns ready and stepped out ready for battle. These fun loving cowboys weren't looking for that kind of fun." Seeing that they were in serious trouble, the cowboys then attempted to make peace by inviting the Métis to a dance at "the home ranch" (probably the D-S of Granville Stuart). However, the Métis feared that if they attended "real trouble would most likely develop." Instead, they prudently "chose to travel to the Little Rocky Mountains and lived there for a while."[47] After successfully confronting the cowboys and forcing their retreat, the Métis knew better than to attend a dance where the ranch hands would probably seek revenge. Instead, they took the safest course and left the region for a period of time. Since most of the cowboys were temporary workers who moved on after the summer work, the Métis could avoid trouble by spending the summer elsewhere and returning home in the fall.

Cowboy harassment of the Métis represents one aspect of the social struggles between the Métis and Euro-American newcomers. Ranch hands, as temporary summer workers, doing the drudgery of cattle work, occupied one of the lowest positions on the West's social scale. Sensitive to negative attitudes toward them, cowboys developed their own codes of conduct and rules of inclusion, and drew strict boundaries between themselves and those they perceived to be beneath them. In their opinion, these lower groups included the non-Métis professional buffalo hunters, the wolfers, and the "breeds." "The cowpunchers" romanticized their own lifestyle and considered themselves to be "a totally different class from these other fellows on the frontier."[48]

Like many cowboys, Teddy Blue Abbot did not associate the Métis lifestyle with the freedom and romance of either cowboy or Indian life. Although he wished that he could have been "a Sioux Indian a hundred years ago," Abbott never expressed a desire to be Métis. That the Métis lifestyle was not romanticized in the same way as that of the Indian or cowboy is one of the mysteries of U.S. western myth development. One might have thought that their lives, colorful and free roaming, would have appealed to the popular imagination in the way that their voyageur ancestors are romanticized in Canada and the Great Lakes region. Perhaps their hard, dirty work was too closely associated with that of the despised professional buffalo hunters and wolfers, or their ways and language too foreign. Their French heritage did not help their popularity on the range. Neither the French, nor Catholics in general, were popular. Westerners such as Abbott regarded the French as effeminate and Catholics as not sufficiently independent of the controlling influences of an autocratic church. Neither were candidates for the rugged individualism favored in the western image.[49]

Cattlemen and, especially, their hired workers, the cowboys, did fit this role. But for all of its subsequent romantic portrayal and lasting image in the American mind, the reign of cowboys on the Montana plains extended only from the early 1880s to the winter of 1886–1887. After this disastrous winter, in which so many Métis and Indians also suffered, 40 to 90 percent of Montana's cattle were dead (region totals differed), and large-scale, open-range ranching, made profitable by wintering cattle without hay or protection, was at an end.[50]

With the bankruptcy of many large cattle companies that resulted from the winter's losses, control of the range shifted from large partnerships and corporations to smaller livestock and farming operations—usually individual, family-owned businesses. The cowboy passed into legend, replaced by the all-purpose "hired hand."[51]

Although disastrous for the cowboy, in the short term the winter of 1886–1887 provided some benefit to the Spring Creek Métis. Expert skinners, they found work salvaging what was left of the dead animals. After rancher Oscar Stevens lost three thousand sheep just east of the Judith Mountains, the Larocques (LaRocques), Doneys, Joe Lafountain (LaFountain), and other Métis families skinned the dead animals. "We moved over and made camp near the dead sheep and the men skinned them all," remembered Isabelle Larocque, who was a member of the party.[52]

However, the long-term consequences of the shift from large-scale ranching to smaller operations after the disastrous winter were ultimately detrimental to the Métis. Even though before 1887 ranchers sought legislation that was hostile to Indian and Métis interests, especially to their freedom to travel and hunt unmolested, and even though the cowboy employees sometimes harassed Métis, the large cattle outfits left the environment much as it had been when buffalo grazed there. The person-to-square-mile ratio remained low. Despite overgrazing, there was relatively little pressure on small game and vegetable resources important to the Métis, and deer and elk were still available. The scattered ranches and small towns provided odd jobs for ready cash. The Métis in the Judith Basin, although no longer prosperous, could survive.

The change to smaller ranches did not diminish employment opportunities. Ranchers now knew that they must provide hay for the winter. Hay had to be cut, stacked, and later fed. Irrigation systems had to be built to increase the hay supply. Fences were needed to keep cattle where they could be protected and fed. The new-style ranches provided steady year-round employment for Métis families, but they also altered the nature of the plains environment. As the smaller, more-intensive ranch operations spread, the number of cattle on the range actually grew.[53] These ranchers increased their utilization of the land in their efforts to better manage their herds. Fences now cut across the prairie; "trespassers" were unwelcome and easier to spot. Intense use of creek bottoms and other game-rich areas eliminated game habitat. Game decreased and Métis families could no longer depend on hunting for food. They had to look for new ways to support themselves. As Métis families faced these developments in their new homeland, they adapted. They became homesteaders themselves or worked for local ranchers. Some turned to a closer association with their Indian relatives.

MONTANA MÉTIS AS "CREE": THE 1885 REBELLION AND THE MONTANA MÉTIS

Just before the winter of 1886–1887 altered the livestock industry so dramatically in favor of smaller, more-intensive operations, events in Canada led to an escalation of rancher/Métis tensions. The 1885 Northwest Rebellion in Saskatchewan and the consequent relocation of Canadian Métis and Crees had a profound effect on non-Métis' attitudes toward and identification of Montana Métis. Although the problem originated earlier, Montana Métis after the Rebellion would be thoroughly confused and identified with their Cree relatives.

Since at least the 1870s, Montanans had referred to the Métis as "Cree half-breeds" or used the terms "Cree" and "breed" interchangeably. This confusion was, in part, due to generations of Métis and Cree intermarriage and cooperative hunting. Montanans noted that breed hunting parties almost always included Crees (and often Chippewas, with whom Montanans also confused both Métis and Crees). The term "Cree" seems to have persisted because the Métis language, Michif, was derived, in part, from that language and because many Métis also spoke Cree. There was an additional, less benign reason for reference to the Métis as Cree. A longstanding backcountry insult, especially in the Canadian Northwest, was to call one a "woods Cree." Identifying the Métis as Crees not only served to diminish them by denying their long history and unique heritage, but also added insult by equating them with a people subject, in the West, to ridicule.[54]

After the 1885 Rebellion, the term "Cree," in reference to the Métis, became even more widespread. To understand how this came about, a brief overview of the Rebellion is necessary. The conflict's roots lay in earlier events in Manitoba, where, despite legislation and assurances, the Canadian government ignored or took years to recognize Métis land claims stemming from the 1869–1870 Red River Resistance. Unable to secure title to their land and suffering intense harassment, many Métis relocated, hoping to maintain their way of life farther west. Some joined relatives who had already followed the great herds onto the Saskatchewan plains. By the early 1880s, however, railroads and Euro-American agriculturists were again threatening Métis settlements. As in the late 1860s, surveyors divided the land into orderly squares with no regard for traditional Métis river-lot land ownership patterns and no guarantee of Métis land title. Fearing a loss of homesteads and civil rights similar to the aftermath of the 1869–1870 Resistance, the Métis organized to protect their communities and economic base.[55] Joined by Cree allies, they took a stand in Saskatchewan near the settlement of Batoche.

In Montana, reactions to the uprising varied. At first, despite some fear that the local tribes and Métis might unite and join the Rebellion, many Montanans supported the Métis cause. Anti–Canadian resentment ran high in Montana, especially in the trading towns that had lost lucrative business when the Canadian Mounted Police shut down their illegal whiskey trade. A June 1884 article in the *Sun River (Montana) Sun*, reflected an open, even sympathetic, attitude toward growing unrest in the north. The editor reported that

> a delegation of four half-breed gentlemen from the Saskatchewan country, N.W.T., arrived here a few days ago to confer with Louis Riel, and if possible prevail upon him to return to their country with them, for the purpose of explaining and proving certain rights promised them by the Canadian government at the time of the confederation. . . . Mr. Riel says that he is an American citizen and that he considers the land over which the stars and stripes wave his home,

and now only goes [to Saskatchewan] to assist his people. . . . Mr. Riel has our best wishes for the success of his mission.[56]

Indeed, though the Rebellion caused some nervousness in Montana, business interests were delighted with the increased need for their supplies and freighting services. The Fort Benton firm, I. G. Baker and Company, reportedly grossed eighteen thousand dollars during the disturbance by selling and transporting supplies. But while non-Métis Montanans temporarily profited from the northern unrest, Montana Métis ultimately suffered.[57]

The first Montana Métis loss was that of their most effective spokesman. When Riel left Montana to support the protests and help protect Métis rights in Saskatchewan, he had been teaching at St. Peter's Mission school. Here, had he not been called away, he might have trained a new generation of Métis leaders and remained an effective spokesman for Métis causes and political organization. The events of 1885 cut short that possibility and took from Montana Métis their most sophisticated spokesman. After Riel's execution for his leading role in the 1885 Rebellion, no one leader spoke for all Montana Métis or united western U.S. and Canadian Métis in a single cause.

For the Spring Creek Métis, the loss of Riel meant an increasing isolation from the international Métis community. Even though after the Rebellion leader Gabriel Dumont settled temporarily three miles east of Lewistown with his wife's brother, David Wilkie, and sister, Judith Wilkie Berger (wife of Pierre Berger), the Spring Creek band suffered from the lack of an influential spokesperson. Although a respected leader and hero of the resistance, Dumont did not have the contacts or language and political skills to replace Riel as a uniting force in Montana.[58]

Ultimately of greater consequence to Montana Métis than the loss of Riel was the stream of Cree and Métis refugees into Montana after the defeat. In Montana Canadian Crees and Métis hoped to avoid Canadian authorities and feared repression by joining relatives in territory already familiar to them from years of buffalo hunting. Despite sporadic army harassment suffered on the Milk River since the 1870s, Cree bands under Little Bear (Imasees) and Little Poplar, with their Métis relatives and allies, sought refuge there after the defeat. On discovering their presence, U. S. First Cavalry troops took Little Bear and his followers into custody, escorting them to Fort Assiniboine. Army officials attempted to deport the Crees to Canada, where they were wanted in connection with the 1885 deaths of white settlers at Frog Lake, Alberta. The longstanding dispute between the Canadian and U.S. governments as to the nationality of these Métis and Crees created enough questions as to the legality of their deportation that the State Department denied permission for such action.[59]

Nevertheless, Cree and Métis troubles were not over. With game gone, they suffered during the harsh winters. Without government recognition as a U.S. Indian tribe, they received no food or supplies. During the winter of 1886–1887 many died in the heavy snows and forty-below-zero temperatures. Augusta-area ranchers, particularly Sam Ford, helped all that they could, but their resources were insufficient to prevent large-scale suffering and death. Although officers at nearby Fort Shaw provided some food, Congress delayed making appropriations for assistance. Unwelcome on already disease- and hunger-plagued reservations, the Crees and Métis found food where they could. On the Milk River several bands survived by eating coyotes poisoned by ranchers. The myth that the Métis and Crees would eat anything probably sprang from these devastating times.[60]

Gradually, numbers of Métis refugee families settled down in isolated valleys along the Front Range of the Rocky Mountains. Some joined relatives and friends in the St. Peter's Mission area. In the valleys of the Front Range, they found small game, raised gardens, and worked on nearby farms and ranches. Here, where many of their descendants may be found today, they lived quietly in relative security and freedom from harassment. Other refugee families joined relatives among the Spring Creek band. Best known among these was Gabriel Dumont, who, as mentioned earlier, fled to the Lewistown area after the Rebellion. Dumont's wife, Madeleine Wilkie, daughter of Jean Baptiste and Amable Azure Wilkie, followed soon after in the company of her sister's husband, Patrice Fleury. The Dumonts stayed with Madeleine's brother, David Wilkie, near their sister, Judith Wilkie Berger. Gabriel's relatives, Edouard and Jean Dumont, and Baptiste Parenteau, along with their families, also came to the area.[61]

Additional Métis and Cree refugees joined relatives living along the Milk River. Unwanted on the nearby reservations, they found work where they could. When economic opportunities and game proved insufficient, they moved south across the Missouri River and attempted to reach better hunting in the Judith Basin. The army, however, fearing the complaints of politically powerful ranchers in the Basin, turned them back. On the now-depleted Milk River hunting grounds these Cree and Métis families faced an uncertain future.[62]

In 1888 Cree problems worsened as much of the northern-Montana Indian land was opened to settlement. Powerful cattle interests had long insisted on the reduction of Montana's reservations. The fact that the reservations were already insufficient to support Montana's Indian population had little effect on the outcome. For the Crees, such reductions meant that they would have no chance of finding a home on existing reservations and little hope for the establishment of a new one on their behalf.[63]

Suffering hunger and poverty, the Cree and Métis refugees, as well as resident relatives who could not find enough game to support their families, suffered renewed harassment. As bands of poverty-stricken Crees and Métis traveled across Montana making a poor living from hunting scarce game or selling buffalo bones and polished horns, frightened settlers demanded deportation. Unsupported rumors of cattle and horse depredations circulated wildly, while settlers exaggerated the numbers of Cree and Métis refugees. The approximately two hundred refugees soon became, in the minds of Montanans, closer to two thousand. The Fort Benton *River Press* led the attack, insisting on the deportation of "these lazy, dirty, lousy, breech-clouted, thieving savages" who were "a constant source of trouble, in that they secretly kill cattle, fire the ranges and commit innumerable petty crimes and offenses too numerous to mention."[64]

During these difficult times, the word "Cree," as used by the press and other Montanans, became a pejorative but pervasive term that included all nonstatus (that is, nonreservation) Indians and people of mixed-Indian ancestry with Canadian connections. The use of French or Cree languages, or temporary residence in Canada, provided all the proof needed for such a connection. The association of the Métis with the Saskatchewan Rebellion intensified the general impression of a Métis Canadian national identity. That Cree bands were their chief allies in the resistance solidified the association. As Cree poverty and dislocation became more visible, and calls for deportation more vocal, the Métis were swept up in the fury.

Despite the consequences of the 1885 Northwest Rebellion for the Montana Métis, it is important not to exaggerate its effect on attitudes toward them. The Rebellion exacerbated existing tensions, but, as mentioned earlier, negative attitudes, prejudice, discrimination, and outright harassment had occurred earlier. Nevertheless, after the Rebellion, Métis ways of being identified and of identifying themselves were altered in both subtle and not so subtle ways. Prejudice against them and fears of reprisal after the Rebellion led many Métis to publicly identify themselves differently than they had before 1885. As Euro-Americans increasingly designated the Métis as Indian or Cree, the Métis themselves began to take on alternative public identities. After the Rebellion, not only did an acknowledged Métis ethnicity become a liability but, to a great extent, it disappeared in the minds of Euro-American Montanans. The furor over Canadian Métis and Crees altered the Euro-American perception of who the Métis were and left a lasting legacy of their Canadian Cree identity.[65]

CHIPPEWA CHOICES: TURTLE MOUNTAIN TIES

The Crees were not the only nonreservation Indians who returned to traditional Montana hunting areas during the 1880s. A band of Turtle Mountain Chippewas led by Little Shell, a respected third-generation Turtle Mountain chief, sought refuge there from poverty in Dakota. The story of the Little Shell band is one of a long struggle to preserve a Turtle Mountain, Dakota, homeland or, failing that, to secure land in Montana. The difficulties began in October 1863, when the Red Lake and Pembina Chippewas ceded their Dakota lands to the government. The Turtle Mountain band, once part of the Pembina Chippewas, never relinquished the Turtle Mountains. Métis and Chippewa bands had continued to hunt and live in the area while traveling back and forth from buffalo hunts in Montana and Canada.[66]

By the early 1880s many Métis of Chippewa ancestry joined the Turtle Mountain Chippewas and Métis. With the buffalo gone, they moved back to the familiar territory of the Turtle Mountains to find game. The Métis who returned were also aware that executive orders of December 21, 1882, and March 29, 1884, had created a small reservation for the Turtle Mountain Chippewas. As Pembina Métis, they felt entitled to participate in reservation negotiations.[67]

By 1884 twelve hundred Métis and about thirty-one full-blood Chippewa families resided in the Turtle Mountain vicinity. Throughout the 1880s and 1890s, as economic opportunities disappeared elsewhere, more Métis returned to the area from the plains of Canada and Montana. Many hoped for land allotments or homestead opportunities as a means to support themselves. But the returning Métis remembered their exclusion from the 1863 treaty negotiations and realized that they might again be prevented from participating unless they established Chippewa tribal status. In that year, Governor Alexander Ramsey, conducting negotiations for the federal government, had ruled that only Indians were eligible for aboriginal title to land. Half-breeds, he determined, could not claim such title. This left the Métis with little option but to assert their rights to their traditional territories, not as Métis aboriginals, but as Chippewas.[68]

The Chippewas, for their part, favored the participation of their Métis relatives as a strategy to increase numerical strength and negotiating power. They realized that the reduced reservation size insisted upon by government negotiators provided too little land for the economic survival of the band. Increased population figures, they hoped, would bolster their negotiating position and provide the numerical evidence that more land was needed.[69]

While many Chippewas saw advantages to Métis participation in treaty negotiations, some Métis were less sure. A large number of Métis favored individually owned allotments, either as half-breed allotments or as homesteads under the Homestead Act, and they rejected the idea of commonly held reservation land. As noted previously, Métis leader Louis Riel led the opposition to Métis reservation enrollment. Fearing the political and social consequences of such a move, he advocated a political distancing from Indian relatives and rejected the concept of a Métis Indian identity. In Riel's opinion, any assumption of an Indian identity risked losing basic civil rights such as the right to vote. The best way to ensure Métis prosperity in Dakota Territory, he believed, was through the political power of a strong Métis voting block. Political or legal association with Indian relatives could only weaken this strategy.[70]

But Riel, at first busy in Montana and, after 1885, lost to the Métis effort, had only limited influence on the Métis returning to the Turtle Mountain area. These families felt that they were entitled to join their Chippewa relatives and participate in reservation negotiations. Although they joined their Chippewa relatives, most Métis did not, as Riel had feared, lose their Métis values or abandon their way of life. While acknowledging a Chippewa ancestry, they continued to live as they traditionally had. They built homes and churches. They welcomed Catholic priests and established their communities around the unifying principles of their religion. Although often fluent in Chippewa and Cree, among themselves they spoke English, French, or, most often, Michif. They continued to enjoy their traditional music and dances, so unlike those of either their Euro-American or their Indian relatives and neighbors. Now that the buffalo were gone, many resumed the more sedentary habits of their early Red River days. They farmed and raised gardens. Although they continued to hunt and trap available game, they also collected buffalo bones and took wage labor on farms, ranches, and railroads. They allied themselves with their Chippewa relatives and neighbors, but maintained their own communities and customs. As the Chippewas determinedly retained their traditional dances and ceremonies despite pressure from church and government officials, the Métis avoided Indian celebrations and held on to their own unique ways.[71]

Distinctions between Chippewas and Métis were based on way of life, observed customs, religion, and type of work. It was never a simple matter of genetic heritage. Turtle Mountain Chippewas of the period avoided wage labor and farming, as they had for decades. They retained traditional religious observances and ceremonies and considered anyone who did not ineligible for recognition as a full-blood, regardless of his or her ancestry. A "full blood" designation required a life lived in a traditional Chippewa manner, not a total absence of European ancestors.[72]

As the Chippewas and Chippewa Métis worked out the terms of their coexistence, other Pembina Métis returned to the area. In 1886 a group of Pembina Métis from the Spring Creek band came back to the Turtle Mountains. Alexander Wilkie, with a party of friends and relatives, moved back to his boyhood home to be with his aging parents and to take part in treaty negotiations. Son of Métis leader Jean Baptiste Wilkie, Alexander, like his father, was concerned about Métis rights to land that they had hunted on for generations. He believed that he could not effectively fight for the recognition of Métis aboriginal land rights from distant Montana.[73]

Wilkie had followed closely the negotiations for a Turtle Mountain reservation. The U.S. government, he knew, had failed to honor the original land grant, had continually endeavored to reduce the reservation's size, and had persisted in an attempt to remove the Turtle Mountain people to White Earth Reservation in Minnesota. Furthermore, in 1883, Special Agent Cyrus Beede had determined that the Métis residing on the Turtle Mountain Reservation were there illegally, identifying them as Canadian Métis. Using the Beede report as justification, the executive order of 1884 drastically reduced the reservation's size from that guaranteed just two years before. An 1882 executive order had established a reservation of about twenty-two townships, including good farmland, but the 1884 order slashed its size to two townships, each unsuitable for farming.[74]

Needless to say, the 1884 executive order did not alleviate the contention and controversy at Turtle Mountain. Disputes erupted over boundaries, taxation, and land claims by the new Euro-American settlers. The Chippewas continued to demand that reservation boundaries be restored to their 1882 position. Issues of reservation size, tribal membership, and severalty (individually owned allotments) split the Turtle Mountain community. The full-blood faction, led by Chief Little Shell, insisted that the reservation size be increased. In support of this end, he favored including all Turtle

Mountain Métis on reservation rolls regardless of their place (or nation) of birth. The constant movement of Métis and Chippewa families back and forth across state and national borders meant that Turtle Mountain and Pembina families often had members born on both sides of the international boundary and in a number of states.[75]

Little Shell did more than welcome Chippewa Métis to Turtle Mountain. He supported a Grand Council resolution finding "that all the mixed blood descendants of our tribe belonging to our said band are hereby recognized to be Indians for all intents and purposes, and are fully entitled to the benefits hereof the same as any of the full bloods of our said tribe and band." This resolution temporarily foiled government attempts to exclude Métis participation in reservation negotiations and thus eliminate their numerical and practical support. The government's past practice, as in Ramsey's 1863 treaty negotiations, had isolated the Chippewas and diminished their numbers by excluding mixed-bloods. In those treaty negotiations, government officials dealt directly only with full-bloods and attempted to satisfy Métis claims separately. Thus the Chippewas lost the numerical strength of the Métis, and the Métis, in turn, were refused aboriginal status in their own right. Learning from that experience, some Turtle Mountain Métis whom government officials had listed as Pembina Chippewa half-breeds in the 1863 treaty sought and won recognition as Turtle Mountain Chippewas. From this time on, many Métis families would identify themselves and be recognized by the Turtle Mountain community as Chippewas.[76]

There was no consensus, however, in the Turtle Mountain community over who would have reservation rights or on the amount of land Chippewa negotiation leaders should continue to claim. Some factions disagreed with Little Shell and his supporters' position that all Turtle Mountain relatives be enrolled. After years of stalemate, they were willing to compromise. Suffering from poverty and desperate to resolve reservation boundaries, a growing number agreed to government demands that Canadian-born Métis and other families whose eligibility officials had found questionable be excluded from the reservation. By 1892, when Congress finally addressed the problems at Turtle Mountain, the community was impoverished, discouraged, and divided.[77]

Congress authorized the McCumber Commission, as it came to be called, in August 1890 to obtain a relinquishment to Chippewa territory in the Turtle Mountain, Dakota, area and to remove the Chippewas to an already established Minnesota reservation. The commissioners were also expected to determine who, among the Chippewas and mixed-descent residents, were entitled to enrollment, a question that had been hotly disputed since the 1884 executive order eliminated many from the rolls to justify a drastic reduction in reservation land.[78]

The appointed commissioners did not come to Turtle Mountain until 1892. In the meantime, conditions on the reservation, including near starvation, were so difficult that Little Shell, the principal leader of resistance to the 1884 executive order decrees, moved his followers to the Milk River of Montana. Here he hoped to find enough game to support his people. From Montana, he continued to fight for a suitable reservation. On August 28, 1891, from Wolf Point, Montana, he wrote to the commissioner of Indian Affairs proposing an exchange of land in the Turtle Mountain area for a reservation on the Milk River adjacent to the Fort Peck Reservation. Commissioner Morgan, however, bowing to Montana land and cattle interests, was not inclined to assign any of the public domain to the Chippewas.[79]

In the meantime, at Turtle Mountain, Indian Agent John Waugh appointed a committee of thirty-two full-blood Chippewas and sixteen Métis to represent the Turtle Mountain people in negotiations with the commission. That Waugh appointed this committee while Little Shell and his followers were away was probably by design, since it was Little Shell who led the opposition to relinquishment of any land claims. Many of Waugh's appointees had been waiting since 1882 for a resolution to the reservation controversy. Worn down by poverty and Euro-American settler pressure, they were anxious for a settlement and ready to compromise with government demands. They believed that if they did not work out an agreement soon, they might lose their remaining land. But Waugh's action left Little Shell and his band without representation on the committee. Even more damaging to the Little Shell supporters, Waugh then chose five committee appointees to review a list of those persons eligible for enrollment. Subsequently, this committee of five struck 112 families (525 individuals) from the rolls, including, not surprisingly, Little Shell's followers.[80]

In September 1892 the commissioners finally arrived under the direction of P. J. McCumber. When they asked for the standing committee's report (that of the council of thirty-two), Little Shell protested. He denounced the omission of families dropped by the committee. Maintaining that many of these people were absent from the reservation only because they had gone to Montana to find food, Little Shell argued forcefully for their inclusion on the rolls. Additionally, Red Thunder, chief councilman to Little Shell, pleaded eloquently for the inclusion of excluded mixed-descent families. "When you (the white man) first put your foot upon this land of ours you found no one but the red man and the Indian woman, by whom you have begotten a large family," he stated and then pointed dramatically to the mixed-descent persons attending. "These are the children and descendants of that woman; they must be recognized as members of this tribe."[81]

Disregarding the protests, the commission not only struck more families from the rolls, but did so without consulting Little Shell or his representatives. The commission posted this new list of official Turtle Mountain families on the church door without further debate. Agent Waugh followed up immediately, on October 15, with a demand "that all persons except those mentioned in said notice are directed to withdraw from the limits of the reservation." Without consultation or recourse, these families were forced to leave their homes and land under threat of arrest. But the anguish of Little Shell and the excluded families was not over. On October 22, the officially recognized tribal members renounced their claim to 9.5 million acres, retaining only the two townships of the previously established (1884) reservation. In return, the government agreed to pay $1 million (approximately ten cents an acre, hence the name "Ten Cent Treaty," by which this agreement would be known). Little Shell and other excluded families protested both the treaty and the means by which it was secured. Nevertheless, disregarding the protests, President Benjamin Harrison sent the treaty to the Senate for ratification on December 3, 1892.[82]

The negotiations irreparably divided the Turtle Mountain community. Families were split, as is evident from the large number of family names found both on lists of the excluded and among the council of thirty-two. The Spring Creek band, too, divided along lines of protestors/excluded and treaty supporters/enrollees. Alexander Wilkie and his father, Jean Baptiste, served on the council of thirty-two. His son-in-law, Octave LaFountain, Octave's brother, Elzear, as well as many other relatives, were among those who signed the McCumber Agreement of October 22, 1892. The Spring Creek Métis followers of Little Shell included the Pierre Berger family (Pierre's wife, Judith, was Alexander Wilkie's sister), the Benjamin Kline family, three of the Doney brothers (two of whom were married to LaFountains), the Moise (Mose) LaTray family, the Pierre and Katherine Laverdure family, and the Edward Wells family. The McCumber Commission excluded all of these Little Shell supporter families from the rolls. Recognized by Little Shell as Turtle Mountain Chippewas, these Spring Creek families remained his followers through subsequent years of protest against the McCumber Agreement.[83]

The battle over the Ten Cent Treaty did not end in 1892; Congress did not ratify the treaty until 1904. Years of bitter dispute, poverty, and waiting followed. By 1898 an aging and tired Little Shell sadly complained of the long wait to have his people's claims heard and of his despair at seeing them "so poor and going hungry." In the meantime, Little Shell and his followers had returned again to Montana, hoping to avoid the poverty in the Turtle Mountain area. Many settled along the Milk River near the present-day town of Havre, where a number of their descendants live today. Some wandered from city to city, much as the Crees did, looking for work. Others joined relatives in the Lewistown area. All suffered dislocation and poverty.[84]

For the Spring Creek band, the Turtle Mountain Reservation negotiations had several long-term repercussions. The band lost an effective spokesman in Alexander Wilkie, who returned permanently to Turtle Mountain. Many of Wilkie's in-laws and their relatives went with him. Octave LaFountain and his wife, Marie Josephine Wilkie, Alexander's daughter, and their large family also moved to Turtle Mountain. Octave's brother Bernard had died near Spring Creek, but his wife, Julienne Wilkie, and daughter Rose, also left, as did Octave and Bernard's brother Elzear. Elzear, his wife, Mary Rose Turcotte, and their large family eventually returned to the Lewistown area (Roy), but not until about 1902. Much of the remaining Spring Creek band united behind Little Shell, and his cause became a unifying factor and a basis for political organization in the next century.[85]

Little Shell's acceptance of mixed-descent descendants of Turtle Mountain Chippewas as Indian tribal members, and government acknowledgement of many mixed-descent persons—such as the Wilkies—as Turtle Mountain Chippewas, had a profound effect on the way some members of the Spring Creek band identified themselves. They realized that their potential aboriginal rights or claims could only be secured as enrolled Chippewas. As Pembina half-breeds they received no government recognition, nor were they able to participate in Turtle Mountain negotiations. A Chippewa Indian, rather than a Chippewa Métis identity, became a more realistic alternative.

During the years of controversy, the Spring Creek Métis did not suffer the poverty of Little Shell followers who fled the difficult economic conditions at Turtle Mountain. With their small acreages, available game, and local wage-work opportunities, they had the means to adjust to new economic conditions. Less well-established Little Shell followers were forced to assume a more migrant lifestyle in order to support themselves with wage labor and a small amount of hunting. Under such conditions they came in closer contact with Cree bands who were also experiencing economic hardship and displacement.[86]

MONTANA'S LANDLESS INDIANS

The ambiguous status and the poverty of the Little Shell band led to their association, in the minds of many Euro-Americans, with Cree bands struggling to survive in postbuffalo Montana. As noted earlier, the Crees and Chippewas were culturally similar, had a history of intermarriage, and continued to intermarry in Montana. The confusion had unfortunate consequences for the Little Shell band. After 1885 Euro-American Montanans tended to view all nonreservation Indians as Canadian Crees who had no right to be in Montana. The Chippewas, in addition to facing expulsion from the Turtle Mountain Reservation, now had to contend with resentment directed toward them as supposed Canadian Indians.[87]

Cree problems in Montana had continued to escalate through the 1880s and early 1890s. Unable to secure a Montana reservation, they moved through the state making a living wherever possible. Their reception in the small towns and cattle ranges of Montana was mixed. When a small Cree band came through Lewistown selling polished buffalo horns, merchants apparently appreciated their business, as the band used their income from the horns to buy clothing and flour. Language proved no barrier with so many Cree-speaking Métis in the area. Frank Daniels, a Spring Creek band member, acted as their interpreter. The only recorded complaint came from D. M. Crowley, whose dog was missing. Crowley feared his pet "made a sumptuous feast for the dusky braves, as Indians are partial to good fat dog meat." Area ranchers were not so complacent. In August of 1892, James Fergus complained to Montana Governor J. K. Toole that "twenty lodges of Canadian Cree Indians camped on Doe Creek [probably Dog Creek] last night. Traveling So[uth] killing game. Please remove them." He made no accusations of cattle depredations but felt entitled to demand that the Indians be removed.[88]

Although their stay in the Lewistown area was relatively quiet, the Crees were forced to move on by rancher opposition to their hunting and fear that they might steal cattle. Their reception elsewhere was less friendly, and calls for the removal of "these dirty Crees," as the Anaconda *Standard* headlined them, grew shrill. Throughout Montana, Euro-American immigrants to the state accused the Crees of being thieves, transmitters of disease, and a general nuisance. Montana's worsening economic situation left residents with little patience for the less fortunate. Suffering from the mine and factory closures of the "panic of 1893," mine and related industry workers, who made up the largest segment of the state's larger towns' populations, faced major layoffs and hunger themselves. Livestock owners, still trying to adjust to new cattle-raising techniques necessitated by the disastrous winter of 1886–1887, were also struggling for economic survival. These Montanans opposed any effort to provide reservation land or any other benefits to the "Canadian beggars." In January 1896, Governor John Rickards responded to such sentiments and, in a letter to Secretary of State Richard Olney, insisted that the Crees be removed: The Cree were "wards of the British government ... [and] an intolerable nuisance constantly violating our game laws, foraging our herds, and not infrequently looting isolated cabins. The patience of our people has been sorely tried."[89]

Finally, by 1896, opposition to the Cree presence grew so strong that the army arranged to remove them to Canada. Knowing that the Crees still feared reprisal and arrest for their part in the 1885 Rebellion and Frog Lake murders, the Canadian and U.S. governments reached an agreement that they hoped would appeal to the Crees. The U. S. Army would transport the bands north to a reservation provided by the Canadians on the Saskatchewan River. For its part, the Canadian government would provide amnesty for all those involved in the Rebellion. With this agreement, the army hoped that the Crees would leave Montana peacefully.

A dispute arose, however, between Governor Rickards and Canadian officials over the fate of Métis persons associated with the Crees. A. E. Forget of the Commissioner of Indian Affairs Office in Regina explained to the Montana governor that many "Crees" who had moved south after the Rebellion had since applied for and received certificates officially terminating their status as treaty Indians. The process, he explained, had provided a means to discharge "'half-breeds' from our Indian treaties. Many of these persons are now therefore not Indian in the eye of the law." Furthermore, since "these persons having now resided for ten years (more or less) on United States soil ... it is assumed that it is not the intention of the United States Government to disturb them." Indeed, disturbing them was what Governor Rickards had in mind. He planned to deport "all Cree whether they hold certificates or not."[90]

While Governor Rickards insisted that the army act, Great Falls attorney John Hoffman, who had previously defended Cree interests, attempted to prevent the deportation, pointing out that Congress had funded but not actually authorized such actions. Furthermore, he argued, the order to deport only mentioned "Canadian Crees." Hoffman insisted that there were many U.S. citizens among the Crees.[91]

Ignoring the dispute, First Lieutenant J. J. Pershing of the 10th Cavalry (later a World War I general) arrested a camp of Crees near Great Falls. For two months Pershing and his African American Troop D covered a thousand miles "rounding up" most of the Crees who were deported. Montanan sightseers traveled to the collection points and train stations to watch as the troops escorted the Crees north. Apparently, no one commented on the irony of the scene in which African American soldiers, whose rights as citizens had been so recently won, were ordered to deny the civil liberties of another harassed ethnic group.[92]

Major J. M. J. Sanno of the 3rd Infantry, in charge of the Cree deportation, reported that 537 "Canadian Cree Indians" with their horses and carts were "delivered" to Canadian authorities. Conditions of the removal ranged from the humiliation—being handled like cattle and loaded into boxcars—of arrest for the lucky, to a two-hundred-mile journey on foot for those not so fortunate. Of those forced to walk to the Canadian boundary, an unknown number died of cold and disease. As Great Falls attorney Hoffman charged, not all of the deported "Crees" were actually Cree. Caught up in the arrests were non-Canadian Assiniboines, Gros Ventres, Chippewas, and Métis.[93]

On arrival in Canada, and contrary to promises that all would receive amnesty, officials arrested Little Bear (Imasees) and Lucky Man for complicity in the Frog Lake murders. This broken promise and hunger on the Canadian reserve convinced the Crees to return to Montana. By fall of that year (1896), they were once again south of the boundary. After the expensive and unproductive 1896 removal campaign, Montanans temporarily gave up on Cree deportation, and, for a time, few suggested ridding the state of "Canadian Indians." Cree suffering was not over, however. Unable to secure a reservation and, as Indians, not eligible to apply for homesteads, they continued to travel in search of jobs, markets for their polished horns, and food.[94]

At this time, other groups also became associated with the nonreservation Indians in Montana. Joining the Crees during the difficult years after their deportation and return was a Chippewa band led by Rocky Boy. The origins of the band are unclear, but it was probably made up of Pembina and Turtle Mountain Chippewas who were closely associated with Pembina Métis and Crees. The band had apparently moved northwest during the 1870s and at that point came into closer contact with the Crees. Rocky

ETHNIC LABELS

Boy was married to Little Bear's cousin or aunt (accounts conflict). During the late 1890s and early 1900s the Little Bear Crees and Rocky Boy Chippewas were indistinguishable to most Montanans as the bands traveled through the state in search of food and work.[95]

The Rocky Boy Chippewas faced the same difficult conditions in Montana as other nonreservation Indians. Cree harassment and deportation affected not just those Crees, Chippewas, and Métis who were actually deported, but all Montana nonreservation Indians and Métis. Métis families, too, especially those who spoke Michif or French, or who had to travel in search of work, were often confused with the Crees and Chippewas. The Spring Creek band, settled quietly on their small farms, escaped actual harassment and deportation, but they could not escape prevailing attitudes. Many Spring Creek band members began to identify themselves as Little Shell or Turtle Mountain Chippewas to avoid harassment and deportation as Canadian Crees. If Euro-Americans insisted on confusing them with their Indian relatives, they wanted it to be clear that they were American Chippewas and not Canadian Crees. Yet despite their early residence in the Judith Basin and association with the Turtle Mountain Chippewas, they also endured the stigma of "Canadian Indians." Non-Métis Montanans forgot or ignored the band's long history as a separate people in the "Cree" hysteria that swept Montana.

• • •

As the century closed, Montana Métis families made the adjustment from a buffalo-hunting economy to wage labor, small-scale farming, and the hunting and trapping of small game. They learned English, educated their children, and took jobs while maintaining their distinctive lifestyle. The lack of economic opportunity forced some families to move from place to place in search of work. In this they were much like nonreservation Indians in Montana, who were prevented from hunting on rangeland, now controlled by livestock owners,and on reservation land, now controlled by the Bureau of Indian Affairs. Mixed bands of Chippewas, Crees, and Métis became a familiar sight on the outskirts of Montana towns.

Some Métis families became more closely associated with the Turtle Mountain Chippewas, the Little Shell Chippewas, or the bands that came to be known as the Rocky Boy Chippewas and Little Bear Crees. These families realized that their only chance to preserve their aboriginal claims to a land base depended on a tribal identity. Though it was government Indian policy that necessitated the formal adoption of an Indian identity, it was family ties that determined the tribal identity to which a family would ascribe and where it would settle. Government policy instituted a framework of formal identification and provided a corresponding vocabulary for that identity but could not determine the way families would make use of the opportunities they found under such policies. Whatever formal identity Métis families adopted in response to government policy, as extended families and bands they retained their sense of community and belonging and the recognition that they were different from fullbloods or whites.

The Métis also retained a sense of difference from other mixed-bloods. Their identity was family and band based, rooted in common values and lifestyle. The actual combination of Indian and Euro-American ancestry played only an auxiliary role; it did not determine Métis identity. Other Montanans of mixed-Indian and Euro-American descent did not identify with the Métis; nor did the Métis necessarily recognize them as members of their community. Despite the efforts of leaders such as Louis Riel to unite all mixed-descent Indian/Euro-American groups politically, they remained distinct both politically and socially.

The Spring Creek band, like all Montana Métis, suffered from prevailing attitudes and from confusion with "Canadian Crees." But established on small farms and able to find wage labor, they did not endure the same harassment and poverty. Although they were the longest continuous and probably the most prosperous Métis community in Montana, their influence within the larger community declined from 1885 to 1900. They lost their most effective leaders with the death of Louis Riel (1885), the move of Alexander Wilkie to Dakota (by 1886), and the death of Francis Janeaux (1887). By the end of the 1890s, the Spring Creek band no longer controlled or influenced Lewistown-area institutions. Increasingly, their organized political efforts centered on the Little Shell and Turtle Mountain Chippewas. Like other Montana Métis, they grew more comfortable with an Indian identity just as the Euro-American community, ignorant of their long separate history and unique culture, ascribed them as such.

CHAPTER 5

Métis, Indian, and White

Ethnic Negotiation in the Twentieth Century, 1900–1919

Through the next decade and a half the Spring Creek families maintained their kinship networks and communities both on Spring Creek and as they began to move within the large, roughly triangular area formed by the Milk River in the north and Lewistown in the south. Euro-American settlers continued to identify the Spring Creek families as Indian and to confuse them with their Native relatives. During these years the Métis negotiated a public identity with powerful government forces and with the Euro-American public while maintaining a private identity centered on a flexible web of kinship ties.

The new century brought fresh challenges from the very first years. In 1900, Little Shell, spokesperson for the Turtle Mountain treaty protest, died and left the movement without leadership. Four years later the U. S. Congress ratified the Ten Cent Treaty, which contained provisions that were almost identical to the 1892 McCumber Agreement. The treaty officially rejected those individuals previously dropped from the Turtle Mountain tribal rolls, including the followers of Little Shell. Also in 1900, the arrival of rail lines to within a hundred miles of Lewistown changed the character of the Judith Basin and touched the lives of all Métis living there. Three years later, the "Jawbone Railroad" provided service directly to Lewistown, thus removing a primary obstacle to the area's agricultural settlement. Through glowing descriptions distributed by railroad and state agency publications, the Judith Basin came to the attention of prospective settlers as one of the last "garden" spots open to homesteading. These developments between 1900 and 1904 altered dramatically both the hopes of the Métis people and the realities of their lives.[1]

"CHANGES IN THE LAND": A NEW CENTURY

The Métis had watched as cattle replaced the buffalo along the Judith and Musselshell rivers of central Montana. Other newcomers, trickling in since 1890, arrived in force with the railroads, transforming the prairie yet again. The homestead rush, which had bypassed the Judith Basin because of its Indian population, dry climate, harsh winters, and lack of transportation, had at last arrived. The railroads not only transported settlers in and their produce out but also, through their publications and advertisements, boosted the basin as a garden paradise. The publications, aimed at making their lines more profitable, described the uninviting climate as healthful, the untested land as fertile, and the semiarid area as well watered and empty. The Judith Basin—newly cleared of buffalo, Indian peoples, and vast open-range cattle operations—now experienced a population boom that transformed the land and dramatically impacted the lives of the Métis people.[2]

Prior to the boom, farming in Montana was small scale and precarious. According to the 1870 census, there were only 851 farms in all of Montana. Because of inadequate transportation, most were close to population centers, particularly mining towns, which provided markets for their produce. These first Montana farms usually lay on fertile and protected creek bottoms since land elsewhere on the semiarid plains lacked adequate water for sustained crop production. Central Montana's average yearly precipitation is fourteen inches. Lewistown receives the highest amount (17.47 inches, mostly in the form of snow), nearby Valentine averages 12.57 (as low as 7.62 in dry years), and Denton, to the west of Lewistown, averages 15.74 inches. These amounts fall well within the ten to twenty inches of precipitation that define a region as semiarid. Those farmers responding to the railroad publicity of the early 1900s were used to far different conditions, more like the thirty inches and long growing season that the farm country of Pennsylvania experienced during the first decades of the twentieth century.[3]

The railroad publicity ran counter to long-held beliefs about the Great Plains's agricultural suitability. The western Great Plains's semiarid climate had earned it the unflattering designation of "Great American Desert" very early. "These plains," observed Alexander Philip Maximilian, prince of Wied-Neuwied, who visited Montana in 1833, "which are dry in summer, and frozen in winter, have certainly much resemblance . . . with the African deserts." Later visitors publicized similar descriptions, including

John Palliser, leader of the 1857 British North American Expedition to the Canadian plains, who popularized the "desert" concept and convinced many Canadians and Americans that the western plains were useless for agriculture. As late as the early twentieth century, school texts still referred to the area between the ninety-eighth meridian and the Rocky Mountains as the Great American Desert.[4]

Despite this reputation, a gradual change in popular attitudes toward the western plains's agricultural potential became evident in the 1890s. Technological innovations and new farming techniques supported a reassessment of its agricultural potential. Steel plows, drills, harrows, and discs, as well as automatic binders and steam-powered threshers, made large-scale agriculture possible in areas of hard soils and tough prairie grasses. "Dry farming" techniques, in which half of a farmer's cropland lay fallow each year, and improved grain varieties solved some of the problems caused by low precipitation. These techniques increased yields, but, like expensive machinery, made large-scale planting necessary, something beyond the means of the small farmer.[5]

In addition to the new methods that made plains agriculture possible, the availability of land drew the attention of a land-hungry populace. As the U.S. government opened Indian land to homesteading, farmers took advantage of the 1862 Homestead Act. This legislation provided 160 acres to anyone over twenty-one, citizen or not, who paid a low filing fee and "proved up" the land by living on it for five years, plowing land, and erecting a home. Many farmers complained that 160 acres could not support a family in dry states such as Montana, and in response, Congress passed the 1877 Desert Land Act, which provided for the sale of 640 acres at $1.25 an acre if the owner would irrigate part of his property. Since, at this time, irrigation was impossible in most of Montana, and few homesteaders had the money to attempt it, the legislation did very little for farmers, although ranchers took advantage of its loopholes to enlarge their holdings. In 1909 and 1912, the Enlarged Homestead Act and the Three-Year Homestead Act increased the offered land to 320 acres and reduced the "proving up" period to three years, but after the end of the World War I agricultural boom years, even these changes did little to help farmers on the dry plains.[6]

Although new legislation and new farming techniques enhanced the desirability of Montana land, the railroad had the greatest impact on the Judith Basin. It is difficult to imagine the isolation of Lewistown during the late nineteenth century, when other Montana towns had rail or water transportation. Wagon, stage, or cart travel, like that the Métis used so effectively, were the only options. Reverend James M. Vermaat, a Roman Catholic priest, vividly described prerailroad traveling conditions. "There were three ways to reach Lewistown in those days," remembered Vermaat. "There was one stage line from Great Falls, a distance of 127 miles, as the crow flies, leaving Great Falls one morning at seven o'clock and arriving at Lewistown the next morning at ten A.M., after traveling all night in the old time stage coach." An alternate route from Billings "required two days and a half staging," and a third, the fastest, left Fort Benton on the Missouri River early in the morning and arrived in Lewistown between nine and eleven in the evening, if all went well. Describing the journey as an "ordeal," Vermaat wrote of travel "across the trackless waste of dry and hilly country" during which, in summer, "you are under a burning sun, and in the winter, the mercury reaches 38 degrees below zero." With the coming of the railroad, exhausting long journeys were no longer necessary and, more important to farmers, there was an economical way to haul stock and grain to market.[7]

Railroads brought something else in their wake. A nationwide promotional campaign by state and local agencies, newspapers, chambers of commerce, business people, and, above all, railroad companies brought the homestead boom to Montana. Personal testimonials, like that of a former Iowa farmer, became a popular promotional device: "I sold my land in Iowa for twice what I paid for land in Montana, and the Montana land yields twice what the Iowa land yielded." A leaflet issued by the Montana Department of Publicity for the Bureau of Agriculture, Labor, and Industry stressed the "salubrity" of the "healthful and exhilarating" climate and cited a report assuring readers that the "average temperature in Montana is about the same as in New York or Pennsylvania." The leaflet failed to mention the extremes of heat and cold that made up such an average and disingenuously described Montana winters as "capricious, but . . . warm, sunlit and inviting," with only an occasional "cold snap [that] adds vigor to the universal energy of the people." Overlooking entirely the winter of 1886–1887 that had devastated the Montana stock-raising industry, the state publication noted that "except upon the plains of the extreme eastern border of the state, the blizzard is unknown. . . . Great herds of cattle and flocks of sheep feed throughout the winter on every bench and plain, and these are given but little shelter, food or attention." Quoting another "expert," the author assured the reader, "It is doubtful if there is another state in the Union where the climate taken the year round is so delightful as that of Montana."[8]

Ben Kline (after 1901). Courtesy of Lewistown (Mont.) Public Library, Brenner Collection.

Such tactics attracted thousands of hopeful homesteaders. By 1919, Fergus County's population had reached over forty thousand. Lewistown also grew, becoming a distribution center for the region. Lewistown's population increased from less than eleven hundred in 1900 to three thousand by 1910, while numerous small agricultural towns sprang up in the surrounding country where only Métis and the occasional rancher had lived since 1879.[9]

MÉTIS HOMESTEADING

As the surge of Euro-American settlers reached central Montana, Spring Creek Métis families felt the impact of the homestead boom and the railroads. Land in the relatively well-watered Spring Creek drainage filled with settlers, and Métis families (especially young couples) had to move to less desirable land to the east and south. A number of families, particularly those who had secured homesteads before the boom, remained near Spring Creek, especially on its tributaries, Boyd and Breed creeks, where they had settled in 1879. Still others moved north to former hunting

TABLE 3
Spring Creek/Lewistown-Area Métis Families, *1900 Montana Census*

Township/Range
15/18 (Lewstown), 15/19 (East Boyd Creek), 16/19 (Ruby Gulch, Limekiln Canyon), 16/20 (Gilt Edge)

Family name ([followed by] wife's maiden name or resident daughter's married name)[1]	# persons	# families	Color or race	Occupation	Can read English	Can write English	Can speak English[3]	Home owned (O), rented (R), or tent (T)	Mixed Blood: Has this Indian any white blood (?)
Belgarde (Laverdure)[2]	3	1	In	1 laborer	1 y / 1 n	1 y / 1 n	2 y	O	½
Benneay (LaFountain)	3	1	W	1 farmer / 1 day laborer	1 y / 2 n	1 y / 2 n	3 y	O	
Berger (Gourneau LaFramboise Wilkie Kiplin Ouelllette)	34	5	In	4 laborers / 2 farmers / 2 farm laborers	25 y	25 y	27 y	O	½
					5 n	5 n	3 n		
Beujah?/Beauchamp?	5	1	In	1 day laborer	2 n	2 n	1 y / 1 n	T	¼
Daniaux (Dagneau/Daniels Beauchamp Laverdure)	6	2	In	1 farmer / 1 farm laborer	2 y / 2 n	2 y / 2 n	3 y / 1 n	1 R / 1 O	1: ?, 5: ½
Desy (Janeau)	3	1	W	1 day laborer	2 y	2 y	2 y	R	
Doney (LaFountain)	19	2	In	2 farmers / 1 farm laborer	3 n / 12 y	3 n / 12 y	2 n / 13 y	1 O / 1 R	1: 0, 4: ⅙ 1: ¼, 11: ¼, 2: ½

Dumont	3	1	In	1 teamster	1 y 1 n	1 y 1 n	1 y 1 n	1 O	¼
Faillant (Gardipee)	12	2	In	3 day laborers	2 y 3 n	2 y 3 n	4 y 1 n	T	1: 0, 6: ⅛, 5: ¼
Ferguson (Fleury)	5	1	In	2 farm laborers	2 y 3 n	1 y 3 n	2 y 2 n	1 R	5: ¼ 29: ¼
Fleury (Wilkie, Wells, Walker, Landry, Ferguson)	32	5	In	3 farm laborers 2 day laborers 2 farmers	6 y 12 n	6 y 12 n	13 y 5 n	5 O	1: ½ 1: ⅝ 1: ⅞
Gardipie (LaRocque, Doney)	38	7	In	2 laborers 3 farm laborers 2 day laborers 1 farmer 2 teamsters	9 y 11 n	9 y 11 n	16 y 4 n	2 O 1 R 4 T	4: 0, 6: 1/32, 1: 1/16 8: ⅛, 9: ¼, 7: ½, 3: ¾
Goulet	2	1	In	1 freighter	2 y	2 y	2 y	O	½
Johnson (LaTray)	6	1	W	1 day laborer	2 y 1 n	2 y 1 n	3 y	O	
Klein (St. Pierre, LaRocque)	9	1	In	1 farmer 2 freighters	5 y 4 n	5 y 4 n	9 y	O	½
Kozlowski (LaTray)	7	1	W	1 quartz miner	2 y 1 n	2 y 1 n	3 y	O	
LaFontaine (Wilkey)	2	1	In	1 wood chopper	2 n	2 n	2 y	O	½
LaFramboise	1	1	In	1 farm laborer	1 n	1 n	1 y	O	½
Langevin	8	1	In	1 farmer 3 farm laborers	7 y	6 y 1 n	7 y	O	1: ½, 7: ¾
LaPlante (Laveillé)	3	1	In	1 teamster	1 y 1 n	1 y 1 n	2 y	T	½

TABLE 3 (continued)
Spring Creek/Lewistown-Area Métis Families, *1900 Montana Census*

Township/Range
15/18 (Lewstown), 15/19 (East Boyd Creek), 16/19 (Ruby Gulch, Limekiln Canyon), 16/20 (Gilt Edge)

LaRoque (Klein)	10	2	In	1 farmer	1 y 3 n	1 y 3 n	4 y		3: ½, 2: ¼, 5: ½
LaTray	9	1	In	2 day laborers 1 washer-woman	5 y 2 n	5 y 2 n	5 y 2 n	O	½
Laveillé	1	1	In	1 day laborer	n	n	y	T	½
Laverdure (Janeau, Turcotte, Charette)	30	6	In	1 freighter 3 laborers 4 farm laborers 2 sheep herders	8 y 12 n	8 y 12 n	16 y 4 n	4 O 1 R 1 T	3: ¾, 15: ½, 11: ¼
Lefferts (LaTray)	6	1	W	1 quartz miner	1 y 1 n	1 y 1 n	2 y	R	
Mingelkoch (Wells)	3	1	W	1 saloon keeper	1 y	1 y	1 y	O	
Morase	9	2	W	2 limemen	6 y	6 y	6 y		
Morgan	8	1	In		1 y 1 n	1 y 1 n	2 y	R	1: ½, 7: ½
Ouellette	1	1	W	Housemaid	1 n	1 n	1 y		
Ouellette (Berger, Dumont, Frederick)	37	6	9 In	5 freighters 1 farmer 1 laborer	13 y 11 n	14 y 10 n	21 y 3 n	4 O	36: ½ 1: ?
Paul	8	2	In	1 freighter 1 lime burner	2 y 3 n	2 y 3 n	5 y	O	½
Pratt (Juneau, Laverdure)	8	1	W	1 farmer	4 y 1 n	4 y	4 y	O	

Rocheleau (Berger)	9	1	In	1 teamster	3 y 1 n	3 y 1 n	3 y 1 n	T	9: ½
Ross	8	1	In	1 freighter	2 y 2 n	2 y 2 n	3 y 1 n	O	½
Sharette/Charette	1	1	In	1 farm laborer	1 y	1 y	1 y	T	½
Spence (Sinclar)	5	1	In	1 teamster	1 y 2 n	1 y 2 n	3 y	T	½
Swan (Berger)	2	1	W	1 day laborer	1 y 1 n	1 y 1 n	2 y	T	
Sweney	3	1	1 W 2 In	1 farmer	1 y 1 n	2 n	2 y	O	1: ½, 1: ½
Tivies	2	1	In		1 y	1 y	1 y		½
Tivies	1	1	W	Cook	1 n	1 n	1 y		
Turcotte	3	1	In	1 laborer	2 y	2 y	2 y		½
Unlisted names	13		In	6 "peddlar[s] of Indian trinkets"	9 n	9 n	2 y 7 n	3 T	0
Wells	38	6	In	2 freighters 1 day laborer 2 laborers 2 farm laborers 1 farmer	13 y 11 n	13 y 11 n	20 y 4 n	3 O 3 R	½

1. Column headings are as found in original census document.
2. Spellings of names are approximations of those recorded by the census enumerator. In some cases they are difficult to read.
3. That the number of persons reading, writing, or speaking English does not equal the number of individuals is explained by the fact that the enumerator did not list children not yet in school under the English proficiency categories.

? Census enumerator's handwriting illegible
In Indian
n no
W White
y yes

TABLE 4
Members of the Spring Creek Métis Families Listed as White in *1900 Montana Census*

Family name maiden name or resident daughter's married name)[1]	# persons	# families	Color or race	Occupation	Can read English	Can write English	Can speak English	Home owned (O), rented (R), or tent (T)
Benneay[2] (LaFountain)	3	1	3 W	1 farmer 1 day laborer	1 y 2 n	1 y 2 n	3 y	O
Desy (Juneau)	3	1	3 W	1 day laborer	2 y[3]	2 y	2 y	R
Johnson (LaTray)	6	1	6 W	1 day laborer	2 y 1 n	2 y 1 n	3 y	O
Kozlowski (LaTray)	7	1	7 W	1 quartz miner	2 y 1 n	2 y 1 n	3 y	O
Laverdure (A Métis minor living with Juneau)	1	1	1 W		1 y	1 y	1 y	
Lefferts (LaTray)	6	1	6 W	1 quartz miner	1 y 1 n	1 y 1 n	2 y	R
Mingelkoch (Wells [Métis])	3	1	3 W	1 saloon keeper	2 y	2 y	2 y	O
Ouellette	1	1	W	Housemaid	1 n	1 n	1 y	
Pratt (wife and children, Juneau)[4]	8	1	8 W	1 farmer	4 y 1 n	4 y	4 y	O

Sheilds (wife and children, Morase)[5]	8	2	8 W	1 dealer, wood ? 2 limemen[6]
Swan (Berger)	2	1	2 W	1 day laborer	1 y 1 n	1 y 1 n	2 y
Tivies	1	1	W	Cook	1 n	1 n	1 y	T

1. Column headings are as found in original census document. A family is defined as a person or group of persons living together in a dwelling.
2. Spellings of names are approximations of those recorded by the census enumerator. In some cases they are difficult to read.
3. That the number of persons reading, writing, or speaking English does not equal the number of individuals is explained by the fact that the enumerator did not list children not yet in school under the English proficiency categories.
4. Virginia Laverdure Janeaux (Juneau) married Peter Pratt, a non-Métis farmer, after the death of Francis Janeaux, her first husband. She, five of her children, and a niece lived with him and are designated as white in the schedule.
5. Margaret Daignon Morase married Peter R. Sheilds, a non-Métis farmer, after the death of Paul Morase. She and six of her children lived with him and are designated as white in the schedule.
6. Limemen worked at the lime kilns in Limekiln Canyon north of Lewistown.

lands in north-central Montana and southern Saskatchewan. Although most homesteaded and several took up Turtle Mountain Chippewa allotments or received Canadian half-breed scrip, few had the economic resources necessary for profitable large-scale agricultural operations. A majority depended wholly or in part on the wage labor of at least some family members. While Spring Creek band members took advantage of a variety of employment opportunities, they continued to maintain kin-based enclaves within roughly a fifty-mile radius north and east of Lewistown.

The 1900 census indicates the variety of options pursued by Métis families at the turn of the century (see table 3). The census enumerator found at least sixty-seven Métis families in the Lewistown vicinity and to the east. As was often the case in previous censuses, enumerators missed a number of families. Still, the information collected gives an indication of the family groups who remained in the area and of their occupations.[10]

Of the Métis families who continued to live close to Lewistown in 1900 (from Lewistown to nine miles east), thirty males were laborers, twenty-three were farmhands, sixteen were farmers (three of whom were Euro-American men married to Métis), and thirteen were freighters. Fewer males engaged in other kinds of wage labor and were teamsters, limemen, or sheepherders. The enumerator listed only one person as woodchopper, a job traditionally held by Métis, but these workers (possibly quite a few) may have been in the mountains securing firewood at the time. Non-Métis married to Métis women included three laborers and a saloon owner. Few Métis women worked outside the home or farm. Of those who did, one was a washerwoman, one a housemaid in a "white" home, and one a cook in a "white" household. Like Euro-American women, the enumerator listed virtually all Métis women as housekeepers regardless of their actual activities.[11]

Though the census data must be examined with care, it suggests modest prosperity—a view supported by the number of families owning homes (thirty-seven). An additional eleven families rented homes, and sixteen lived in tents. The tent figure was probably higher in the summer months (the enumerator visited in June and July) and among those working in or near the gold-boom town of Giltedge, where housing was in short supply and tents common for all residents. In a short period of time, the Spring Creek Métis families had adapted to a dramatically changed economy that was now totally dominated by Euro-American newcomers.

By 1900, the families had found a variety of jobs and continued, as they had in the late 1880s and 1890s, to own small farming and livestock operations.

As economic conditions required, groups of related families moved east of Lewistown, establishing Métis enclaves where they settled. By the 1910s, land available under the Homestead Act could no longer be found close to Spring Creek, which encouraged Métis families to apply for homestead land or Turtle Mountain allotments farther east, in the Giltedge, Roy, Flat Willow, and Winnett area (over fifty miles east of Lewistown).

Table 5 shows the location of Métis homesteads and Indian allotments in Fergus County. The last column of the table indicates that most applicants from the original Spring Creek families "proved up" on their homesteads and received a deed (Final Certificate, FC) or paid cash for their land before meeting all of the Homestead Act requirements (Commuted to Cash, CC). A number of applicants voluntarily relinquished their homesteads, some taking up homestead land elsewhere in the county. Of those who did not prove up and did not receive a deed, most were individuals who applied for Turtle Mountain allotments and were rejected as ineligible. Some who were rejected, such as Elizabeth Berger Swan and Mary Ernestine Wells Fleury, took up homestead land elsewhere under the Homestead Act provisions. But the widespread ineligibility for Turtle Mountain allotments, in addition to the coming depression, would be a major factor in a redistribution of Métis families that would take place in the 1920s and 1930s.

As in 1879, Métis families in the early 1900s clustered in a patchwork of loose, kinship-defined enclaves. Again, they preferred space around themselves, access to streams and suitable garden land, and relatives living within a few miles. The experiences of several families illustrate variations on a theme of movement within geographical areas bound by kinship networks. One group of families relocated northeast of Lewistown, forming an enclave in the Roy area. Between 1901 and 1916 the related, and still intermarrying, LaFountain, Doney, LaRocque, Davis, and Gardipee families applied for homestead land or Turtle Mountain Chippewa allotments here. They engaged in wage labor for ranchers, stage lines, and livery stables and ran their own small farms and livestock operations. Sarah LaRocque, born in 1904 and still living in Roy, remembers the early years there as happy times with many traditional Métis celebrations among the families.[12]

Other families moved farther from Spring Creek, including a few who joined relatives in Canada. John and Philomene Ouellette Wells, for example, traveled to Saskatchewan, later returned to north-central Montana, and eventually moved back again to Saskatchewan. The Wells family had arrived on Spring Creek with the original families in 1879. Its members had homesteaded land on the outskirts of Lewistown, built a log house,

TABLE 5
Métis Homestead Applications, 1900–1915
(within present-day boundaries of Fergus Co.)

Family Name	Section	Type	Disposition
Township 14N/Range 18E			
Fleury, Dolar[1]	20	HE	CC
Wells, Pete	20		Can
Township 18N/Range 18E			
LaTray, Joseph	8	Hd	Hd
LaTray, Joseph	8	Hd	Hd
Township 15N/Range 19E (East Boyd Creek)			
Lafontaine, B.	9	HE	FC
Berger, Fran.	17	HE	FC
Kline, Ben	25	Coal	
Wells, Rose	34	HE	CC
Laverdure, Louis	35	Hd	FC
Township 16N/Range 19E (Ruby Gulch, Limekiln Canyon)			
Swan, Joseph, Jr.	28	HE	FC
Township 17N/Range 19E			
Wilke, Wm.	6	HE	FC
Township 18N/Range 19E			
Paul, Martin	11	Hd	FC
Township 14N/Range 20E			
Daniels, F. J.	25	Hd	FC
Township 15N/Range 20E (Cheadle area)			
Ouellette, Sarah	2	Hd	Rel
Charette, Isacc	11	HE	Can
Ouellette, J. M.	12		Rel
Wells, Rosa	18	DLE	Rel
Fleury, Eliz.	18		Can
Lafontain, Jos.	21	HE	H
Lafontain, Jos.	22	DLE	
Lafontain, Jos.	26	DLE	
Laverdure, Th.	32	Hd	FC
Township 16N/Range 20E (Giltedge area)			
Gardipee, Paul	12	HE	Rel
Latray, Mose	29		Rel
LaTray, Louis	29	Hd	FC
Township 17N/Range 20E			
Larocque, Joseph	34	Hd	FC

Family Name	Section	Type	Disposition
Township 18N/Range 20E (Armells area)			
Doney, Mary	18	IA	Rej
Fayant, Abe.	18	IA	Rej
Doney, Stephen	20	IA	Rej
Township 13N/Range 21E			
Fleury, Va.	13	Hd	CC
Township 14N/Range 21E (Forest Grove area)			
Berger, Justine	10	HE	FC
Daniels, Frank	19	Hd	FC
Township 15N/Range 21E			
LaTray, Mose	2	DLE	Rel
LaTray, Mose	9	DLE	FC
LaTray, Louis	11	DLE	Can
LaTray, Janice	12	Hd	FC
Berger, Vitaline?	25		Rel
Berger, Vitaline	25	IA	Rej
Laverdure, Fred	25	IA	Rej
Laverdure, Fred	25	Hd	FC
Turcotte, James	35	Hd	FC
Berger, Betsey	35	IA	Rej
Berger, Martin	35	IA	Rej
LaTray, James	35	Hd	FC
Township 16N/Range 21E (Fort Maginnis area)			
LaRock, Raphael	7	Hd	FC
Doney, Sarah	18	Hd	CC
Berger, Wm.	20	Hd	Rej
LaTray, Mose	30	HE	FC
Lefferts, Wm.	33		
Charette, Jos.	34	DLE	FC
Township 17N/Range 21E			
LaRocque, Ch.	1	HE	Am
LaRocque, Bernie	1	IA	Rej
Davis, Owen	1	IA	Rej
Doney, Pete	1	Hd	
Gardipee, Mary	2	Hd	FC
LaRoqne, Archie	2	IA	Rej
LaRocque, Wm.	2	IA	Rej
Gardipie, Gabe.	2		Can
LaRoqne, Wm.	3	IA	
Fayant, Julia	4	IA	Rej
Fayant, Jos. H.	4	IA	Rej
Fayant, Angela	4	IA	Rej

TABLE 5 (continued)
Métis Homestead Applications, 1900–1915
(within present-day boundaries of Fergus Co.)

Family Name	Section	Type	Disposition
Fayant, Blanch	9	IA	Rej
Fayant, J. H.	10	IA	Rej
Guardipie, J. B.	11	Hd	FC
Gardipi, J. B.	11	Hd	FC
Gardipi, M. M.	11	Hd	FC
Gardipee, Gabe.	12	Hd	
LaRoque, Leo	12	IA	Rej
LaRocque, Ch.	12	IA	Rej
LaRoque, Ch.	12	Hd	Rel
Davis, Owen J.	12	Hd	FC
LaRocque, Sam.	13	IA	Rej
Gardipi, Gabe.	13	Hd	FC
Laroque, Raph.	14	Hd	FC
Laroque, Jos.	14	IA	Rej
Larocke, Ambr.	14	Hd	FC
Swan, Robert	23	HE	Rej
Gardipee, John	23	HE	Rel
Gardipee, John	24		Rel
Township 18N/Range 21E			
Lafonten, Ezie	13	HE	Rel
Doney, Sarah	13	Hd	FC
Doney, John A.	13	HE	Am
Lafontain, Al.	23	IA	TM
Doney, David	23	DLE	Rel
Doney, John R.	24	HE	Am
Doney, David	24	Hd	Rel
Doney, Jos. Fr.	25	HE	FC
Lafontain, Ezear	25	IA	TM
Lafontain, Ezear	26	IA	TM
Lafontain, Maxim	26	IA	TM
Lafontain, Collin	26	IA	TM
Lafontain, Anthony	26	IA	TM
Lafontain, Ed.	27	IA	TM
Fayant, Florence	33		Rej
Lafontain, Martin	33		Rej
Swan, Rebecca	35	IA	Rej
Swan, H. M.	35		Rej
Swan, W. J.	35		Rej
Swan, Eliz.	35		Rej

Family Name	Section	Type	Disposition
Township 19N/Range 21E			
Doney, Thomas	5	IA	Rej
Doney, Clemence	5	IA	Rej
Doney, Madeline	5	IA	Rej
Township 12N/Range 22E			
Laframboise, Justine (Paul)	1	IA	Rej
Rocheleau, Cath.	1	IA	Rej
LaFramboise, Isadore	1		FC
Berger, Teddy	12	IA	Rej
Wells, Joe	13	Hd	Rel
Township 13N/Range 22E			
Laverdure, Henry	12	IA	Rej
Laveradure, Sophia	12	IA	Rej
Berger, Gladys	22	IA	Rej
Quelitte, Elizzy Berger	23	IA	Rej
Quelette, Rob.	23	IA	Rej
Fleury, Ernestine	23	IA	Rej
Quellette, Robert F.?	23	Hd	FC
Fleury, Ernestine	23	Hd	FC
Berger, Judith	25	Hd	FC
LaFramboise, Isidore	25	HE	FC
Berger, Louis?	26	Hd	FC
Berger, Betsey	26	Hd	Rel
Fleury, Mary E.	26	Hd	Rel
Berger, Arthur	26	Hd	FC
Wells, Edward	26	Hd	FC
Fleury, Ernestine	26	Hd	FC
Berger, Gladys	27	HE	FC
Berger, Arthur	27	Hd	FC
Wells, Edward	28	Hd	Am
Wells, Joe	28	Hd	FC
Township 14N/Range 22E			
Paul, Mary	11	IA	Rej
Ouellette, J. M.	21	Hd	Can
Laverdure, Sarah			Rel
Township 16N/Range 22E			
LaTray, Rosellie	21	DL	Rel
Township 17N/Range 22E (Black Butte area)			
Doney, Joe	5	Hd	Rel
Davis, Simon	5	IA	Rej

TABLE 5 (continued)
Métis Homestead Applications, 1900–1915
(within present-day boundaries of Fergus Co.)

Family Name	Section	Type	Disposition
Davis, Owen	6	Hd	FC
Davis, Alexzina	6	IA	Rej
Gardepi, Vital.	6	Hd	Rel
Gardepi, Gabe.	7	Hd	Am
Fayant, Ellen	7	Hd	Rel
LaRocque, John	7	Hd	Rel
Township 18N/Range 22E (Roy area)			
Doney, James	18	Hd	FC
Champagne, M. P.	19	IA	TM
Doney, Fred	19	Hd	Rel
LaRoque, M. A.	20	IA	Rej
Champagne, Flor.	24	IA	TM
Champagne, Flor.	24	IA	TM
Champagne, Rosalie	26	IA	TM
Lafountaine, Elzear	26	IA	
Champagne, Philomene	27	IA	TM
Champagne, Fred.	27	IA	Rej
LaRoque, Angela	29	IA	Rel
Lafontaine, Emma	29	IA	TM
Lafontaine, Jn.	29	IA	TM
Lafontain, Adel	30	IA	Rel
Lafontain, Jos.	30	IA	Rel
Champagne, J. F.	30	IA	TM
Lafontaine, Mary Rose	30	IA	TM
LaRoque, L. T.	31	IA	Rej
LaRoque, Eli	31	IA	Rej
Laroque, Joseph	31	DL	FC
Township 13N/Range 23E			
Daigneau, Lizie	31	HE	FC
Township 14N/Range 23E			
Scharette, Th.	18	Hd	FC
Laverdure, Lina	18	IA	Rej
Laverdure, Alb.	19	IA	Rej
Laverdure, Ralph	20	HE	FC
Charette, John	20	Hd	CC
Paul, Elzear	23		HC
Daniels, Peter	23	Hd	CC
Dagneau, Fr.	23	HE	Rel
Lavallée, Rosa	23	HE	CC

Family Name	Section	Type	Disposition
Paul, Rose	23	DL	Rel
Paul, Rose	23	IA	Rej
Paul, William	25	IA	Rej
Paul, Anna	25	IA	Rej
Laverdure, Marg.	27	HE	CC
Laverdure, Barney	31	HE	Rel
Laverdure, Sarah	31	IA	Rej
Berger, Filamine	31	Hd	FC
Ouelette, Frank	32	HE	FC

Township 15N/Range 23E (Grass Range area)

Berger, Patrick	5	Hd	

Township 13N/Range 24E (Eastern edge of Fergus Co.)

LaFramboise, Isadore	34	DL	FC

Township 14N/Range 24E

Charette, Louie	18	Hd	CC
Paul, Fred	18	IA	Rej
Paul, Walter	18	IA	Rej
Paul, Rose	18		FC
Charbonneau, George J.	18	Hd	

Township 15N/Range 24E

Laverdure, Natalie	9	IA	Rej
Laverdure, Agatha	9	IA	Rej
Laverdure, Agatha C.	29	IA	Rej
Laverdure, Ida	29	IA	Rej

Township 16N/Range 24E

Berger, Moses	14	DL	Rel
Berger, David	14	Hd	FC
Berger, Moses	14	Hd	FC
Berge, Mose	15	Hd	FC
LeTray, Frank	15		FC
Turcotte, Maggie	20	IA	Rej
Turcotte, Jos.	20	IA	Rej
Laytray, Joe	21	Hd	Rel
Berger, Moses	21	IA	Rej
Klyne, Gabriel	27	IA	Rej
Berger, John H.	27	IA	Rej
Kemph, Jennette	27	IA	Rej
Berger, Laura A	28	IA	Rej
Kemph, Carrie	28	IA	Rej
Wells, Clara	29	IA	Rej
Wells, Anthony	29	IA	Rej
Kemph, Teddy W.	33	IA	Rej

TABLE 5 (continued)
Métis Homestead Applications, 1900–1915
(within present-day boundaries of Fergus Co.)

Family Name	Section	Type	Disposition
Berger, Wm.	33	Hd	Rel
Berger, Raymond	34	IA	Rej
Lafontain, Eliza	35	IA	Rej
Berger, Mary	35	IA	Rej
Township 17N/Range 24E			
Paul, Wm. J.	13	Hd	FC
Paul, Lillian	13	DL	Rel
Paul, Wm J.	13	HE	FC
Wilkie, Wm.	14	DL	FC
Fontain, Frank	19	Hd	FC
Wilkie, Blanch	23	DL	FC

1. Spellings are as found in the Bureau of Land Management documents.

Am	Amended
Can	Cancelled. "Land actions cancelled are done by the Government for failure to comply with law or regulation."
CC	Commuted to cash. A cash payment made to receive patent.
CE	"A cash sale entry is involved. The notation often refers to the sale of public land under the provisions of the Land Law of 1820; however, it was sometimes used for Preemption Act of 1841, commuted Homestead Act and other entries."
Coal	Coal Withhold. "Refers to the sale of land under Coal Lands Sale Act of 1873."
DL/DLE	Denotes an entry made under the provisions of the Desert Land Act of 1877 as amended.
FC	"This denoted the issuance of a final certificate by local land office officials. The document implies that an entry person has proved up under provisions of the law and is entitled to a patent."
G	"Division of the General Land Office [that] handled actions regarding preemption laws, townsite applications, and the sale of Indian lands."
H	Case closed by "H" ("H" was the General Land Office division, known as the "Contest Divison," that adjudicated agricultural entry contest actions).
Hd	See HE
HE	Homestead Act Entry. "Can denote the Homestead Act of 1862, Reclamation Act of 1902, Forest Homestead Act of 1906, Enlarged Homestead of 1909, and sometimes the Stock-Raising Homestead Act of 1916."
IA	Indian Allotment as provided for in the Dawes Act of 1887.
Pre	"The land is being taken under the provision of the Preemption Act of 1841."
Rel	Relinquishment. "Entry person voluntarily gives up his/her right to the entry in question."
Rej	Rejected
TM	Turtle Mountain Band

Key source: Bureau of Land Management, District Office, Billings, Mont.

For full names, year of entry, and year of disposition, see Martha Harroun Foster, "We Know," 495–508.

MÉTIS, INDIAN, AND WHITE   199

and raised horses. With his brother Daniel, John Wells supplemented his income by hauling freight, but, when the railroad reached Lewistown, he realized that the heyday of Métis freighting was over. By 1901 Philomene, John's brother, Edward, and Edward's grandson and daughter had applied for Canadian half-breed scrip. They hoped to farm and raise livestock near relatives in Saskatchewan. The death of John's stock from "swamp fever" brought the family back to Montana, but John, Philomene, and their younger children returned to Canada in 1918. Today, descendants of John and his siblings can be found near other relatives on the Milk River, Saskatchewan River, and Spring Creek drainages as well as in the towns between.[13]

Some Wells relatives remained closer to Spring Creek, including John Wells's niece, Mary Ernestine Wells Fleury. (Her efforts to raise a large family after the death of her husband were recounted in the previous chapter.) Descendants of Mary Ernestine continue to live in Lewistown today. In 1979 her great-granddaughter, Treena LaFountain, with her husband, Robert, and other descendants of the Spring Creek families celebrated Métis culture and history in the Lewistown Métis Centennial Celebration, an event that has been held annually to this day.

Though many Spring Creek families moved within the rough triangle formed by the Milk River on the north and Lewistown on the south, representatives of almost all of the original families stayed within thirty miles of Spring Creek. Several remained near where they originally settled in 1879. They continued to run small farms and livestock operations until economic reversals between 1919 and 1925 necessitated a new set of adaptive measures for many. After 1919, most Métis, like over 50 percent of Montana farmers, suffered foreclosure or voluntarily gave up their land in a nationwide agricultural depression that hit Montana particularly hard. Between 1919 and 1925 grain and cattle prices plummeted, and the value of Montana farmland fell by 50 percent. As a result, Montana had the highest rate of farm bankruptcy in the United States, with twenty thousand mortgages foreclosed. One-hundred-and-sixty-acre parcels that could not support a family in the best of times provided next to nothing during the following years of drought. Many who were not actually foreclosed upon saw the handwriting on the wall and relinquished their homesteads voluntarily before the inevitable occurred.[14]

For the Métis, there were additional obstacles to holding on to their homesteads and allotments in hard times. Problems with the English language made them especially vulnerable to speculators and quasi-legal maneuvering. Conrad Anderson, a rancher in Roy, recalled an instance in which his neighbor, Joe LaFountain, was apparently cheated out of his land. Joe "farmed quite extensively and with cattle did pretty well, for a time," Anderson wrote. However, "Joe could not read or write and because of that a couple of 'Slick Sharks,' . . . through some shady deal, had Joe foreclosed on and took his cattle and farm equipment." According to Anderson, Joe retaliated, but to no avail. "A few days later one of these men got the scare of this life. In a fight . . . in Roy, Joe knocked the fellow down where upon he [Joe] grabbed an ax and pretending to bash his [the "shark's"] head in, made him beg for his life." The tale became a legend among the Roy homesteaders, but did nothing to restore LaFountain's land, cattle, and equipment.[15]

Victimized by "shady deals" or, like over half of all homesteaders, simply by hard economic times, most Métis lost their homesteads after 1919. Métis families differed, not in their loss, but in that, after losing their farms, they tended to stay in Montana and not leave for Washington, Oregon, or California, as did sixty thousand Euro-American Montana farmers. After 1919 Spring Creek Métis families followed several strategies, all within familiar geographical locations connected and interwoven by kinship networks. They found work in the Lewistown/Roy/Flat Willow areas, they moved north to the Zortman region south of Fort Belknap Reservation, or they joined relatives farther north, along the Milk River. As the Spring Creek families both spread north and maintained their Lewistown enclave, they consolidated bonds with Milk River relatives. The Milk River–Spring Creek kinship network became one of the two principal Métis kinship systems in Montana (the second included the Front Range communities).[16]

The families who moved north retained ties to the area. Some returned to Lewistown, occasionally after a generation of absence. Such a family was that of Ken Doney, whose parents moved to the Landusky area (south of Fort Belknap Reservation), where he was born in 1933. Ken, grandson of Gregory Doney and great-grandson of Lalley Doney (both brothers of original Lewistown settlers), moved to Lewistown in the 1960s, and became the town's first Métis sheriff in 1987. The experience of Lewistown's first Métis mayor, Robert LaFountain (grandson of original settler, Ezear (Elzear) "Joe" LaFountain), provides another variation on this theme of regional, kinship-bound mobility. Robert LaFountain's father, Albert, was born and first homesteaded in the Roy area before eventually moving to Lewistown.[17]

As was common throughout Métis history, movement within a kinship-bound region characterized the decades after 1900. For the Spring Creek families, this kinship-bound area did not change significantly from that of 1879: the rough inverted triangle defined on its northern base by the Milk River and on its southern point by Lewistown.

SOCIAL REALITIES, 1900–1916

The 1900 census, which provides much useful employment information, also documents changing attitudes toward Montana Métis. Consistent with the tendency to ascribe an Indian identity to Métis noted in the previous chapter, most Métis families are found in the Indian population schedule, not in the general population schedule. The race designation reflects the enumerator's opinion, since it was his responsibility to make the decision as to a person's "color" rather than a family representative or the individuals themselves. In Fergus County the enumerators were invariably Euro-American males.[18]

The few Métis families not recorded by the enumerator as Indian were either headed by a white male or were Métis working in a white household. One exception was the Métis couple John and Elizabeth Swan, who, for reasons that cannot be clearly determined, were also listed as white. The enumerator listed a Métis cook (Tivies) and a Métis housemaid (Ouellette), who were working in white homes, as white even though he recorded others of their family name (and almost certainly their relatives) as Indian. Of the Métis families headed by white males, two were those of Virginia Laverdure Janeaux Pratt and Margaret Daignon (Daniels/Daigneau) Morase Sheilds. These Métis widows and their resident children by their previous marriages are listed as white. Although, as noted earlier, their deceased husbands, traders Francis Janeaux and Paul Morase, were probably Métis, the Lewistown Euro-American community regarded them as French Canadian. Evelyn Janeaux, daughter of Francis and Virginia Janeaux, married Irene Desy, who, although possibly Métis, was a relatively prosperous farmer and also regarded as French Canadian. Additionally, at least one LaFountain woman, three LaTray women, and one Wells married Euro-Americans before 1900, and they and their children, if any, are listed as white.

The white identity of John and Elizabeth Swan is both interesting and confusing, as both were Métis. Elizabeth, who publicly identified herself as being of mixed descent, applied for a Turtle Mountain Chippewa allotment (her request was denied) and later became active as a Little Shell Chippewa spokesperson. The enumerator possibly made his assumption of white identity based on the couple's facility with the English language and their Euro-American lifestyle (which both adopted during school years at St. Peter's Mission). The fact that they were living in a tent probably did not signal an Indian lifestyle to the enumerator, as it was a common practice among Euro-Americans in the boom years of Giltedge, a gold town.[19]

Gender also profoundly influenced ascribed identity, and, at first glance, it would appear that if the enumerator determined the head of family to be white, then the rest of the family would automatically be listed as white. But this was not universally true. The enumerator recorded as Indian the family of Henry Sweney, a white Euro-American born in Vermont. He also listed as Indian the Métis children of George Morgan, a deceased non-Métis from Pennsylvania, and his wife, Frances Berger Morgan (daughter of Spring Creek leader, Pierre Berger). Perhaps the lack of a white male actually present in the household influenced his decision in this case. The evidence indicates that a white identity was more complex than simply belonging to a family headed by a white male. Still, it is a powerful indicator, since nine of the ten Métis families designated as white (except the Swans) were headed by non-Métis.

As the enumerator's assumptions about Métis identity show, although Métis and Euro-American families interacted, worked together, and lived as neighbors, Euro-Americans viewed the Métis as "different," often as Indian. The Métis also saw themselves as distinct, but distinct from both Indians and Euro-Americans. Memoirs, interviews, and other documentation from early in the century show that Métis families continued to celebrate their difference by retaining traditional Métis customs and lifeways. Regardless of what they called themselves or were labeled by their neighbors, their strong kinship networks and unique culture persisted.

Descendants of the original Spring Creek families, Sarah LaRocque of Roy and Marie Ehlert of Lewistown (great-granddaughter of Elizabeth Berger Swan) both remember traditional Métis celebrations being held regularly until World War II. Sarah (born in 1904) remembers her parents holding New Year's dinners and dances in the Roy house where she still lived until recently. Starting at Christmas, her neighbors and relatives moved from house to house, eating at each place. When evening came they removed the furniture from one or two rooms of the house and danced "jigs" and "quadrilles" all night to the music of a fiddler. A favorite, as it had been for decades (and still is), was the "Red River Jig." The big celebration came on New Year's Day, with traditional foods served all day and dancing all night. Howard Paul, whose grandparents lived outside of

Grass Range (and about forty miles east of Lewistown), remembers that when he was about six years old (probably in 1919) his family traveled to the Desy ranch near Lewistown for New Year's celebrations that lasted from after Christmas until after New Year's Day. Art LaPier, a well-known fiddler who was born in 1918, played in Lewistown many times. His stories of these days reflect the enthusiasm with which the Métis celebrated and danced. "The only time my grandmother would dance was New Year's," he remembered. "She was crippled all her life—she had two canes. But she'd get two or three drinks of that wine or whatever it was and she'd get out there and jig with no canes. She and my grandfather wore moccasins. He jigged backwards, I'll tell you, the old timers could jig." Participants' recollections of these events—of the music, dances, food, and enthusiasm—are much like those of the 1880s and earlier.[20]

Descendants of the Spring Creek families also tell of their mothers and grandmothers preparing traditional medicines and foods. Sarah LaRocque remembers her mother and the neighboring Doneys using traditional remedies, which the women made from local plants. As noted in the previous chapter, Treena LaFountain reported that her great-grandmother, Mary Ernestine Wells Fleury, was known as a healer and used traditional Métis remedies. Marie Ehlert has quite vivid memories of traditional medications. As children, they dreaded getting sick because their mother or grandmother would rub the afflicted person's chest with terrible-smelling goose grease, a favorite Métis remedy. Marie's grandmother, like Mary Ernestine Wells Fleury and her daughter, also prepared traditional foods, including pemmican, "bullet," or *le boulet/les boulettes* (a form of meatballs), *rubbaboo* (rabbit, sage hen, or duck stew), *la galet* (bannock bread), and a tallow pudding called "son of a bitch in a sack." Chokecherry syrup was a favorite, and women used chokecherries and Juneberries in their pemmican. Mary LaMare Johnson, who grew up early in the century near the Milk River town of Malta, described her family's preparation of pemmican.

> You mash up your dry meat real fine and then you mixed dry cherries [chokecherries] in there. You had to mash it together and put sugar in there—quite a bit of sugar, and you put melted shortening in it. Mix it real good and then you pound real good—pounded and let it set till it got real hard. . . . Then when it was ready to eat you just kind of broke it up in chunks.

Métis women continue to prepare these foods for celebrations and rounds of visiting today.[21]

Clothing, for the older generation, also remained distinctive. Gregory Doney and Mary Ernestine Wells Fleury, for example, wore traditional Métis clothing well into the twentieth century. Mary Ernestine's descendants remember her always wearing a long dark dress, gray shawl, and large cross until her death, in 1952. For many of those years she also wore moccasins. Walt Coburn, who ranched south of Fort Belknap, remembered Gregory Doney wearing brightly quilled moccasins and "a gay colored Hudson's Bay voyageur sash knotted around his middle . . . [with] the long fringes swinging."[22]

Most members of the Spring Creek families spoke some English; nevertheless, what primarily set them apart was language. According to the 1900 census, 224 Métis living in the Lewistown vicinity spoke English, whereas thirty-five did not. It is no coincidence that all members of the Métis families listed as white spoke English. Yet many families, whether they knew English or not, still used the "old language." Furthermore, their English was often heavily accented and distinguished by a non-English sentence structure. Longtime resident Walt Coburn recalled that the Métis families south of Fort Belknap in the 1920s and 1930s, including former Spring Creek families such as the Doneys, "spoke a strangely blended mixture of Cree and French and cow-country American." This blend set the Métis apart and sometimes made them an object of ridicule. As noted earlier, popular central-Montana cowboy Teddy Blue Abbott made good-natured fun, in the harsh Montana style, of "those French breeds'" use of English. John Moran, Mose LaTreille (LaTray), and Joe Doney (the later two listed as English speakers in the 1900 census) all suffered Abbott's humor.[23]

The Catholic church continued to be a center of the Spring Creek families' lives. Those who lived close enough continued to attend St. Leo's Catholic Church, as they had since its creation. Even so, they remained distinct and often apart in church. Helen Chandler, an early Lewistown resident, remembered that in 1900 "there were a lot of half-breeds" at church (St. Leo's). "In fact, half of one side of the church was filled with half-breeds." When local historian Anna Zellick asked Chandler, "And you didn't socialize much with these people, did you?" Chandler answered, "No, except in Sunday school." That the Métis sat apart from the rest of the congregation was confirmed by Lewistown native Sue Eastman, who remembered that as late as the 1930s the Métis families sat together—by then in the back of the church. Accentuating their physical separation were concepts of proper church attire. While Euro-American women wore colorful clothing and covered their heads with bright scarves and fashionable hats, the Métis women continued to wear long black dresses and to cover their heads with dark shawls.[24]

It is unclear whether the tendency of Métis families to remain apart in church was their choice or due to Euro-American unwillingness to socialize with them. But regardless of their feelings about their fellow parishioners, the Métis continued to attend church, and the more prosperous families contributed financially to church upkeep. Contribution lists for the year 1910 include two members of the Berger family (the original Spring Creek band leaders), the widow and the daughter-in-law of former Spring Creek band trader Francis Janeaux, the widow of trader Paul Morase, and former trader Ben Kline. These are members of the relatively affluent Spring Creek families, and ones that continued to live in or very near Lewistown. They are also individuals who were more likely to be listed as white in the 1900 census. In addition to Swans, LaTrays, and Gardipees, these same families contributed throughout the 1910s and early 1920s.[25]

St. Leo's church records provide a glimpse into other social relationships. When an individual was baptized, usually as an infant, the parents selected two sponsors to serve as godparents for the child. The parish baptismal records show that Métis families who stayed in the Lewistown area invariably selected other Métis for these positions. Since Métis couples often had large families, and each child usually had different sponsors, the baptismal records give a good indication of the ties that the family wished to reinforce.

Recent literature suggests that Native fur-trade women (Indian and Métis) used godparenting as a tool to extend their kinship networks and to enlarge family alliances, helping to consolidate their trade relationships and ensure their family's prosperity. This practice continued in the Lewistown fur-trade families of Janeaux and Morase. But with the exception of the trader families, most Spring Creek band women who married Euro-Americans between 1900 and 1916 appear to have followed a different strategy. They used godparenting not to extend their kinship alliances outward, but to reaffirm existing Métis networks. Now surrounded and outnumbered by a large, socially dominate Euro-American society, the Métis intermarried with their new neighbors, as they had often done throughout their history. But they used fictive kin arrangements, such as godparenting, to cement existing Métis kinship networks at the same time that they introduced new members into their community.[26]

Two patterns emerged. In one case, trader families tended to use godparenting to extend and consolidate kinship ties to the Euro-American community. For example, Evelyn Janeaux Desy (daughter of trader Francis Janeaux) and her husband, Irene Desy, (a rancher who self-identified as French Canadian), twice asked non-Métis to sponsor their children. Former trader and Lewistown businessman Paul Morase and his wife, Margaret Daigneau (Daniels/Daignon), selected the Crowleys, prosperous non-Métis business people. In contrast, most Métis selected other Métis as godparents. The Berger, Doney, Daigneau/Daniels, Fleury, Laverdure, LaTray, Ouellette, Ross, Swan, and Turcotte families always listed Métis sponsors (with the exceptions of non-Métis married to Métis relatives, and of the parish priests, who were sometimes asked to be godparents). The remaining Métis families listed only an occasional non-Métis as a sponsor. Even among Métis married to Euro-Americans, an overwhelming number of nontrader families selected Métis godparents, thus reinforcing their Métis kinship ties.[27]

An increase in non-Métis sponsors might be expected in the younger generation, which began to intermarry with Euro-Americans at a greater rate and, presumably, became more involved with the Euro-American community. However, the appearance of non-Métis sponsors did not occur along generational lines, but along occupational ones. The families of former traders, who also tended to become Lewistown business people, more often included their non-Métis associates and neighbors as sponsors. The nontrader families continued to select Métis sponsors for their children.[28]

Like godparenting relationships, the majority of marriages continued to be between Métis from 1900 to 1916. Intermarriage between Métis and Euro-Americans became more common, however, with many such unions occurring between Métis and newly arrived southeastern Europeans. Like the Métis, these new arrivals were devout Catholics. Also like the Métis, they experienced discrimination and ridicule for their lack of English-language skills, their difference in dress, and other aspects of their lifestyle. The intermarriage of ethnically diverse Catholics was a natural development. Although prejudice in the larger community probably limited intermarriage overall, there is no record of the church itself discouraging ethnically mixed marriages. In fact, for the Roman Catholic Church during these years, the phrase "mixed marriage" had an altogether different meaning. Repeated articles in the *Lewistown Catholic Monthly* warn parishioners not of the dangers of ethnic intermarriage, but of marriage outside the faith.[29]

As the Spring Creek families both strengthened their ties to Métis kin and welcomed new non-Métis family members, the terms that they used to identify themselves to the non-Métis community became quite complex and situational. The term "breed," once common, became a private word used among family members, since the larger community most often employed it in a pejorative sense. The terms "Indian" and "white" were the more socially acceptable choices, ones that might avoid ridicule or criticism. Few Métis born after the 1930s remember their families using the word "half-breed," "Métis," "Mitsif" or any similar term outside the family. Treena LaFountain, a Fleury and Wells descendant, remembers that her family always used "breed" among themselves. Her grandmother used "Mitsif," but Treena never understood, and no one ever explained, what that term meant. She thought that when her Grandmother called her "you little Mitsif," she was (affectionately) calling her a "brat"! Marie Ehlert, on the other hand, remembers that her family, the Bergers, always identified themselves as "Indian," although they were very conscious of their difference from reservation Indians.[30]

The Spring Creek band families who were ascribed a white identity and/or self-identified as white invariably had close kinship ties to the Euro-American community, often over many generations. They usually preferred the designation "French Canadian." This term, while deemphasizing an Indian ancestry (yet not necessarily excluding it), emphasized a French/Catholic heritage that could and often did include Métis culture and lifestyle. Self-identification as French Canadian could, but did not necessarily, represent a rejection of a Métis identity or Métis kinship ties.

One family that identified as French Canadian was that of Frances Morgan Shoup, who was born in Lewistown in 1922. Frances, whose mother's father was Ben Kline and whose father's mother was Frances Berger Morgan (daughter of Spring Creek leader Pierre Berger), remembers her family always describing themselves as French Canadians, "never as Indian." As far as she knows, her grandmother (Frances Berger Morgan) was the only Berger not to identify as Indian and was very consistent in avoiding that designation. Frances Shoup remembers that neither her mother nor her father's mother ever went "to any Indian meetings . . . and I think she was about the only one of them [the Bergers] that didn't." Frances's grandfather, Ben Kline, and his family followed a generations-long tradition of family identification as French Canadian or German and a family tendency to marry non-Métis.[31]

By 1900 a few Spring Creek Métis families were identifying as white and were so identified by the larger Euro-American community. At the same time, non-Métis identified the bulk of the Spring Creek Métis families as Indian. As Métis families took an active roll in tribal affairs and applied for Turtle Mountain allotments, this trend was consolidated.

TRIBAL RECOGNITION AND MÉTIS ETHNIC IDENTITY

As in the 1890s, the Chippewa and Cree experience in Montana had a profound effect on both the identity ascribed to Métis and on how they identified themselves, especially in public situations. In the Euro-American mind, Montana Métis, whether associated with an Indian band or not, became confused, sometimes even synonymous, with Canadian Crees. As noted previously, the Crees suffered continual harassment through the 1890s and were repeatedly "rounded up" and deported to Canada. Their treatment had a deeply felt, if indirect, effect on the Spring Creek band. Several Spring Creek families had relatives among the Little Bear Crees, Rocky Boy Chippewas, and Métis recently arrived from Canada, as well as strong kinship ties to the Turtle Mountain Chippewas. As relatively prosperous residents and landowners in the Judith Basin, they escaped the worst treatment afforded Canadian Crees. They were not swept up in the deportations as other Métis had been. Even so, they did not escape the prejudice and ill will directed at the "Crees," nor did they escape inclusion under the label.

Though the treatment of Cree and Chippewa bands in Montana affected the Spring Creek Métis, events at Turtle Mountain more directly concerned them and had both particular relevance to their future and to the way the Euro-American community regarded them. Through the 1890s Little Shell and other Chippewa leaders had fought ratification of the 1892 McCumber Agreement, which drastically cut the Turtle Mountain Reservation's size and removed many families from the rolls. Little Shell insisted that the government enlarge the proposed reservation, increase the reimbursement for land relinquished, and loosen requirements for enrollment so that those families who had, of necessity, been away from the reservation for extended periods of time not be excluded. Eligibility disputes revolved around the question of who had lived continuously in the Turtle Mountain area, a requirement that eliminated Little Shell and his followers. Residency, not "blood quantum," was the issue since the Grand Council of 1892 had resolved that mixed-blood descendants were to be recognized as Turtle Mountain Chippewas and to receive benefits equal to those of full-bloods."[32]

Controversy over the 1892 agreement and deep factional divisions prevented its passage for twelve years. Finally, in 1904 Congress ratified the Turtle Mountain treaty. A combination of the death of Little Shell in 1900, worsening conditions and near starvation on the reservation, and the departure for Canada of many Métis families who had given up hope that they would be reinstated on tribal rolls led to tribal acceptance of the treaty. Ratifying most of the provisions of the 1892 McCumber Agreement, the treaty did not expand the reservation to its pre-1892 size, nor did it reinstate families who had been removed from the rolls. In 1904 the infamous Ten Cent Treaty, as it came to be known, became law.[33]

Another controversial provision of the treaty provided for allotment of reservation land in severalty. The distribution of 160-acre parcels began in 1906. The small size of the reservation precluded the settlement of all families at Turtle Mountain and forced many to take land on the public domain far from the reservation. Only 326 individuals secured allotments on the reservation, while 650 allottees were forced to take up land elsewhere. One hundred and forty-nine of these secured land in Montana. Under the provisions of the agreement, the fourteen hundred dependents of the allottees also had rights to allotments. With reservation land already taken up by the original allottees, the dependents also had to find land far from the reservation in the Dakotas and Montana.[34]

In addition to those who qualified, many others applied for allotments, unsure if they were eligible. At least eighty-one Métis applied for allotments in Fergus County east of Lewistown. Some of these, such as the Champagne family, were Turtle Mountain enrollees who were not members of the Spring Creek band; most of the applicants, however, were. Of the Spring Creek band members, only those individuals who met the necessary condition of residence at Turtle Mountain during the 1880s qualified for enrollment and allotments. These individuals included the Wilkies and descendants of Calixte and Charlotte Adam LaFountain, who had returned to Turtle Mountain from Spring Creek in the early 1880s. Most Spring Creek band members had been living in the Spring Creek drainage of Montana during those years and—judged to be nonresidents of the Turtle Mountain area—did not qualify.

Ezear (Elzear) LaFountain (son of Calixte and Charlotte) and his wife, Mary Rose Turcotte, did qualify for enrollment. Ezear and his family had traveled back to Turtle Mountain with his brothers and their wives' family, the Wilkies, in the early 1880s and so were able to establish the fact of their residence. Enrollment officials denied the applications of other Spring

Creek families, most of whom resided in Montana during the last decades of the 1800s. Those families rejected as ineligible and refused allotments included members of the Spring Creek families of Doney, Fayant, Swan, Laverdure, Berger, Ouellette, Davis, Paul, Turcotte, Kline, and Wells. Ineligibility must have been particularly disappointing and economically debilitating for these families, as government allotment agents took as long as seven years to reject their allotment applications.[35]

With all of the difficulty in securing allotments, obtaining allotted land did not necessarily improve one's chance for prosperity in the harsh environment of the Montana plains. The treaty provided 160 acres from the public domain. Much of this land remained unsettled only because it was isolated and unproductive. Even on the best land in the western prairies, 160 acres could not support a family, as the homesteaders quickly discovered. Summertime grass for a horse and a cow would be all a family could expect these acres to provide unless a stream ran through the property. A stream might provide water to irrigate a garden or encourage longer streamside grass that could be cut for winter hay, but there are few streams on the Montana plains and many dry up in summer. For those families who persevered and obtained patent to their land, life remained harsh. They were now subject to taxes, and some, in an attempt to raise cattle or crops, had borrowed to buy stock, seed, and equipment. Exacerbating their situation was the drought that began on the Montana and Dakota plains in 1914 and persisted into the 1920s and 1930s. As prices fell and costs rose, it became impossible for many families to pay their taxes and repay loans. The Métis and Turtle Mountain Chippewas would not be the only families to lose their farms, but, by 1920, close to 90 percent of the Turtle Mountain allottees who had received patents had lost their land.[36]

Both the loss of allotted land to taxes and ineligibility for allotments caused a bitterness among Turtle Mountain and Little Shell people that is still strong today. Many could not understand how they could lose land that was due them as Native people. "Somehow they just took it away from us," recalled Mary La Mere Johnson when asked about her family's loss of allotted land. "I don't know, we lived on it too for quite a few years. And the first thing you know they just took it away from us."[37]

The treaty and enrollment controversies had an additional effect on Montana Métis, whether eligible for tribal membership or not. The process of applying for enrollment and allotments encouraged a renegotiation of public identity. Aspiring Turtle Mountain families might continue to self-identify as Métis (or breed) within the Métis community, but to the rest of the world and in any public documents they were Chippewas. They recognized the role that the U.S. government played in assigning this public identification and their need to adapt to the consequent ramifications. "Let the Government settle our affairs *so that we may know who and what we are*," was a persistent demand as early as the 1880s. Although referring here to national identity, the comment reflects the broader dilemma caused by the government's ability not only to define national identity, but ethnic identity as well. It demonstrates that the Métis understood the realities of their situation and the extent of the government's power.[38]

For families omitted from the Turtle Mountain rolls, enrollment battles had a similar effect. Most waited years for confirmation of their status. As they reacted to their exclusion from the rolls and organized politically to protest, they found it mandatory to do so as Chippewas—protesting as Métis could serve no purpose. Consequently, over the years they met under various titles—Red Bear Chippewas, Landless Indians, or Little Shell Chippewas—but not as Métis.[39]

Many Spring Creek Métis participated in the meetings held to denounce the Ten Cent Treaty and the exclusion of so many families from the Turtle Mountain rolls. Henry Paul, chairman of the Little Shell Chippewas from 1983 to 1984, remembers a 1920 gathering east of Lewistown. "A large meeting of Landless Little Shell Indians took place at my grandparents' [home]," he recalled. "Approximately 40–50 tribal members came from all over." Recounting efforts to secure the support of state officials, Paul wrote that "Roy Ayers was running for governor of Montana [and] was asked what he was going to do about the 'Ten Cent Treaty' and payments for the lost lands." Spring Creek Métis served as officers and organizers. An important figure in the continued protest was Elizabeth Swan, granddaughter of Spring Creek band leader Pierre Berger and his wife, Judith Wilkie, who was secretary of the Little Shell organization through the 1930s and 1940s.[40]

Even as the Little Shell families protested, they, like the Turtle Mountain band, were required to draw up lists of eligible members. And again, the federal government played a decisive part. In compliance with Bureau of Indian Affairs instructions, these lists, which came to be known as the Roe Cloud Rolls, included both eligible individuals and their degree of Indian "blood." The blood quantum information was necessary because Section 19 of the 1934 Indian Reorganization Act stipulated that, if other provisions were not met, one had to be of "one-half or more Indian blood" to qualify as Indian. Again the government placed the burden on individuals to prove their Indian blood and, in doing so, discounted Métis ancestry. The "one half rule" not only emphasized Chippewa ancestry but also effectively eliminated a legal Métis identity under the act. Any Métis admitting to one half Indian ancestry was Indian under the law.[41]

Like the enrollment process at Turtle Mountain, organization of the Little Shell band and federal regulations governing the compilation of official rolls affected the way that Spring Creek Métis identified themselves and were identified by the larger community. Little Shell members now tended to refer to themselves as Chippewas, and the publicity surrounding their protest and organization solidified this tendency among Euro-American Montanans. Since many Spring Creek families participated in Little Shell activities, and individuals from most of the original families were listed in the 1937 Roe Cloud Roll, they also began to identify publicly as Chippewas.

There were exceptions to identification as Little Shell Chippewas among the Spring Creek Métis families, however. Descendants of the trader families of Janeaux, Morase, and Kline more often avoided an Indian identity, and most members of the LaFountain family, as mentioned above, were Turtle Mountain enrollees. Nor did all of the eligible Spring Creek band members wish to enroll, and, to this day, their descendants are unaffiliated. As a consequence of these diverging patterns of identification, Spring Creek family public identification became more flexible and situational. Spring Creek Métis, even within the same family, began to identify differently—as Indian, white, or (privately, for the most part) as breed.[42]

Despite the adoption of more varied identifiers, Little Shell families, including Spring Creek members and relatives, maintained their kinship networks and communities. Over the years, Little Shell families as well as their nonaligned and Turtle Mountain relatives moved within the large, roughly triangular area formed by the Milk River in the north and Lewistown in the south. Within this triangle most Métis families were bound by extensive kinship networks, and certain towns became centers for Little Shell families. Despite an influx of Euro-American agriculturists, towns from Havre (on the Milk River) to Wolf Point (on the Missouri River, about thirty miles downstream from its confluence with the Milk) developed sizable and often physically discrete Métis communities. After 1930 Zortman (fifty miles south of the Milk River), Chinook, and Havre (both on the Milk River), and Augusta (east of Great Falls) had Métis communities consisting almost exclusively of families affiliated with or related to the Little Shell or Turtle Mountain Chippewas. The Spring Creek and Milk River

Métis, already bound by generations of kinship networks, continued to intermarry, tying the families into a complex web of kin-based relationships that included Turtle Mountain, Little Shell, and unaffiliated Métis, plus new Euro-American relatives. Doney, Berger, Laverdure, and other names familiar among the Spring Creek band became associated with Zortman and the Milk River communities. For example, quite a number of present-day Zortman/Milk River families trace their ancestry to the Doney brothers (Gregory, Joseph, John M., and Lalley), three of whom settled on Spring Creek and later at Roy and the Missouri River, before moving north.[43]

Although their closest kinship ties were to the triangle families, the Spring Creek Métis were also already related to and continued to intermarry with Métis along the Front Range of the Rocky Mountains. The struggle of these Métis and their Indian relatives for recognition and a reservation indirectly, but profoundly, affected the public identification of the Spring Creek Métis and their treatment by the larger Euro-American community. In the late 1870s the Front Range families had clustered around the St. Peter's Mission area near present-day Cascade, but, by the turn of the century, they had developed a number of enclaves from the Blackfeet Reservation south along the foothills and small mountain ranges of the Rocky Mountain Front. Canadian Métis and Little Bear Crees had joined the Front Range families after the 1885 Rebellion. As noted earlier, Little Bear and his Cree and Métis followers struggled over the next several decades to obtain a Montana reservation. Euro-American Montanans, for their part, persisted in calling for their expulsion to Canada.[44]

Efforts late in the 1890s to secure land for the Little Bear Crees on the Flathead Reservation of Montana had collapsed as had previous attempts. Like the Little Bear band, the Rocky Boy Chippewas, who had been moving from place to place within Montana since at least the early 1890s, also failed to receive permission to locate on the Flathead Reservation (or anywhere else). In spite of their growing poverty, and amid near starvation in wintertime, the Rocky Boy band had as little support from the Montana congressional delegation and the Montana public in general as had the Crees. In fact, Montanans persisted in confusing the two groups and in labeling the Chippewas "Canadian Crees" who were illegal "vagabonds" for whom Montanans had no obligation.[45]

After the turn of the century, conditions worsened for both bands. With agricultural settlement came game depletion, which destroyed both food sources and supplies of fur-bearing animals. It became impossible to earn a living by trapping as they had for generations. A 1918 report to the

Board of Indian Commissioners reflected the poverty of the Rocky Boy band. "For many years these Indians were tramps, vagrants, objects of charity, panhandlers, and casual laborers around Great Falls, Havre, Big Sandy, Box Elder, and other Montana towns," the author observed. "The white people of Montana looked upon Rocky Boy's people with contempt and called them scavengers and alley cats, because many of them gleaned their food from garbage cans." When Thralls W. Wheat, clerk of the Allotting Service, compiled a list of Rocky Boy Chippewas in 1909, he also commented on the condition of these people.

> I find that the Indians belonging to this band are very poor. Nearly all of them are camped in the neighborhood of slaughter houses near the towns and cities, and their food is limited to bread and refuse that they receive from these slaughter houses. They obtain their flour, clothing, bedding, camp equipage, etc., by selling bead work, and polished cow horns made into hatracks. A few of the young men work on ranches, and at cutting wood. They seem to be willing to work after they receive employment, but they are backward about looking for work.
>
> These Indians know no home except ragged filthy tents. They have lived in tents during the past winter, and from the condition of their tents, bedding, stoves, etc., I believe that they must have suffered greatly. They sleep on the ground and have very little bedding. Most of their stoves are improvised from old wash-tubs.

Others reported the hunger and desperation that Wheat observed. Fred Nault, later a Rocky Boy enrollee, personally witnessed the conditions at Great Falls in the late 1920s and 1930s. "I've seen 75 to 100 men go down into the city dump at Great Falls to pick up junk to sell," he wrote in his memoirs, "and whenever the bakery bread wagon would come to throw stale bread and pastry over the bank a lot of them almost came to blows they were so hungry."[46]

Unwelcome outside the towns where they sought food, the Chippewa and Cree bands suffered both hunger and harassment by local officials. The apprehension of five Chippewa-Crees near Helena illustrates their vulnerability to arrest for even the slightest "crimes." "Half a dozen residents of Lenox," reported the *(Helena) Montana Daily Record*, complained "to the county attorney that the Indians were making themselves obnoxious in that vicinity; that in addition to flirting with fire water, had purloined chickens, allowed their horses to range on the Lenox lawns, and had in some instances used insulting language in the presence of women, and in other instances appeared in scant attire before the children of the neighborhood." Accusations of such "crimes" justified the band's removal from the community without trial.[47]

Eventually conditions became so bad that the destitute bands won the support of a few sympathetic and influential citizens of Helena and Great Falls. The editors of the *Great Falls Daily Tribune* also joined efforts to protect the Indians' rights and provide needed supplies. In several articles, the *Tribune* defended the homeless bands and publicized the conditions they suffered.

> When they [Rocky Boy band] seek to kill game to provide for the winter the game wardens get after them for killing game reserved by law for the white man's amusement. When they camp near a city and seek to glean a living off what the white man throws away the police order them to move on. When they camp in the country the ranchers threaten to shoot their ponies because they are believed to be diseased, and perhaps they are. They are accorded just one privilege in this land that belonged to their forefathers, and that is to die of hunger.[48]

As their circumstances worsened, the landless bands intensified efforts to secure support for a reservation. Rocky Boy, less burdened than Little Bear by the stigma of being Canadian Cree, was more successful in winning the sympathy of prominent Montanans. By 1908, with the help of individuals such as illustrator Charlie Russell and businessman and writer Frank Linderman, plus a number of business people, efforts to secure a reservation for the Rocky Boy band began in earnest. Initial attempts to locate the band on the Blackfoot or Fort Belknap reservations failed when reservation officials, like those on the Flathead Reservation, opposed situating the band within their boundaries or on allotments nearby. A variety of problems and misunderstandings subverted every effort to secure land, including the hostility of some of Montana's Native people toward the Métis members of the band. Fort Peck Reservation briefly became a possibility for settlement of the band until the agent there assured government officials that the resident Indians (traditional enemies of the Métis) would never tolerate "French mixed bloods" on or near their land. The comment of Fort Peck's reservation agent reflects the double bind under which the Rocky Boy Chippewas labored. When the argument suited opponents, they might be accused of being Canadian Crees and therefore the responsibility of Canada. On the other hand, since many members of the band were Métis, they might be accused of being "French breeds" and not Indian at all.[49]

Determining the actual identity of Rocky Boy band members was another problem. In the course of efforts to secure allotment or reservation land, Indian Inspector Frank C. Churchill requested a census of the Rocky Boy band. Allotting agent Thralls W. Wheat compiled a roll in 1909, attempting to exclude any of the Rocky Boy band who were "properly wards of the Canadian government." He listed 120 Indians "affiliated" with Rocky Boy's band. Most were Chippewas, but also present were Sioux, Assiniboines, and Blackfeet, all peoples with whom the Chippewas had been intermarrying for some time. Wheat did not exclude half-breeds from the rolls. John C. Ewers, historian of the Rocky Boy Chippewa-Crees, estimated that if Métis had been omitted, the extensively intermarried Rocky Boy Chippewa band would have been reduced to seventy-five Indians. Ewers identified the half-breed families as Denny, Momy, Mosney, Papin, Peletier, La Fromboise, Smith, and Gardipee. Most of these family names are also common among the Little Shell and Turtle Mountain Chippewas.[50]

Wheat's inclusion of Métis on the Chippewa rolls did not end efforts to exclude them. Even as Little Bear Crees won acceptance for their admittance to the rolls, new efforts to drop the Métis were underway. A new roll of "Rocky Boy's band and 'No–reservation Indians' in the state of Montana," compiled in 1912 by Supervisor of Indian Schools Fred A. Baker, included 386 persons, thereby tripling the number of enrollees. Baker found it impossible to distinguish Rocky Boy Chippewas from Little Bear Crees and reluctantly concluded that the attempt was fruitless. While prepared to accept related Little Bear Crees, Baker remained hostile to inclusion of Canadian half-breeds. "As is usual in all such cases," he wrote in 1912, "when reservations are to be allotted or tribal funds divided there were on hand a large number of *interlopers*, half-breed Canadian Crees and Chippewas who claimed membership in Rocky Boy's Band." Baker complained that Rocky Boy and the older Indians were "inclined to be exceedingly liberal in their decisions as to who were members of the band." Apparently he expected Rocky Boy to exclude Métis relatives, thereby reducing the government's responsibility and expense. As in the past, it was the half-breeds accused of being Canadian who were deemed interlopers. The long Métis history in Montana or as associates and relatives of the Chippewas was again overlooked or dismissed.[51]

Despite the efforts of some officials to exclude the Métis, Little Bear was even more disposed than Rocky Boy to include mixed-descent relatives on his proposed rolls. The roll of July 16, 1917, which listed Little Bear band members in addition to those on the 1909 Wheat roll, reflects Little Bear's desire to enroll mixed-descent families. It increased the number of eligible individuals to 451. The roll listed Métis more closely associated with the Front Range families than with the Lewistown/Milk River triangle and the Spring Creek band. Among them were Allery, Belcourt, Bushie, Courchane, Capalette, Dechamp, Demontyne, Favel, Hamline, Houle, Henderson, Jackson, Ladue, Larance, Morrisette, Sangray, Valley, and Walls families.[52]

As disputes over eligibility for Rocky Boy and Little Bear enrollment continued, Rocky Boy petitioned Baker for a reservation near the Bear Paw Mountains of north-central Montana, just south of the Milk River, near Havre, Montana. The government had recently closed Fort Assiniboine and was preparing to open its large land holdings to Euro-American settlement. Rocky Boy, an astute politician, was able to secure support for a reservation on fort land from crucial Great Falls and Helena politicians and business people (who, although sympathetic to the Rocky Boy band, did not want them in their own backyard). Opposing the move were the Havre residents, whose hostility to the proposed reservation erupted in a series of newspaper editorials.[53]

Labeling Rocky Boy and his band "trifling, lazy, renegade Chippewa Indians" and "human scavengers," the *Havre Plaindealer* charged that, "located near Havre, they would inevitably become a charge upon the bounty and charity of local people. There is no earthly reason why these people should be sluffed [*sic*] off by the government on Havre."[54] Havre citizens' hostility toward the Chippewa-Crees was certainly racially motivated, but another basis for it lay in the fear that a reservation would take large amounts of county land off the tax rolls, thus crippling the growing community's economy. Havre business people led the resistance to any reservation in the county. Their financial success, they believed, depended upon large numbers of Euro-American agriculturists who would patronize local stores, buy farm machinery, take out loans, and pay taxes.[55]

In the face of such opposition, it took until 1916 to finally establish Rocky Boy's Reservation for the Rocky Boy and Little Bear bands. All concerned hoped that this land base, close to the game-rich Bear Paw Mountains, would end the bands' poverty. But not all landless Indians in Montana benefited from the new reservation. Officials submitted only 658 names to Washington, and 206 of those were denied enrollment. The final roll of July 16, 1917, included just 451 individuals. Some of those omitted eventually won enrollment, but many more joined the Little Shell band members in the growing ranks of Montana's "Landless Indians."[56]

After securing a reservation, Rocky Boy enrollees retained their close ties to Canadian Cree kin, as well as to Montana and Canadian Métis relatives, and continued to intermarry extensively with them. Because of the large number of Métis enrollees, Rocky Boy's Reservation, during its early years, had a distinctly Métis flavor. A visitor reported that many of the Rocky Boy Indians "wore the brilliant sashes of the Canadian Indians" (the traditional Métis Assumption sash). Even though numerous enrollees were Métis, only a few were closely related to the Spring Creek families. Just six individuals born in Lewistown or members of the original Spring Creek families qualified for enrollment at Rocky Boy. These included members of the Ladue (Ledoux), Wells, Gardipee, Ducharme (married to an Ouellette/Wallett), and Nomee families.[57]

Although kinship ties were less close, the process of establishing Rocky Boy's Reservation directly influenced the ascribed and public self-ascribed identity of the Spring Creek band, as it did all Montana Métis. Rocky Boy enrollment, more so than at Turtle Mountain, required documenting one's identity as an Indian; a half-breed label could threaten eligibility. Even though many enrollees were Métis, the general public and influential supporters alike were unwilling to support half-breed enrollment. Frank Linderman, a strong supporter of the reservation and of Indian rights, expressed a common attitude toward mixed-Indian descent people while testifying in defense of several arrested Chippewa-Crees. "I am not here pleading for the Indian who gets drunk, or the Indian who steals, or the half-breed Indian," he announced. His equating of half-breeds with drunks and thieves, as persons not deserving of help or consideration, illustrates the widespread hostility that Métis faced. Wallace Stegner, who grew up on the Canadian border just north of the Milk River, noted that, according to early-twentieth-century notions, "an Indian was a thieving, treacherous, lousy, unreliable, gut-eating vagabond, and that if anything a halfbreed was worse." It was against such widely held beliefs that Linderman fought on behalf of Indians. However, in the case of the Métis, he and other Indian supporters like him, concurred.[58]

Arising out of and compounding the public ill feeling described by Linderman and Stegner were continuing efforts to deny U.S. citizenship and residency to Canadian half-breeds. Responding to the interests of readers who shared such sentiments, the *Lewistown News Argus* publicized

Bureau of Immigration and Naturalization rulings that severely limited non-European immigration and citizenship. In 1907 the *News Argus* reported that the bureau had confirmed the ineligibility of "half-breed Canadian Indians" for U.S. citizenship. Strengthening this ruling was a 1909 district court case that found persons who were half white to be half-breeds and, as such, belonged to neither of the parent "races." Such a person could not be considered eligible for citizenship. In Montana, enforcement of such laws was not applied to settled, tax-paying, longtime residents such as the Spring Creek Métis, who continued to enjoy the benefits of citizenship such as voting. Nevertheless, these rulings left all Montana Métis fearful and in danger of being denied citizenship on three fronts—their Indian ancestry, their mixed ancestry, and their Canadian roots (if any). Since, in Montana, the application of strict immigration laws was often directed at Canadian Cree half-breeds, these rulings added to the pressure to prove either one's birth on U. S. soil or one's U. S. Indian, as opposed to Métis, ancestry. For those Métis who were born in Canada (and had not become naturalized citizens earlier), the only chance of legal U.S. residency seemed to be enrollment at Rocky Boy's. "French breeds" remained in danger of deportation. Again, the publicity left the impression that all Métis were illegal Canadian half-breeds with no rights to U.S. residency or citizenship.[59]

Like the struggle for enrollment, citizenship legislation encouraged a specific Indian public identity for those Métis who secured Rocky Boy enrollment. No longer in public documents or publications were Rocky Boy Métis referred to as "French breeds." And since, in Montana, French Breeds were associated with Canada (and possible deportation), the Chippewa-Crees were unlikely to identify themselves as Métis, Michif, or Mitsif as did many Turtle Mountain enrollees. For mixed-descent people in Montana, even more than for those of North Dakota, a mixed-blood designation risked not only losing rights as Indians but also as U.S. residents. Rocky Boy enrollment meant not only a land base—it also secured legal residence in the United States and a measure of respect as a tribal Indian that could not be found as a Canadian half-breed. Prospective enrollees hoped that it would end harassment by immigration agents and local law enforcement. Ironically, publicity surrounding the creation of Rocky Boy's tended to raise hostility toward "half-breed interlopers," even while public support for Cree and Chippewa Indians rose.

Throughout the first nineteen years of the twentieth century, government designations and Euro-American public opinion made it necessary for both enrolled and rejected Montana Métis to seek redress as Indians. In negotiating their Native rights, the Métis also negotiated a public identity. The process of establishing eligibility for enrollment at Rocky Boy's intensified an Indian self-identification, as did the protests of the Little Shell band. At the same time, the enrollment process solidified the ascribed Indian identity of the mixed-descent followers of Little Bear, Rocky Boy, and Little Shell.

For the Spring Creek Métis, like all Montana Métis, there was simply no opportunity or advantage to declare a Métis identity while fighting for rights as Native Americans or for U.S. citizenship. Even the words "Métis," "Michif," and "Mitsif" went out of use and were seldom heard in Montana after the 1930s. Euro-American Montanans occasionally used the word "breed," but with a pejorative connotation that had nothing to do with a distinct cultural group. Denied a way to express their unique identity, negotiating an Indian identity came closest to meeting their needs and self-perceptions. Nevertheless, ascription by the Euro-American community and public self-ascription by the Rocky Boy and Little Shell bands of an Indian identity coexisted with a strong feeling among Métis that they were unique. A private Métis identity survived, centered on strong kinship ties and a sense of community.

• • •

The new century brought dramatic social and economic change to central Montana. Government policy and attitudes toward breeds restricted ethnic choices, giving mixed-descent identity neither legal standing nor social acceptance. In response, Métis families renegotiated their public identity even as they maintained a strong sense of their distinctiveness, added new ethnically diverse family members, and strengthened generations-old kinship bonds. For the Spring Creek band, as for other Montana Métis, identity became increasingly complex, multilayered, and situational, but remained rooted in the kinship network.

Pressure on Métis identity had begun before the turn of the century. The public outcry over Canadian Crees "roaming" Montana had encouraged the impression among Euro-American Montanans that the Métis were Cree and Canadian. A combination of powerful national, state, and local developments at the turn of the century further encouraged both the ascription to Métis of an Indian identity and a public self-ascribed Indian identity by the Métis. Between 1900 and 1919, government regulation of enrollment necessitated the documentation of Indian ancestry and forced Rocky Boy, Turtle Mountain, and Little Shell Métis to emphasize their Indian heritage at the expense of a public Métis identity. For those not enrolled or determined to resist government policies, an Indian identity became the only politically viable alternative for effective protest. An Indian identity became not just a political expedient, but also a political necessity. Furthermore, close and generations-old kinship ties made an alliance with Indian relatives a natural alternative. By 1916 the official government enrollment of Rocky Boy Chippewa-Crees and Turtle Mountain Chippewas, as well as organized Little Shell band protests, defined the possible public Métis identities for the twentieth century—all of them Indian.

Yet some Métis avoided an Indian identity. Many continued to insist that they were breeds, especially among family and friends. Others self-identified as white, particularly families with long traditions of business ties, intermarriage, and strong kinship bonds with Euro-Americans. These families often described themselves as French Canadian, thus signaling a commitment to their unique cultural heritage while maintaining a white identity.

Métis families' primary reliance on kinship to define who they were modified the influence of ascribed identities and subsumed them under preexisting kinship networks. Although many Métis families began to call themselves Indian, they realized that a Euro-American ascription of an Indian identity did not necessarily provide legal status, tribal enrollment, or tribal acceptance. The reality of their ethnic identity, their private sense of who they were, still lay within the family.

CONCLUSION

"Piyish Tout Ni Pouyoun"

For the Spring Creek Métis, ethnic identity rested on kinship ties, which supported a deep sense of belonging, and a continuing recognition of difference from both Indian and Euro-American groups. Ethnic boundaries among the Spring Creek Métis were sometimes dramatically porous, allowing individuals to seemingly join or drop out at will. Yet, at the same time, Métis families retained strong feelings of "we" and "them" that provided a sure sense of who they were and who they were not. While negotiating a public identity with powerful forces of the U.S. government, the Roman Catholic Church, and Euro-American public opinion, the Spring Creek Métis maintained a private identity that reflected their knowledge of who they were.[1]

Despite restrictions on possible formal or legal ethnic identities, Métis identity continues to be, as it has always been, flexible, multilayered, multifaceted, and permeable. Formal, publicly recognized identifications such as Chippewa or Cree did not negate a Métis identity. Government and other institutions mandated certain public identities, but they were just one layer that coexisted with a multilayered, situational identity that could survive government, church, or other institutional and popularly ascribed identification. The very *variety* of their kinship bonds supported a Métis identity. In families that might have Cree, Chippewa, or other tribal relatives plus a variety of Euro-American relatives and in-laws, a Métis identity might be the only one inclusive enough to encompass and accept all members of the family.

It was this absorbent, inclusive nature of Métis ethnicity that sustained it, allowing kinship ties, no matter to which ethnic group, to enrich, rather than destroy, a sense of unique ethnicity. Such flexibility allowed government ethnic definition, prejudice in the larger community, poverty after the decimation of the bison, and other potentially destructive forces to be used by Métis families to reinforce their sense of separateness, while simultaneously including other ethnic groups. In the 1800s a Métis person may have had ancestors who were Chippewa, Cree, African, Iroquois, English, Scot, French, and Hawaiian, as well as a number of other Native and European ancestries. By the early twentieth century, Métis families may have included all of these plus Lithuanian, Polish, Croatian, or any other of the numerous ethnic groups who settled in central Montana at the turn of the century.

For the Spring Creek Métis, as for all peoples, ethnic identity evolves on many levels. Public identities—those used outside the kinship group—are especially complex and multipurpose. Multiethnic descent requires an ability to be comfortable with and to operate efficiently under multiple public identities. It is not unusual for a Métis to assume, at various points in her or his life, an Indian, white, or Métis identity. Because there was very little opportunity to publicly identify as Métis between the late 1890s and the 1920s, most families negotiated Indian or white identities. The terms "Métis," "Michif," and others like them were seldom heard in Montana by the 1920s. To the Euro-American community, even the term "breed" referred to a type of Indian, although usually a degenerate one. Nevertheless, by the 1970s, as part of a nationwide ethnic renewal, Métis identity flowered again. A private identity that had persevered—supported by kinship networks and maintained by elders—became public once more.

This study finds that the pervious boundaries of a multilayered and situational Métis identity grounded in an extensive kinship network provided a framework from which these families could maintain their sense of who they were despite challenge and change. They were able to absorb labels and rigid ethnic definitions as layers that did not disrupt their private sense of self. The porous flexibility allowed easy acceptance of new members as well as ascribed public identities. In this, the experience of the Spring Creek Métis supports the ethnic theories of anthropologist Fredrik Barth. Such theories emphasize the volitional, evolving aspects of ethnic identity that are constantly negotiated between an individual's and a family's self-ascription on the one hand and social assignment by outside forces on the other. This tension between self-ascription and ascription, between an individual or family's sense of who they are and the possibilities for identification presented by outside forces is particularly relevant to the Métis experience.[2]

Sociologist Joane Nagel, in examining American Indian identity writes, "Just as ethnic identity is both volitional and ascribed, ethnicity is constructed by individuals and ethnic groups themselves, as well as by social, economic, and political outsiders. Ethnic boundaries are constructed from within and from without, propped up by both internal and external pressures."[3] For people such as the Métis, common threads of profound importance unite and provide a sense of commonality—they constitute the forces "from within." For the Spring Creek Métis, ties of kinship are at the heart of ethnic identification. It is from the framework of family and kin that they negotiated (and continue to negotiate) challenges from macro factors such as government regulations, church policy, or economic dislocation. An intricate and powerful web of kinship—consanguineous, affinal, and fictive (adoption and godparenting)—connected the central-Montana Métis families, providing social and economic stability and a strong sense of who they were.

Viewing ethnic identification from the perspective of the kinship network illuminates a powerful element often missing from studies of ethnicity. The Spring Creek Métis experience underscores gender in the establishment of kinship networks and the role of those networks in ethnic negotiation. The role of women is particularly difficult to uncover unless a close investigation is made of the kinship network in order to ascertain matrilineal ties. Métis identity, as well of that of other groups, would benefit from a close investigation of women's roles, at the family level, in the adaptive and enduring nature of kinship networks.

As important as exploring issues that affect ethnic identification is the placement of the Métis experience at the heart of U.S. history. In much of the northern plains, the Great Lakes area, and the Mississippi River drainage Métis were central to the story of early settlement. Nevertheless, their role in the history of the United States has been and continues to be overlooked and misunderstood. The absence of Métis in the history of the American people is all the more remarkable for the fact that across the frontier they were often the first non-Indian residents and founders of many settlements, much as they were in central Montana. For central Montana, like many other areas of the country, the complete story cannot be told without reference to the role of people of mixed descent.

As it is relevant to the way we see U.S. history, the nature of Métis identity is also relevant to the way we in the United States look at our own ethnic identity. The permeable boundaries of Métis kinship-centered inclusiveness allow members to move between layered identities. Thus, at least as far as the Métis were concerned, their members might freely sustain membership in ethnic communities of both their parents, or of all their grandparents. Nor was ethnic community restricted by genetic ancestry—adoption and fictive kinship relations were also prevalent. Perhaps such a model of inclusive multiethnic identification has relevance today. In a country where ethnicity has been alternately dismissed (melting pot theories) or sharply drawn by concrete, immutable definitions and lists of markers that serve to determine authenticity with enrollment lists and blood quantum restrictions, a flexible, inclusive ethnic identity that allows individuals to acknowledge all aspects of their heritage and ancestry might more satisfactorily address the needs of our growing multiethnic population.

The Métis model recognizes a mestizo population but not one that has "melted" into an undifferentiated mass dominated and defined by one powerful group. The Métis example would suggest a "Mestizo America" in which each family recognized its unique heritage and comfortably assumed various levels of identity reflecting its component aspects. The Métis provide a microcosm of a North America in which multicultural societies develop and flourish despite intentional and unintentional attempts to melt them into one faction's ideal or separate them into prescribed ethnicities that do not recognize their multifaceted ancestry. Métis are true citizens of North America. They are our past and our future.[4]

APPENDIX

Signatories of Petition to N. A. Miles, Musselshell River, August 6, 1880

Bold text: member of the group that moved to Spring Creek in the summer of 1879.
Underlined text: moved to the Spring Creek area after 1879.
* Parent, sibling, or child of Spring Creek band member.
Note: Several names, for instance, Jean Charette, are so common it is impossible to identify the individual with certainty.

Alexandre Wilkey
Pierre Berger Sr.
Antoine Ouilette
Baptis Gariépy Sr
Isidore Berger
Jean Baptis Berger
Bernard Berger
Jacques Berger
Pierre Berger Jr.
Isaïe Berger
Binjamin Klyne
Joe Lyonnais [Doney]
Baptis Adams Sr.
Norman Marion
Jean Bellehumeur
Narcisse Cardinal
André Alary Jr.
Baptiste Gariépy Jr.
François BelleHumeur
Gabriel Amyot
Jonas Hamlin Sr.
Patrice Hamlin
Jonas Hamlin Jr.
Sévère Hamlin Sr.
André Alary Sr.
Jonas Rainville
Baptiste Alary
Antoine Houle
Alexandre St Matt
William Davis Jr.
Sévère Hamlin Jr.
George Lambert.
L.M. Jérôme
Ambroise Houle
Michel St Denis
Alexandre Azur

Louis St Matt
Louis Gariépy
François Amyot Jr.
Joseph Parisien
Abraham Boyer
<u>Pierre Charbonneau</u>
<u>Elie Gariépy</u>
Baptiste Bellegarde
Octave Lafontaine
Joseph Ouellette
Baptiste Ledoux
Cléophas Ducharme
François Ouellette
Moïse Ouellette
Charles Alary
William Laframboise
Baptiste Turcotte*
Moïse Latreille
Pierre Laverdure Sr.
Daniel Laverdure*
François Laverdure*
William Davis Sr.*
Michel Davis*
Joseph Davis*
Michel Vivier
Hyacinthe George
<u>Jean Charette</u>
Bernard Lafontaine
Charles Norwest
François Daigneau
Pierre Léveillé
Baptiste Alary Sr.
Moïse Fagnant*

Pierre Beauchamp
Antoine Fleury Sr.
Antoine Fleury Jr.
<u>Louis Fleury</u>
Edouard Wells
Arthur Amyot
Joseph Amyot
Baptiste Lafontaine*
François Amyot Sr.
Joseph Charette
Thomas Larance
Thomas Bird
Baptiste Larocque
Bonaventure Cardinal
Léonide Gariépy
Salomon Hamelin
<u>Joseph Larocque</u>
William Fagnant*
Antoine Lafontaine
Xavier Fagnant*
Moïse Adam
Théophile Fagnant
Elzéar Hamelin
Jean Marie Lyonnais
Patrice BelleHumeur
Baptiste Gariépy
Johnny Leclair
Jacques Cardinal
Pierre Cardinal
Narcisse Cardinal Jr.
Jérémie Adam
Xavier Laverdure*

Appendix source: Riel, *Writings*, 2:223–26.

Abbreviations

AICRJ	*American Indian Culture and Research Journal*
ARCIA	Annual Report of the Commissioner of Indian Affairs
BLM	Bureau of Land Management
BR	*The Benton (Montana) Weekly Record*
CIA	Commissioner of Indian Affairs
CSHSND	Collections of the State Historical Society of North Dakota
CSHSW	Collections of the State Historical Society of Wisconsin
HBC:CND	The Publications of the Hudson's Bay Record Company Minutes of Council Northern Department of Rupert Land
JFP	James Fergus Papers
LNA	*The Lewistown (Mont.) News Argus*
LPL	Lewistown Public Library, Lewistown, Montana
MA	*The (Maiden, Mont.) Mineral Argus*
MBSC	Merrill G. Burlingame Special Collections, Montana State University, Bozeman, Montana
MHSA	Montana Historical Society Archives, Helena, Montana
MLSC	Mansfield Library Special Collections, University of Montana, Missoula, Montana
NAC	National Archives of Canada, Ottawa, Ontario
NARG	National Archives, Washington, D.C., Record Group
Serial	Congressional Document Serial Set Number
SHSND	State Historical Society of North Dakota
SPM	St. Peter's Mission
SPMP	St. Peter's Mission Papers
UCA	Ursuline Center Archives, Great Falls, Montana
WHS	Wisconsin Historical Society
WPA	Works Progress Administration, Federal Writers Project

Notes

INTRODUCTION

1. Several years earlier, Ken Doney, as sheriff, became Fergus County's (of which Lewistown is the county seat) first Métis to be elected to county office.

2. Some Métis, as noted, are members of recognized Indian tribes and, as such, do have a land base and official recognition, but as Indians, not Métis.

3. That Spring Creek band families founded the *longest continuously occupied* Métis community in Montana is not to suggest that there were not Métis families in Montana far earlier. For example, Fort Benton was the home of Métis families decades before, and many Métis settled on the Milk River and the western front of the Rocky Mountains earlier than the Spring Creek band came to Spring Creek.

4. Spring Creek (referred to on recent maps as Big Spring Creek) flows from Big Springs, about three miles southeast of the central Montana town of Lewistown, through the town, and continues in a northwesterly direction to meet the Judith River. The Milk River flows from the eastern edge of Glacier Park near St. Mary's Lake, northeasterly to Alberta, where it parallels the boundary line for some one hundred miles before turning south into Montana again. Thence, it flows through north-central Montana to join the Missouri River near Fort Peck.

5. Lying in the heart of central Montana, the Judith Basin is formed by the tributaries of the Judith River (one of which is Spring Creek). The Musselshell River, the Snowy Mountains, the Little Belt Mountains, and, in the north, the Missouri River, surround the basin, forming a roughly circular area approximately one hundred miles in diameter.

6. For an overview of theories of ethnicity, see Hutchinson and Smith, *Ethnicity*.

7. Barth, *Ethnic Groups;* Clifford, *Predicament,* 281 ("We were different").

8. Nagel, *Ethnic Renewal,* 20–21. For a lucid yet concise examination of constructed ethnicity, see *Ethnic Renewal,* 19–42.

9. Ibid., 21.

10. Unidentified respondent to a question posed by the author, "Is it possible to be both Indian and Métis?" (discussion session, 1997 Métis Celebration, Lewistown, Mont.) The general consensus was yes.

11. Barth, "Emerging Issues," 21–23.

12. Nash, "Hidden History."

13. In the United States, Jacqueline Peterson broadened historians' understanding of both ethnogenesis and who the Métis people are with her study of the Great Lakes Métis ("Prelude to Red River"). For recent works, see Thorne, *Many Hands;* Sleeper-Smith, *Indian Women and French Men;* and Murphy, *Gathering of Rivers.*

14. For the best introduction to Métis scholarship, see the collection of studies in Peterson and Brown, *New Peoples.* A comprehensive but Eurocentric portrayal is Giraud's *Métis.* The most popular account is probably Joseph Kinsey Howard's *Strange Empire.* For a more recent work with a stimulating perspective, see Ens, *Homeland.* Thorne's *Many Hands* is an excellent account of the métis experience on the lower Missouri River, as are Sleeper-Smith's (*Indian Women and French Men*) and Murphy's (*Gathering of Rivers*) accounts of mixed-descent families in the Great Lakes area.

Chittenden, *American Fur Trade;* Richard White, *American West;* and *Middle Ground;* Malone, Roeder, and Lang, *Montana,* 48–50.

15. *AICRJ* 6 (1982); Peterson and Brown, *New Peoples.*

16. Dusenberry, "Waiting," 119–36.

17. Dusenberry, "Rocky Boy Indians" and "Waiting"; Burt, "Nowhere Left" and "Crooked Piece"; Morris and Van Gunten, "Oral History"; Franklin and Bunte, "Montana Métis Community"; Hogue, "Disputing the Medicine Line."

18. The following works discuss "whiteness" as a social construction: Allen, *White Race;* Frankenberg, *White Women;* Horsman, *Race and Manifest Destiny;* Haney-López, *White by Law;* Roediger, *Wages of Whiteness;* Pascoe, "Miscegenation Law."

19. For a discussion of the early use of "half breed," see Brown, *Strangers,* 172; and "Linguistic Solitudes," 150.

20. For a discussion of Métis/métis usage, see Brown, "Genesis and Rebirth," 136; Peterson and Brown, *New Peoples,* 6.

CHAPTER 1

1. The Red River of the North forms the North Dakota–Minnesota border, flowing northward through Manitoba to Lake Winnipeg. It is part of the Hudson Bay drainage rather than the Missouri River system. Since it flows northward, the southern portion, which is within the United States, is the upper river.

2. Dickason, "'One Nation,'" 30 ("began to look"); Peterson, "Many Roads," 39.

3. Joseph Kinsey Howard, *Strange Empire,* 39; Peterson, "Many Roads," 42, 45; Giraud, *Métis,* 1:281; John Foster, "Plains Métis," 379. "In the seventeenth century the term *coureur de bois* meant anyone who voyaged into the wilderness to

trade for furs. Until 1681 laws forbade the practice, hence the name had a pejorative sense, meaning virtually an outlaw" (Eccles, *Canadian Frontier*, xi). Later the term was used interchangeably with "voyageurs," men who originally were paid company employees manning the fur trade canoes (110).

4. For further discussion, see chapters 2–3.

5. This is a growing field, but informative studies of Indian and Métis women include: Albers and Medicine, *Hidden Half;* Axtell, *Indian Peoples;* Klein and Ackerman, *Women and Power;* Shoemaker, *Negotiators of Change* (this work contains an especially informative introduction); Van Kirk, *Many Tender Ties;* Sleeper-Smith, *Indian Women and French Men;* Murphy, *Gathering of Rivers*. Additionally, there are a number of excellent studies of specific groups of Native women.

A pioneering work in the field of women's roles in the fur trade is Van Kirk's *Many Tender Ties*. Jennifer Brown, Lucy Murphy, and Susan Sleeper-Smith have also made important contributions to the study of mixed-descent women's roles in establishing and maintaining kinship networks and community.

6. Peterson, "Many Roads," 41–42, 52, 59, 63.

7. Coues, *New Light;* Donna Valley Russell, *Michigan Censuses* (1710 Census, Detroit, 5; 1750 Census, Detroit, 16; 1765 Census, Detroit, 30; 1779 Census, Detroit, 40-45); "Commercial History of Milwaukee," 4:253–89, CSHSW; Thwaites, "Fur Trade on the Upper Lakes," 234–474; Thwaites, "The Mackinac Register"; *1830 Michigan Census; 1850 Wisconsin Census*.

8. See Brown, *Strangers*, for a compelling discussion of the companies' roles.

9. Brown, *Strangers*, 5–8.

10. Ibid., 6.

11. Giraud, *Métis*, 1:316–17, 322–23; Brown, *Strangers*, 69, 216–20. Many of these descendants retained their Cree identity, as some continue to do today.

12. Van Kirk, "'Custom,'" 199 (n. 47); John Foster, "Métis," 86; Brown, "Centrifuge," 214; Brown, *Strangers*, 67–68, 76–77, 155, 159, 216–20.

13. See note 12; Nute, *Voyageur*, 36; Brown, "Genesis and Rebirth," 140.

14. Giraud, *Métis*, 1:281, 264 ("nearer to the Indian"); John Foster, "Plains Métis," 379; Gardener, "Ethnology," 372–73.

15. John Foster, "Plains Métis," 383. Diane Payment and Jennifer Brown note the Cree spelling as Otipemisiwak (Payment, *"Free People,"*; and Brown, "Métis, Half-breeds," 24).

16. Peterson, "Prelude," 53; "Many Roads," 64.

17. Havard, "French Half-Breeds," 311; Nasatir, *Before Lewis and Clark* 1:32–33; Joseph Kinsey Howard, *Strange Empire*, 25–26.

18. Nasatir, *Before Lewis and Clark*, 1:5, 8–9, 33–34; "Anglo-Spanish Frontier," 291; "Jacques D'Eglise"; and "Spanish Explorations."

19. The tripmen, or voyageurs, were the workers of the fur trade, manning the canoes and boats that carried furs and supplies. Chittenden, *American Fur Trade*, 57 (four-fifths), 99; Havard, "French Half-Breeds," 311–13.

20. For an account of the métis of the lower Missouri River, see Thorne, *Many Hands*. Nasatir, *Before Lewis and Clark*, 1:247, 267, 292, 300.

21. Nasatir, *Before Lewis and Clark*, 2:645–46, 667; Chittenden, *American Fur Trade*, 127.

22. Larpenteur, *Forty Years*, 92.

23. I use "Ojibwa" and "Chippewa" in this context rather than Anishinaabe because they are the terms employed historically. "Chippewa," as mentioned earlier, is the term still in use in Montana today.

24. For an excellent summary of early Anishinaabe history and their movement into present-day Minnesota, see the first chapter of Meyer, *White Earth Tragedy*. For an account of the Ojibwas in western Canada, see Peers, *Ojibwa of Western Canada*. Tyrrell, *Thompson's Narrative*, 281; Chaboillez, "Journal," 265, 270, 408 (n. 146); Hickerson, "Genesis," 303–305. La Vérendrye, *Journals*, 9, 95–96, 134–39, 147, 185, 186. The conflict with the Sioux, who were hard-pressed from the east themselves, continued for decades. For an account of the Sioux struggles with the often tenuous Ojibwa/Cree/Assiniboine alliance, see Hickerson, "Genesis," 289, 295, 306, 332, 382. By the 1840s Edwin Denig of Fort Union reported that the Crees and "Chippeway" "are so mingled . . . and with difficulty to be considered a distinct people" (*Five Indian Tribes*, 100). Henry Youle Hind reported in 1858 that people of Cree and Ojibwa descent were known as "Bungays" (*Narrative*, 1:333).

I use the word "Sioux" here rather than a more precise and more appropriate Lakota, Nakota, or Dakota because of the variety of groups involved.

25. Coues, *New Light*, 1:79–81; Joseph Kinsey Howard, *Strange Empire*, 31; Chaboillez, "Journal," 265, 398 (n. 107); Hickerson, "Genesis," 301, 334 (n. 41).

26. Lounsberry, *North Dakota*, 1:41; Thwaites, *Lewis and Clark*, 6:108–110; Hickerson, "Genesis," 126.

27. James H. Howard, "Plains-Ojibwa," 21–22, 59–61. See Van Kirk, *Many Tender Ties*, for women's roles in the fur trade. For a discussion of the literature concerning Ojibwa women, see Bruce M. White, "Woman Who Married a Beaver," 109–47.

28. Coues, *New Light*, 1:268–69; Lounsberry, *North Dakota*, 49.

29. Hickerson, "Genesis," 320, 326–27; Delorme, "Turtle Mountain Chippewa," 123; Hesketh, *Turtle Mountain Chippewa*, 110–11; James H. Howard, "Turtle Mountain Chippewa," 37.

30. John Foster, "Plains Métis," 383; Hickerson, "Genesis," 326.

31. Joseph Kinsey Howard, *Strange Empire*, 50; Sealey and Lussier, *Métis*, 45–46.

32. Coues, *New Light*, 1:n. 442; Glover, *Thompson's Narrative*, 165; Lounsberry, *North Dakota* 1:47–48, 51–52 (in canoe); Masson, *Les Bourgeois*, 1:401–403. For more information, see Martha Harroun Foster, "We Know," chap. 2. Sources for the survey of Spring Creek family names include: Bradbury, *Travels;* Coues, *New Light;* Fleming, *Minutes;* Giraud, *Métis;* Hafen, *Mountain Men;* Masson, *Les Bourgeois;*

Morice, *Dictionnaire;* Nasatir, *Before Lewis and Clark;* Thwaites, "Commercial History of Milwaukee," 4: 253–89; "Fur Trade on the Upper Lakes"; and "Mackinac Register of Marriages"; Stewart Wallace, *Dictionary;* W. S. Wallace, *Documents;* St. Louis Genealogical Society, "Catholic Marriages"; Olson, "St. Charles Co."

33. Havard, "French Half-Breeds," 311. For an account of the settlement of Red River Colony, see Giraud, *Métis;* Joseph Kinsey Howard, *Strange Empire;* Morton, *Canadian West;* Ross, *Red River;* Stanley, *Birth of Western Canada.*

34. For the production of pemmican, see Belcourt, "Letter," November 25, 1845, St. Paul, in Hesketh, *Turtle Mountain Chippewa,* 5:143, 145; Chittenden, *American Fur Trade,* 802; Robinson, *Great Fur Land,* 117, 163–65.

35. Ross, *Red River,* 17–18; Sealey and Lussier, *Métis,* 43–44; Schenck, "Against All Odds," 35, 50; Wheeler-Voegelin and Hickerson, *Red Lake,* 66.

36. For an informative account of the Pemmican War, the Battle of Seven Oaks, and the controversy surrounding their historical interpretation, see Coutts and Stuart, *Seven Oaks,* especially Dick, "'Seven Oaks,'" 65–70 and Brown, "Commentary," 90–93. For a firsthand account from the perspective of a British settler, see Ross, *Red River.* For the dating of Métis nationalism, see Brown, "Genesis and Rebirth," 140; Dickason, "'One Nation,'" 31; Peterson, "Many Roads," 37; Joseph Kinsey Howard, *Strange Empire,* 32; Sealey and Lussier, *Métis,* 51. Peterson, "Many Roads," 37 (burst upon"), 64 ("not merely"). Peter Bakker notes that the Métis language, Michif, developed after 1815 in the Great Plains buffalo camps (*Language*).

37. Brown, *Strangers,* 173. For the NWC–HBC merger, see Pritchett, *Red River,* i, 221–22; Galbraith, *Hudson's Bay Company,* 6–8.

38. Innis, *Fur Trade,* 288; Brown, *Strangers,* 199–220. For a comparison of two Red River Settlement communities and the origins of their populations, see Ens, *Homeland.*

39. Ens, *Homeland,* 20; Dawson, "Journal," 19; Keating, *Narrative,* 221–27; Arnold, *Old Pembina,* 102–14.

40. Giraud, *Métis,* 2:71; Rich, *Journal,* 32 ("an uneducated"); Ens, *Homeland,* 20. For discussions on settling the Métis near the Settlement, see Nute, *Documents,* 354; Fleming, *Minutes,* 3:382; Ross, *Red River,* 235–37; Giraud, *Métis,* 2:71; Ens, *Homeland,* 20–21, 51; Sealey and Lussier, *Métis,* 44–45.

41. MacLeod and Morton, *Cuthbert Grant;* Fleming, "Minutes," 3: 216; Sealey and Lussier, *Métis,* 45.

42. Ens, *Homeland,* 20; Giraud, *Métis,* 2:168–69. Spring Creek band members related to Cuthbert Grant included the Edward Wells family. Edward Wells, Sr., married Isabelle McGillis, sister of Marie McGillis, Grant's wife. Edward Wells was the son of Josephte Grant, the sister of Cuthbert Grant. Therefore, in the tangled kinship relations typical of the Métis families, Edward Wells was both a nephew and brother-in-law of Grant (Wells Family Papers; Fleury Family Papers; letter of Henri Letourneau, August 27, 1955, Calgary, Alberta, and letter of L. G. Wells, May 8, 1973, Vancouver, B.C. ([Fleury Family Papers]; *1850 Minnesota Census,* 73/73).

43. Ens, *Homeland*, 28 (regardless); Martin, *Hudson's Bay Company*.

44. Brasser, "Métis Art," 221–29; Robinson, *Great Fur Land*, 49; Joseph Kinsey Howard, *Strange Empire*, 301; Dusenberry, "Waiting," 121; Lederman, "Métis Fiddling," 11–18; Vrooman, "Medicine Fiddle," 19–29; Bakker, *Language;* John C. Crawford, "What Is Michif?," 231–41; and "Speaking Michif," 47–55; Laverdure and Allard, *Michif Dictionary*.

45. Giraud, *Métis*, chaps. 17 and 18, 2:139–76. In fact, this translation of Giraud titles chaps. 17 and 18 "The Circumstances of Nomadism" and "The Consequences of Nomadism."

46. A large body of literature examines these changing attitudes. For example, see Horsman, *Race*. R. David Edmunds discusses the effects of racism on the Métis of the Great Lakes area ("'Unacquainted,'" 185–93). Peterson, "Many Roads," 39; Atwater, *Indians of the Northwest*, 180.

47. Keating, *Narrative*, 2:43 ("The settlement"); Giraud, *Métis*, 2:168; Sprenger, "Métis Nation," 121–22.

48. Sprenger, "Métis Nation," 123–27, 132; Samuel Wood, "Report," 41–42; Ens, "Dispossession," 126–29. Also see continued discussion in chap. 2, "Environmental Change and the Robe Trade."

49. Roe, *North American Buffalo*, 371; Ens, *Homeland*, 38–39.

50. Burlingame, "Buffalo in Trade," 264–78 (robe trade); Larpenteur, *Forty Years*, 90–97, 92 ("many half-breed families").

51. Hornaday, *Extermination*, 443–44 (buffalo robes); Rife, "Kittson," 232–34.

52. U.S. Department of War, "Report of Captain Jonathan Pope," 20, 27–31. Gilman, Gilman, and Stultz describe the extensive Red River cart trails developed by the Métis for transporting robes to markets in St. Paul in *Red River Trails*. Ens, in *Homeland* (28–92), discusses the growth of both HBC and freetrader buffalo product production during these years. Joseph Kinsey Howard, *Strange Empire*, 55 ("The cart").

53. Ross, *Red River*, i, 246.

54. Ibid., 244 (cost), 245 ("the great rendezvous"), 245–50. Thirteen years later, Isaac Stevens, reporting for the Exploration and Surveys Party to the Pacific Ocean, noted a similar organization still in practice ("Reports," 65).

55. Ross, *Red River*, 248 (an English half-breed); Stevens, "Reports," 65 ("I was much"); Swan, "Brief History," 1, 3.

56. Ross, *Red River*, 246 ("tents"), 248.

57. James H. Howard, "Plains-Ojibwa," 21–22; Wheeler-Voegelin and Hickerson, *Red Lake*, appendix C, 5.

58. Murray, "Turtle Mountain Chippewa," 18; Way shaw wush koquen abe, speech, 190–91; Samuel Wood, "Report," 24 (decline of bison noticed). For a discussion of factors leading to the extermination of the buffalo, see chap. 2 of this study (*"We Know"*).

59. John Foster, "Country-Born," 180–82; Judd, "Native Labour," 305–14; Ens, *Homeland,* 75; Camp, "Turtle Mountain Plains," 76–77; Gluek, *Minnesota,* 60–65.

60. Rife, "Kittson," 225–52; Gluek, *Minnesota,* 53–54; Ross, *Red River,* 376 ("Le commerce est libre"), 377.

61. Woolworth, "Sumner's Expedition," 94; Belcourt, "Mixed Blood or Half-Breeds," 14.

62. Denig, *Five Indian Tribes,* 105; Belcourt quoted in Samuel Wood, "Report," 1–36, 27 (families and livestock), 40 (5,000) ("the half-breeds") ("the descendents").

63. *(St. Paul) Minnesota Pioneer,* January 23, 1850, as quoted in Rife, "Kittson," 242–43 ("Their dress"); Rife, "Kittson," 244 ("most of the year"); Belcourt, "Mixed Blood or Half-Breeds," 93–94; Hind, *Narrative,* 1:255 (floods); Woolworth, "Gingras," 17, 20–21.

Historian Nancy Woolworth comments on the isolated nature of these Métis communities. She writes that "between 1851 and 1858, the district elected Norman W. Kittson as Councilor and Joseph Rolette, Jr. and Antoine B. Gingras as its representatives to the Territorial Legislature. The sessions met in January in St. Paul, and the three men therefore had to walk almost 700 miles on snowshoes behind dog sleds to attend" ("Gingras," 20).

64. Havard, "French Half-Breeds," 311; Charles D. Denney Papers; ("Family of Jean Baptiste Wilke," 562; "Family of Michael Klyne and Madeline Beauchemine," 289.001); *1850 Minnesota Census;* St. Boniface (Manitoba) Roman Catholic Church, "Registre des Baptemes, Mariages and Sepultures, 1825–1834"; Gail Morin, "Individual Narrative of Charlotte Pelletier," June 26, 2003.

65. See chap. 2 for genealogical diagrams. *1850 Minnesota Census,* Pembina Dist., no. 54, 94 (household and visitation numbers), (parents of Judith Wilkie Berger), 108, 75 (Klynes), 73 (Isabell and Edward Wells), 93; *Half-Breed Script Applications, 1886–1901, 1906; Index: Half-Breed Script Applications, 1886-1901, 1906;* Charles D. Denney Papers ("Family of Jean Baptiste Wilke," 562; "Family of Michael Klyne and Madeline Beauchemine," 289.001); Picton, "Collection"; St. Florent Roman Catholic Church, "Mission de St Florent"; Assumption Roman Catholic Church, Records; Devine, "Métis or Country-Born?"; Devine, conversation, July 2003; Morin, *Metis Families; Manitoba Scrip;* and "Individual Narrative of Charlotte Pelletier," June 26, 2003, and telephone conversation, July 2003.

66. See Martha Harroun Foster, "We Know," table 2, 145–46, for specific individuals' names and residence numbers. *1850 Minnesota Census.* Another column in the census recorded the individuals' race. Census instructions included abbreviations for black (B), mulatto (M), Indian (I), and a blank space for white. All of the Pembina residents have blank spaces in this category, indicating that the census taker considered these people to be white, not Indian. There is also the possibility that he felt the subject of race, in a region such as the Red River Valley, too politically charged and simply ignored the column. The 1860 census

taker would have a different approach and opinion. For the role of the census enumerator in determining race, see Thornton, *Holocaust and Survival*, 216.

67. Thorne, *Many Hands*, 135; Gates, "Indian Allotments"; Samuel Wood, "Report," 3–4, 6–9 ("Half-breed Reserves").

68. In 1817, several local Chippewa and Cree leaders negotiated a treaty with Thomas Selkirk (as proprietor of the Red River Settlement) and the HBC that ceded territory along the Red River and its tributaries. Other Crees and the Assiniboines resented Chippewa participation in the treaty negotiations, claiming the area as theirs (Ross, *Red River*, 412). The United States recognized Chippewa control of the area in the 1825 Prairie du Chien Treaty in an attempt to bring peace between the Sioux and the Chippewas. Wheeler-Voegelin and Hickerson, *Red Lake*, 93, 130, 129 ("several hundred half-breeds"); Ross, *Red River*, 411–12 ("If we may judge").

69. Wheeler-Voegelin and Hickerson, *Red Lake*, 131, appendix C, 6–7; Ross, *Red River*, 411–12.

70. "Treaty with the Chippewa . . . 1854," 2.

71. Ibid., throughout, especially 3.

72. Ibid., 3, 27, 32, 85, 142; Wub-e-ke-niew, *We Have the Right*, 322–26. For a list of Spring Creek band individuals who were accepted or rejected, see Martha Harroun Foster, "We Know," table 2, 145–46.

73. Wheeler-Voegelin and Hickerson, *Red Lake*, 147, 163 ("Today the Pembina") ("to a certain extent").

74. Wheeler-Voegelin and Hickerson, *Red Lake*, appendix C (8), 166.

75. "Treaty with the Chippewa . . . 1863," 653–55 ("related"); Horr, *Chippewa Indians*, 6:277–78 ("in lieu of"). For a list of case numbers, see Martha Harroun Foster, "We Know," table 2, 145–46.

76. Wheeler-Voegelin and Hickerson, *Red Lake*, 163.

CHAPTER 2

1. Ens, *Homeland*, 76; Giraud, *Métis*, 2:133–34.

2. Giraud, *Métis*, 2:280; Ens, *Homeland*, 76; Dobak, "Killing," 45–48; Burlingame, "Buffalo in Trade," 280.

3. Burlingame, "Buffalo in Trade," 274–76 (1831, Fort Union); Larpenteur, *Forty Years*, 63–64, 72–80, 90–97. As noted previously, Métis trading and working at Fort Union included Jacques Berger, probably the father of Pierre Berger, who would lead the Spring Creek band (*Forty Years*, 90–97); Malone, Roeder, and Lang, *Montana*, 55. The steamboat era in Montana began when the *Yellowstone* reached Fort Union, near Montana's eastern border, in 1832 (Malone, Roeder, and Lang, *Montana*, 55; Chittenden, *American Fur Trade*, 338–39). Dobak, "Killing," 42–46 (42 [Fort Benton], 46 [products of 115,000 buffalo]); Giraud, *Métis*, 2:135.

4. *Pembina (North Dakota) Pioneer*, August 7, 1879; Thomson, "Fort Pembina," 9–11.

NOTES TO PAGES 54–58

5. Sprenger, "Buffalo Hunting," 123–29; Samuel Wood, "Report," 41–42; Ens, "Dispossession or Adaptation?" 126–29.

6. Sealey and Lussier, *Métis*, 37; Hesketh, *Turtle Mountain Chippewa*, 107–109 (Way shaw wush koquen abe's speech); Hornaday, *Extermination*, 489 ("very scarce"); Denig, *Five Indian Tribes*, 118 ("appear in full") (emphasis added).

7. Hayden, "Geology and Natural History," 12:151.

8. Hind, *Narrative*, 1:180.

9. The classic works supporting overhunting as the principal cause of the buffalo's extinction include Hornaday, *Extermination;* and Burlingame, "Buffalo in Trade," 262–91. A recent article supporting this view is Dobak, "Killing," 33–52. For the role of environmental factors, see Flores, "Bison Ecology," 465–85; Isenberg, "Return of the Bison," 179–96; Koucky, "Buffalo Disaster," 23–30. Kenneth and Sally Owens explore the role of disease in the disappearance of the buffalo in "Buffalo and Bacteria." Also, see Isenberg, "Policy of Destruction" and *Destruction of the Bison*. Owens and Owens, "Buffalo and Bacteria," 66 (resistance to disease); Jamison, "Edmonton Hunt," 29 ("before the buffalo"). Blackleg is an often-fatal infectious disease caused by a soil bacterium.

10. Hayes, *Animal Health*, 139; Owens and Owens, "Buffalo and Bacteria," 66–67; Koucky, "Buffalo Disaster," 28.

11. Roe, *North American Buffalo*, 396; Ens, *Homeland*, 77–78, 117.

12. Ens, *Homeland*, 111, 117; Woolworth, "Gingras," 26–27. Gerhard Ens points out another factor encouraging the Métis to move their hunts farther west: because of increased border control, it was becoming too expensive to transport robes across the boundary at Red River to the lucrative U.S. markets. Farther west the herds still gathered in great numbers and border supervision was sporadic (*Homeland*, 117).

13. Fear of miscegenation and the notion that mixed-descent children combined the worst attributes of their parents can be found in nationally read popular literature early in the nineteenth century. Cooper, in *The Prairie*, makes his attitudes clear. The main character, Natty Bumppo, works as a trapper in the Missouri River country. He says of the area mixed-bloods, "The half-and-halfs that one meets in these distant districts are altogether more barbarous than the real savage" (24). Cooper's character Ester Bush, wife of a settler who was offered an Indian wife, angrily asks her husband, "Would ye disgrace color, and family, and nation, by mixing white blood with red, and would ye be the parent of a race of mules!" (346). Brian Hubner examines Cooper's works in "'A Race of Mules,'" 61–74.

14. Marble, "Red River." Works that consider the portrayal of Métis in nineteenth-century popular literature include: Hubner, "'A Race of Mules'"; Scheick, *The Half-Blood;* Smits, "'Squaw Men,'" 29–61; and Sprenger, "Buffalo Hunting."

15. Joseph Rolette was a member of the Minnesota Territorial Assembly from 1853 to 1855 and of the Territorial Council from 1855 to 1857 (Libby, "Gazetteer of Pioneers," 1:378–79). Marble "Red River," 582.

16. Marble, "Red River," 606.
17. Ibid., 584–85.
18. Ibid., 588–89. This image of Métis drudgery even entered the U.S. Congressional Record when Governor Stevens's exploration party reported that on the women "depend all the drudgery of camp duties" (Stevens, "Reports," 56, 66).
19. Marble, "Red River," 595.
20. Dawson, "Surveying," 19; Ens, *Homeland*, 78, 213–14.
21. Some of these camps include: Touchwood Hills, Souris River, Saskatchewan Forks, the Fort Edmonton area, Lac la Biche, St. Laurent, Prairie Ronde, Lac Ste. Anne, La Coulée Chapelle, Lac la Vielle, and Coulées Cheminée (Ens, *Homeland*, 118, 213–14; Sealey and Lussier, *Métis*, 99–100). For a history of the Batoche community, see Payment, *"Free People."*

The Milk River flows from the eastern edge of Glacier Park near St. Mary's Lake, northeasterly to Alberta, where it parallels the boundary line for some one hundred miles before turning south into Montana again. Thence it flows through north-central Montana to join the Missouri River near Fort Peck.

Explorer Captain John Palliser, describing the area, wrote of "arid prairies" along the forty-ninth parallel, where his party was "in great want of water, and the heat was very great while traveling through burning sand" (Palliser, *Journals*, 7, 139–45). Others supported this idea of "the Great American Desert." See, for example, Russell, *Red River Colony*, 66.

22. Cunningham, *Montana Weather*, 6–8. Stegner, *Wolf Willow*, 3; Stegner grew up just north of the Montana-Saskatchewan border (6).
23. Larpenteur, *Forty Years*, 75–76 ("which abounded"). For Métis moving into the traditional territory of the Assiniboines and Gros Ventres, see "ARCIA, 1854," 189–90; Stevens, "Report," S. Ex. Doc. 78, 148–49; Ewers, "Chippewa Cree," 52–56; Kline, interview, 2; Van Den Broeck, "Sketch," 1; Shambow, interview, 5; Guardipee, "Eli Guardipee's Story," 2–3.
24. It is possible that Tom "Lavatta" was Tom Lavallée. It might be noted here that one person could handle several carts at once by tying one draft animal to the cart in front, much the way a pack string of horses is handled by one rider. Guardipee, "Eli Guardipee's Story," 3–4 ("great camp of breeds"). Dodson is located about forty-five miles east of Havre on the Milk River of north-central Montana.
25. Guardipee, "Eli Guardipee's Story," 4.
26. This account is taken from the reminiscences of Clemence Gourneau Berger in "Judith Basin," 11–12.
27. Ibid., 11.
28. Ibid.
29. Ibid.
30. Ibid. (emphasis added).
31. For the traveling of missionaries, see O'Connell, "Juneaux's Trading Post," 1; SPM "Baptismal Register." For Fort Benton records, see SPM, "Marriage

Register" 1, no. 1; 1, no. 3; 1, no. 5; 2, no. 7; 3, no. 13; 19, no. 95. (Alexis Gardépée had two of his children baptized at Fort Campbell near Fort Benton in September 1858 [SPM, "Baptismal Register," 1, no. 14].) O'Connell, "Juneaux's Trading Post," 2 (Pierre Laverdure); SPM, Baptismal Register, 104, no. 2271 (Gardepi baptism).

32. Giraud, *Métis*, 2:405; O'Connell, "Juneaux's Trading Post," 1.

33. O'Connell, "Juneaux's Trading Post," 1.

34. Shambow, interview, 6.

35. Van Den Broeck, "Sketch," 1; Kline, interview, 2.

36. For the Janeaux family name, see Fonda, "Early Wisconsin," 218–19; Grignon, "Recollections," 292; Morice, *Dictionnaire*, 136; Pratt, "Reminiscences," 130–33; *1850 Wisconsin Census*, Milwaukee County. O'Connell, "Juneaux's Trading Post," 1–2 (Janeaux on the Missouri River). Kline, interview, 2 (Fort Stevenson). Fort Stevenson was south of present-day Minot, North Dakota, on the bend of the Missouri River. Kline, interview, 2 (Milk River).

37. O'Connell, "Juneaux's Post," 1–2; Van Den Broeck, "Sketch,"1–2 (Janeaux appointed deputy); *War of the Rebellion*, Series 1, vol. 48, part 1, 636–38, 784–85, 979–80, 636 ("rejecting all overtures"), 636–37 ("Half-breed traders"), 637 ("break up the trading"), 638 ("It seems impossible"); Utley, *Indian Frontier*, 76–81; JFP, box 17, folder 20.

38. Wright to E. P. Smith, commissioner of Indian Affairs, Washington, D.C., June 2, 1873, NARG 75, M234, roll 497; Wright refers to I. G. Butler and Bro., which he probably confused with the I. G. Baker firm. No I. G. Butler is listed as having a business in early Fort Benton (Leeson, *Montana*, 502). Baker owned the oldest trading post in Fort Benton still in operation at the time. He had bought out Pierre Choteau, Jr., and the American Fur Company in 1866. He also had posts on the Milk River, including one at the mouth of Frenchman's Creek (Bradley, "Manuscript," 345–47). For one version of I. G. Baker's and T. C. Power's involvement in the liquor business, see Sharp, *Whoop-Up Country*, especially 38–41, 214–15. Sharp, *Merchant Princes*, 8–9.

39. *BR*, "Half-Breeds," October 17, 1879.

40. Kline, interview, 2 (Ben Kline was a valuable employee because he spoke English [Van Den Broeck, "Ben Kline," 2]); O'Connell, "Juneaux's Trading Post," 1–2; Kline, interview, 3 ("It was necessary").

41. Kline, interview, 2–3. Kline also took for granted Biedler's enthusiasm for "running down bootleggers, which was one of their main duties at that time," since, Kline suspected, Biedler "consumed considerable of the condemned material" (Ibid.).

42. Michif is the French-Cree language used widely by the Métis at the time and still in use in Métis communities today, including those near and on Turtle Mountain Reservation. For more information, see John C. Crawford, "What Is Michif?," 231–41; and "Speaking Michif," 47–55; and Laverdure and Allard, *Michif Dictionary*.

H. M. Robinson wrote from his own observations, but also freely incorporated the works of others. He typically denied any indication of Métis independence or ability, and therefore stressed the place of a few able leaders in an otherwise (in his view) primitive, irrational, and superstitious "mongrel" population (Robinson, *Great Fur Land*, 4, 48, 50, 109).

43. Ibid., 276.

44. Begg, *North-West*, 2:85.

45. When Janeaux arrived on the Milk River, he already may have been connected to the LaFountain and Fagnant families of Red River Settlement and Qu'Appelle, Saskatchewan, who hunted on the Milk River in the 1870s. He may also have been related to several of the Milk River families from early nineteenth-century associations in the Great Lakes area (see the Charlotte Adam Network diagram).

46. Betsy Kiplin Berger, "Sporty," 1.

47. Riel, *Writings*, 2:225,357; and 5:221, 225, 229; "Treaty with the Chippewa ... 1854," Ex. Doc. No. 193, schedule B, 27. Pierre Berger, Sr., and Pierre, Jr., were issued scrip no. 138 and no. 5 under the 1863–1864 Treaty with the Chippewa of the Red Lake and Pembina Bands (Wub-e-ke-niew, *We Have the Right*, 323). For Judith Wilkie's marriage and for Jean Baptiste Wilkie, see Swan, "Brief History," 1, 8; Thackeray, *Centennial Celebration*, 14; Marie Granot Ehlert (great-great-granddaughter of Judith Wilkie Berger), interview, July 16, 1996; SPM, "Baptismal Register," 127, no. 2659; SPM, "Marriage Register," 19, no. 93; *1880 Montana Territorial Census*, Meagher County, Judith Basin; Swan, "Brief History," 6–8 (Wilkie/LaFountain relationship), 1, 7 (Wilkie/Fleury relationship); *1850 Minnesota Census*, Pembina District.

48. Joseph Kinsey Howard, *Strange Empire*, 49–50.

49. Stegner, *Wolf Willow*, 8.

50. There are many works that address the 1869–1870 Manitoba Resistance. For an introduction to the period, see Joseph Kinsey Howard, *Strange Empire;* W. L. Morton, *Manitoba;* and Ens, *Homeland*. Arthur S. Morton, *Canadian West*, 920; Sprague, "Government Lawlessness," 415–41; Ens, *Homeland*, 139.

51. Ens, *Homeland*, 151–54.

52. For historians who adopted this "primitive" reversion interpretation, see the works of George F. G. Stanley, and Giraud. Gerhard Ens convincingly argues that "the dispersal of the Red River Métis between 1850 and 1875 should not be seen primarily as the self-inflicted exile of a 'primitive' people nor the forced dispossession by the Canadian government. Rather, it should be seen as an adaptive, innovative response to new economic opportunities ("Dispossession or Adaptation?" 122.)

Giraud, *Métis*, 2:388–90, 389 (criticism of Métis by the clergy), 642 (n. 117), 388 ("These are people") (breaking into Métis homes).

53. Giraud, *Métis*, 2:416 ("entered into"); Rich, *Hudson's Bay Company*, 2:515 ("efforts at husbandry"); Stanley, *Birth of Western Canada*, 8 ("indolent, thoughtless and improvident"). Sprenger lists many examples of how historians of the fur trade and of Canada portrayed the Métis as "irrational, incomprehensible, and non-adaptive" in "Métis Nation," 120–35.

54. Williams to Acting Asst. Adjt. Gen., February 6, 1878, NARG 75 M666, roll 362. For the Cree-Métis relationship in Montana, see the work of Larry Burt, who has documented the troubled history of the Crees in Montana. Burt, "Crooked Piece," 47 (Crees and Métis camping together on the Milk River).

55. O'Connell, "Ft. Turney," 1.

56. Sweitzer to Asst. Adjt. Gen., March 8, 1875, NARG 75, M234, roll 503, 3; Black to Asst. Adjt. Gen., December 5, 1879, NARG 75, M234, roll 518, 4.

57. Alderson to Smith, May 1, 1874, NARG 75, M234, roll 498, 4; Terry to Sweitzer, March 23, 1875, NARG 75, B234, roll 503 ("break up").

58. Koury, *Military Posts*, 6.

59. *BR*, October 17, 1879 ("These Canadian"); Thornton to Evarts, November 15, 1879, NARG 75, M234, roll 517, 2 ("British half breeds"); Turner, *North-West Mounted Police*, 1:498 ("all the half-breeds"); Dept. of Indian Affairs, Canada, "Annual Report, 1879" (Ottawa: 1880), 88.

60. Black to Potter, November 26, 1879, 2; Black to Asst. Adjt. Gen., January 28, 1880, 6; Kline, interview, 4. Ben Kline reported that "the Sioux Indians later robbed the breeds of all of their ponies and they were finally forced to travel about on their carts by putting their cows in the shafts in lieu of ponies" (Kline, interview, 4). The Métis received no assistance or compensation from the government to ease their predicament. Ewers, "Chippewa Cree," 85.

61. Ewers, *Blackfeet*, 72. Giraud, *Métis*, 2:413–14 (buffalo disappear in Canada). Jamison reported that the great herds were gone from Alberta and "the nearby plains" by 1877 ("Edmonton Hunt," 24). Garcia, *Tough Trip*, 184–85; Giraud, *Métis*, 2:414.

62. Swan, "Brief History," 1; Van Den Broeck, "Sketch," 2–3.

63. Swan, "Brief History," 1; Van Den Broeck, "Sketch," 2–3.

The sources for the relationships are listed in the notes for the kinship network diagrams. The Gayion family may be that of Joseph Gagnon and Margaret Chartier. The couple had a boy, Herman, in the Judith Basin about September 21, 1879. The family may have been connected to Margaret Daignon (Daniels), wife of Spring Creek band trader Paul Morase. Margaret Daignon sponsored the baby at baptism (SPM, "Baptismal Register," 127, no. 2664).

Cottonwood Creek runs north just west of present-day Lewistown and joins Spring Creek near Hanover, a few miles northwest of Lewistown. Spring Creek flows from Big Springs about three miles southeast of Lewistown, through the town, and continues in a northwesterly direction to meet the Judith River. Confusingly, north of Lewistown, near Brooks, Warm Spring Creek (an entirely different stream) also flows northwest and joins the Judith River about ten miles north of the confluence of Spring Creek and the Judith. As mentioned above, today Spring Creek is often referred to as Big Spring Creek.

64. Swan, "Brief History," 3–5; Van Den Broeck, "Sketch," 3 ("killed lots of them") ("whole week to"). As mentioned above, Gayion may be an alternative spelling of Gagnon, in which case the family had a long history in St. François Xavier and Pembina.

65. The most effective illustration of the Spring Creek band kinship network would have been a large circle. In this way the interrelatedness of the band members would be easier to see. Although I have divided the band into "networks," the divisions are somewhat artificial in the sense that all families are connected, and the patterns can take various forms on paper.

Sources for Spring Creek band family networks include: Clemence Gourneau Berger, "Judith Basin"; Ehlert, interview, July 16, 1996, and subsequent conversations; Fleury Family Papers; Kline, interview; LaFountain Family Papers; Robert and Treena LaFountain, interviews, September 17, 1995, July 26, 1996; "*Mineral Argus* and *Fergus County Argus* Index to Deaths"; Fergus County Genealogical Society, "Index to Births" and "Index to Marriages"; SPM, "Baptismal Register," 127, no. 2659; SPM, "Marriage Register," 19, no. 93; Shoup, interview, July 16, 1996; Sprague and Frye, *Genealogy;* George F. G. Stanley, Thomas Flanagan, and Claude Rocan, "Biographical Index," in Riel, *Writings*, Vol. 5; Swan, "Brief History;" Joseph Kinsey Howard Papers; Thackeray, *Centennial Celebration;* "Treaty with the Chippewa . . . 1854," Ex. Doc. No. 193, schedule B, 27; *1850 Minnesota Census, 1860 Minnesota Census,* Pembina District; *1880 Montana Census,* Meagher County, Judith Basin; Van Den Broeck, "Sketch,"; Walraven, interview, July 30, 1996; Wells-Norlin, interview, July 13, 1997; Wells Family Papers; Zilba, conversation, August 24, 1997; Zwolle and Quiring, *LaTray Family Genealogy;* Charles D. Denney Papers ("Family of Jean Baptiste Wilke," 562; "Family of Michael Klyne and Madeline Beauchemine," 289.001); *Half-Breed Script Applications, 1886–1901, 1906; Index: Half-Breed Script Applications, 1886–1901, 1906,* "Collection de Picton"; St. Florent Roman Catholic Church, "Mission de St. Florent"; Assumption Roman Catholic Church, Records, Pembina, N.Dak.; Devine, "Métis or Country-Born?"; Devine, conversation, July 2003; Morin, *Metis Families; Manitoba Scrip;* and telephone conversations, July 2003.

66. Sleeper-Smith, *Indian Women and French Men;* Murphy, *Gathering of Rivers.*

67. Black to Asst. Adjt. Gen., January 28, 1879 (Miles broke up the Métis camps). Miles, *Personal Recollections,* 306, 309 (Sitting Bull) ("sharp engagement") ("location of such").

68. Turner, *North-West Mounted Police,* 1:466 ("future all property"); Miles, *Personal Recollections,* 309 ("living in that") ("practically British subjects"), 310 ("This people had") ("determined") ("gathered them"). Reference to this campaign is

also found in the following: U.S. Secretary of War, *Annual Report, 1879,* "Miles's Report" (September 1879), 61–64; *Army and Navy Register* 16 (August 2, 1879), 954; Virginia Weisel Johnson, *The Unregimented General: A Biography of Nelson A. Miles* (Boston: Houghton Mifflin, 1962), 217–21; Turner, *North-West Mounted Police,* 1:461–74.

69. Turner, *North-West Mounted Police,* 1:466.
70. Kline, interview, 3.
71. Ibid., 3–4.
72. Leeson, *Montana,* 501. In the chapter "Pioneers of Chouteau County," for example, Leeson lists several Métis living in Fort Benton in 1862–1863 (496, 501). Ewers, "Chippewa Cree," 148–55.

CHAPTER 3

1. Black to Asst. Adjt. Gen., December 5, 1879, NARG 75, M234, roll 518, 4 ("hostile Sioux"); ibid., December 27, 1879, NARG 75, M234, roll 518, 1 ("committed . . . no depredations").

2. Ibid., December 27, 1879, NARG 75, M234, roll 518, 1 ("all Canadian Half-Breeds"); Potter to Black, November 3, 1879, NARG 75, M234, roll 518 ("authorized by") ("see they are removed"); Black to Asst. Adjt. Gen., January 28, 1880, NARG 75, M234, roll 518, 3 ("destitute condition").

3. Asst. Adjt. Gen. to Col. Ruger, November 6, 1879, NARG 75, M234, roll 518 ("to act in") ("If these halfbreeds"); Black to Potter, Helena, November 26, 1879, NARG 75, M234, roll 518, 1 ("American Half Breeds"); Black to Asst. Adjt. Gen., January 28, 1880, NARG 75, M234, roll 518, 6 ("if those Half Breeds").

4. Black to Asst. Adjt. Gen., January 28, 1880, NARG 75, M234, roll 518, 7.

5. Black to Potter, Helena, November 26, 1879, NARG 75, M234, roll 518, 2.

6. Sherman to Headquarters, "Endorsements," January 3, 1880, NARG 75, M234, roll 518.

7. Potter to Black, December 5, 1879, NARG 75, M234, roll 518.

8. Flanagan, *Riel,* 97–101; Stanley, *Riel,* 230 (John Ireland). Riel was also connected by marriage to several families who had members in Dakota and Montana, including the Poitra, Gladu, and Lavallée families (Riel, *Writings,* 5:262–63, 287–88, 326).

9. Flanagan, *Riel,* 103 (envisioning a confederacy); Riel, *Writings,* 2:205, 5:287. Riel also possibly had relatives (of in-laws) among the hunters. Riel's sister Octavie was married to Louis Lavallée. At least one family of that name was hunting with the Métis on the Milk River that summer.

10. *BR,* December 19, 1879 (Milk River camp); Riel, *Writings,* 2:208. "There are many buffalo," he wrote, "I have seen immense numbers of them." (translation by author).

11. Riel, *Writings,* 2:210, 218–19 (hunting rights); Flanagan, *Riel,* 105 ("The Half Breeds are"), 106–109.

12. Riel, *Writings,* 2:220–21, 223–27.

13. "Chippewa Half-Breeds of Lake Superior," Ex. Doc. 193.

14. Colonel Nelson A. Miles (Riel politely addressed him as "General," his Civil War rank) was stationed at Fort Keogh on the Yellowstone River, near present-day Miles City. Riel, "Petition," *Writings*, 2:223–26 (a copy of the petition may also be found in Martha Harroun Foster, "We Know," 314–17); Flanagan, *Riel*, 110.

15. Flanagan, *Riel*, 110; Riel, *Writings*, 234.

16. Flanagan, "Riel and the Dispersion," 179–90.

17. Sources for family relationships include the following: "Treaty with the Chippewa . . . 1854"; Wub-e-ke-niew, *We Have the Right; 1850 Minnesota Census, 1860 Minnesota Census*, Pembina District; *1880 Montana Census*, Meagher County, Judith Basin; SPM, "Baptismal Register," and "Marriage Register"; Stanley, Flanagan, Rocan, "Biographical Index," in Riel, *Writings*, 5:207–360; Flanagan, "Riel and the Dispersion," 1186–87; and Sprague and Frye, *Genealogy*.

If more information were available concerning the remaining ten men, it is plausible that we would find that their marriages, or those of family members, also united them to the other signatories. Some of the names are very common, making it difficult to identify several individuals with certainty. For specific information on family relationships, Pembina treaty applications, and Pembina census participation of the petition signatories, see Martha Harroun Foster, "We Know," 314–21.

18. Flanagan, "Riel and the Dispersion," 187.

19. Flanagan, *Riel*, 110; Riel, *Writings*, 2:227; Ewers, "Chippewa Cree," 87–89. For information on whiskey suppliers, see Sharp, *Whoop-Up Country*, especially 39–42, 214–15; Sharp, *Merchant Princes*, 8–9.

20. Granville Stuart to Fergus, January 21, 1886, JFP; Malone, Roeder, and Lang, *Montana*, 123, 162 (Granville Stuart was territorial council president in 1883); Ewers, "Chippewa Cree," 89 (Department of Interior rejects plan); Flanagan, *Riel*, 110.

21. Riel, *Writings*, 2:228.

22. Carroll, Montana, was a rough trading village 150 miles below Fort Benton, on the Missouri River, and about sixty miles north of the Spring Creek Métis community (Lewistown). The Spring Creek settlement was located on the Carroll Trail, which ran from Carroll to Helena. Flanagan, *Riel*, 110–11; Joseph Kinsey Howard, *Strange Empire*, 338 ("A squalid"); *BR*, September 17, 1880; Schultz, *My Life*, 201–202.

23. Schultz, *My Life*, 202.

24. Riel, *Writings*, 229 (n. 1); Flanagan, *Riel*, 111. Flat Willow Creek, southeast of Lewistown, flows north of the Snowy Mountains, eastward into the Musselshell River. Schultz, *My Life*, 203, 206 ("a banner season").

25. Ewers, "Chippewa Cree," 87; *1880 Montana Census*, Meagher County, Judith Basin. Another problem associated with estimating the Métis population through

the 1880 Census is that the enumerators entered a variety of racial designations in the "color" column. For example, most of the Spring Creek band is enumerated as "Indian."

"Wood hawks," as they were known, cut wood for the steamers making their way to Fort Benton. Several Spring Creek band members, including Mose LaTray and the Doney brothers, occasionally made a living in this way. ("Mose LaTray—The Woodhawks," in Deal and McDonald, *Heritage Book*, 575–76.)

St. Peter's Mission, founded in 1863 close to the Teton River near present-day Choteau, Montana, was moved three times before locating permanently between the Sun and Dearborn rivers, about fifteen miles west of present-day Cascade (Bradley, "Manuscript," 315–16; Tabor, "History of St. Peter's," 5).

26. Overholser, *Fort Benton*, 288.

27. Koury, *Guarding*, 15, 18; Swan, "Brief History," 4; Vulcan, *MA*, March 27, 1884.

28. Koury, *Guarding*, 3–4, 8, 13–14, 30; "Reedsfort"," *MA*, March 24, 1884. Called Camp Lewis after a former major of the Seventh Infantry, W. H. Lewis, the summer camp gave the town of Lewistown its name (Koury, *Guarding*, 31).

29. Swan, "Brief History," 4, 6; Vern Anderson, "LaTray Family"; D. Jackson, "Early History," 1–2; Deal and McDonald, *Heritage Book*, 564, 566.

30. Swan, "Brief History," 6; Homestead Entry Applications.

31. Breed Creek is a tributary of Spring Creek, which parallels Boyd Creek just to the south. Van Den Broeck, "Sketch," 3; Swan, "Brief History," 3, 6–7; Homestead Entry Applications.

32. Swan, "Brief History," 3, 6–7.

33. E. C. Abbott and Smith, *We Pointed*, 192. According to Isabelle Larocque (LaRocque), Joe Doney first settled in Chicago Gulch, a tributary of Ford's Creek, north of what would become the site of Fort Maginnis. Joe Larocque settled both there and in nearby Collar Gulch (Larocque, interview, in Conrad Anderson, "Roy," 22).

34. For filing dates, see Martha Harroun Foster, "We Know," 323–24.

35. These families are also more likely to be counted in the census, since the hunters were away hunting at census time. *1880 Montana Census*, Meagher County, Judith Basin.

36. Isaie Berger was a carpenter and his father, Pierre, a blacksmith.

37. Homestead Entry Applications; Richard White, *American West*, 147 (national average).

38. The later designation of some Métis families (exclusive of those descended from Canadian Crees who moved south after 1885) as Landless Indians has different historical roots, stemming from the exclusion of the Little Shell Band of Chippewa (many of whom were Métis) from the Turtle Mountain Reservation rolls in the 1890s. As will be seen in the following chapter, these Métis became "landless" (i.e., lacking reservation land or a recognized homeland) by the refusal of authorities to acknowledge their Turtle Mountain tribal status.

39. Any sort of statistical analysis of birthplace using the census data would be distorted by the absence of so many hunting families, therefore it is not attempted here. *1880 Montana Census*, Meagher County, Judith Basin, Sup. Dist. 78, Enumerator Dist. 23.

40. Ibid.

41. Ibid.; Chouteau County, Fort Benton, Enumerator Dist. 3; Meagher County, Musselshell Valley, Sup. Dist. 78, Enumerator Dist. 23.

42. *1880 Montana Census*, Chouteau County, Shonkin Creek, Enumerator Dist. 4.

43. Stuart, *Forty Years*, 2:142–44.

44. Ibid., 2:134.

45. Swan, "Brief History," 4–5.

46. Ibid., 5.

47. Paul, interview; Ehlert, interview, July 16, 1996; Shoup, interview, July 16, 1996; LaRocque, interview.

48. As noted below, the Spring Creek band members spoke French, Chippewa, Cree, and Michif. Most informants identified their speech and that of their parents and grandparents as "Cree" or "Chippewa," when actually it was Michif (John C. Crawford "What Is Michif?" 232, 238). For a discussion of Michif, see John C. Crawford, "What Is Michif?," 231–51; Laverdure and Allard, *Michif Dictionary*. Schultz, *My Life*, 202 ("They were").

49. Joseph Kinsey Howard, *Strange Empire*, 345. The reading and writing skills of the Spring Creek band are not reflected in the 1880 census, where the enumerator lists even trader Francis Janeaux (whose letters survive) as illiterate. This may have been, in part, because he only questioned the residents about their ability to speak and write English, although that does not explain his listing Janeaux as illiterate (*1880 Montana Census*, Meagher County, Judith Basin). Arthur Maritz was the first teacher and taught briefly before Brassey (Mercy Jackson, "Public and City Schools of Fergus County," 1). Swan, "Mrs. Swan," December 22, 1968, *LNA*, and Shoup, interview (attended school in Pembina) (Francis Janeaux and Ben Kline spoke English); Mercy Jackson, "Lewistown Schools," 1; Deal and McDonald, *Heritage Book*, 157–58.

50. Swan, "Brief History," 3, 7–8. Elizabeth Swan wrote that the hymns were sung in "French or Cree." As noted above, many informants referred to the Michif language as "Cree" (John C. Crawford, "What Is Michif?," 232, 238). Joseph Kinsey Howard, *Strange Empire*, 344–45 ("astonished").

51. Garcia, *Tough Trip*, 260–61.

52. Swan, "Brief History," 7.

53. Ibid.

54. Naturalization Applications, Fergus County, Mont.; "Naturalization Record Index, 1887–1910," Lewistown Genealogy Society; Martha Harroun Foster, "We Know," 285–86, 329–30.

55. Joseph Kinsey Howard, *Strange Empire*, 345. The Monet dit Bellehumeur family was known by both names, Monet (Monette) and Bellehumeur. Four Bellehumeur families, including a Michael Bellehumeur (the name of Marguerite's great-grandfather) are found among the applicants for land under the half-breed provisions of the 1854 Chippewa Treaty. The 1850 U.S. census, Pembina District, Minnesota Territory, includes sixteen "Monisette" (a variant spelling of Monette) families. Joseph Kinsey Howard, *Strange Empire*, 346 ("The romance"); and Howard Papers, box 16, folder 2, ("very dark"). Alex C. Botkin, political ally of Riel in Montana, also commented on Marguerite's appearance and illiteracy, writing that she "looked like a full-blood Indian and was illiterate" (Botkin, "John Brown," 18–22).

56. For the genealogy of the Bellehumeur family see: Riel, *Writings*, 2:294, 5:308, and Sprague and Frye, *Genealogy*.

57. Stanley, *Riel*, 244; Riel, *Writings*, 2:243 ("that C.A. broadwater"). Wilder's Landing was on the Missouri River near Carroll.

58. Riel, *Writings*, 2:246–54, 253 ("reach public opinion"); Flanagan, *Riel*, 111–12.

59. See Malone, *Battle for Butte*, for a lively account of Montana politics and mining, including reports of flagrant bribery and outrageous electoral fraud.

60. Martin Maginnis, incumbent congressman (1872–1884) representing Montana Territory, was editor of the *Helena Independent*, not surprisingly a Democratic newspaper. Riel, "An Open Letter," *Helena Daily Herald*, October 20, 1882, and *(Fort Benton) River Press*, October 25, 1882 (A copy is also reprinted in Riel, *Writings*, 2:257–58); Botkin, "John Brown," 18–22.

For an intriguing study of Métis voting and the role of Louis Riel, see Mumford, "Métis and the Vote," 38–45.

61. Many early Montanans married Indian women. The non–Red River Métis half-breed population was relatively large in this sparsely populated state. When Riel used the term "half-breed," he, of course, intended no disrespect. For him, as for other Métis, it was simply the English translation of the French word "métis." Riel, *Writings*, 2:259 ("White men married"), 271–72. Riel wrote,

> There are at St. Peter's Mission, near Fort Shaw, about twenty-five Half-breed families who are willing and trying to farm. There are fifty of them settled in the Judith Basin and its close vicinity. There were seventy of them settled in the neighborhood of Wilder's Landing last winter, eighty others at the mouth of the Musselshell and further down towards Fort Peck. How many more Half-breed families live separated from each other and scattered over the Territory? In all they are more numerous than any one Indian tribe in Montana.

Wilder's Landing was just east of Carroll on the Missouri River. Malone, *Battle for Butte*, 65–66.

62. Malone, *Battle for Butte,* 66.

63. Stanley, *Riel,* 246–47. Riel himself was not yet a citizen. He had declared his intention to become a citizen on May 17, 1880, but it was not finalized until March 16, 1883, after he had fulfilled the residency requirement (Riel, *Writings,* 2:166–67, 220–21). Riel to editor of the *(Helena) Weekly Herald,* December 21, 1882 ("to use their influence").

64. *(Helena) Weekly Herald,* December 21, 1882.

65. Sharp, *Whoop-Up Country,* 114–15; Stanley, *Riel,* 247; *BR,* May 19, 1883 ("complicity") ("the leader") ("were British"); Overholser, *Fort Benton,* 363; Sharp, *Merchant Princes,* 8–9; *BR,* "The Herald to Louis Riel," September 1, 1883; Stanley, *Riel,* 253–54. Rocky Point was a trading hamlet on the Missouri River near Carroll.

66. "Louis Riel. A Refutation," *(Helena) Weekly Herald,* June 11, 1885 ("attempting to incite"); Stanley, *Riel,* 253; Malone, Roeder, and Lang, *Montana,* 73–74; "Unjust Censure," *Benton Record,* September 8, 1876; "The Herald and Louis Riel," *BR,* September 1, 1834 ("a gentleman") ("a low scoundrel").

67. "Half-Breeds," *Benton Record,* October 17, 1879 ("these Canadian half-breeds"); *BR,* April 28, 1883 ("another of his absurd") ("animal, fox-like cunning"); *Great Falls Tribune,* July 16, 1885 ("the meanest creature").

68. Two years later the charges against Riel were repeated. The following is a defense of Riel by H. P. Rolfe of Helena:

> I notice a late number of the *Independent* reiterates the old story of Louis Riel's illegally "voting a large number of half-breeds, who it was alleged by many prominent citizens were not citizens, nor had they ever declared their intention to become such." The *Independent* is behind the times. The above story was a campaign lie and has served its purpose. Louis Riel committed the crime of voting an opposition ticket to the *Independent*'s and that was all. He was indicted by a Chouteau County grand jury (after vainly searching for other charges) for "attempting to incite Urbain Delorme and Jerome St. Matt to vote, he knowing they had not declared their intentions to become citizens of the United States."
>
> I have in my possession proof that these two men had declared their intentions in Dakota and had voted, pre-empted land and had performed all acts of citizenship. Riel was put to much trouble and expense by this political persecution for one or two terms and then the case was dismissed by the Democratic District Attorney for the simple reason that there was not the shadow of evidence against Riel. Should the *Independent* desire anything further, I can produce the sworn statements of the Postmaster of Pembina, Dakota, the Deputy Collector of Customs of Minnesota, the Judge of Probate, and of other respectable citizens of Pembina county, Dakota. Very respectfully,
> H.P. Rolfe

("Louis Riel: A Refutation from H. P. Rolfe, Esq.," *(Helena) Weekly Herald*, June 11, 1885)

69. Riel, *Writings*, 2:257 (Special Deputy Marshall), 329, 360 ("no interest") ("flat poor").

70. For example, Riel wrote that the Métis were "too civilized for the Indians" and could not "stay nor live with them" (*Writings*, 2:272).

71. Ibid., 2:284.

72. Swan, "Brief History," 8.

73. Straham, "Resources of Montana Territory," 50 ("profits") ("We know that"); Price, *Memories*, 103 ("I am going").

74. Conrad Anderson, "Roy," 19 (Anderson wrote, "The ranchers only took possession of the well watered creeks and springs").

75. Malone, *Battle for Butte*, 11–12, 85.

76. Guardipee, "Story," 12 (Blackfeet winter on the Judith River); Schultz, "Last Years," box 8, folder 25, James W. Schultz Papers, MBSC ("favorite winter hunting"). T. C. Power, J. H. McKnight of Fort Shaw, and H. P. Brooks organized the Judith Cattle Company on Warm Spring Creek in the summer of 1878. By 1885 they controlled a range of twenty-five to thirty square miles (Leeson, *Montana*, 1287). Schultz, "Red Armenians," 18 ("never again").

77. Malone, Roeder, and Lang, *Montana*, 118; Sparlin, *Trail Back*, 16. Granville Stuart often complained about the ineffectiveness of the soldiers charged with controlling Indian "trespassing." The following is a typical journal entry (although it refers to Martinsdale, south of the Snowy Mountains): "There are thirty soldiers stationed here, and it is a good safe place for them as there are some settlers below to keep the Indians off them" (*Forty Years*, 2:137).

78. Granville Stuart, a major supporter of an effective army presence in the Judith Basin, had been a prospector and small merchant when he became bookkeeper for Hauser's First National Bank of Helena. In 1879 Stuart, Hauser, and Davis formed a corporation, known as the DHS ranch, with Stuart as manager (Stuart, *Forty Years*, throughout, 2:154–58). Stuart to James Fergus, April 15, 1883, Granville Stuart Papers; Stuart to Samuel T. Hauser, July 30, 1881, box 6, folder 62, Samuel T. Hauser Papers ("the presumption").

79. MacMillan, "Andrew Jackson Davis," 85, 93 (Stuart's losses). An example of Fergus's sympathy for the Indian cause is his letter of December 28, 1889. Fergus wrote to "Friend McGaughlin" in reference to the Indian question that "you say . . . we are giving them lands, and feeding them. We cannot give a man that that belongs to him even if it has been forced from him and if we had not taken their land and killed their Buffalo we would not need to feed them they could feed themselves" (JFP, box 2, folder 5, 2). Fergus's views were not typical among Euro-American Montanans. Fergus to Granville Stuart, December 4, 1881, Samuel T. Hauser Papers, box 6, folder 35 ("the Big Spring"); Stuart to J.

Fergus, December 12, 1881, Granville Stuart Papers ("We are certainly") ("the breeds").

80. Doane, Letters, March 21, 1882 (burning Métis homes); July 10, 1882 ("halfbreed and Cree").

81. Giraud, *Métis*, 2:416.

82. Burt, "Nowhere Left," 198; Doane to Mary Doane, Letters, 1882 (date incomplete) ("everything is in"). After 1882 the army concentrated on the removal of Crees, sending them back across the line into Canada. The campaign was "vicious" and thorough, but the army's preoccupation with the Crees did not end the harassment of the Métis, for, in their enthusiasm, the soldiers often swept up Métis traveling with their relatives. For an account of the tragic circumstances of the Crees during these years, see Burt, "Nowhere Left," and Ewers, "Chippewa Cree," 78.

83. Schultz, *My Life*, 209 ("Crees and Red River"); Dobak, "Killing," 49 (disappearance of buffalo) ("living on dogs"); *BR*, May 7, 1880 ("were selling their furs").

84. Malone, Roeder, and Lang, *Montana*, 141. For a discussion of the Blackfeet "winter of starvation," see Ewers, *Ethnological Report* and *Blackfeet;* Schultz, "Red Armenians," 18–19; West, "Starvation Winter," 2–19. Joseph Kinsey Howard, *Strange Empire*, 356–57; Linderman, *Pretty-shield*, 250–51 ("We believed").

85. *BR*, August 24, 1882 ("The Gros Ventre").

86. Hornaday, *Extermination*, 503 (100,000 hides), 506 (I. G. Baker), 512 (herds gone).

87. Chittenden, *American Fur Trade*, 2:814 ("wild and unprotected"); Ens, *Homeland*, 156 ("social and economic").

88. Joseph Kinsey Howard, *Strange Empire*, 344.

89. Peers, *Ojibwa of Western Canada*, 207.

CHAPTER 4

1. "Eldorado," *MA*, December 10, 1885 ("Big Spring creek half-breed settlement"); *MA*, March 27, 1884.

2. Dissly, *Short History*, 7–10.

3. Conrad Anderson, "Roy," 16, 23; Vern Anderson, "LaTray Family," 4; Torgerson, "With a Smile"; Leslie G. LaTray, obituary, *LNA*, August 13, 1997; "Dedication Old Post Office," *LNA*, September 17, 1931; Donovan, *First Hundred Years*, 21 (Turcotte is spelled "Jarcot"), 9 (wood hawks); Ewers, "Chippewa Cree," 111 (buffalo bones); Burlingame, "Buffalo in Trade," 289–90; Price, *Memories*, 60. Big Sandy lies just north of the Missouri River, between the Judith Basin and the Milk River.

4. Treena LaFountain, interview, July 26, 1996; Ehlert, interview, July 16, 1996.

5. Fleury genealogy, Fleury Family Papers; Swan, "Brief History," 6.

6. When buffalo hide was no longer available, Métis women used burlap sacks to make containers. Treena LaFountain, interview, July 26, 1996.

7. Ibid.

8. "Indian Allotment Application," Fleury Family Papers; Homestead Entry Applications, Fergus County; also see chapter 6 (Mary Ernestine Fleury homestead); Treena LaFountain, interview, July 26, 1996.

9. "Poll Lists" (election of October 24, 1864) includes: Juneau, Antoine/56*/Fort Benton/Choteau City; Lafontain, P. M./13*/Willow Cr., Fort Owen/Missoula County; Lavalllie, John/63*/Hell Gate Precinct/Missoula County; LeDoux, Isadore/47*/Deer Lodge Precinct/Deer Lodge City (* These numbers indicate the order within precinct). *Fergus County Argus,* August 19, 1886 (1886 Fergus County elections); "Poll Books"; Moses, "Benjamin Kline," 3 ("directed the political"). Mercy Jackson, "History of Fergus County," 7; Dissly, *Short History,* 13.

10. Swan, "Brief History," 9 (cemetery); Vermaat, *History,* 14 (Ouellette); Deal and McDonald, *Heritage Book,* 229 (committee).

11. Deal and McDonald, *Heritage Book,* 229 (McDonnell recollections); Swan, "Brief History," 9 ("Our little").

12. An example of distortions inadvertently caused by early Euro-American accounts is resident Mercy Jackson's history of Lewistown. Often quoted locally, her history lists the first marriage license in Fergus County as that of two non-Métis couples in 1886. She is undoubtedly correct, but although this was the first marriage recorded in county records, it was by no means the first marriage. Such "facts," though correct in a strict sense, distort reality, since the earliest marriages were Métis who saw no reason to register their family events at the courthouse or to obtain licenses (Jackson, "Lewistown," 3).

13. Swan, "Brief History," 11; Vermaat, *History,* 14.

14. Vermaat, *History,* 17.

15. Donovan, *First Hundred Years,* 16 (land); *MA,* January 15, 1885, and February 19, 1885; "Reports, Fergus County Superintendent of Schools, 1887–1906," 4, 85, 150, 172, 250, and "Minutes," Fergus County Superintendent of Schools, April 14, 1900, Book 1, S.D. No. 1, as cited in Zellick, "History of Lewistown School," 21–23. Despite the much-appreciated efforts of Stacey Vestal, business manager for the Lewistown School District, to locate the originals of these documents, they apparently have disappeared from a closet of the old Lewistown Junior High, which had served as a repository for the school system's historical documents. This account is dependent on portions of the documents recorded by Lewistown historian and former teacher Anna Zellick in her history of the Lewistown School District.

16. Mercy Jackson, "Public and City Schools," 1; Zellick, "History of Lewistown School," 23.

17. Swan, "Mrs. Swan," 14; Moss, "Report of Supervisor Moss," 2 ("About thirty white girls attend but they are separate in every way from the Indian girls"). By this time, St. Peter's Mission School was located between the Sun and Dearborn rivers, about fifteen miles west of present-day Cascade, Montana.

18. McBride, *Bird Tail*, 71; Swan, "Mrs. Swan," 14; "Program of Daily Recitations" and "Course of Study"; "Ursuline Annals," June 29, 1896 ("the white girls").

19. Swan, "Mrs. Swan," 14.

20. Moss, "Report of Supervisor Moss," 1, 3.

21. Palladino, *Indian and White*, 113–14.

22. Ibid., 115.

23. Lusk to Price, August 6, 1883, Miscellaneous file, SPMP; McBride, *Bird Tail*, 163; Palladino, *Indian and White*, 277; Woodstock Letters 10:319.

24. McBride, *Bird Tail*, 208 (student lists), 72 (photographs); Tabor, "Great Falls Yesterday," 1; SPM, "Marriage Register," 14, no. 71 and McBride, *Bird Tail*, 208 (Ford family). By 1897 Sadie Pambrun would attend the Indian school, not the white academy (McBride, *Bird Tail*, 145).

25. McBride, *Bird Tail*, 73, 101, 111; Tabor, "Great Falls Yesterday," 5.

26. Tabor, "Great Falls Yesterday," 5.

27. "Names of boys having White Fathers enrolled at St. Peter's Mission Montana," August 11, 1895, SPMP.

28. "Ursuline Annals," May 23, 1895.

29. Schuflet, interview, 14.

30. Garcia, *Tough Trip*, 194 and throughout.

31. Ibid., 83, 91, 182, and throughout.

32. Ibid.; Stocking, "Ft. Benton Memories," 9 ("the crossing").

33. Mary Hunter Doane, "Trip," 1.

34. Alderson and Smith, *Bride Goes West*, 146–47.

35. Garcia, *Tough Trip*, 38 ("that Injun louse"); Stegner, *Wolf Willow*, 57. Persons suspected of having lice combed their hair with a fine-toothed comb to remove the lice and nits, or eggs.

36. E. C. Abbott and Smith, *We Pointed*, 136, 182. Granville Stuart was managing partner of one of the largest ranches in the area (the DHS or D-S). He was also well educated and respected, becoming, in 1883, the Montana Territorial Council president.

37. E. C. Abbott and Smith, *We Pointed*, 141–42.

38. Mary Hunter Doane, "Address," 3–4.

39. For Stuart's campaign to remove Native people, see Stuart to Fergus, July 26, 1885, JFP, 1; Stuart to Fergus, September 26, 1885, JFP; Fergus to Stuart, December 4, 1881, Samuel T. Hauser Papers. "Senate Resolution on the Death of the Late Mary Stuart Abbott," February 5, 1967, Helena, Mont., copy available Mary Stuart Abbott Papers, Fergus Co. SC 978.6292, LPL, 1 ("full-blood").

40. Worthen, "Fergus," 15.

41. Fergus to Andrew Fergus, October 8, 1893, JFP, MLSC.

42. Stuart, reported vigilante leader, later justified the actions of the group, arguing that because of "enormous losses the young struggling stock-growing

industry faced certain annihilation unless immediate steps should be taken to protect it" (Stuart, *Forty Years*, 156). Malone, Roeder, and Lang, *Montana*, 163.

43. Stuart, *Forty Years*, 2:214, 221. An "armed posse" hung Narcisse Laverdure and Joe Vardner without trial in June 1884, at Judith Landing (on the Missouri River). The men were accused of stealing seven horses. A month later the vigilantes hung Sam McKensie near Fort Maginnis, a few miles from Lewistown (Stuart, *Forty Years*, 2:198–99).

44. I. Larocque, interview in Conrad Anderson, "Roy," 23 (spelling of Métis names as found in document).

45. Conrad Anderson, "Roy," 20–21.

46. *Register of Criminal Actions*, case no. 27, (Ledoux and Falcon), 122, 157, 395, 302, 339, 300, 448, 180, 283, 289, 336, 507.

47. I. Larocque, interview in Conrad Anderson, "Roy," 23.

48. Although not all cowboys were Euro-American, in the Judith Basin most were until after 1887. E. C. Abbott and Smith, *We Pointed*, 101–102.

49. Ibid., 145.

50. Stuart, *Forty Years*, 232–37; Toole, *Montana*, 146–47. Toole estimates the number of cattle in Montana at 500,000 before the winter and 82,000 by the end (146–47). Central-Montana rancher David Hilger wrote that "the winter of 1886–7 was the coldest and with more snow than any other winter I can recall after 59 years residence in the state. Eighty percent of the cattle and sheep died that winter" (Hilger, "Early Days on Dog Creek," David Hilger Papers, 3). Malone, Roeder, and Lang, *Montana*, 165–68.

51. Gressley, *Bankers and Cattlemen*, 244–47.

52. I. Larocque, interview, in Conrad Anderson, "Roy," 23.

53. Malone, Roeder, and Lang, *Montana*, 166.

54. Noyes, *Chinook*, 21; Garcia, *Tough Trip*, 34, 319; Dusenberry, "Waiting," 119.

55. For example, see Beal and MacLeod, *Prairie Fire*; Flanagan, *Riel and the Rebellion*.

56. *Sun River (Montana) Sun*, June 12, 1884.

57. Joseph Kinsey Howard, *Strange Empire*, 502.

58. Mueller to Kessler, October 31, 1952, Oscar Mueller Correspondence. Elizabeth Swan remembered that Mrs. Dumont died soon after her arrival and was buried near the Berger homestead. In 1889 her remains, with those of other Métis, were reburied in the present Catholic cemetery (Swan, interview, and Mueller to Kessler). Woodcock, *Dumont*, 229, 234.

59. For a readable and sympathetic but declensionist version of these events, see Joseph Kinsey Howard, *Strange Empire*. For a classic, if not sympathetic, overview, see Stanley, *Birth of Western Canada*. Burt, "Nowhere Left," 196–99, 203; Burt, "Crooked Piece," 45, 49–50; *(Fort Benton) River Press*, December 30, 1885, and June 6, 1888; *Great Falls Tribune*, August 1, 1901.

60. *Helena Independent,* January 9, 1887; Raymond Gray, "History of the Cree Nation," January 16, 1942, 6–13 (also p. 107); "Relief for the Cree Indians," Ex. Doc, 341, 1–4; Dusenberry, "Displaced," 3–4; *Helena Independent,* January 27, 1887; and "Territorial Indian Appropriation," February 2, 1887 (officers from Fort Shaw provide food).

61. Franklin and Bunte, "Montana Métis Community," 73 (Front Range families); Woodcock, *Dumont,* 232; Riel, *Writings,* 5:357.

62. These refugee families often melted into existing Métis communities, making any estimate of their numbers difficult. Ewers, "Chippewa Cree," 96.

63. Stuart (former president of the Montana Stockgrowers' Association) to Fergus, January 21, 1886, JFP; Stuart, *Forty Years,* 226.

64. Burt, "Crooked Piece," 48–50; Burt, "Nowhere Left," 203; Ewers, "Chippewa Cree," 94, 111; Worthen, "Judith Basin," 60; *(Fort Benton) River Press,* May 28, 1890 ("these lazy"); and February 11, 1891 ("a constant source").

65. Dusenberry, "Waiting," 119, 126, 134.

66. "Turtle Mountain Band of Chippewa Indians," S. Doc. 444, 1, 3, 31–32, 104.

67. Hesketh, *Turtle Mountain Chippewa,* 113–14; "Turtle Mountain Band of Chippewa Indians," S. Doc. 444, 101–103.

68. "Turtle Mountain Band of Chippewa Indians," S. Doc. 444, 142 (1884 population). For the growth of the Métis population in the Turtle Mountain area during the 1880s, see Ens, "After the Buffalo." Wheeler-Voegelin and Hickerson, *Red Lake,* 8.

69. This policy was officially stated in the "Minutes of the Grand Council Proceedings of January 29, 1892," S. Doc. 444, 119.

70. Riel, *Writings,* 2:284.

71. Ens, "After the Buffalo," 7–8.

72. Rebecca Kugel has examined Minnesota Ojibwes (Objiwas) who distinguished themselves from the Métis, in part, by the work that they were willing to perform and by their deep suspicion of wage labor and dependence on European employers. "To work like a Frenchman," something an Ojibwe man would not do, defined Métis ethnic identity for the Ojibwes (Kugel, "To Work").

73. Swan, "Brief History," 8.

74. Camp, "Working," 21–24; Hesketh, *Turtle Mountain Chippewa,* 113–14; "Executive Order for a Reservation," S. Doc. 444, 101; Murray, "Turtle Mountain Chippewa," 23.

75. Hesketh, *Turtle Mountain Chippewa,* 123–27; "Reservation of the Turtle Mountain Band of Chippewa Indians," S. Doc. 444, 156; "Preamble and Resolutions," S. Doc. 444, 108–13; "Minutes of the Grand Council Proceedings of January 29, 1892," S. Doc. 444, 118–19.

76. "Minutes of the Grand Council Proceedings of January 29, 1892," S. Doc. 444, 119 ("that all the mixed blood"). Wheeler-Voegelin and Hickerson, *Red Lake,* appendix C, 8.

77. Dusenberry, "Waiting," 127–32.
78. S. Rep. 693, S. Doc. 444, 1–2.
79. "Turtle Mountain Band of Pembina Chippewa Indians," S. Doc. 154, 20.
80. "Turtle Mountain Band of Chippewa Indians," S. Doc. 444, 117–24; "Report of the Commissioner of Indian Affairs for 1892."
81. "Turtle Mountain Band of Chippewa Indians," S. Doc. 444, 33–34.
82. Ibid., 31–43, 41 ("that all persons"). Waugh directed that they "withdraw from the limits of the Turtle Mountain Reservation at once or be arrested" (41). "Report of the Turtle Mountain Indian Commission, 1893," House Ex. Doc. 229, 9–23.
83. "Turtle Mountain Band of Chippewa Indians," S. Doc. 444, 41–42, 45–46; "Report of the Turtle Mountain Indian Commission, 1893," House Ex. Doc. 229, 16–18 (signers of the McCumber agreement); Franklin and Bunte, "Supplemental Report," 112.
84. "Turtle Mountain Band of Pembina Chippewa Indians," S. Doc. 154, 26 ("so poor"): Dusenberry, "Waiting," 131–34; LaCounte, "Saga," 8.
85. "Commissioners' Report." S. Doc. 444, 18–19; "Turtle Mountain Chippewa Indian Census, 1892"; "LaFountain Genealogy." For the Elzear LaFountain family, see St. Leo's Roman Catholic Church, "St. Leo's Parish Baptisms," 1:15 and "LaFountain Genealogy."
86. Dusenberry, "Waiting," 134.
87. Morris, "Chief Little Shell Tribe," 8, 18; Denig, *Five Indian Tribes*, 100; Dusenberry, "Waiting," 127, 133–34.
88. Donovan, *First Hundred Years*, 22 ("made a sumptuous"); Fergus to Toole, August 31, 1892, JFP ("Twenty lodges").
89. Dusenberry, "Displaced," 4 ("these dirty Crees") ("Canadian beggars"); Gray, "History of the Cree Indians," February 11, 1942, 6–7 (also pp. 21–22); February 10, 1942, 2 (also p. 17); Malone, *Battle for Butte*, 54–55. *Senate Report*, vol. 4, no. 821, 54th Cong. 1st sess., as partially reproduced in Dusenberry, "Displaced," 6 ("wards").
90. Forget, CIA, Regina, NT, to governor of Montana (J. E. Rickards), Helena, April 1, 1896, *Senate Report*, ("had provided"); Dusenberry, "Displaced," 6; *Great Falls Tribune*, June 11, 1896; Gray, "History of the Cree Indians," February 27, 1942, 12 (also p. 43), 13 (also p. 44) ("all Cree").
91. Gray, "History of the Cree Indians," February 11, 1942, 6 (21); Dusenberry, "Displaced," 6; Ewers, "Chippewa Cree," 107–109.
92. *Great Falls Tribune*, June 19, 1896; Pershing, "Autobiography," 5:11, John J. Pershing Papers; Smythe, "John J. Pershing," 20–21 ("rounding up"); Dusenberry, "Displaced," 6–7.
93. Ewers, "Chippewa Cree," 107–10, 108 (537); Gray, "History of the Cree Indians," March 3, 1942, 11 (13); *Great Falls Daily Leader*, July 9, 1896; Dusenberry, "Displaced," 6–7; *(Helena, Mont.) Daily Independent*, "Men 206, Dogs 200 . . . Vagabond Crees," June 26, 1896.

94. Dusenberry, "Displaced," 7 (arrests); Wessel, "Rocky Boy's," 18 ("Canadian Indians"); Burt, "Crooked Piece," 50.

95. Ewers, *"Chippewa Cree,"* 63, 117, 145–47; Dusenberry, "Displaced," 10 (identity of Rocky Boy's wife); and *Montana Cree,* 40; Wessel, "Rock Boy's," 33.

CHAPTER 5

1. Congress ratified the Ten Cent Treaty with Senate Bill 196 and House Bill 12,689. For information, see "Ten Cent Treaty," ARCIA, 1903, 228; "Report Amending Senate Bill 196"; Camp, "Turtle Mountain Plains: Chippewas," 152, 143; Worthen, "Central Montana," 14 (Jawbone railroad). Sources for central Montana include Worthen, "Central Montana"; Dissly, *Short History.* For central Montana as a "garden," see Hall, "Montana," 1, 10–12; Malone, Roeder, and Lang, *Montana,* 238–41.

2. Cronon, *Changes in the Land,* ("Changes in the Land"); Hall, "Montana," 1, 9–13; Malone, Roeder, and Lang, *Montana,* 238–41.

3. *1870 Montana Census;* Malone, Roeder, and Lang, *Montana,* 233; Gieseker, "Soils," 24; Cunningham, *Montana Weather,* 8; Department of Climatology (cited August 16, 1999), available online at http://www.ems.psu.ed/pa.climatology/state/div06pcp.html.

4. Thwaites, *Early Western Travels,* 42; Malone, Roeder, and Lang, *Montana,* 232.

5. Malone, Roeder, and Lang, *Montana,* 236–37.

6. Gates, *Public Land Law,* 245; Malone, Roeder, and Lang, *Montana,* 237–38.

7. Vermaat, *History,* 9–10.

8. Malone, Roeder, and Lang, *Montana,* 238–39; Hall, "Montana," 1, 10–12.

9. Freeman, "Geography and Geology," 12 (Fergus County's population); *MA,* June 11, 1885; *Thirteenth Census of the United States,* vol. 2 (Washington, D.C.: WPO, 1913), 1154.

10. Tables 3 and 4.

11. Limemen worked the lime kilns that processed limestone into lime.

12. For the relationship of the LaFountain, Doney, LaRocque, Davis, and Gardipee families, see Spring Creek band diagrams, chapter 2. For their settlement of the Roy area and additional information, see Conrad Anderson, "Roy," 27 and Martha Harroun Foster, "We Know," 422, 510–11. St. Leo's Roman Catholic Church, "St. Leo's Parish Baptisms"; Franklin and Bunte, "Montana Métis Community," 104b; Roy History Committee, *Homestead Shacks,* 81–83, 159, 483. For Sarah LaRocque (daughter of Ralph and Isabelle LaRocque), see St. Leo's Roman Catholic Church, "St. Leo's Parish Baptisms," 1893–1918; LaRocque, interview.

13. John Wells was the son of Edward "Neddy" Wells and Isabelle McGillis. His wife, Philomene Ouellette, was the daughter of Antoine Ouellette and Angelique Bottineau (Wells Family Papers). "Canadian Scrip Applications, 1900–1901"; Fleury Family Papers; Homestead Entry Applications. For specific information and scrip application numbers, see Martha Harroun Foster, "We Know," 511.

14. Malone, Roeder, and Lang, *Montana,* 280–85; Martha Harroun Foster, "We Know," 495–508.

15. Conrad Anderson, "Roy," 24.

16. Malone, Roeder, and Lang, *Montana,* 283 (Malone reported that Montana had the highest bankruptcy rate in the United States and that it was the only state to lose population during the 1920s); Conrad Anderson, "Roy," 24; Roy History Committee, *Homestead Shacks;* R. L. Polk, *Lewistown City Directory;* Franklin and Bunte, "Montana Métis Community," 66–69.

The second major Métis kinship network in Montana is that of the Rocky Mountain Front Range families. The original Front Range families were already related to the Spring Creek band and Milk River families in the 1870s, when they settled near St. Peter's Mission. After 1885 Canadian Métis and Crees joined them in establishing communities along the Front Range.

17. Doney, interview, July 24, 1996. Because Métis families intermarried often, it is not unusual to have a situation like that of Ken Doney's family in which his great-grandfather on his mother's side (Florence Rita Doney, daughter of John William Doney) and his grandfather on his father's side (Richard Doney) were brothers. Robert LaFountain, interview, October 17, 1995.

18. Tables 3 and 4; Thornton, *Holocaust and Survival,* 216.

19. Elizabeth identified her people as "Red River half breeds" when writing their history (Swan, "Brief History," 1). Sinclair, interview, 56; LaPier, interview, 73; Homestead Entry Applications.

20. LaRocque, interview; Treena LaFountain, interview, July 26, 1996; Ehlert, interview, July 16, 1996; LaPier, interview, 81–84; Franklin and Bunte, "Supplemental Report," 21. The author witnessed similar enthusiasm for jigging at the 1997 Métis celebration in Lewistown, where a woman in her nineties rolled her wheelchair onto the floor to jig.

21. LaRocque, interview; Treena LaFountain, interview, July 26, 1996; Ehlert, interview, July 16, 1996; Johnson, interview, 88–89 ("You mash"). Mary Johnson also described how her mother made prepared wild berries called *"ta quite ma nanna."* First she washed and dried the berries so that they would last until needed. When ready to use them, her mother would "soak and boil them and put sugar in. Then they'd cook them in grease. Put quite a bit of grease in the pan" she explained, "and then you put sugar in there. . . . After they cook a while you put in a little flour. To tell you the truth, they were good. We'd have them for winter, of course we didn't eat them every day because if we did they wouldn't last" (88). Johnson's instructions for drying meat are as follows: "When you first hung it to dry and then built a fire underneath the deal and let it smoke. The smoke kept the flies away from the meat. And we smoked it, not all the time it was drying, just for a while, and it'd take probably a couple of days to dry— just depends on how thin you can slice it" (89). Métis women prided themselves on how thin and how quickly they could slice meat. The thinness and length of the strips one was able to cut was a measure of skill and a source of respect.

22. Treena LaFountain, interview, July 26, 1996; Franklin and Bunte, "Supplemental Report," 14 ("a gay").

23. Robert LaFountain, interview, October 17, 1995; Ehlert, interview, July 16, 1996; LaRocque, interview; Franklin and Bunte, "Supplemental Report," 14 ("spoke a strangely blended"); *1900 Montana Census,* Fergus County; E. C. Abbott and Smith, *We Pointed,* 182.

24. Chandler, interview; Eastman, interview, July 23, 1996.

25. *Lewistown Catholic Monthly,* "Detail of Pew Rent," December 1919–February 1920, 3:1–4; December 1922, 6:1, 5; June 1923, 6:9, 3; August 1923, 6:11, 3. By 1940, the "General Statement of Individual Accounts" included members of the following Métis families: Berger, Desy, Desmarais, Fleury (including Mrs. E., probably Ernestine), Gardipee, LaTray, LaFountain, Laverdure, Ledoux, LaPier, Swan, Tivies, Turcotte, and Wells families. ("General Statement of Individual Accounts of St. Leo's Parish, from January 1st 1935 to January 1st 1941," St. Leo's file, Great Falls Diocese Archives, Great Falls, Mont.

26. For a discussion of fur-trade women, kinship ties, and Catholicism, see Sleeper-Smith, "Women, Kin, and Catholicism," 423–52.

27. For specific examples, see Martha Harroun Foster, "We Know," 514. St. Leo's Roman Catholic Church, "St. Leo's Parish Baptisms."

28. St. Leo's Roman Catholic Church, "St. Leo's Parish Baptisms"; "St. Leo's Parish Marriages."

29. Monkelin, interview, 24–26; Zellick, interview. Several informants note that prejudice toward "breeds" continued through this period (and, to an extent, continues today). For example, Sue Eastman (of Euro-American descent) remembered that she would "never even have considered dating a Métis, much less marrying one." She reported, "Oh, I just wouldn't have done that. People just didn't do that." Treena and Robert LaFountain as well as others confirm these attitudes (Eastman, interview; Treena LaFountain, interview, July 26, 1996; Robert LaFountain, interview, July 26, 1996; Shoup, interview, July 15, 1996). "What Do You Know?" *Lewistown Catholic Monthly* 5, no. 4 (March 1922): 5.

30. Treena LaFountain, interview, September 17, 1995, July 26, 1996; Ehlert, interview, July 16, 1996.

31. Shoup, interview, July 15, 1996. An excellent paper that explores the Métis identity of the Klyne (Kline) family is Devine, "Métis or Country-Born?"

32. "Turtle Mountain Band of Chippewa Indians," S. Doc. 444, 21, 22; "Grand Council of 1892," S. Doc. 444, 119.

33. Camp, "Working," 27–29.

34. "Turtle Mountain Indians," Ex. Doc. 229, 2–3; "Report of the Turtle Mountain Indian Commission, 1893," Ex. Doc. 229, 15; "Letter from the Secretary of the Interior . . . Turtle Mountain Indians," 2–4; Murray, "Turtle Mountain Chippewa," 30–32; Camp, "Working," 30.

35. Table 5; Homestead Entry Applications (allotment information); "Turtle Mountain Allotment and Census Records"; Swan, "Brief History," 8 (Alexander Wilkie and family return to Turtle Mountain). Spring Creek band members

submitted applications as early as 1911, but were not rejected until 1914 or as late as 1918 (Homestead Entry Applications; for dates of Spring Creek Band member rejection, see Martha Harroun Foster, "We Know," 495–508).

36. Little Shell member John Sinclair described the allotments to interviewer C. Patrick Morris. "There wasn't a water hole for fifty miles and no firewood, nothing. There was no way they could even survive out there." (Sinclair, interview, 47). Mary La Mere Johnson described her family's allotment as "badlands" and remembered that "it wasn't good land for farming or anything like that" (Johnson, interview, 49). Camp, "Working," 36.

37. Johnson, interview, 49.

38. "Reservation of the Turtle Mountain Band of Chippewa Indians," H. Rep. 632 (emphasis added).

39. For reference to Red Bear Chippewas see Franklin and Bunte, "Supplemental Report," 23.

40. Franklin and Bunte, "Supplemental Report," 21 ("A large meeting"); Sinclair, interview, 56; LaPier, interview, 73.

41. Under provisions of the 1934 Indian Reorganization Act, BIA Field Representative Henry Roe Cloud supervised the compilation of several versions of the rolls. In 1979 Little Shell historian C. Patrick Morris described the Roe Cloud roll as the "pivotal document in determining the present ethnic identity of the Little Shell people" (Morris and Van Gunten, "Chief Little Shell Tribe," 132). The most accessible copy of the Indian Reorganization Act may be in Albert L. Hurtado and Peter Iverson, eds. *Major Problems in American Indian History* (Lexington, Mass.: D. C. Heath, 1994), 451–54.

42. Cloud, "Basic Membership Roll" (this roll is not the current basic membership roll). There has been argument ever since about the completeness of the Roe Cloud rolls. Many families were omitted.

43. Sinclair, interview, 47; Franklin and Bunte, "Montana Métis Community," 79–87, 104b; Roy History Committee, *Homestead Shacks,* 159, 483; Doney, telephone conversation, September 10, 2000; *1900 Montana Census,* Fergus County, no. 321/323, no. 319/321 (Doney homesteads).

44. In the 1890s, as the Spring Creek band and their relatives along the Milk River strengthened their bonds to the Little Shell Chippewas, Métis farther to the west became more closely associated with the Rocky Boy and Little Bear bands. Although many Métis living near St. Peter's, Cascade, the Teton River Canyon, and the Dearborn Canyon were related to the Spring Creek Métis, they, like other Front Range families, lived near and intermarried with Canadian Métis who moved to Montana after 1885, and with Chippewas and Crees of the Rocky Boy and Little Bear bands. Some Front Range Métis also developed close ties with other Native groups, including intermarriage with neighboring Blackfeet (Franklin and Bunte, "Montana Métis Community," 66–69).

45. For descriptions of the conditions faced by the Rocky Boy Chippewa-Crees and their struggle for a reservation, see Burt, "Crooked Piece," 45–51, and "Nowhere Left," 195–209; Ewers, "Chippewa Cree," 81–136; Dusenberry, "Displaced" and *Montana Cree*, 40; Wessel, "Rocky Boy's," throughout.

46. McDowell, "Report," 359 ("For many Years"); Wheat to Commissioner, April 20, 1909, 2 ("I find") (a section of this letter is reproduced in Dusenberry, "Displaced," 9–10); Nault, "Fred Nault," 19; Sinclair, interview, 118–19.

47. *(Helena) Montana Daily Record*, October 28, 1912.

48. Gray, "Montana Landless Indians," April 9, 1942, 11–12.

49. Frank Linderman Papers; Dusenberry, "Displaced," 1 (public support for a Rocky Boy reservation); secretary of the interior to Churchill, December 1908, file 900-08-307.4 ("French mixed bloods").

50. Ewers, "Chippewa Cree," 127.

51. Ewers, "Chippewa Cree," 127–28 ("as is usual") (emphasis added); Wheat to commissioner of Indian Affairs, April 20, 1909; "Census of Rocky Boy's Band"; "Tentative Roll of Rocky Boy Indians"; Wessel, "Rocky Boy's," 22, 38.

52. Ewers, "Chippewa Cree," 128–31.

53. Wessel, "Rocky Boy's," 38–48. Comments on the running dispute between Havre citizens and the *Great Falls Tribune*, which supported Rocky Boy, are found in numerous articles, including *Great Falls Tribune*, November 4, 1909; November 5, 1909; November 6, 1909.

54. *Havre Plaindealer*, January 11, 1913; March 15, 1913.

55. Wessel, "Rocky Boy's," 40–43.

56. Dusenberry, "Displaced," 14. Dusenberry writes that the 1917 roll included 452 individuals. Ewers's figure of 451 is used here (Ewers, "Chippewa Cree," 131).

57. McDowell, "Report," 360, 361 ("wore the brilliant"); "Tentative Roll of Rocky Boy Indians"; McLaughlin, "Family History," throughout; St. Leo's Roman Catholic Church, "St. Leo's Parish Baptisms"; "St. Leo's Parish Marriages."

58. *(Helena) Montana Daily Record*, October 28, 1912 ("I am not here pleading"); Stegner, *Wolf Willow*, 50 ("An Indian was").

59. Donovan, *First Hundred Years*, 72 ("*News Argus* report"); In re Knight, 171F.299, 300 (N.D.N.Y. 1909) as cited in Haney-López, *White by Law*, 59, 241, n. 28 (1909 district court ruling). A Supreme Court decision of 1884 (*Elk v. Wilkins*) ruled that since Native Americans' allegiance was to their tribe, they were not U.S. citizens, nor did they acquire citizenship by being born in the United States (112 U.S.94 [1884]). It was not until the Nationality Act of 1940 that all persons born in the United States, including "Indian, Eskimo, Aleutian, or other aboriginal tribe" automatically received citizenship. American citizenship was also denied on the basis of being neither of "white" nor of African descent. Since 1790, naturalization had been limited to "free white person[s]." With the enactment of the Fourteenth Amendment, African Americans were eligible for citizenship, but other "non-white" ethnic groups were denied such citizenship on the

basis that they were nonwhite (Ibid., 41–42.) See also Rogers Smith, *Civic Ideals: Conflicting Visions of Citizenship in U.S. History* (New Haven, Conn.: Yale University Press, 1997).

For Métis voting on Spring Creek, see "Poll Books," 1884–1888 and "Voter Registration Index, 1928–1932" (copies available at the Lewistown Genealogical Society, Lewistown Public Library, Lewistown, Mont.).

CONCLUSION

1. "Piyish tout ni Pouyoun." ["Finally I'm finished everything."] Michif translation by Norman Fleury, director of the Michif Language Program for the Manitoba Métis Federation and cochair of the Michif Language Recovery Program of the Métis National Council. The author wishes to thank Norman Fleury and Lawrence J. Barkwell of the Manitoba Métis Federation for their assistance with this title.

2. Barth, *Ethnic Groups;* and "Enduring."

3. Nagel, *Ethnic Renewal,* 32.

4. Nash, "Hidden History."

Bibliography

BOOKS AND ARTICLES

Abbott, E. C. "Teddy Blue," and Helena Huntington Smith. *We Pointed Them North: Recollections of a Cowpuncher.* 1939. Reprint, Norman: University of Oklahoma Press, 1971.

Albers, Patricia, and Beatrice Medicine, eds. *The Hidden Half: Studies of Plains Indian Women.* Washington, D.C.: University Press of America, 1983.

Alderson, Nannie T., and Helena Huntington Smith. *A Bride Goes West.* 1942. Reprint, Lincoln: University of Nebraska Press, 1969.

Allen, Theodore. *The Invention of the White Race.* London: Verso, 1994.

Arnold, H. N. *History of Old Pembina.* Larimore, N.Dak.: 1917.

Atwater, Caleb. *The Indians of the Northwest, Their Manners, Customs etc. etc., or, Remarks Made on a Tour to Prairie du Chien and Thence to Washington City in 1829.* Columbus, Ohio: 1831.

Axtell, James, ed. *The Indian Peoples of Eastern America: A Documentary History of the Sexes.* New York: Oxford University Press, 1981.

Baird, Henry S. *Recollections of the Early History of Northern Wisconsin.* Vol. 4. Madison, Wis.: CSHSW, 1859.

Bakker, Peter. *A Language of Our Own: The Genesis of Michif, the Mixed Cree-French Language of the Canadian Métis.* New York: Oxford University Press, 1997.

Barkwell, Lawrence J., Leah Dorion, and Darren R. Préfontaine. *Metis Legacy: A Metis Historiography and Annotated Bibliography.* Winnipeg, Manitoba: Pemmican, 2001.

Barth, Fredrik. "Enduring and Emerging Issues in the Analysis of Ethnicity." In *The Anthropology of Ethnicity: Beyond "Ethnic Groups and Boundaries,"* edited by Hans Vermeulen and Cora Govers, 11–31. Amsterdam: Het Spinhuis, 1994.

——. *Ethnic Groups and Boundaries: The Social Organization of Culture Difference.* Boston: Little, Brown, 1969.

Beal, Bob, and Rod MacLeod. *Prairie Fire: The 1885 North-West Rebellion.* Edmonton, Alberta: Hurtig Press, 1984.

Begg, A. *History of the North-West.* 3 vols. Toronto: Hunter, Rose, 1894–95.

Berger, Clemence Gourneau. "Metis Come to Judith Basin." *Lewistown (Mont.) Daily News.* December 31, 1943. Reprinted in *The Trail Back,* edited by Alberta C. Sparlin. Great Falls, Mont.: Blue Print and Letter, 1976.

Billon, Frederick L. *Annals of St. Louis in Its Early Days under the French and Spanish Dominations.* St. Louis: Nixon-Jones, 1886.

———. *Annals of St. Louis in Its Territorial Days, from 1804–1821.* St Louis: Nixon-Jones, 1888.

Binnema, Theodore, Gerhard J. Ens, and R. C. MacLeod. *From Rupert's Land to Canada: Essays in Honour of John E. Foster.* Edmonton: University of Alberta Press, 2001.

Blair, Emma H., ed. *The Indian Tribes of the Upper Mississippi Valley and Region of the Great Lakes.* 2 vols. Cleveland: 1911.

Botkin, Alex C. "The John Brown of the Half Breeds." *Rocky Mountain Magazine* 1 (September 1900): 18–22.

Bradbury, John. *Travels in the Interior of America in the Years 1809, 1810, and 1811.* 1819. Reprint, Lincoln: University of Nebraska Press, 1986.

Bradley, James H. "Lieut. James H. Bradley Manuscript." In *Contributions to the Historical Society of Montana.* Vol. 9. Helena: Montana Historical Society, 1922.

Brasser, Ted J. "In Search of Métis Art." In Peterson and Brown, *New Peoples,* 221–30.

Brown, Jennifer S. H. "Diverging Identities: The Presbyterian Métis of St. Gabriel Street, Montreal." In Peterson and Brown, *New Peoples,* 195–206.

———. "Fur Trade as Centrifuge: Familial Dispersal and Offspring Identity in Two Company Contexts." In *North American Indian Anthropology: Essays on Society and Culture,* edited by Raymond J. DeMallie and Alfonso Ortiz, 197–219. Norman: University of Oklahoma Press, 1994.

———. "Linguistic Solitudes and Changing Social Categories." In *Old Trails and New Directions: Papers of the Third North American Fur Trade Conference,* edited by Carol M. Judd and A. J. Ray, 147–59. Toronto: University of Toronto Press, 1980.

———. "The Métis: Genesis and Rebirth." In Cox, *Native People, Native Lands,* 136–47.

———. "Métis, Halfbreeds, and Other Real People: Challenging Cultures and Categories," *History Teacher* 27, no. 1 (November 1993).

———. *Strangers in Blood: Fur Trade Company Families in Indian Country.* Norman: University of Oklahoma Press, 1980.

———. "Woman as Centre and Symbol in the Emergence of Métis Communities." *Canadian Journal of Native Studies* 3, no. 1 (1983).

———, W. J. Eccles, and Donald P. Heldman, eds. *The Fur Trade Revisited: Selected Papers of the Sixth North American Fur Trade Conference, Mackinac Island, Michigan, 1991.* East Lansing: Michigan State University Press, 1994.

———, and Elizabeth Vibert, eds. *Reading Beyond Words: Contexts for Native History.* Peterborough, Ontario: Broadview Press, 1998.

"The Buffalo Hunt." *Nor'Wester,* August 28, 1860.

Burlingame, Merrill G. "Buffalo in Trade and Commerce." *North Dakota Historical Quarterly* 3, no. 4 (July 1929): 262–91.

Burt, Larry. "In a Crooked Piece of Time: The Dilemma of the Montana Cree and the Metis." *Journal of American Culture* 9 (Spring 1986): 45–52.

———. "Nowhere Left to Go: Montana's Crees, Metis, and Chippewas and the Creation of Rocky Boy's Reservation." *Great Plains Quarterly* 7, no. 3 (1987): 195–209.

Camp, Gregory S. "Working Out Their Own Salvation: The Allotment of Land in Severalty and the Turtle Mountain Chippewa Band, 1870–1920." *AICRJ* 14, no. 2 (1990).

Campbell, Marjorie Williams. *The North West Company.* New York: St. Martin's Press, 1957.

Chaboillez, Charles Jean Baptiste. "Journal of Charles Jean Baptiste Chaboillez, 1797–1798." Edited by Harold Hickerson. *Ethnohistory* 6, no. 3 (Summer 1959).

Champlain, Samuel de. *The Works of Samuel de Champlain.* Edited by Henry P. Bigger. Toronto: Champlain Society, 1922–36.

Charbonneau, Hubert. "Le comportement démographique des voyageurs sous le régime français." *Histoire Sociale [Social History]* 11, no. 21 (May 1978): 120–33.

Chittenden, Hiram Martin. *The American Fur Trade of the Far West.* 1935. Reprint, Lincoln: University of Nebraska Press, 1986.

Clifford, James. *The Predicament of Culture: Twentieth-Century Ethnography, Literature, and Art.* Cambridge, Mass.: Harvard University Press: 1988.

Cooper, James Fenimore. *The Prairie.* 1927. Reprint, New York, Dodd, Mead, 1954.

Coues, Elliott W., ed. *New Light on the Early History of the Greater Northwest.* Vol. 1. 1897. Reprint, Minneapolis: Ross and Haines, 1965.

Coutts, Robert, and Richard Stuart, eds. *The Forks and the Battle of Seven Oaks in Manitoba History.* Winnipeg: Manitoba Historical Society, 1994.

Cox, Bruce Alden, ed. *Native People, Native Lands: Canadian Indian, Inuit and Métis.* Ottawa: Carleton University Press, 1987.

Crawford, John C. "Speaking Michif in Four Métis Communities." *Canadian Journal of Native Studies* 1 (1983): 47–55.

———. "What Is Michif? Language in the Métis Tradition." In Peterson and Brown, *New Peoples,* 231–42.

Cronon, William. *Changes in the Land: Indians, Colonists, and the Ecology of New England.* New York: Hill and Wang, 1883.

Cunningham, Carolyn, comp. *Montana Weather: From 70 Below to 117 Above.* Helena: Montana Magazine, 1982.

Curot, Michel. *A Wisconsin Fur Trader's Journal, 1803–04.* Edited by Reuben Gold Thwaites. Madison, Wis.: CSHSW, 1911.

Dawson, George M. "Surveying the International Boundary: The Journal of George M. Dawson, 1873." *Saskatchewan History* 21, no. 1 (Winter 1968).

Deal, Babbie, and Loretta McDonald, eds. *The Heritage Book of Central Montana.* Fergus County Bi-Centennial Heritage Committee, 1976.

Delorme, David. "History of the Turtle Mountain Chippewa Indians." *North Dakota History* 22, no. 2 (July 1955).

Denig, Edwin Thompson. *Five Indian Tribes of the Upper Missouri: Sioux, Arickaras, Assiniboines, Crees, Crows.* Edited by John C. Ewers. Norman: University of Oklahoma Press, 1961.

Densmore, Frances. *Chippewa Customs.* 1929. Reprint, St. Paul, Minn.: Ross and Haines, 1979.

Department of Climatology. Pennsylvania State University, College Park, Pa. Available from http://www.ems.psu.ed/pa.climatology/state/div06pcp.html.

Devine, Heather. "Ambition Versus Loyalty: Miles Macdonell and the Decline of the North West Company." In Fiske, Sleeper-Smith, and Wicken, *New Faces of the Fur Trade,* 247–82.

———. "*Les Desjarlais:* The Development and Dispersion of a Proto-Métis Hunting Band, 1785–1870." In Binnema, Ens, and Macleod, *From Rupert's Land,* 129–58.

———. "Roots in the Mohawk Valley: Sir William Johnson's Legacy in the North West Company". In Brown, Eccles, and Heldman, *Fur Trade Revisited,* 217–42.

Dick, Lyle. "Historical Writing on 'Seven Oaks': The Assertion of Anglo-Canadian Cultural Dominance in the West." In Coutts and Stuart, *Seven Oaks,* 65–70.

Dickason, Olive P. "From 'One Nation' in the Northeast to 'New Nation' in the Northwest: A Look at the Emergence of the Métis." *AICRJ* 6 (1982): 1–23.

Dissly, Robert L. *A Short History of Lewistown.* Lewistown, Mont.: Great Falls Savings and Loan, 1979.

Dobak, William A. "Killing the Canadian Buffalo, 1821–1881." *Western History Quarterly* 27, no. 1 (Spring 1996).

Donovan, Roberta. *The First Hundred Years: A History of Lewistown, Montana.* Lewistown: Central Montana Publishing, 1994.

Douaud, Patrick. "Canadian Métis Identity: A Pattern of Evolution." *Anthropos* 78 (1983): 71–88.

Dusenberry, Verne. "The Métis of Montana." In *The Redman's West.* 1965.

———. *The Montana Cree: A Study in Religious Persistence.* 1962. Reprint, Norman: University of Oklahoma Press, 1998.

———. "Montana's Displaced Persons: The Rocky Boy Indians." *Montana Magazine of History* 4 (Winter 1954): 1–15.

———. "Waiting for a Day That Never Comes: The Dispossessed Métis of Montana." *Montana: The Magazine of Western History* 6 (1958). Reprinted in Peterson and Brown, *New Peoples,* 119–36.

Eccles, W. J. *The Canadian Frontier, 1534–1760.* New York: Holt, Rinehart and Winston, 1969.

———. *The French in North America, 1500–1783.* East Lansing: Michigan State University Press, 1998.

Edmunds, R. David. "'Unacquainted with the Laws of the Civilized World': American Attitudes toward the Métis Communities in the Old Northwest." In Peterson and Brown, *New Peoples,* 185–94.

Ens, Gerhard J. "After the Buffalo: The Reformation of the Turtle Mountain Métis Community, 1879–1905." In Fiske, Sleeper-Smith, and Wicken, *New Faces of the Fur Trade,* 139–52.

———. "Dispossession or Adaptation? Migration and Persistence of the Red River Métis: 1835–1890." *Historical Papers: The Canadian Historical Association* (1988): 120–44.

———. *Homeland to Hinterland: The Changing Worlds of the Red River Métis in the Nineteenth Century.* Toronto: University of Toronto Press, 1996.

Ewers, John C. *The Blackfeet: Raiders on the Northwestern Plains.* Norman: University of Oklahoma Press, 1958.

———. *Ethnological Report on the Blackfeet and Gros Ventre Tribes of Montana.* New York: Garland, 1974.

———. "Ethnological Report on the Chippewa Cree Tribe of the Rocky Boy Reservation and the Little Shell Band of Indians." In *American Indian Ethnohistory: North Central and Northeastern Indians.* Vol. 6. Edited by David Agee Horr, 1–170. New York: Garland, 1974.

———. "Mothers of the Mixed-Bloods: The Marginal Woman in the History of the Upper Missouri." In *Probing the American West: Papers from the Santa Fe Conference,* edited by K. Ross Toole et al., 62–70. Santa Fe: Museum of New Mexico Press, 1962.

Fiske, Jo-Anne, Susan Sleeper-Smith, and William Wicken. *New Faces of the Fur Trade: Selected Papers of the Seventh North American Fur Trade Conference, Halifax, Nova Scotia, 1995.* East Lansing: Michigan State University Press, 1998.

Flanagan, Thomas. *Louis "David" Riel: Prophet of the New World.* Toronto: University of Toronto Press, 1979.

———. "Louis Riel and the Dispersion of the American Métis." *Minnesota History* 49, no. 5 (Spring 1985): 179–90.

———. *Riel and the Rebellion: 1885 Reconsidered.* Saskatoon, SK: Western Producer Prairie Books, 1983.

Fleming, R. Harvey, ed. *Minutes of Council, Northern Department of Rupert Land, 1821–31.* Vol. 3. Toronto: Champlain Society, 1940.

———, ed. *The Publications of the Hudson's Bay Record Society: Minutes of Council, Northern Department of Rupert Land, 1821–31.* London: Champlain Society, 1940.

Flores, Dan. "Bison Ecology and Bison Diplomacy: The Southern Plains from 1800 to 1850." *Journal of American History* 78, no. 2 (September 1991): 465–85.

Fonda, John H. "Early Wisconsin." In CSHSW. Vol. 5. Madison, Wis.: WHS, 1907.
———. "Reminiscences of Wisconsin." In CSHSW. Vol. 5. Madison, Wis.: WHS, 1907.
Foster, John. "The Métis and the End of the Plains Buffalo in Alberta." *Alberta: Studies in the Arts and Sciences* 3, no. 1 (1992): 61–77.
———. "The Métis: The People and the Term." *Prairie Forum* 3, no. 1 (1978).
———. "The Plains Métis." In *Native Peoples: The Canadian Experience*, edited by Bruce Morrison and R. C. Wilson, 375–403. Toronto: McClelland and Stewart, 1986.
———. "Some Questions and Perspectives on the Problem of Métis Roots." In Peterson and Brown, *New Peoples*, 73–94.
———. "Wintering, the Outsider Adult Male and the Ethnogenesis of the Western Plains Métis." In Binnema, Ens, and Macleod, *From Rupert's Land*, 179–92.
Frankenberg, Ruth. *White Women, Race Matters: The Social Construction of Whiteness*. Minneapolis: University of Minnesota, 1993.
Franklin, Robert, and Pamela Bunte. "A Montana Métis Community Meets the Federal Acknowledgment Process: The Little Shell Chippewa of Montana and 25 CFR S83.7(b), the 'Community' Criterion." In *Proceedings of the International Conference on the Métis People of Canada and the United States, May 16–18, 1996*, edited by William Furdell, 55–104. Great Falls, Mont.: University of Great Falls, 1996.
Freeman, O. W. "Geography and Geology of Fergus County." Fergus High School Bulletin no. 2. Lewistown, Mont.: 1919.
Galbraith, John S. *Hudson's Bay Company as an Imperial Factor, 1821–1869*. Berkeley: University of California Press, 1957.
Garcia, Andrew. *Tough Trip through Paradise, 1878, 1879*. Edited by Bennett H. Stein. 1967. Reprint, San Francisco: Comstock Editions, 1986.
Gardner, W. H. "Ethnology of the Indians of the Valley of the Red River of the North." In *Annual Report of the Smithsonian Institution*. Washington, D.C.: GPO, 1871.
Gates, Paul. *History of Public Land Law Development*. Washington, D.C.: Public Land Law Review Commission, 1968.
———. "Indian Allotments Preceding the Dawes Act." In *The Frontier Challenge*, edited by John Clark. Lawrence: University Press of Kansas, 1971.
Gieseker, L. F. "Soils of Fergus County, Preliminary Report, Soil Reconnaissance of Montana." Bulletin No. 355. Bozeman: Montana State College Experiment Station, 1938.
Gilfillan, Joseph A. "The Ojibways in Minnesota." Vol. 9. Minnesota Historical Society Collections. St. Paul: Minnesota Historical Society, 1901.
Gilman, Rhoda R., Carolyn Gilman, and Deborah M. Stultz. *The Red River Trails: Oxcart Routes between St. Paul and the Selkirk Settlement, 1820–1870*. St. Paul: Minnesota Historical Society, 1979.

Giraud, Marcel. "France and Louisiana in the Early Eighteenth Century." *Mississippi Valley Historical Review* 36, no. 4 (1949–50): 657–74.

———. *Le Métis Canadien: Son role dans l'histoire des Provinces de l'Ouest.* Paris: Travaux et Memoires de l'Institute d'Ethnologie, 1945.

———. *The Métis in the Canadian West.* Translated by George Woodcock. 2 vols. 1945. Reprint, Edmonton: University of Alberta Press, 1986.

Glover, Richard, ed. *David Thompson's Narrative, 1784–1812.* Toronto: Champlain Society, 1962.

Gluek, Alvin C., *Minnesota and the Manifest Destiny of the Canadian Northwest: A Study in Canadian-American Relations.* Toronto: University of Toronto Press, 1965.

Gorham, Harriet. "Families of Mixed Descent in the Western Great Lakes Region." In Cox, *Native People, Native Lands*, 37–55.

Gressley, Gene N. *Bankers and Cattlemen.* New York: Alfred A. Knopf, 1966.

Grignon, Augustin. "Augustin Grignon's Recollections." In CSHSW. Vol. 3. Madison, Wis.: WHS, 1857.

Hafen, LeRoy R., ed. *French Fur Traders and Voyageurs in the American West.* Lincoln: University of Nebraska Press, 1997.

———, ed. *The Mountain Men and the Fur Trade of the Far West: Biographical Sketches by Scholars of the Subject and with Introductions by the Editor.* Arthur H. Clark: Glendale, Calif., 1965–1972.

Hall, J. H. "Montana." Department of Publicity of the Bureau of Agriculture, Labor and Industry of the State of Montana. Helena, Mont.: Independent Publishing / State Printers, 1912.

Haney-López, Ian F. *White by Law: The Legal Construction of Race.* New York: New York University Press, 1996.

Harmon, Daniel Williams. *A Journal of Voyages and Travels in the Interior of North America.* New York: A. S. Barnes, 1903.

Harpole, Patricia C., and Mary D. Nagle, eds. *Minnesota Territorial Census 1850.* St. Paul: Minnesota Historical Society, 1972.

Harrison, Julia D. *Métis: People between Two Worlds.* Vancouver: Douglas McIntyre, 1985.

Havard, V. "The French Half-Breeds of the Northwest." 2 vols. In *Report of the Smithsonian Institution, 1879.* Washington, D.C.: GPO, 1880.

Hayden, Ferdinand V. "On the Geology and Natural History of the Upper Missouri." In *Transactions of the American Philosophical Society.* Vol. 12. Philadelphia: C. Sherman, Son, 1863.

Hayes, Jack, ed. *Animal Health.* Washington, D.C.: GPO, 1984.

Henry, Alexander. "Report of Northwest Population, 1805." In Coues, *New Light.*

———. *Travels and Adventures in Canada and the Indian Territories Between the Years 1760 and 1776.* New York, 1809.

Hesketh, John. "History of the Turtle Mountain Chippewa." In CSHSND. Vol. 5. Edited by O. G. Libby. Grand Forks, N.Dak.: SHSND, 1923.
Hickerson, Harold. "The Genesis of a Trading Post Band: The Pembina Chippewa." *Ethnohistory* 3, no. 4 (Fall 1956).
Hind, Henry Youle. *Narrative of the Canadian Red River Exploring Expedition of 1857 and of the Assiniboine and Saskatchewa Exploring Expedition of 1858.* 2 vols. London: Longman, Green, Longman, and Roberts, 1860.
Hogue, Michel. "Disputing the Medicine Line: The Plains Crees and the Canadian-American Border, 1876–1885." *Montana: The Magazine of Western History* 52, no. 4 (Winter 2002): 2–17.
Hornaday, William T. *The Extermination of the American Bison.* Washington, D.C.: GPO, 1889.
Horr, David Agee, ed. *Chippewa Indians.* 7 vols. New York: Garland, 1974.
Horsman, Reginald. *Race and Manifest Destiny: The Origins of American Racial Anglo-Saxonism.* Cambridge, Mass.: Harvard University Press, 1981.
Howard, James H. "The Plains-Ojibwa or Bungi: Hunters and Warriors of the Northern Prairies with Special Reference to the Turtle Mountain Band." Anthropological Papers. Vermillion: University of South Dakota, 1965.
———. "The Turtle Mountain Chippewa." *North Dakota Quarterly* 26, no. 2 (Spring 1958).
Howard, Joseph Kinsey. *Strange Empire.* 1952. Reprint, St. Paul: Minnesota Historical Society Press, 1994.
Hubner, Brian. "'A Race of Mules': Mixed-Bloods in Western American Fiction." *Canadian Journal of Native Studies* 15, no. 1 (1995): 61–74.
Hutchinson, John, and Anthony D. Smith, eds. *Ethnicity.* Oxford, U.K.: Oxford University Press, 1996.
Innis, Harold A. *The Fur Trade in Canada.* 1930. Reprint, Toronto: University of Toronto Press, 1970.
Isenberg, Andrew C. *The Destruction of the Bison: An Environmental History, 1750–1920.* New York: Cambridge University Press, 2000.
———. "The Return of the Bison: Nostalgia, Profit, and Preservation." *Environmental History Review* 2, no. 2 (April 1997): 179–96.
———. "Toward a Policy of Destruction: Buffaloes, Law, and the Market, 1803–83." *Great Plains Quarterly* 12 (Fall 1992): 227–41
James, Edwin, ed. *The Captivity and Adventures of John Tanner.* Minneapolis: Ross and Haines, 1956.
Jamieson, Frederick C. "The Edmonton Hunt." *Alberta Historical Review* 1, no. 1 (April 1953).
Jetté, René. *Dictionnaire généalogique des familles du Québec: des origines à 1730.* Montreal: University of Montreal Press, 1983.
Judd, Carol M. "Native Labour and Social Stratification in the Hudson's Bay Northern Department, 1770–1870." *Canadian Review of Sociology and Anthropology* 17, no. 4 (1980): 305–14.

Keating, William H. *Narrative of an Expedition to the Source of St. Peter's River.* 2 vols. London: George B. Whittaker, 1825.
Klein, Laura F., and Lillian A. Ackerman, eds. *Women and Power in Native North America.* Norman: University of Oklahoma Press, 1995.
Kohl, J. G. *Kitchi-Gami: Wanderings Round Lake Superior.* 1860. Reprint, Minneapolis: Ross and Haines, 1956.
Koucky, Rudolph W. "The Buffalo Disaster of 1882." *North Dakota History* 50, no. 1 (Winter 1983): 23–30.
Koury, Michael J. *Guarding the Carroll Trail: Camp Lewis, 1874–1875.* Bellevue, Nebr.: Old Army Press, 1969.
———. *Military Posts of Montana.* Bellevue, Nebr.: Old Army Press, 1970.
La Vérendrye, Pierre Gaultier de Varennes de. *Journals and Letters of Pierre Gaultier de Varennes de La Vérendrye and His Sons.* Vol. 16. Edited by Lawrence J. Burpee. Toronto: Publications of the Champlain Society, 1927.
LaCounte, Larry. "A Saga of Struggle and Contribution in Two Nations." In *The Metis Centennial Celebration Publication, 1879–1979,* edited by Bill Thackeray. Lewistown, Mont.: Metis Centennial Celebration Committee, 1979.
Larpenteur, Charles. *Forty Years a Fur Trader on the Upper Missouri.* 1933. Reprint, Lincoln: University of Nebraska Press, 1989.
LaTray, Leslie G. "Les." Obituary. *LNA,* August 13, 1997.
Laverdure, Patline, and Ida Rose Allard. *The Michif Dictionary: Turtle Mountain Chippewa Cree.* Winnipeg, Manitoba: Pemmican, 1983.
Leary, James P., ed. *Medicine Fiddle: A Humanities Discussion Guide.* Marquette: Northern Michigan University, 1992.
Lecompte, Janet. "The Choteaus in the St. Louis Fur Trade." In *A Guide to the Microfilm Edition of Research Collections of the American West: Papers of the St. Louis Fur Trade,* edited by William R. Swagerty. St. Louis: Missouri Historical Society, 1991.
Lederman, Anne. "Old Native and Métis Fiddling: An Ethnomusicological Perspective." In Leary, *Medicine Fiddle.*
Leeson, M. A. *History of Montana, 1739–1885.* Chicago: Warner, Beers, 1885.
Lewiston (Mont.) News Argus, "Dedication of Marker at Old Post Office Thursday," September 17, 1931.
Libby, O. G., ed. "Gazetteer of Pioneers." In *Collection of the State Historical Society of North Dakota.* Vol. 1. Bismarck: 1906.
Linderman, Frank B. *Pretty-shield.* 1932. Reprint, Lincoln: University of Nebraska Press, 1972.
Lockwood, James H. "Early Times and Events in Wisconsin." In CSHSW. Vol. 2. Madison, Wis.: WHS, 1903.
Long, John. "Treaty No. 9 and Fur Trade Company Families: Northeastern Ontario's Halfbreeds, Indians, Petitioners, and Métis." In Peterson and Brown, *New Peoples,* 137–62.

Lounsberry, Clement A. *North Dakota: History and People.* 3 vols. Chicago: S.J. Clarke, 1917.

Lowie, Robert H. *Indians of the Plains.* 1954. Reprint, Lincoln: University of Nebraska Press, 1982.

Lussier, Antoine S., and D. Bruce Sealey, eds. *The Other Natives: The-les Métis, 1700–1885.* Winnipeg: Manitoba Métis Federation Press, 1978–1980.

Mackenzie, Alexander. *Voyages from Montreal through the Continent of North America . . . in 1789 and 1793.* 1801. Reprint, Toronto: Courier Press, 1911.

MacLeod, M. A., and W. L. Morton. *Cuthbert Grant of Granttown: Warden of the Plains of Red River.* Toronto: McClelland and Stewart, 1963.

Madill, Dennis F. K. "Riel, Red River, and Beyond: New Developments in Métis History." In *New Directions in American Indian History,* edited by Colin Calloway. Norman: University of Oklahoma Press, 1988.

Malone, Michael P. *The Battle for Butte: Mining and Politics on the Northern Frontier, 1864–1906.* Seattle: University of Washington Press, 1981.

———, Richard B. Roeder, and William L. Lang. *Montana: A History of Two Centuries.* 1976. Reprint, Seattle: University of Washington Press, 1991.

Marble, Manton. "To Red River and Beyond." Pt. 1. *Harper's New Monthly Magazine* 21, no. 123 (August 1860): 289–311.

———. "To Red River and Beyond." Pt. 2. *Harper's New Monthly Magazine* 21, no. 125 (October 1860): 581–606.

———. "To Red River and Beyond." Pt. 3 *Harper's New Monthly Magazine* 22, no. 129 (February 1861): 306–22.

Martin, Archer. *The Hudson's Bay Company Land Tenures and the Occupation of Assiniboia.* New York: Clowes, 1898.

Masson, L. R. *Les Bourgeois.* 2 vols. 1889–1890. Reprint, New York: Antiquarian Press, 1960.

McBride, Genevieve, O.S.U. *The Bird Tail.* New York: Vantage Press, 1974.

McDonnell, John. "John McDonnell's Journal." In Masson, *Les Bourgeois.*

McKenney, Thomas L. *Sketches of a Tour of the Lakes, of the Character and Customs of the Chippeway Indians and of Incidents Connected with the Treaty of Fond de Lac.* 1827. Reprint, Minneapolis, 1959.

Meyer, Melissa L. *The White Earth Tragedy: Ethnicity and Dispossession at a Minnesota Anishinaabe Reservation, 1889–1920.* Lincoln: University of Nebraska Press, 1994.

Miles, Nelson A. *Personal Recollections and Observations of General Nelson A. Miles.* Chicago: Werner, 1897.

Miller, J. R. "From Riel to the Métis." *Canadian Historical Review* 69 (January 1988).

Morice, A. *Dictionnaire historique des Canadiens et des Métis français de l'ouest.* Québec: Laflamme and Proulx, 1908.

Morin, Gail. *The Manitoba Scrip.* Pawtucket, R.I.: Quintin Publications, 1996.

———. *Metis Families: A Genealogical Compendium.* Pawtucket, R.I.: Quintin Publications, 1996.

Morton, Arthur S. *A History of the Canadian West to 1870–71.* Toronto, 1939.

———, ed. *The Journal of Duncan McGillivray of the North West Company at Fort George on the Saskatchewan, 1794–1795.* 1929. Reprint, Fairfield, Wash.: Ye Galleaon Press, 1989.

Morton, W. L. *Manitoba: A History.* 2nd ed. Toronto: University of Toronto Press, 1967.

———. "The North West Company: Pedlars Extraordinary." *Minnesota History* 40, no. 4 (1966).

Mumford, Jeremy. "Métis and the Vote in Nineteenth-Century America: A Westward Journey." *Journal of the West* 39 (Summer 2000): 38–45.

Murphy, Lucy Eldersveld. *A Gathering of Rivers: Indian, Métis, and Mining in the Western Great Lakes, 1737–1832.* Lincoln: University of Nebraska Press, 2000.

Murray, Stanley N. "The Turtle Mountain Chippewa, 1882–1905." *North Dakota History* 51, no. 1 (Winter 1984).

Nagel, Joane. *American Indian Ethnic Renewal: Red Power and the Resurgence of Identity and Culture.* Oxford, U.K.: Oxford University Press, 1996.

Nasatir, A. P. "The Anglo-Spanish Frontier in the Illinois Country during the American Revolution, 1779–1783." *Illinois State Historical Society Journal* 21 (1928).

———, ed. *Before Lewis and Clark: Documents Illustrating the History of the Missouri, 1785–1804.* 2 vols. 1952. Reprint, Lincoln: University of Nebraska Press, 1990.

———. "Jacques D'Eglise." *Mississippi Valley Historical Review* 14 (1927): 47–56.

———. "Spanish Explorations of Upper Missouri." *Mississippi Valley Historical Review* 14 (1927): 57–71.

Nash, Gary B. "The Hidden History of Mestizo America." *Journal of American History* 82 (December 1995): 941–62.

Noyes, Al. J. *In The Land of Chinook or, The Story of Blaine County.* Helena, Mont.: State Publishing, 1917.

Nute, Grace Lee, ed. *Documents Relating to Northwest Missions, 1815-1827.* St. Paul: Minnesota Historical Society, 1942.

———. *The Voyageur.* New York: D. Appleton, 1931.

O'Connell, Samuel. "Ft. Turney, on Milk River, 31 August 1875." *BR*, September 11, 1875. Copy held by MHSA (Samuel O'Connell Papers. SC 597, box 1, folder 1).

Overholser, Joel. *Fort Benton: World's Innermost Port.* Helena, Mont.: Falcon, 1987.

Owens, Kenneth N., and Sally L. Owens. "Buffalo and Bacteria." *Montana* (Spring 1987): 65–67.

Palladino, L. B., S.J. *Indian and White in the Northwest: A History of Catholicity in Montana, 1831 to 1891.* 1893. Reprint, Lancaster, Pa.: Wickersham, 1922.

Palliser, John, et al. *Journals, Detailed Reports and Observations Relative to Captain Palliser's Exploration of a Portion of British North American during the Years 1857, 1858, 1859 and 1860.* London, 1862.

Pascoe, Peggy. "Miscegenation Law, Court Cases, and Ideologies of 'Race' in Twentieth-Century America." *Journal of American History* 83, no. 1 (June 1996): 44–69.
Payment, Diane. *"The Free People—Otipemisiwak": Batoche, Saskatchewan, 1870–1930.* Ottawa: National Historic Parks and Sites, Parks Canada, 1990.
———. "Plains Métis." In *Handbook of North American Indians,* edited by Raymond J. Demallie, 13:661–76. Washington, D.C.: Smithsonian Institution, 2001.
Peers, Laura. *The Ojibwa of Western Canada, 1780–1870.* St. Paul: Minnesota Historical Society, 1994.
———, and Jennifer S. H. Brown. "'There Is No End to Relationship Among the Indians': Ojibwa Families and Kinship in Historical Perspective." *History of the Family: An International Quarterly* 4 (2000): 529–55.
Peterson, Jacqueline. "Ethnogenesis: The Settlement and Growth of a 'New People' in the Great Lakes Region, 1702–1815." *AICRJ* 6 (1982): 23–64.
———. "Many Roads to Red River: Métis Genesis in the Great Lakes Region, 1680–1815." In Peterson and Brown, *New Peoples,* 37–72.
———. "Prelude to Red River: A Social Portrait of the Great Lakes Métis," *Ethnohistory* 25 (1978).
———, and Jennifer S. H. Brown, eds. *The New Peoples: Being and Becoming Métis in North America.* Winnipeg: University of Manitoba Press, 1985.
Pratt, Alexander F. "Reminiscences of Wisconsin." In CSHSW. Vol. 1. Madison, Wis.: WHS, 1903.
Price, Con. *Memories of Old Montana.* Hollywood, Calif.: Highland Press, 1945.
Pritchett, John. *The Red River Valley, 1811–1849.* New Haven, Conn.: Yale University Press, 1942.
R. L. Polk and Company. *Fergus County Directory.* Helena, Mont.: R. L. Polk, 1904–1918.
———. *Lewistown City Directory.* Helena, Mont.: R. L. Polk, 1904–1918.
Rich, E. E. *George Simpson's Journal of Occurrences in the Athabaska Department and Report 1820–21.* Toronto: Champlain Society, 1838.
———. *The History of the Hudson's Bay Company, 1670–1870.* 2 vols. London: Hudson's Bay Record Society, 1959.
———, ed. *Journal of Occurrences in the Athabasca Department by George Simpson, 1820 and 1821, and Report.* Toronto: Champlain Society, 1938.
Riel, Louis. *The Collected Writings of Louis Riel.* Edited by George F. G. Stanley. 5 vols. Edmonton: University of Alberta Press, 1985.
Rife, Clarence. "Norman Kittson, a Fur Trader at Pembina." *Minnesota History* 6, no. 3 (September 1925).
Robinson, Henry Martin. *The Great Fur Land, or Sketches of Life in the Hudson's Bay Territory.* New York: G. P. Putnam's Sons, 1879.
Roe, Frank Gilbert. *North American Buffalo: A Critical Study of the Species in Its Wild State.* 1951. Reprint, Toronto: University of Toronto Press, 1970.

Roediger, David R. *The Wages of Whiteness: Race and the Making of the American Working Class.* London: Verso, 1991.

Ross, Alexander. *Report of the Proceeding Connected with the Disputes between the Earl of Selkirk and the NWC, at the Assizes, Held at York, in Upper Canada, October 1818.* London: B. McMillan, 1819.

———. *The Red River Settlement: Its Rise, Progress, and Present State.* 1856. Reprint, Minneapolis: Ross and Haines, 1957.

Roy History Committee. *Homestead Shacks over Buffalo Tracks: History of Northeastern Fergus County.* Bozeman, Mont.: Color World Printers, 1990.

"Running the Buffalo." *Nor'Wester,* September 11, 1862.

Russell, Alexander J. *The Red River Colony, Hudson's Bay and Northwest Territories, Considered in Relation to Canada.* Montreal: G. E. Desbarats, 1870.

Russell, Donna Valley, ed. *Michigan Censuses, 1710–1830.* Detroit: Detroit Society for Genealogical Research, 1982.

Saunders, Richard M. "The Emergence of the *Coureur de Bois* as a Social Type." *Canadian Historical Association Historical Reports* (1939): 22–33.

Sawchuk, Joe. *The Métis of Manitoba: Reformulation of an Ethnic Identity.* Toronto: Peter Martin, 1978.

Scheick, William J. *The Half-Blood: A Cultural Symbol in Nineteenth Century Fiction.* Lexington: University of Kentucky, 1979.

Schenck, Theresa M. "Against All Odds . . . and with the Help of Our Friends: The Native Role in Establishing the Red River Colony, 1812–1817." *North Dakota Quarterly* 65, no. 4 (1998).

Schultz, James W. "America's Red Armenians: The Blackfeet Starve to Death, but the Indian Bureau Blocks Private Relief." *Sunset Magazine,* November 1922.

———. *My Life as an Indian.* 1907. Reprint, New York: Fawcett Columbine, 1981.

Sealey, D. Bruce, and Antoine S. Lussier. *The Métis: Canada's Forgotten People.* Winnipeg: Manitoba Métis Federation Press, 1975.

Seilstad, Margaret Jackson. "George R. Jackson Family History." In Deal and McDonald, *Heritage Book,* 155–60.

Sharp, Paul F. *Merchant Princes of the Plains.* Helena: Montana Historical Society Press, 1955.

———. *Whoop-Up Country: The Canadian-American West, 1865–1885.* Minneapolis: University of Minnesota Press, 1955.

Shoemaker, Nancy, ed. *Negotiators of Change: Historical Perspectives on Native American Women.* New York: Routledge, 1995.

Skinner, Alanson. "Notes on the Eastern Cree and Northern Saulteaux." *Anthropological Papers of the American Museum of Natural History* 9 (1911).

Slaughter, Linda W. "Fort Randall." In CSHSND. Vol. 1. Bismarck, N.Dak.: SHSND, 1903.

Sleeper-Smith, Susan. "Furs and Female Kin Networks: The World of Marie Madeleine Réaume L'Archevêque Chevalier." In Fiske, Sleeper-Smith, and Wicken, *New Faces of the Fur Trade*, 53–74.

———. *Indian Women and French Men: Rethinking Cultural Encounter in the Western Great Lakes*. Amherst: University of Massachusetts Press, 2001.

———. "Women, Kin, and Catholicism: New Perspectives on the Fur Trade." *Ethnohistory* 47, no. 2 (Spring 2000): 423–52.

Smits, David D. "'Squaw Men,' 'Half-Breeds,' and Amalgamators." *AICRJ* 15, no. 3 (1991): 29–61.

Smythe, Donald, S.J., "John J. Pershing." *Montana* 28, no. 1 (January 1968).

Sparlin, Alberta. *The Trail Back*. Great Falls, Mont.: Blue Print and Letter, 1976.

Sprague, Douglas N. "Government Lawlessness in the Administration of Manitoba Land Claims, 1870–1887." *Manitoba Law Journal* 10, no. 4 (1980): 415–41.

———, and R. P. Frye. *The Genealogy of the First Metis Nation: The Development and Dispersal of the Red River Settlement, 1820–1900*. Winnipeg, Manitoba: Pemmican, 1983.

Sprenger, George Herman. "The Métis Nation: Buffalo Hunting Versus Agriculture in the Red River Settlement, 1810–1870." In Cox, *Native People, Native Lands*, 120–35.

Stanley, George F. G. *The Birth of Western Canada: A History of the Riel Rebellions*. 1936. Reprint, Toronto: University of Toronto Press, 1960.

———. *Louis Riel*. Toronto: McGraw-Hill Ryerson, 1963.

Stebbins, Susan. "Métis Women among the Iroquois." In *Proceedings of the International Conference on the Métis People of Canada and the United States*, edited by William Furdell. Great Falls, Mont.: University of Great Falls, 1996.

Stegner, Wallace. *Wolf Willow: A History, a Story, and a Memory of the Last Plains Frontier*. Lincoln: University of Nebraska Press, 1955.

Stuart, Granville. *Forty Years on the Frontier as Seen in the Journals and Reminiscences of Granville Stuart*. Edited by Paul C. Phillips. 2 vols. 1925. Reprint, Glendale, Calif.: Arthur H. Clark, 1967.

"The Summer Hunt." *Nor'Wester*, August 14 and 18, 1860.

Sunder, John E. *The Fur Trade on the Upper Missouri, 1840–1865*. Norman: University of Oklahoma Press, 1965.

Swagerty, William R. "Marriage and Settlement Patterns of Rocky Mountain Trappers and Traders." *Western Historical Quarterly* 11, no. 2 (April 1980): 159–80.

Swan, Elizabeth Berger. "Mrs. Swan, One of Lewistown's Earliest Residents Recalls Memories of Her Childhood, School Days." *LNA*, December 22, 1968. Copy held by MBSC.

Thackeray, Bill, ed. *The Métis Centennial Celebration Publication*. Lewistown, Mont.: Métis Centennial Celebration Committee, 1979.

Thomas, L. G., ed. *Prairie West to 1905*. Toronto: Oxford University Press, 1975.

Thomson, William D. "History of Fort Pembina: 1870–1895." *North Dakota History* 36, no. 1 (Winter 1969).

Thorne, Tanis C. *The Many Hands of My Relations: French and Indians on the Lower Missouri*. Columbia: University of Missouri Press, 1996.

Thornton, Russell. *American Indian Holocaust and Survival: A Population History since 1492*. Norman: University of Oklahoma Press, 1987.

Thwaites, Reuben Gold, ed. "Commercial History of Milwaukee." In CSHSW. Vol. 4. Madison, Wis.: WHS, 1859.

———. *Early Western Travels, 1748–1846*. 32 vols. Cleveland, Ohio: A. H. Clark, 1904–1907.

———, ed. "Fur Trade in Wisconsin." In CSHSW. Vol. 19. Madison, Wis.: WHS, 1910: 375–487.

———. "Fur Trade on the Upper Lakes." In CSHSW. Vol. 19. Madison, Wis.: WHS, 1910: 234–374.

———. "The Mackinac Register of Marriages, 1725–1821". In CSHSW. Vol. 18. Madison, Wis.: WHS, 1908.

———. *The Original Journals of the Lewis and Clark Expedition*. New York: Dodd, Mead, 1904–1905.

———. "Register of Baptisms, 1695–1821". In CSHSW. Vol. 19. Madison, Wis.: WHS, 1910.

———, ed. "Register of Internments, 1743–1806." In CSHSW. Vol. 19. Madison, Wis.: WHS 1910.

———. "Register of Marriages, 1787." In CSHSW. Vol. 19. Madison, Wis.: WHS, 1910.

———, ed. "Travels and Explorations of the Jesuit Missionaries in New France, 1610–1791." In *Jesuit Relations and Allied Documents: Iroquois, Ottawas, Lower Canada*. 73 vols. Cleveland: Burrows, 1899.

Toole, K. Ross. *Montana: An Uncommon Land*. Norman: University of Oklahoma Press, 1959.

Torgerson, Kristen. "With a Smile and a Horse He Keeps Peace." *LNA*, August 3, 1997.

Truteau, Jean Baptiste. "Journal of Truteau on the Missouri River, 1794–1795." In *Before Lewis and Clark: Documents Illustrating the History of the Missouri, 1785-1804*, edited by A. P. Nasatir. 1952. Reprint, Lincoln: University of Nebraska Press, 1990.

Turner, John Peter. *The North-West Mounted Police, 1873–1893*. 2 vols. Ottawa: E. Cloutier, King's Printer, 1950.

Tyrrell, J. B., ed. *David Thompson's Narrative of Explorations in Western America, 1784–1812*. 1916. Reprint, New York: Greenwood Press, 1968.

———. *Samuel Hearne's Journey from Prince of Wales Fort in Hudson's Bay to the Northern Ocean 1769–1772*. Toronto: Champlain Society, 1911.

Utley, Robert M. *The Indian Frontier of the American West, 1846–1890*. Albuquerque: University of New Mexico Press, 1983.

Van Kirk, Sylvia. "'The Custom of the Country': An Examination of Fur Trade Marriage Practices." In *Essays on Western History*, edited by Lewis H. Thomas. Edmonton: University of Alberta Press, 1976.

———. *Many Tender Ties: Women in Fur Trade Society, 1670–1870*. Norman: University of Oklahoma Press, 1980.

Vermaat, James M. *History of the Foundation of the First Convent of the Congregation of the Daughters of Jesus in the United States of America at Lewistown, Montana*. San Antonio, Tex.: 1928.

Vrooman, Nicholas. "Tale of the Medicine Fiddle: How a Tune Was Played and the Metchif Came to Be." In Leary, *Medicine Fiddle*, 19–29.

Wade, Mason. *The French Canadians*. Toronto: Macmillan Co. of Canada, 1965.

Wallace, Stewart. *Dictionary of Canadian Biography*. London: Macmillan, 1963.

Wallace, W. S. *Documents Relating to the North West Company*. Toronto: Champlain Society, 1934.

———. "The Pedlars From Quebec." *Canadian Historical Review* 4 (December 1932): 387–402.

Warren, William W. *History of the Ojibwa Nation*. Minneapolis: Ross and Haines, 1957.

West, Helen B. "Starvation Winter of the Blackfeet." *Montana Magazine of History* 9 (Winter 1959): 2–19.

"What Do You Know about the Church's Protest against Mixed Marriages?" *Lewistown Catholic Monthly* 5, no. 4 (March 1922).

Wheeler-Voegelin, Erminie, and Harold Hickerson. *The Red Lake and Pembina Chippewa*. Vol. 1, *Chippewa Indians*. Edited by David Agee Horr. New York: Garland, 1974.

White, Bruce M. "The Woman Who Married a Beaver: Trade Patterns and Gender Roles in the Ojibwa Fur Trade." *Ethnohistory* 46, no. 1 (Winter 1999).

White, Richard. *"It's Your Misfortune and None of My Own": A History of the American West*. Norman: University of Oklahoma Press, 1991.

———. *Middle Ground: Indians, Empires, and Republics in the Great Lakes Region, 1670–1815*. Cambridge, UK: Cambridge University Press, 1991.

Williams, Glyndwr, ed. *Andrew Graham's Observations on Hudson's Bay, 1769–91*. London: Hudson's Bay Record Society, 1969.

Wishart, David J. *The Fur Trade of the American West, 1807–1840*. Lincoln: University of Nebraska Press, 1979.

Wood, W. Raymond, and Thomas D. Thiessen. *Early Fur Trade on the Northern Plains: Canadian Traders among the Mandan and Hidatsa Indians, 1738–1818*. Norman: University of Oklahoma Press, 1985.

Woodcock, George. *Gabriel Dumont: The Metis Chief and His Lost World*. Edmonton: Hurtig, 1975.

Woodstock Letters: A Record of Current Events and Historical Notes Connected with the Colleges and Missions of the Daughters of Jesus in North and South America. Vol. 10. Woodstock, Md.: Woodstock College Press, 1881.

Woolworth, Nancy L. "Captain Edwin V. Sumner's Expedition to Devils Lake in the Summer of 1845." *North Dakota History* 28, no. 3 (Fall 1964).

———. "Gingras, St. Joseph and the Métis in the Northern Red River Valley, 1843–1873." *North Dakota History* 42, no. 4 (Fall 1975).

Wub-e-ke-niew. *We Have the Right to Exist: A Translation of Aboriginal Indigenous Thought.* New York: Black Thistle Press, 1995.

UNPUBLISHED DOCUMENTS

Abbott, Mary Stuart. Papers. Fergus Co., SC 978.6292. LPL.

Anderson, Conrad. "History of Roy, Montana." (n.d.) Fergus County Collection. SC 978.6292. LPL.

Anderson, Vernon. "The LaTray Family and Their Part in Central Montana History." Term paper, December 1, 1975, College of Great Falls, Great Falls, Mont. Copy held by LPL.

Assumption Roman Catholic Church. Assumption Parish Records. Pembina, N.Dak.

Berger, Betsy Kiplin. As told to Elizabeth Berger Swan. "Sporty and the Bear Claw." File 542. MBSC.

Camp, Gregory S. "The Turtle Mountain Plains: Chippewas and Métis, 1797–1935." Ph.D. diss., University of New Mexico, 1986.

Cloud, Henry Roe, comp. "Basic Membership Roll of the Landless Indians of Montana." 1937. Little Shell Office, Great Falls, Mont.

"Course of Study, Daily Programs, List of Text Books for Girls Dept., St. Peter's Mission, Mont., 1896." SPMP. Miscellaneous file. UCA.

Denney, Charles D. Papers. Glenbow Archives, Calgary, Saskatchewan.

Devine, Heather. "Métis or Country-Born? The Case of the Klynes." Paper presented at the Annual Meetings of the Canadian Historical Association, Learned Societies Conference, St. John's, Newfoundland, Canada, May 31–June 14, 1997.

Doane, Gustavus C. Gustavus C. Doane Letters. Doane Papers. SC 28. MHSA.

Doane, Mary Hunter. "Address by Mrs. Doane" (n.d.), Mary Hunter Doane Papers. Manuscript file 292. MBSC.

———. "Trip from Ft. Ellis to Ft. Assiniboine" (n.d.), Mary Hunter Doane Papers. Manuscript file 292. MBSC.

Fergus County Genealogical Society. "Index to Births." Lewistown, Mont., December 20, 1883–December 26, 1900.

———. "Index to Marriages." Lewistown, Mont., December 20, 1883–December 26, 1900.

———. "*Mineral Argus* and *Fergus County Argus* Index to Deaths." Lewistown, Mont., December 20, 1883–December 26, 1900.

Fergus, James. Papers. Col. 28. MHSA.

———. Papers. MLSC.

Fleury Family Papers. In possession of Treena LaFountain, Billings, Mont.

Foster, John. "The Country-Born in the Red River Settlement, 1820–1850." Ph.D. diss., University of Alberta, 1973.

Foster, Martha Harroun. "'We Know Who We Are': Multiethnic Identity in a Montana Community." Ph.D. diss., University of California Los Angeles, 2000.

Franklin, Robert, and Pamela Bunte. "Supplemental Report." In "Supplemental Evidence and Analysis in Support of Federal Acknowledgment of the Little Shell Tribe of Chippewa Indians of Montana," December 12, 1994. Copy available at Little Shell Tribal Headquarters, Great Falls, Mont.

Gray, Raymond. "History of the Cree Indians." Raymond Gray Papers. WPA Records, 1935–1942, col. 2336, box 18. MBSC.

———. "History of the Cree Nation." Raymond Gray Papers. WPA Records, 1935–1942, col. 2336, box 18. MBSC.

———. "History of the Montana Landless Indians." Raymond Gray Papers. WPA Records, 1935–1942, col. 2336, box 18. MBSC.

Guardipee, Eli. "Eli Guardipee's Story." As told to John B. Ritch. Eli Guardipee Reminiscence. SC 772. MHSA.

Hansen, Matthew. "The South Fork of the Teton River: A History of Its People." Paper, June 1980.

Hauser, Samuel T. Papers. Col. 37. MHSA.

Heidenreich, Virginia L. "The Fur Trade in North Dakota." Bismarck, N.Dak.: 1990. SHSND.

Hilger, David. Papers. SC 854. MHSA.

Howard, Joseph Kinsey. Papers. Col. 27. MHSA.

Jackson, Dorman. "Early History, Lewistown and Missions." 1974. Catholic History File. St. Leo's Catholic Church Library, Lewistown, Mont.

Jackson, Mercy. "History of Fergus County from the Early Days." Mercy Jackson Papers. Col. 544. MBSC.

———. "Lewistown." Mercy Jackson Papers. Col. 544. MBSC.

———. "Lewistown Schools." Mercy Jackson Papers. Col. 544. MBSC.

———. "Public and City Schools of Fergus County." Mercy Jackson Papers. Col. 544. MBSC.

Kugel, Rebecca. "To Work Like a Frenchman": Ojibwe Men's Definitions of Métis Men's Ethnicity in the Early Nineteenth Century." Paper presented at the American Society for Ethnohistory Annual Meeting, November 1998.

LaFountain Family Papers. In possession of Donna LaFountain Walraven, Black Eagle, Mont.

"LaFountain Genealogy." In possession of Donna LaFountain Walraven, Black Eagle, Mont.

LaTray, Leslie G. Speech, Bicentennial dinner, September 21, 1975. In Vernon Anderson, "The LaTray Family."

Lewistown Catholic Monthly. "Detail of Pew Rent, Repairs, Fuel and Light Collections," 1919–1923. Copy held in the Great Falls Diocese Archives, Great Falls, Mont.

———. "Financial Report of St. Leo's Church," 1919–1923. Copy held in the Great Falls Diocese Archives, Great Falls, Mont.

Linderman, Frank B. Papers. MF 382. MHSA. Originals held by MLSC.

Lusk, Charles. Communication. Washington, D.C., Bureau of Catholic Indian Missions, to Hiram Price, Commissioner of Indian Affairs, August 6, 1883. Miscellaneous file, SPMP, UCA.

MacMillan, Donald. "Andrew Jackson Davis: A Story of Frontier Capitalism, 1864–1890." Master's thesis, University of Montana, 1967.

McLaughlin, James. "Family History of So-Called Rocky Boy Indians Residing in the State of Montana." May 7–30, 1917. Copy available at Little Shell Office, Great Falls, Mont.

Morin, Gail. "Individual Narrative of Charlotte Pelletier." Information provided to author June 26, 2003.

Morris, C. Patrick, and Robert Van Gunten. "An Oral History of the Chief Little Shell Tribe of Chippewas of Montana." 1979. MBSC.

Moses, W. W. "Benjamin Kline of Lewistown Oldest Judith Basin Settler Still Rugged Despite 81 Years." Ca. 1903, Central Montana History Collection, SC 978.6292. LPL.

Moss, William M. "Report of Supervisor Moss on St. Peter's Mission School, Montana." To Superintendent of Indian Schools, August 14, 1895, SPMP, Miscellaneous file. UCA.

Mueller, Oscar. Oscar Mueller Correspondence. SC978.6292. LPL.

Nault, Fred. "Fred Nault: Montana Metis and Told by Himself." Chippewa-Cree Research, Rocky Boy School, Rocky Boy Reservation, Mont., 1977.

O'Connell, Samuel. "Juneaux's Trading Post on Milk River, Montana Territory: Story of Medicine Lodge known as Juneaux's Post." Samuel O'Connell Papers. SC 597, box 1, folder 1. MHSA.

Olson, Edna McElhiney, ed. "St. Charles Co., Missouri Marriages, 1792–1863." St. Charles, Mo., 1969.

Pershing, John. "Autobiography." John J. Pershing Papers. Box 380. Library of Congress, Washington, D.C.

Picton, Pierre. "Collection de l'abbée Pierre Picton." Société Historique St. Boniface, Manitoba.

Podruchny, Carolyn. "'Sons of the Wilderness': Work, Culture and Identity among Voyageurs in the Montreal Fur Trade, 1780–1821." Ph.D. diss., University of Toronto, 1999.

Potter, Carroll H., Capt. 18th Inf. Letters. 1879. M234, roll 518, NARG 75.

"Program of Daily Recitations." SPMP. Miscellaneous file. UCA.

Schultz, James W. "Last Years of the Buffalo." James W. Schultz Papers. Box 8, folder 25. MBSC.
St. Boniface Roman Catholic Church. "Registre des Baptemes, Mariages and Sepultures, 1825–1834. St. Boniface—Manitoba, Canada—Photocopies of Original Records Saved from Fire—June 6, 1825–November 25, 1834." Collection of the Genealogical Forum, Portland, Ore., n.d.
St. Florent Roman Catholic Church. "Mission de St. Florent [Lebret] Roman Catholic Registre des Baptemes, Mariages and Sepultures." Qu'Appelle, Saskatchewan.
St. Francis Xavier Roman Catholic Church. "Register of Baptisms, Marriages and Deaths—St. Francis Xavier Church—Manitoba, Canada—1834–1851. St. Francis, Manitoba."
St. Leo's Roman Catholic Church. "St. Leo's Parish Baptisms." Lewistown, Mont.
———. "St. Leo's Parish Marriages." Lewiston, Mont.
St. Louis Genealogical Society. "Catholic Marriages, St. Louis, Missouri, 1774–1840." St. Louis, Mo., n.d.
St. Peter's Mission. "Baptismal Register." Great Falls Diocese Archives, Catholic Pastoral Center, Great Falls, Mont.
———. "Marriage Register." Great Falls Diocese Archives, Catholic Pastoral Center, Great Falls, Mont.
———. Papers. UCA.
Stocking, Winfield Scott. "Ft. Benton Memories." Winfield Scott Stocking Papers. SC 797. MHSA.
Stuart, Granville. Letters. James Fergus Papers. Col. 28. MHSA.
———. Papers. University of Montana microfilms. Western American Collection, Missoula, Mont. (originals held at Yale University Library).
Swan, Elizabeth Berger. "A Brief History of the First Catholic Pioneers of Lewistown, Montana." File 541. MBSC. Also held by LPL and in the Joseph Kinsey Howard Papers. Col. 27, MHSA.
Tabor, Isabell Lewis. "Great Falls Yesterday." WPA, 1939. Copy held by Diocese of Great Falls Archives, Great Falls, Mont.
———. "History of St. Peter's Mission." In "Great Falls Yesterday." WPA, 1939. A copy held by Diocese of Great Falls Archives, Great Falls, Mont.
"Tentative Roll of Rocky Boy Indians, May 30, 1917." SC 903, 1/1, MHSA.
"Ursuline Annals." SPMP. UCA.
Van Den Broeck, Victor. "Sketch of Ben Kline's Life, Gathered by Father Van Den Broeck During Many Private Conversations with His Friend Ben." Ben Kline Reminiscences. SC 942. MHSA.
"Voter Registration Index, 1928–1932," Fergus Co., Mont. Prepared by Lewiston, Mont. Genealogical Society.
Wells Family Papers. In possession of Gloria Wells-Norlin, Bozeman, Mont.
Wessel, Thomas R. "A History of the Rocky Boy's Indian Reservation." N.d. Montana State University Library, Bozeman, Mont.

Worthen, C. B. "Central Montana History." MC 76, box 1, folder 17. MHSA.
———. "Fergus: A Miniature of the West." Paper presented at the Montana State Librarian's Annual Convention, Lewistown, Mont., October 10, 1927. C. B. Worthen Papers. Fergus County Collection. SC 978.6292. LPL.
———. "Judith Basin." Worthen Collection. MC 75, box 2, folder 3. MHSA.
Zellick, Anna. "A History of Fergus County." Master's thesis, University of Chicago, 1945.
———. "History of Lewistown School District No. One, 1882–1982." Lewistown Heritage Committee, 1984. A copy is held by the Lewistown Genealogical Society.
Zwolle, Lily B., and Mary Ann Quiring, comps. "LaTray Family Genealogy." Lewistown, Mont., 1985.

INTERVIEWS

Abbott, Mary Stuart. Interview by Oscar Mueller. N.d., manuscript file 298, box 2, MBSC.
Chandler, Helen. Interview by Anna Zellick. Lewistown, Mont., August 7, 1978. Copy held by Lewistown City Library, Lewistown, Mont.
Doney, Ken. Interview by author. Lewistown, Mont., July 24, 1996.
Eastman, Sue. Interviews by author. Lewistown, Mont., July 1996.
Ehlert, Marie. Interviews by author. Lewistown, Mont., July 1996.
Johnson, Mary La Mere. Interview. In "An Oral History of the Chief Little Shell Tribe of Chippewas of Montana," edited by C. Patrick Morris and Robert Van Gunten.
Kline, Ben. "Ben Kline." Interview by Oscar Mueller. December 2, 1931. Ben Kline Reminiscences. SC 942. MHSA.
LaFountain, Robert. Interviews by author. Billings, Mont., October 1995; July 1996.
LaFountain, Treena. Interviews by author. September 1995; July 1996.
LaPier, Art. Interview by Patrick Morris. In "An Oral History of the Chief Little Shell Tribe of Chippewas of Montana," edited by C. Patrick Morris and Robert Van Gunten.
LaRocque, Sarah. Interview by Nicholas Vrooman. Roy, Mont. In "When They Awake: Metis Culture in Contemporary Context." Video. Great Falls, Mont.: Institute for Metis Studies, University of Great Falls, 1995.
LaTray, Joe. Interviews by Vernon Anderson. 1975. In Vernon Anderson, "The LaTray Family."
Monkelin, Daisy Tuss. Interview by Anna Zellick. Lewistown, Mont., November 13, 1969. Copy (SC 495) held by MHSA.
Paul, Howard. Interview by Nicolas Vrooman. Great Falls, Mont. In "When They Awake: Metis Culture in Contemporary Context." Video. Institute for Metis Studies, University of Gt. Falls, Gt. Falls, Montana, 1995.

Schuflet, Lula. Interview. 1980. In *The First Hundred Years: A History of Lewistown Montana*, edited by Roberta Donovan. Lewistown, Mont.: Central Montana Publishing, 1994.

Shambow, Louis. Interview by A. J. Noyes. December 17, 1916. Louis Shambow (Chambeau) Reminiscence. SC729, 1/1. MHSA.

Shoup, Frances Morgan. Interview by author. Lewistown, Mont., July 15–16, 1996.

Sinclair, John. Interview by Patrick Morris. In "An Oral History of the Chief Little Shell Tribe of Chippewas of Montana," edited by C. Patrick Morris and Robert Van Gunten.

Swan, Elizabeth Berger. Interview by Oscar Mueller. Lewistown, Mont., n.d. Fergus County Collection. Oscar Mueller Correspondence. SC978.6292. LPL.

Walraven, Donna LaFountain. Interview by author. Great Falls, Mont., July 30, 1996.

Wells-Norlin, Gloria. Interview by author. Bozeman, Mont., July 13, 1997.

Zellick, Anna. Interview by author. Lewistown, Mont., July 18, 1996.

Zilba, Stella Helen. Conversation with author. Lewistown, Mont., August 24, 1997.

GOVERNMENT DOCUMENTS

Canadian Government Documents

"Canadian Scrip Applications, 1900–1901." RG15, NAC.

Half-Breed Script Applications, 1886–1901, 1906. Vol. 1333–1371, MF no. c-14944–c-15010, RG15–21, NAC.

Index: Half-Breed Script Applications, 1886–1901, 1906. MF no. c-14943, RG15–21, NAC.

U.S. Bureau of the Census

1830 Michigan Census, Michilimackinac and Chippewa Counties.
1840 Wisconsin Territorial Census.
1850 Minnesota Territorial Census, Pembina District.
1850 Wisconsin Territorial Census, Milwaukee, Brown, and Dodge Counties.
1860 Minnesota Territorial Census, Pembina District.
1870 Montana Territorial Census.
1880 Montana Territorial Census.
1900 Montana Census.

Local, State, and Federal U.S. Government Documents

"Annual Report of the Commissioner of Indian Affairs, 1854." (ARCIA) Washington, D.C.: A. O. P. Nicholson, 1855.

Belcourt, George Antoine. "The Mixed Blood or Half-Breeds." In "Turtle Mountain Band of Chippewa Indians." 56th Cong., 1st sess, S. Doc. 444, Serial 3878.

Black, Lieut. Col. H. M. Letters. 1879, 1880, M234, roll 518. NARG 75.

BIBLIOGRAPHY

Bottineau, John B. "List de familles Métis Americaine de Pembina." Records of the Bureau of Indian Affairs (BIA), Irregular Shaped Papers no. 114. NARG 75.

"Census of Rocky Boy's Band of Chippewa Indians of Montana By T. W. Wheat, Clerk, Allotting Service, 8–14 April 1909." SC903, 1/1 MHSA. Original held by Office of Indian Affairs, April 27, 1909, File 31599.

"The Chief, Little Shell, Here Speaks." Belcourt, N.Dak., January 26, 1898. 55th Cong., 2nd sess., S. Doc. 154, p. 26, Serial 3600.

"Chippewa Half-Breeds of Lake Superior." U.S. Congress. House. 42nd Cong., 2nd sess., Ex. Doc. 193, Serial 1513.

"Commissioner's Report of the Agreement with the Turtle Mountain Indians." 56th Cong., 1st sess., S. Doc. 444, Serial 3878.

"Commissioner's Reports for 1906." Serial 5118.

"Commissioner's Reports for 1907." Serial 5296.

Crawford, T. M. ARCIA. Washington, D.C.: GPO, 1844.

"Executive Order for a Reservation Embracing the Turtle Mountain." 56th Cong., 1st sess., S. Doc. 444, Serial 3878.

"Forget, A. E. Commissioner of Indian Affairs (CIA), Regina, Northwest Territories, to Governor of the State of Montana (J. E. Rickards), Helena, April 1, 1896." In *Senate Report, 1895–1896*. Vol. 4. 54th Cong., 1st sess.

Homestead Entry Applications. Montana Tract Book, roll 36. BLM, District Office, Billings, Mont.

"Letter from the Secretary of the Interior Relative to Agreement between the Turtle Mountain Indians in North Dakota and the Commission Appointed under the Act of July 13, 1892." 54th Cong., 1st sess., S. Doc. 23, Serial 3347.

McDowell, Malcolm. "Report on the Rocky Boy's Band, Montana." Annual Report Board of Indian Commissioners, 1918.

"Minutes of the Grand Council Proceedings of January 29, 1892." 56th Cong., 1st sess., S. Doc. 444, Serial 3878.

"Naturalization Record Index, 1887–1910." Office of the Clerk of Court, Fergus County, Mont.

"Poll Books." Meagher and Fergus County, 1884–1888. MF 311. MHSA.

"Poll Lists." (For the election of October 24, 1864, to establish Montana as a territory). Records of the Montana secretary of state. Record Series 250, 6/18–25. MHSA.

"Preamble and Resolutions." January 7, 1891, 56th Cong., 1st sess., S. Doc. 444, Serial 3878.

Ramsey, Alexander. St. Paul, Minn., October 1863, "Northern Superintendency." No. 6. ARCIA, 1863. Washington, D.C.: GPO, 1864.

———, and A. C. Morrill. "Journal of the Proceedings Connected with the Negotiations of the Treaty with the Red Lake and Pembina Bands of

Chippewa—Conducted at the Old Crossing of Red Lake River on the Second of Oct. 1863." Treaty File, Records of the BIA, 1863.

Register of Criminal Actions. Book 1. Fergus County, Office of Fergus County Clerk of Court, Lewistown, Mont.

"Relief for the Cree Indians, Montana Territory." 50th Cong., 1st sess., 1888, Ex. Doc. 341, Serial 2561.

"Report Amending Senate Bill 196 to Ratify Agreement with Turtle Mountain Indians of North Dakota, January 25, 1904." 58th Cong., 1st sess., S. Rep. 471, Serial 4571.

"Report of the Commissioner of Indian Affairs for 1892." Washington, D.C.: GPO.

"Report of the Turtle Mountain Indian Commission, 1893." U.S. Congress. House. 52nd Cong., 2nd sess., Ex. Doc. 229, Serial 3105.

"Reservation of the Turtle Mountain Band of Chippewa Indians." H. Rep. 632. Reprint, 56th Cong., 1st sess., S. Doc. 444, Serial 3878.

S. Rep. 693, 56th Cong., 1st sess., S. Doc. 444, Serial 3878.

Secretary of the Interior to Indian Inspector Frank C. Churchill, December 1908. File 900-08-307.4. NARG 75.

Sherman, Gen. William T. "Endorsements." January 3, 1880, M234, roll 518. NARG 75.

Stevens, Isaac. "Reports of Exploration and Surveys to Ascertain the Most Practicable and Economical Route for a Railroad from the Mississippi to the Pacific Ocean." 36th Cong. 1st sess. H. Doc. 56, Washington, D.C.: GPO, 1855–1860.

———. "Report of Explorations for a Route for the Pacific Railroad, I. I. Stevens, Governor of Washington Territory, 1853." 33rd Cong., 2nd sess., S. Ex. Doc. 78, Serial 758.

Straham, Robert E. "The Resources of Montana Territory." Published at the direction of the Montana Legislature, 1979.

"Ten Cent Treaty." ARCIA, 1903, Serial 4645.

"Treaty with the Chippewa Indians of Lake Superior and the Mississippi, September 30, 1854." In "Chippewa Half-Breeds of Lake Superior." 42nd Cong., 2nd sess., Ex. Doc. 193, Serial 1513.

"Treaty with the Chippewa of Red Lake and Pembina Bands, 1863," 57th Cong., 1st sess., S. Doc. 452. In *Indian Affairs: Laws and Treaties,* Vol. 2, compiled by Charles J. Kappler. Washington, D.C.: GPO, 1903.

"Turtle Mountain Allotment and Census Records, Probated Allotted Lands." M6MC-77-2, roll 193. NARG 75. (LDS Family History Center no. 1028538).

"Turtle Mountain Band of Chippewa Indians," 56th Cong., 1st sess., S. Doc. 444, Serial 3878.

"Turtle Mountain Band of Pembina Chippewa Indians." February 23, 1898, 55th Cong., 2nd sess., S. Doc. 154, Serial 3600.

"Turtle Mountain Chippewa Indian Census, 1892." Little Shell Tribal Office, Great Falls, Mont.

"Turtle Mountain Indians." U.S. Congress. House. 52nd Cong., 2nd sess., Ex. Doc 229, Serial 3105.

U.S. Department of War. "Report of Captain Jonathan Pope to the Secretary of War." 31st Cong., 1st sess., Ex. Doc. 10, S. Doc. 42, Serial 577.

The War of the Rebellion: Official Records of the Union and Confederate Armies. Washington, D.C.: GPO, 1896.

Waugh, John H. "Letters Turtle Mountain Reservation Agency." 56th Cong., 1st sess., S. Doc. 444, Serial 3878.

Way shaw wush koquen abe. "Speech." St. Joseph, Sept 14, 1852. ARCIA. Washington, D.C.: GPO, 1854.

"Wheat, Thralls W. Clerk, Allotting Service, to Commissioner of Indian Affairs, 20 April 1909, Blackfeet Indian Reservation, Browning, Montana." SC903 U.S. Interior Dept., Office of Indian Affairs, Records Folder 1/1, MHSA. Original held by Rocky Boy's Agency, Rocky Boy, Mont.

Wood, Samuel. "Report of Major Wood Relative to His Expedition to Pembina Settlement . . ." 31st Cong., 1st sess., 1850, H. Ex. Doc. 51, Serial 577.

NEWSPAPERS

(all Montana unless noted)
The Benton Record
The Benton Weekly Record
Fergus County Argus
The (Fort Benton) River Press
Great Falls Daily Leader
Great Falls Daily Tribune
Great Falls Tribune
The Havre Plaindealer
The (Helena) Daily Independent
The (Helena) Montana Daily Record
The (Helena) Weekly Herald
The Lewistown News Argus
The (Maiden) Mineral Argus
Pembina (N.Dak.) Pioneer
(St. Paul) Minnesota Pioneer

WEBSITES

Programme De Récherche en Démographie Historique (PRDH).
    http://www.genealogy.umontreal.ca. l'Université de Montréal, Québec.
St. Louis Genealogical Society. Earl Fischer Database of St. Louisans.
    http://www.stlgs.org/efdb/indes.shtml.

Index

All references to illustrations are in italic type.

Abbott, Mary Stuart, 155, 156
Abbott, Teddy Blue, 155, 156, 160, 204
Aboriginals, rights of, 46, 58, 90, 96, 169, 177
Adam, Baptiste, 111, 125
African American soldiers, 176
African Americans, 17
Agricultural disasters, 54
Agricultural potential, of Great Western Plains, 180–81
Agricultural settlement, 29, 30–31, 101. *See also* Scottish agricultural community
AICRJ. *See American Indian Culture and Research Journal* (AICRJ)
Alberta, 22, 23, 57, 74
Alderson, Nannie, 154
Alderson, William W., 76
Allery family, 217
Allotting Service, 214
American Fur Company, 35
American Half Breeds, 92, 123
American Indian Culture and Research Journal (AICRJ), 12
American Indian history, 11
The American Fur Trade of the Far West (Chittenden), 11
Ammunition, sale of, 66–67, 76, 86

Anderson, Conrad, 192–93
Anderson, Reese, 156
Anepeminn (high-bush cranberry), 26
Anti-British, 122–24
Ascription, 5, 7, 40–50, 223
Assiniboine River area, 22, 29
Assiniboines, 26, 27, 35, 43, 47, 79, 94, 117, 133, 176
Atwater, Caleb, 34
Augusta, 212
Ayers, Roy, 211
Azure, Amable, 41
Azure, Charlotte Pelletier, 41, 42
Azure, Gabriel, 64
Azure, Pierre, 41

Baker, Fred A., 216
Baker, I. G., 133
Baker massacre of 1870, 129
Bankruptcy, and cattle ranching, 161–62, 195, 259n16
Barnett, G. P., 137
Barth, Fredrik, 8, 10, 223
Battle of the Little Bighorn, 77
The Battle of Seven Oaks, 30
Beading/embroidery, 139, *141–42*
Bear Creek, 103
Bear Paw Mountains, 217

Beauchamp family, 97
Beaver: depletion of, 15, 27, 39; economy based on, 16, 24, 26; steel traps, 24
Beede, Cyrus, 169
Belcourt, G. A., 40–41
Belcourt family, 217
Benton Weekly Record, 123–24
Berger, Adele, 69, 72
Berger, Anabel, 72, 81
Berger, Clemence Gourneau, 62–65
Berger, Isaie, 62, 114
Berger, Jacque, 36, 72
Berger, John B., 144
Berger, Judith Wilkie, 37, 41, 42, 45, 72, 164, 165; in Spring Creek, 79, *80*, 82, 103
Berger, Pierre: as early Métis leader, 25, 36, 37, 41, 45; in Lewistown, 137, 144, 145; and Spring Creek band, 79, *80*, 81, 95, 103, 114
Berger family, 103, 104, 108, 111, 143, 172, 205–207, 210, 212
Biedler, X., 65, 67, 120
Bighorn River, Mont., 25
Billings, Mont., 137
Biracial identities, 6, 17, 30, 32
Black, H. M., 91–93
Black Butte, 80, 103, 114
"Black Robe of the North," 117
Blackfeet, 35–36, 76, 95, 100, 114, 117, 128, 151
Blackfeet Reservation, 213, 215
Blind Breed Gulch, 103
"Blood quantum," 211–12
Bloods, 76, 79, 100, 117
Bones, processing of, 139
Botkin, Alexander, 121–22
Bowles, John J. ("Jim"), 101
Boyd Creek, 183
Boyd Creek School, 146
Boyer, Frank, 111
Boyer family, 19
Brassey, Edward, 116
Breed Creek, 103, 183
"Breed School," 146

"Breeds," 125, 130, 135, 207, 219; definition of, 89, 153, 156; "French breeds," 216, 219; "Mixed breed," 34; white prejudice toward, 3–4. *See also* "Half-breeds"
British conquest, of Canada, 20
British North American Expedition to the Canadian plains (1857), 181
British policies, 49
British trade organizations, 18–19
Broadwater, Charles A., 66, 121
Brooks, Henry, 129, 158
Brown, Jennifer S. H., 12
Buffalo, 5, 24; and Chippewas, 27–28, 38–39; disappearance of, 54–56, 91, 94, 120, 127–29, 131–35, 136–37, 239n9; diseases of, 55–56; economy based on, 16, 26–27, 35, 38–39, 74, 101, 132; and environmental changes, 51, 54–56, 60, 74, 88; and Hudson's Bay Company, 52–54; hunting of, 22, 32, 61, 80–81, 111; and Milk River Métis, 60–72, 94; and Pembina, 31, 33, 36, 52; and trade, 34–40, 51–54, 60, 100, 111. *See also* Pemmican
Buffalo hunts, 36–40; importance of, 52–54; Red River carts used in, 36–38, 52, *138*, 236n52
Buffalo robes; carts used for, 36–38, 52, *138*, 236n52; and the economy, 35, 38–39, 74; trade in, 51–56, 60, 100, 111; transportation of, 36, 53–54
Bunte, Pamela, 12
Bureau Of Immigration and Naturalization, 218–19
Bureau of Indian Affairs, 177, 211
Burt, Larry, 12
Bushie family, 217
Butte, Mont., 122

C. A. Broadwater & Co., 120, 122
Callihoo, Victoria, 55
Canada: British conquest of, 20; fur country of, 18; Métis in, 4, 11–12, 15, 16, 77–78, 89; mixed-descent people of, 3, 20; Native people in, 11–12

INDEX

Canadian. *See* Euro-Canadians; French Canadian; U.S.–Canadian relations
"Canadian beggars," 175
Canadian border. *See* U.S.–Canadian boundary
"Canadian Crees," 5, 98, 105, 132, 174, 176, 178, 208, 213, 218, 220–21
Canadian Half-Breeds, 91, 216, 219
Canadian Indians, 92, 105, 176
Canadian Métis, 4, 11–12, 15, 16, 89, 94, 125, 169; expulsion of, 77–78
Canadian Mounted Police, 163
Capalette family, 217
Carroll, Mont., 99–102, 117, 119, 123, 246n22
Carroll Trail, 101–102
Catholic church/clergy, 7, 28, 31, 64, 74, 82, 122, 206; in Lewistown, 135, 136, 144, 147; in Spring Creek, 204
Catholic Colonization Bureau, 93
Catholic French-Canadians, 11
Catholicism, of Métis, 64
Cattle ranching: and bankruptcy, 161–62, 195, 259n16; in Judith Basin, 158, 255n50; Métis and cowboys, 157–62, 255n48; Montana businessmen and, 127–31, 158–62; rustlers, 158–59; Spring Creek band and, 114; Stuart and, 158–59, 254n42, 255n43; vigilantes, 158–59; and weather, 161–62
Cattlemen, Euro-American, 90
Census: of 1850 Minnesota Territory, 41, 69, 237n66; of 1870, 180; of 1880, 105–14; of 1900 Montana, 183, *186–91*, 201–208; enumerators of, 201–202; gender, 202; Pembina, 97; race/color in, 113–14, 201
Central-Montana Métis, 134
Chaboillez, Charles Jean Baptiste, 26
Champagne family, 209
Chandler, Helen, 204
Charboneau, Peter, 82
Charboneau, Pierre, 113
Charboneau, Rose, 113
Charboneau (Charbonneau) family, 19, 25, 28

Charbonneau, Toussaint, 25
Charette, John, 82, 143
Charette family, 19
Charles II (king), 20
Cheyennes, 145
Chicago, 19
Chinook, 212
"Chipaways," 26
Chippewa-Métis bonds, 27, 40, 47
"Chippewa rose," 33
Chippewa Treaty of 1854, 44–47, 59, 71, 82, 95
Chippewa Treaty of 1863-1864, 69, 82, 95
"ChippewaCrees" (Chippewa-Crees), 14, 214, 218
Chippewas, 13–14, 22, 29, 35, 176; buffalo hunting of, 27–28, 38–39; hunger of, 213–15; Lake Superior Chippewas, 44, 95; Little Shell Chippewas, 12, 13, 201, 211; and Métis, 24–28, 32, 47, 208, 234nn23–24; Mississippi Chippewas, 44; Pillager Chippewas, 43; Plains Chippewa, 38; Red Bear Chippewas, 211; Red Lake Chippewas, 43, 45; and Red River Settlement, 43. *See also* Pembina band of Chippewa; Rocky Boy Chippewa Crees; Turtle Mountain Chippewas
Chittenden, Hiram, 11
Chouart, Médard, 20
Chouteau County, Mont., 100, 113, 121, 124
Churchill, Frank C., 216
Citizenship: denial of, 218–20, 262n59; and the Milk River Métis, 72–73, 92
Civil rights, of Métis, 78, 88
Clapp, D. E., 76
Clark, W. P., 86
Clothing, of Métis, 204–205
Coburn, Walt, 204
Commissioner of Indian Affairs Office, 175
Community schools, 7

Constitution Act (1982), 12
Contres-maitres (foremen), 28
Cottonwood Creek, 80
Courchane family, 217
Coureurs de bois, 17–18, 232n3
"Coyote french," 125
Crees, 4, 13–14, 117, 130; "Canadian Crees," 5, 98, 105, 132, 174, 176, 178, 208, 213, 218, 220–21; child-rearing and custody practices of, 20; "ChippewaCrees" (Chippewa-Crees), 14, 214, 218; and Euro-American community, 174–78; hunger of, 213–15; as landless Indians, 174–78; Little Bear Crees, 213, 216–17; in Montana, 12, 76, 79, 151; and the Montana Métis, 162–67, 208; Plains Crees, 54; on Red River, 22, 27, 29, 32, 43; as refugees, 165–67, 256n62; trade of, 20, 23–26, 35, 95, 100. *See also* Rocky Boy Chippewa Crees
"Creole," 25
Crowley, D. M., 174
Crows, 35, 79, 98
Custer, George A., 77
Cypress Hills, 60, 62

D-S Ranch, 160
Daigneau (Dagneau). *See* Daniels (Daignon) family; individual Daniels entries
Daigneault family, 143
Daignon. *See* Daniels (Daignon) family; individual Daniels entries
Dakotas, 3, 20, 23, 74, 94
Dakota Territory, 41, 78, 168
Damiani, Joseph, 117–18
Dances, of Métis, 3
Daniels (Daignon), Frank, 69, 82, 111, 174
Daniels (Daignon) family, 108, 206
Davis, A. J., 128, 129
Davis family, 185, 210
Dawson, George, 60
Dawson County, 121
Dechamp family, 217

Delassus, Don Charles Dehault, 25
Delorme, Urbain, 19, 124
Demers, Frank, 125
Democrats, 121–23, 125–26
Demontyne family, 217
Denig, Edward, 54
Denny family, 216
Denton, Mont., 180
Deportation, of Métis, 92
Desert Land Act (1877), 181
Des Groseilliers, Sieur, 20
de Smet, Pierre, 43
Desy, Evelyn Janeaux, 206
Desy, Irene, 144, 201, 203, 206
Detroit, 19
de Varennes, Pierre Gaultier, 23
Dimon, C., 66
Discrimination: against Indians, 3–4, 6; against Métis, 5, 6, 9, 30, 136, 155
dit Beauchemin, Andre Millet, 42
dit Bellehumeur, Jean Baptiste Monet, 118
dit Bellehumeur, Marguerite Monet, 118
dit Bellehumeur, Michel Monet, 119
Doane, Gustavus C., 131, 154
Doane, Mary Hunter, 154, 157
Dodson, Mont., 62
Doney, Gregory and Lalley, 193, 204
Doney, Joseph, 79, 82, 103, 139, 204
Doney, Ken, 193, 259n17
Doney, Philomene LaFountain, 103
Doney family, 19, 109, 111, 143, 161, 172, 185, 203, 206, 210, 213
Douglas, Thomas (Earl of Selkirk), 29
Downing, Laura, 148
Drought, 192, 210
Ducharme family, 218
Dumont, Edouard and Jean, 165
Dumont, Gabriel, 164, 165
Dumont, Madeleine Wilkie, 165
Dumoulin, Sévere, 28
Dusenberry, Verne, 12

Earl of Selkirk (Thomas Douglas), 29
Eastman, Sue, 204

INDEX

Economy: and beaver, 16, 24, 26; and buffalo, 16, 26–27, 35, 38–39, 74, 101, 132; and buffalo robes, 35, 38–39, 74; changes in, 51, 74, 132, 175; and Métis' identity, 5, 7, 9, 13, 18, 50, 74, 88, 131–35; of Rupert's Land, 19–23
Edmonton, Alberta, 56
Educational policy, of Lewistown, 146–52
Ehlert, Marie, 202, 207
1820s, 16
1830s, 19, 32–40
1840s, 32–40, 71
1850s, 40–50, 55
1860s, 40–50, 53–56, 59–72, 88–89
1870s, 59–72, 73–78, 88–89
1880s, 90, 101–14, 137, 143, 146, 158–71
1890s, 143–47, 170–78, 261n44
Engagés, 18, 24
"English halfbreeds," 30, 32
Enlarged Homestead Act, 181
Enrollment policy, 3, 6, 210–12, 216–21
Ens, Gerhard, 32
Environmental changes, 51, 54–56, 60, 74, 88
Ethnicity: family v. community, 10; and Métis' identity, 3–10, 208–21, 222–25; and self-identification, 8; and social assignment, 8; volitional aspect of, 8
Ethnogenesis, 14
Euro-American cattlemen, 90
Euro-American males, fur trade and, 11
Euro-Americans, 4–5; and Crees, 174–78; in Lewistown, 136, 143, 145; lifestyle of, 202; and Métis, 17, 64–72, 73–78, 88, 135, 152–55, 208, 213; and métis, 19; prejudice of, 6, 34, 40, 56–57, 125; and Spring Creek band, 101–102; whiteness, 156–57
Euro-Canadians, 22, 34, 57
Ewers, John C., 89, 100–101, 132, 216, 246n25
Executive orders of 1882 and 1884, 167, 169, 171
Expulsion, 77–78, 86–89, 90

Fagnant, Antoine, 42
Fagnant, Jean, 119
Fagnant, Joseph, 42
Fagnant, Josephte, 42
Fagnant, Marguerite, 42
Fagnant families, 79
Falcon, Peter, 159
Farmers/farming, 31, 32, 74, 105, 111–13, 180
Favel family, 217
Fayant, Alex, 109
Fayant, Mary, 109
Fayant family, 109–10, 210
Feast of the Ascension (1895), 152
Fenian revolutionaries, 93
Fergus, James, 130, 158, 174, 251n79
Fergus County, Mont., 137, 143, 183, 185, 201, 209
Fergus County Register of Criminal Actions, 159
Fiddling, of Métis, 3
First communion, 152
First Peoples. *See* Indians
Fisher, Madeline, 119
Flanagan, Thomas, 97
Flathead Reservation, 213, 215
Flat Willow, 185
Flat Willow Creek, 80, 100
Fleury, Antoine, 28, 72
Fleury, Antoine, Jr., 118
Fleury, Betsy Wilkie, 79
Fleury, Mary Ernestine Wells, 118, 139–43, 185, 192, 203–204
Fleury, Patrice, 165
Fleury family, 19, 143, 206
Foods, of Métis, 203, 259n21
Ford, Louise and Millie, 150
Ford, Sam and Clementia Lapierre, 150–51
Ford Creek, 114, 129
Forget, A. E., 175
Fort Assiniboine, 91, 154, 164, 217
Fort Belknap Reservation, 193, 204, 215
Fort Benton, 53, 64, 66, 74, 100, 101–102, 113, 117, 124, 137
Fort Ellice, Manitoba, 59, 118

Fort Ellis, 76, 154
Fort Janeaux, 67
Fort Laramie Treaty negotiations, in 1851, 43
Fort Maginnis, 99, 102, 129, 137, 139, 157
Fort Peck, 76, 171
Fort Peck Reservation, 215
Fort Rouge, 29
Fort Shaw, 165
Fort Union, 35–36, 52, 54, 238n3
Francis, James, 65
Franklin, Robert, 12
Freemen, 21–22, 28, 29, 39
Free trade movement, 39
Freetraders, 26
"French breeds," 216, 219
French Canadian, 4, 33, 144, 201, 207
"French frontiersmen," 11
Frenchman Creek, 67, 86
French Montreal companies, 20
Frog Lake murders, 164, 175, 176
Front Range, of Rocky Mountains, 4–5, 165, 213
"Full-bloods," 46, 153, 169
Fur trade: in Canada, 18; changes in, 17; end of, 135; Euro-American males in, 11; families, 205–206; importance of, 17; Métis ancestors in, 9, 11, 32; of Missouri River, 23–24, 35; in Montreal, 17, 20, 23; movement of, 19; and Pembina, 27; of Red River, 23–26; regions of, 17, 20, 28; reorganization of, 30–32; and Rupert's Land, 20; studies of, 11; U.S., 16
Fur traders: "free" or "illegal," 18; independence of, 17

Garcia, Andrew, 79, 117, 153–55
Gardepee (Gardepi, Gardipee, Guardipee). *See* Gardipee families; individual entries for Gardepi, Gardipee, and Guardipee
Gardepi, Joseph, 64
Gardepi, Marie Selma, 64

Gardipee, Baptiste, 62
Gardipee, Mary Larocque, 103
Gardipee families, 185, 216, 218
Gayion family, 79, 243n63
Gens libres (freemen), 21
German Silver Cross, 64
Gervais family, 19
Gibbon, John, 76
Giltedge, Mont., 184, 185, 202
Giraud, Marcel, 22, 34, 75
Gladu, Frank, 125
Gladue, Antoine, 65
Glenbow Foundation, in Calgary, Alberta, 12
Godparenting, 205–206
Gourneau, Joseph and Judith McMillan, 62
Grand Council of 1892, 208
Grand Rapids, 19
Grant, Cuthbert, 31–32, 235n42
Grant, Marguerite, 119
Grant, Peter, 26
Grantown, 32
"Great American Desert," 180–81
Great Falls, 215
Great Lakes Métis, 23, 82
Great Lakes region, 11, 15, 17, 18, 232n13; family names of, 19, 82; independent traders and freemen in, 22
Green Bay, 19
Gros Ventres, 79, 94, 117, 133, 176
Guardipee. *See* individual entries for Gardepee, Gardepi, Gardipee, and Guardipee
Guardipee (Gardipee), Eli, 62, 65, 113, 159, 240n24

"Half Breed School," 146
"Half-breeds," 11, 13, 34, 132, 135, 204; American Half Breeds, 92, 123; Canadian Half-Breeds, 91, 216, 219; definition of, 156, 207; "English halfbreeds," 30, 32; as hunters, 57; in Milk River, 61, 66, 76–77; Pembina half-breeds, 71–72; and

politics, 122, 126, 167, 249n61; "Red River half-breeds," 86; treaties relating to, 43–45, 95. *See also* "Breeds"
Hamlin, Sevire, 114
Hamline family, 217
Harassment of Métis, 90–93, 159–60
Harrison, Benjamin, 172
Hatch, Edward A., 53
Hatch expedition, 53–54
Hauser, Samuel T., 127–30
Havre, 212, 217
Hayden, Ferdinand V., 55
Hayt (commissioner), 91
HBC. *See* Hudson's Bay Company (HBC)
Healey, J. J., 123, 125, 131
Helena, Mont., 101–102, 120, 122, 135, 215
Helena Daily Herald, 122
Helena Independent, 120, 121
Henderson family, 217
Henry, Alexander, 27
Hispanic, 6
History of the American West and Middle Ground; Indians, Empires, and Republics in the Great Lakes Region, 1670–1815 (White), 11
Hoffman, John, 175
Hogue, Michael, 12
Homeland, in Montana, 90, 95–99. *See also* Métis, homeland of
Homestead Act (1862), 96, 104–105, *106–12,* 143, 168, 181, 201
Homestead Applications, *194–200*
Homesteads: Judith Basin, 179–81; Spring Creek band, 102–105, 158, 183–201, 247n33, 247n35; Turtle Mountain Chippewas, 183. *See also* 1862 Homestead Act; Enlarged Homestead Act; Three-Year Homestead Act
Hommes libres (freemen), 21
Houle family, 28, 217
Howard, Joseph Kinsey, 36, 72–73, 117, 119, 249n55

Hudson Bay, 20
Hudson's Bay Company (HBC), 16, 19–21, 27, 43, 132; and buffalo trade, 52–54; "English halfbreeds" of, 30, 32; North West Company merging with, 30, 35, 42; policies of, 21, 29, 49, 52; retirees of, 22, 29; and Rupert's Land, 19–20; tensions with, 39; traders of, 23–26, 35
Hunting, of buffalo, 22, 27–28, 32, 38–39, 60–72, 80–81, 94, 111
Hunting rights, 29

I. G. Baker and Company, 164
"Illegal immigrants," 67
Imoda, Camillus, 64, 151
Independent traders, 21–22, 28, 29
Indian Affairs. *See* Office of Indian Affairs
Indian-European contact, 15
Indian Reorganization Act (1934), 211–12, 261n41
Indians: American history of, 11; Canadian Indians, 92, 105, 176; definitions of, 6, 12, 13, 17, 207; discrimination against, 3–4, 6; identity of, 20–21; Landless Indians, 105, 174–78, 211, 218, 247n38; legal position of, 11–12; merging with, 6; Métis and, 3, 9, 19, 40–41, 49, 232n10; as mixed-descent, 20; Plains Indians groups, 38; relatedness to, 7–8; U.S. government's negotiations with, 42–43, 45–46, 136, 167–74; U.S. policy towards, 17. *See also* Non-Indians; specific Indian tribes
Indians of the Northwest, The (Atwater), 34
Intermarriage, 6, 18, 28, 33–34, 134–35, 206–207, 260n29
International boundary line, 16, 31
International law, 17
Inuits, 11–12
Ireland, John, 93
Irish, 122–23
Iroquois, 47

Jackson, George, 116
Jackson, Mercy, 116
Jackson family, 217
Janeaux, Antoine A., 113
Janeaux, Evelyn, 201
Janeaux, Francis Avila: death of, 143, 178; in Milk River, 62, 64–65, 67–71, 81, 242n45; religious participation of, 144; in Spring Creek, 102–103, 113, 114, 116, 118, 123, 133, 134
Janeaux, Virginia Laverdure, 42, 64, 69, 81–82
Janeaux family, 19, 143, 205, 212
Jannot, Philomene, 81
"Jawbone Railroad," 179
Johnson, Mary LaMare (La Mere), 203, 210
Judith Basin, 5, 62, 69, 71, 231n5; homesteading, 179–81; Métis hunters in, 99–101; railroads arriving in, 179–81, 192
Judith Gap, 80
Judith Mountains, 102
Judith River, 80
Juneau family name, 143

Keating, William H., 34
Keller, A. R., 98–99
Kelogg (major), 131
Kinship: godparenting, 205–206; Métis, identity of based on, 5, 7, 9, 18, 39, 49–50, 69, 82, 97, 119, 134, 185, 220–22; Milk River-Spring Creek system of, 193–94, 201, 212–13; sponsors, 206
Kipp, Joseph, 129
Kittson, Norman, 36, 39, 52, 237n63
Kline, Ben, 42, 61, 65, 67, 79–80, 87, 116, *184*, 207, 241n41
Kline family, 143, 151, 172, 210, 212
Klyne, Michel and Madeleine, 42
Koury, Michael, 77

Lac la Biche, 56
La Salle, Sieur de, 24
La Vérendrye, Sieur de, 23, 24
Ladue family, 217, 218
Lafontain (Lafontaine, Lafountain). *See* LaFountain families; individual LaFountain entries
LaFountain, Albert, 193
LaFountain, Antoine, 81, 111
LaFountain, Bernard, 72, 173
LaFountain, Calixte, 72, 81, 82, 209
LaFountain, Charlotte Adam, 42, 72, 81, 82, 119, 209
LaFountain, Elzear (Ezear), 173, 209
LaFountain, Joe, 161, 193
LaFountain, John B., 103
LaFountain, Julienne Wilkie, 173
LaFountain, Mary Rose Turcotte, 173, 209
LaFountain, Octave, 72, 172, 173
LaFountain, Robert E. (mayor), 3, 192, 193, 231n1
LaFountain, Treena, 4, 192, 203, 207
LaFountain families, 19, 79, 109, 143, 185, 212, 258n12
La Fromboise (Laframboise) family, 19, 216
Lake of the Woods, 23
Lake Superior Chippewas, 44, 95
Lake Superior Métis, 46
Lakotas, 65–66, 78, 79, 86, 90–91
Landless Indians, 105, 174–78, 211, 218, 247n38
Landre, (father), 117
Landusky, 193
Lang, William, 11
Language: of Métis, 7, 192; of Missouri River, 25; problems with, 192–93, 204
LaPalme, Dr., 147
LaPier, Art, 203
Larance family, 217
LaRocque. *See* Larocque
Larocque, Isabelle, 159, 160, 161
Larocque, Joseph, 42, 82, 103
Larocque, Madeline Fagnant, 42, 103
LaRocque, Sarah, 185, 202
Larocque family, 19, 161, 185
Larpenteur, Charles, 52, 61
LaTray, Joe, 137

INDEX

LaTray (LaTreille, Latreille), Mose (Moise), 79, 137, 155, 172, 204
Latreille, Madame Félix, 94
Lavallie family name, 143
Lavatta, Tom, 62
Laverdure, Catherine (Katherine) Charette, 41–42, 69, 82, 172
Laverdure, Daniel, 118
Laverdure, Eliza, 42, 69
Laverdure, François, 69
Laverdure, Joseph, 118
Laverdure, Peter, 111
Laverdure, Pierre, 42, 64, 69, *70*, 82, 102, 172
Laverdure (Laverdu) family, 19, 108, 119, 143, 206, 210, 212
Layoffs, 30–31
Leclaire family, 97
Ledoux, Alexander, 159
Ledoux (LeDoux), John, 79, 82
LeDuc family, 19
Leeson, M. A., 89
Le Floch, 74–75
Leighton Bros., 67
Lenox, Mont., 214
L'éveillé family, 19
Lewis, Ed, 150
Lewis and Clark party, 24, 25, 26
Lewis family, 150–51
Lewistown, Mont., 3–5, 15, 80, 104, 133; Berger in, 137, 144, 145; Catholic church in, 135, 136, 144, 147; educational policy of, 146–52; Euro-Americans, 136, 143, 145; growth of, 136–37, 179–83; school system in, 146–52, 253n17
Lewistown-area Métis community, 3, 7, 13
Lewistown/Havre/Glasgow triangle, 4
Lewistown Métis, 4
Lewistown Métis Centennial Celebration, 3, 9, 192
Lewistown/Milk River triangle, 4, 217
Lewistown/Roy/Flat Willow, 193
Lice, Métis and, 154–55, 254n35
Lincoln, W. L., 94–95

Linderman, Frank, 215, 218
Liquor business, 66–67; problems with, 120–21, 123. *See also* Whiskey traffic
Lisa, Manuel, 25
Little Bear, 164, 176
Little Bear Crees, 213, 216–17
Little Belt Mountains, 102
Little Poplar, 164
Little Rocky Mountains, 160
Little Shell, 127, 167, 169–73, 179, 208
Little Shell Chippewas, 12, 13, 201, 211
Livestock industry, 137
Long, Stephen, 31
Lucky Man, 176

Mackinac, 18
Maginnis, Martin, 121, 123
Maiden, Mont., 136, 137
Malone, Michael P., 11
Mandan villages, 24, 25
Manitoba, 20, 22, 39, 74, 94, 163
Manitoba Resistance of 1869-1870, 73–75, 88, 93
Marble, Manton, 57–59
Marriages, of Métis, 18. *See also* Intermarriage
Maximilian, Alexander Philip, 180
McCumber, P. J., 171
McCumber Agreement (1892), 172, 179, 208–209
McCumber Commission, 170
McDonnell, Theresa, 144
McGillis, Isabelle, 42
McKay, William, 59
McKensie, Sam, 159
McKenzie, Kenneth, 35
Meagher County, 121
Medicine Lodge, 67, 76
Mendota, 52
"Mestizo America," 10, 225
métis, 11, 19, 95, 232n14; definition of, 14
Métis: ancestors of, 223; Berger as leader of, 25, 36, 37, 41, 45; in Canada, 4, 11–12, 15, 16, 77–78, 89;

Catholicism of, 64; celebrations of, 202–203; and Chippewas, 24–28, 32, 47, 208, 234nn23–24; civil rights of, 78, 88; clothing of, 204–205; cowboys and, 157–62, 255n48; dances of, 3; definition of, 14, 232n20; of European descent, 15; fiddling of, 3; foods, 203, 259n21; fur trade, 9, 11, 32; generosity of, 57–58; history of, 3, 5, 10–13; hunters, 99–101; hunting rights of, 29; of Indian descent, 15; Indians and, 9, 19, 40–41, 49, 232n10; language of, 7, 192; legal positions of, 11–12; lice and, 154–55, 254n35; marriages of, 18; of Missouri River, 23–28; nationalism of, 29–30; no land base of, 3, 231n2; as nomadic, 33–34, 57–59, 75; no official tribal recognition of, 3; poverty of, 10, 173, 213–14; powwow of, 3; prejudice toward, 10; Protestant persecution of, 73–74; racial stereotypes of, 3; as refugees, 164–67, 256n62; resettlement of, 88; in Rupert's Land, 49, 73–74; social acceptance of, 3; society, 18; study of, 10; survival of, 4, 5; trading rights of, 29; and Turtle Mountain Chippewas, 167–74, 208, 256n68; in the United States, 4, 13; whites and, 4, 9. *See also* specific Métis bands

Métis, homeland of, 90; family relationships, 96–99, 246n17; petition for, 95–99, 120; Riel involved with, 93–96, 98–100

Métis, identity of: ascription, 5, 7, 40–50, 223; authenticity, 6; boundaries, 8–10, 16, 39; class, 13; culture, 5, 7, 33; development of, 5, 7, 10, 12, 17–23; discrimination, 5, 6, 9, 30, 136, 155; during 1670-1800, 17–23; during 1900-1919, 201–21; economic factors, 5, 7, 9, 13, 18, 50, 74, 88, 131–35; ethnicity, 3–10, 208–21, 222–25; Euro-Americans, 17, 64–72, 73–78, 88, 135, 152–55, 208, 213; evolution, 7, 10; gender, 5, 13; government policy, 5, 9, 178; institutional pressures, 5; kinship, 5, 7, 9, 18, 39, 49–50, 69, 82, 97, 119, 134, 185, 220–22; maintenance of, 5, 10, 17; mixed descent, 5; as Native people, 17, 47; negotiations, 6–9; during Northwest Rebellion, 166; outside forces, 8–9; as public, 9; self-ascription, 5, 7, 223; threats to, 88–89; U.S. government, 40–50

Métis, on Milk River: buffalo hunting, 60–72, 94; citizenship, 72–73, 92; deportation of, 92; dress, 64; federal licenses, 66–68; government of, 64; harassment of, 90–93, 159–60; as "illegal immigrants," 67; Judith Basin, moving to, 78–86; life, 62–65; migration of, 73–74, 88; military concerns with, 65–66; Montana businessmen and, 66–69; Riel and, 93–96, 245nn8–9; starvation, 91; suspicions of, 75; weather conditions, 61; as wintering site, 59–72, 60–72, 240n21

Métis–Indian relations, 3;
Métis–Lakota trade, 66
"Métisse," 34
"Michif," 34, 68, 163, 177, 219, 223, 241n42
Michilimackinac, 19, 23, 24
Migration, of Métis, 73–74, 88
Mikinakwatshuanishinabe, 27
Miles, Nelson A., 78, 86–88, 90–91, 95, 98
Military concerns: with Métis, on Milk River, 65–66; with Red River Settlement, 31
Milk River drainage, 4, 20, 56
Milk River/Havre/Zortman area, 96
Mills, Earl, 8
Milwaukee, 19
Mining, 137
Minnesota, 20, 22, 23, 52
Minnesota Territory, 43

INDEX

Minnesota Territory Assembly, 57
Minnesota Territory census (1850), 41, 69, 237n66
Mississippi Chippewas, 44
Mississippi drainage, 18, 22
Mississippi Valley, 15, 52
Missouri drainage, 11
Missouri River, 11; buffalo robes, 52–53, 74; fur trade of, 23–24, 35; language of, 25; Métis of, 23–28
"Mitsif," 207
"Mixed-bloods," 11, 45–50
"Mixed breed," 34
Mixed-descent people, 9, 10, 14, 34, 239n13; of Americas, 6; of Canada, 3, 20; of Dakotas, 3; in Great Lakes area, 17, 19; as Indians, 20; of Montana, 3, 122, 153–54
Momy family, 216
"Mongrelization," 33
Montana, 3–5, 18, 23, 28, 57, 71, 74, 94, 220–21; Crees in, 12, 76, 79, 151; homeland in, 90, 95–99; mixed-descent people of, 3, 122, 153–54; 1900 census of, 183, *186–91*, 201–208; Saskatchewan border with, 73; starvation of tribes in, 132–33; trappers in, 11
Montana businessmen: cattle ranching and, 127–31, 158–62; Métis and, 66–69
Montana Department of Publicity for the Bureau of Agriculture, Labor, and Industry, 182
Montana (Malone, Roeder, and Lang), 11
Montana Métis, 4, 8, 9, 23, 42, 177, 210; as "Cree," 162–67, 208; study of, 10–13, 105. *See also* Spring Creek band
Montana State University, 12
Montana Territory, 67, 77
Montreal: fur trade in, 17, 20, 23; Rupert's Land, 19–20
Moran, John, 19, 204
Morase family, 143, 151, 205, 206, 212

Morase (Morris), Paul, 69, 81, 102–103, 113, 134, 146, 201
Morgan (commissioner), 171
Morgan, Frances Berger, 202, 207
Morgan, George, 202
Morris, Pat, 12
Morrisette family, 217
Mosney family, 216
Moss, William M., 148
Multiethnic descent, 6
Multilingual, 30
Murphy, Lucy Eldersveld, 82
Musselshell Valley, 79, 81, 87, 95, 113

Nagel, Joane, 8, 224
Nash, Gary, 10
Native American. *See* Indians
Native lands, acquisition of, 17
Native matrilineal groups, 17
Native people, 5, 78, 215; attitudes toward, 6; in Canada, 11–12; intermarriage of, 28; Métis' identity as, 17, 47; and North West Company, 21, 28, 30
Native rights, 47–49
Nault, Fred, 214
N-Bar ranch, 137
"New People," 30
New Peoples: Being and Becoming Métis in North America, The (Peterson and Brown), 12
Nez Perce, 63
1900-1919, 179–221
Nomadic, 33–34, 57–59, 75
Nomee family, 218
Non-European racial categories, 17
Non-Indians, 3, 11, 25
Non-Métis, 3, 4, 56, 74, 144
North Dakota, 22, 23, 26, 39
North West Company (NWC), 16, 27, 82; Hudson's Bay Company merging with, 30, 35, 42; and Native people, 21, 28, 30; retirees of, 22; voyageurs of, 21, 23–26, 28; XY company merging with, 27, 28
North West Mounted Police, 77

Northwest Rebellion (1885), 158, 162–67, 175, 213
Norwest family, 97
NWC. *See* North West Company (NWC)

O'Connell, Samuel, 64, 76
Office of Indian Affairs, 38, 66, 241n38
O'Hanlon, Thomas, 99
Ojibwas, 22, 25–26, 256n72
Ojibwas of Western Canada, The (Peers), 134
Old Crossing, 45
Old Northwest, 43
Olney, Richard, 175
Ontario, 23
"O-tee-paym-soo-wuk" (their-own-boss), 22
Ouellette, Antoine, 81, 102
Ouellette, Frank, 65, 72, 81
Ouellette, Philomena, 72, 81
Ouellette (Willett) family, 113, 151, 206, 210

Palladino, L. B., 148–49
Palliser, John, 181
Pambrun family, 150–51
Papin family, 216
Parent family, 19
Parenteau, Baptiste, 165
Parkman, Francis, 11
Paul, Henry, 211
Paul, Howard, 202
Paul family, 143, 210
Peebles, Elizabeth, 146
Peers, Laura, 134
Pelletier (Peletier) family, 19, 41, 79, 216
Pembina, 16; and buffalo, 31, 33, 36, 52; and fur trade, 27; growth of, 24–26, 28, 42; treaty at, 43–44; in U.S. territory, 31
Pembina band of Chippewa, 43, 45, 127; freetraders marrying into, 26
Pembina census, 97
Pembina half-breeds, 71–72

Pembina Métis, 16, 31–32, 40–50, 54, 69, 82, 151, 169
Pembina River, 26, 27
Pemmican, 29, 33, 51, 54, 100, 111. *See also* Buffalo
Pemmican War, 29–31, 54, 235n36
Pend d'Oreilles, 79, 117
Pepin, Simon, 120
Pershing, J. J., 176
Peterson, Jacqueline, 12, 17, 30
Piegans, 79, 101, 117, 132
Pillager Chippewas, 43
"Piyish Tout Ni Pouyoun," 222, 263n1
Plains Chippewa, 38
Plains Crees, 54
Plains Indians groups, 38
Poitra, Frances, 19, 119
Politics: and "half-breeds," 122, 126, 167, 249n61; Spring Creek band and, 118–27
Pope, John, 66
Portage de Prairie, 23
Porter, Ned, 91–92
Poverty, 10, 173, 213–14
Power, Thomas C., 66, 121, 123, 128, 133
Prairie du Chien, 19, 24
Pratt, Virginia Laverdure Janeaux, 201
Preemption Act (1841), 104–105
Pretty Shield, 132
Price, Con, 127
Priests, 60, 64, 71
Provisioners, 29

Qu'Appelle River, 54, 60

Race/color, in census, 113–14, 201
Racial categories, Non-European, 17. *See also* Biracial identities; Triracial descent
Racial prejudice, 30, 33, 56, 236n46
Racial situation, polarized, 16–17
Racial stereotypes, of Métis, 3
Radisson, Pierre Esprit, 20
Ramsey, Alexander, 43–47, 167, 170
Ranchers, Spring Creek band and, 127–31

Red Bear Chippewas, 211
Red Lake, 23
Red Lake Chippewas, 43, 45
Red River, 15, 22, 29, 232n1; ancestors of, 5; carts of, 36–38, 52, *138*, 236n52; Crees on, 22, 27, 29, 32, 43; drainage communities of, 19, 22, 52; 1816 stand at, 23; fur trade of, 23–26; "New People" of, 30; and Spring Creek band, 28, 32, 43–44
"Red River half-breeds," 86
"Red River Jig," 202, 259n20
Red River Métis, 16, 19, 23–28, 39–40; buffalo products, 51–56; changing conditions of, 73–75; emergence of, 29–30; historians' images of, 75, 243n53. *See also* Red River Settlement
Red River Resistance of 1869-1870, 163
Red River Settlement, 16, 19, 22, 28, 109; after Manitoba Resistance, 73–74; Chippewas as part of, 43; Métis as part of, 32, 43, 47; Métis as threat to, 31; as Métis' center of society, 32–40; military problems, 31; starvation, 54. *See also* Red River Métis
Red Thunder, 171
Red River Settlement, The (Ross), 11
Reed, A. S., 101
Reed's Fort, 81, 101
Refugees, 164–67, 256n62
Religious activities, of Spring Creek band, 116–18, 144–46, 205
Republicans, 121–23, 127
Reservations, 42–44, 91, 95, 127; Blackfeet, 213, 215; Flathead, 213, 215; Fort Belknap, 193, 215; Fort Peck, 215; land allotment, 209–11, 215–21, 260n35, 261n36; Rocky Boy's, 217–18; White Earth, 169
Resettlement, of Métis, 88
Retirees: of Hudson's Bay Company, 22, 29; of North West Company, 22
Rickards, John, 175

Riel, Louis, 13, 73, 98–100, 168; accusations against, 123–25, 250n68; execution of, 164, 178; Milk River Métis and, 93–96, 245nn8–9; Spring Creek band and, 118–27, 134–35, 164
Robinson, H. M., 68
Rocky Boy, 176
Rocky Boy Chippewa Crees, 13–14, 177, 208; land for, 213–21, 262n45, 262n53
Rocky Boy's Reservation, 217–18
Rocky Mountains, 23
Roe Cloud Rolls, 211–12
Roeder, Richard, 11
Rolette, Joe, 57–58, 239n15
Roman Catholic Church. *See* Catholic church/clergy
Rose, Magdalena, 72
Ross, Alexander, 11, 36–38, 43
Ross family, 206
Roy, Mont., 185, 192–93, 213
Royal Mounted Police, 124
Rupert (prince), 20
Rupert's Land, 17; charter of, 20; economic life of, 19–23; freemen in, 22, 39; fur trade, 20; and Hudson's Bay Company, 19–20; independent traders in, 22; Métis in, 49, 73–74; Montreal partnerships, 19–20; social life of, 19–23
Russell, Charlie, 215

Sacagawea, 25
Saco, 67
Saginaw, 19
Sangray family, 217
Sanno, J. M. J., 176
Saskatchewan, 22, 23, 39, 57, 74, 94, 185; Montana border with, 73
Saskatchewan River area, 22
Sault Ste. Marie, 18, 19
Sayer, Guillaume, 39
Schools: Boyd Creek School, 146; "Breed School," 146; community, 7; "Half Breed School," 146; in Lewistown, 146–52, 253n17; Spring

Creek band and, 116, 137, 146–52, 248nn48–49, 253n15; St. Peter's Indian School, 147–49; white policy of, 150–52
Schuflet, Lula, 152–53
Schultz, James Willard, 99–100, 115–16, 129, 132
Scottish agricultural community, 22, 33
Scrip distribution, 44–47, 49, 69, 72, 82, 183, 192
Selkirk Settlement, 22, 29
Selkirk Treaty of 1817, 43, 238n68
Semple, Robert, 29
Shambow, Louis, 61, 64–65
Sheilds, Margaret Daniels (Daignon) Morase, 69, 146, 201
Sherman, William T., 92–93
Shonkin Creek, 113
Shoshones, 156–57
Shoup, Frances Morgan, 207
Simpson, George, 31
Sioux, 26, 27, 39, 43, 66, 76, 77, 86, 94, 114, 243n60
Sioux War of 1876, 90
Sitting Bull, 86, 91, 94
Sleeper-Smith, Susan, 82
Smith family, 216
South Bend, 19
Spanish, 24
Spring Creek, Mont., 4, 5, 6, 213, 231n4
Spring Creek band, 4, 7, 9, 14, 41, 222–25, 231n3; ancestors of, 15, 23–26, 28, 97; army's campaign against, 129–31, 252n82; Berger, Judith in, 79, *80*, 82, 103; Berger, Pierre, 79, *80*, 81, 95, 103, 114; buffalo hunting, 80–81; cabins built by, 115; "Canadian Crees" and, 178, 208; Catholic church, 204; cattle raised by, 114; community participation of, 143–52; daily life of, 114–18; in 1880, 105–14, 248n39; and Euro-Americans, 101–102; family names of, *48, 83–85,* 244n65; farming, 105, 111–13; formation of, 79–86, 101–105; homesteads, 102–105, 158, 183–201, 247n33, 247n35; Janeaux in, 69, 102–103, 113, 114, 116, 118, 123, 133, 134; kinship system of, 193–94, 201, 212–13; music of, 115; politics and, 118–27; ranchers and, 127–31; records of, 144–45, 253n12; Red River, 28, 32, 43–44; religious activities of, 116–18, 144–46, 205; Riel and, 118–27, 134–35, 164; schools established by, 116, 137, 146–52, 248nn48–49, 253n15; treaty negotiations, 44–46; voting of, 143; Wilkie in, 95, 103–105, 111, 118, 125, 127, 169, 172–73
Squatters/squatter's rights, 32, 104, 151
"Squaw men," 11
Stack, B. E., 87–88
Starvation: Métis, on Milk River, 91; Montana tribes and, 132–33; Red River Settlement, 54
State Department, 165
St. Boniface, 28
St. Dennis family, 119
Stegner, Wallace, 61, 73, 155, 218
Stevens, Isaac, 37, 38
Stevens, Oscar, 159, 161
St. François Xavier, 16, 40, 52, 56, 69, 82
St. Joseph, N. Dak., 24, 41, 56
St. Laurent, 60
St. Leo's Catholic Church, 145, 204, 205
St. Louis, Mo., 24
St. Matt, Jerome, 124
Stockmen, 128
St. Paul, 52
St. Peter, 52
St. Peter's Indian School, 147–49
St. Peter's Mission, 4, 64, 96, 101, 117, 132, 152, 164, 213
St. Pierre family, 19
Stuart, Granville, 99, 114, 129–30, 156–57, 251nn77–78; cattle ranching and, 158–59, 254n42, 255n43

INDEX

Stuart brothers, 128
Stuart girls, 156–57
Sumner, Edwin, 40
Swan, Elizabeth Berger, 115–18, 144–48, 185, 201, 211, 259n19
Swan, John, 201
Swan family, 206, 210
Swan River areas, 52
Sweitzer, N. B., 76
Sweney, Henry, 202
Sy-co-was-ta-ca-pa, 150, 151

Tabor, Isabell Lewis, 151
Tariffs, 24
Tax collectors, 126
Taxes, 75
T. C. Power and Co., 99, 158
"Ten Cent Treaty," 172–73, 179, 209, 211, 258n1
Terminology, 13–14
Terry, Alfred, 76
Teton River, 100
Therion (father), 145
Thornton, Edward, 77
Three-Year Homestead Act, 181
Tingley, Robert S., 113
Toole, J. K., 174
"To Red River and Beyond" (Marble), 57
Trade networks, 18, 24
Traders. *See* Freetraders; Fur traders; Hudson's Bay Company (HBC); Independent traders
Trappers, in Montana, 11
Tribes: federal recognition of, 3, 6, 12, 208–21; starvation of, 132–33
Tripmen, 24, 233n19
Triracial descent, 6
Truteau, Jean Baptiste, 25
Turcotte, Marie, 69
Turcotte, Vital, 69, 72, 139
Turcotte family, 19, 206, 210
Turtle Mountain, N. Dak., 38, 60, 143
Turtle Mountain Chippewas, 4, 13, 27, 38, 126, 176, 210; homesteads, 183; and Métis, 167–74, 208, 256n68

Turtle Mountain Métis, 151, 208
Turtle Mountain treaty, 209

University of Montana, 12
U.S., British trade competition with, 16
U.S.–Canadian boundary, 72–73, 88; establishment of, 24; Métis north of, 16, 39
U.S.–Canadian relations, 39
U.S. Department of the Interior, 44, 45
U.S. First Cavalry troops, 164
U.S. government: Indians' negotiations with, 42–43, 45–46, 136, 167–74; and Métis identity, 40–50, 179; treaty of 1863-1864, 45–47, 59, 170
U.S. Indian policy, 17
U.S. Senate resolution, in 1864, 46

Valley family, 217
van den Heuvel, John, 145
Van Gorp (father), 147
Van Gunten, Bob, 12
Veiduais family, 143
Vermaat, James M., 145, 182
Violence, 29
Voyageurs, 21, 23–26, 28

"Waiting for a Day That Never Comes: The Dispossessed Métis of Montana" (Dusenberry), 12
Walls family, 217
Walsh (superintendent), 77
War of 1812, 43
Warm Spring Creek, 158
Washpee Wampanoag, 8
Waugh, John, 171–72, 257n82
Way shaw wush koquen abe (Green Setting Feather), 38, 54
Weather, 61, 161–62, 165
Weekly Herald, 124, 125
Wells, Daniel, 192
Wells, Edward, 42, 45, 81, 82, 87, 113, 125
Wells, Edward, II, 46

Wells, John, 185, 192, 258n13
Wells, Marie, 82
Wells, Mary Natalie, 118
Wells, Pauline, 118
Wells family, 19, 143, 151, 172, 185, 192, 210, 218
We Pointed Them North (Abbott), 155
Wheat, Thralls W., 214, 216
Whiskey traffic, 76, 98, 124, 163. *See also* Liquor business
White, 6; definition of, 13, 156–57, 207, 232n18; Métis and, 4, 9; school policy, 150–52
White, Richard, 11
White Earth Reservation, in Minnesota, 169
White Horse Plains, 31–32
Whitemud River, 60
Whiteness, definitions of, 156–57
White River, 35
White Sulphur Springs, 102
Wilder's Landing, Mont., 101
Wilkie, Alexander, 41, 72, 79, 82, 178; in Spring Creek, 95, 103–105, 111, 118, 125, 127, 169, 172–73
Wilkie, David, 164, 165
Wilkie, Jean Baptiste, 37, 41, 42, 44, 58, 71–72, 169, 172

Wilkie, Josephine, 72
Wilkie family, 103, 108, 209
Winnett, Mont., 185
Winnipeg, 19, 23
Winter of 1886-1887, 182
Wintering, 54–57, 75, 99, 128–29
Wintering camps, 56, 61–72, 239n12
Wolf Point, Mont., 171
Women: beading/embroidery of, 139, *141–42;* berry picking by, 140; defined roles of, 18, 27, 224, 233n5; description of, 58–59, 240n18; work of, 139–43, 252n6
Wood, chopping of, 139
Wood, Samuel, 38, 40
"Wood hawks," 139
Wood Mountain, 60, 62
"Woods Cree," 163
Wright, James, 66

XY Company, 21; North West Company merging with, 27–28

Yancktonai Sioux, 76
Yellowstone River, 35

Zellick, Anna, 204
Zortman region, 193, 212